INTERNATIONAL COLLABORATIVE VENTURES IN U.S. MANUFACTURING

INTERNATIONAL COLLABORATIVE VENTURES IN U.S. MANUFACTURING

Edited by

DAVID C. MOWERY

An American Enterprise Institute/Ballinger Publication

*COMPETING IN A
CHANGING WORLD ECONOMY
PROJECT*

BALLINGER PUBLISHING COMPANY
Cambridge, Massachusetts
A Subsidiary of Harper & Row, Publishers, Inc.

This volume was supported by a grant from the Sloan Foundation.

International Standard Book Number: 0-88730-221-1

Library of Congress Catalog Card Number: 87-35831

Printed in the United States of America

Library of Congress Cataloging-in-Publication Data

International collaborative ventures in U.S. manufacturing.

　"American Enterprise Institute/Ballinger publication."
　"Competing in a changing world economy project."
　Includes index.
　1. Technology transfer—Economic aspects—United States.
2. Joint ventures—United States.　3. Competition, International.
I. Mowery, David C.
HC110.T4157　1988　　　338.8'8973　　　87-35831
ISBN 0-88730-221-1

CONTENTS

LIST OF FIGURES

LIST OF TABLES

PREFACE

International "alliances" among manufacturing firms have attracted considerable attention in the 1980s. Managers have raised questions about the structure and control of international collaborative ventures, scholars have become increasingly active in studying the causes and implications of collaboration, and policymakers have voiced concerns about the effects of collaborative ventures on the international competitiveness of American industry. Debate and inquiry in these three intersecting areas have been conducted with relatively few facts or data, however—a small number of prominent ventures are the focus of much of the discussion, with little consideration of the representativeness of these examples.

The project reported in this book began in 1985 as an effort to compare the recent experiences of eight different industries in international collaboration, as a means of expanding the knowledge that underpins discussion of this phenomenon. All of the contributors are either students of technological change, experts on the industry they were asked to discuss, or both. The contributors met twice, once in 1985 to discuss the project and once in 1986 to discuss drafts of the industry studies. The chapters incorporate comments of the contributors and discussions with the editor following the 1986 meeting.

The American Enterprise Institute's Competing in a Changing World Economy supported this project from its inception. We appreciate the support of AEI, as well as the administrative support and comments of Claude Barfield, coordinator of the Competing in a Changing World Economy project, and Robert Benko of the project staff. The views expressed in this book are those of the authors and do not necessarily represent the views of the American Enterprise Institute or the Office of the U.S. Trade Representative.

David C. Mowery
Editor

1 COLLABORATIVE VENTURES BETWEEN U.S. AND FOREIGN MANUFACTURING FIRMS
An Overview

David C. Mowery

The international environment within which U.S. manufacturing firms operate has been transformed during the past three decades. The economic and technological strengths of the United States have declined, and these strengths are more evenly distributed among U.S. and foreign firms. This new international economic environment, combined with changes in product and process technologies and in the industrial and trade policies of the U.S. and foreign governments, has contributed to a recent increase in the number and importance of collaborative ventures between U.S. and foreign firms in product development, manufacture, and marketing.

Many of these interfirm alliances involve significant exchanges of management expertise and technology. Several assessments have expressed concern over the long-term implications of international collaboration for the competitiveness of U.S. industry. Reich and Mankin (1986, pp. 78-79) argue that "the U.S. strategy [in joint ventures with Japan] seems shortsighted. In exchange for a few lower skilled, lower paying jobs and easy access to our competitors' high-quality, low-cost products, we are apparently willing to sacrifice our competitiveness in a host of industries—autos, machine tools, consumer electronics, and semiconductors today, and others in the

Research for this chapter was supported by the American Enterprise Institute's Competing in a Changing World Economy project. Additional support was provided by the Center for Economic Policy Research at Stanford University and the National Science Foundation (PRA 83-10664).

1

future." Other accounts assert that collaborative ventures may produce a "hollow corporation," not engaged in producing goods, employing a small number of highly paid financial and marketing executives and few if any production workers (*Business Week*, 1986). Still other observers view international collaboration as essential to global competitive strategies (Porter and Fuller, 1986; Perlmutter and Heenan, 1986).

The chapters in this book discuss the causes and consequences of collaborative ventures between U.S. and foreign firms in eight manufacturing industries. Chapters 2-5 analyze collaboration in relatively mature industries characterized by high levels of research and development spending: telecommunications equipment, commercial aircraft, integrated circuits, and pharmaceuticals. Chapters 6 and 7 examine young, R&D-intensive industries, biotechnology and robotics; and Chapters 8 and 9 discuss collaborative ventures in mature, less R&D-intensive industries, steel and automobiles. Both the importance of international collaborations and the activities included in collaborations, which range from research partnerships to agreements covering the marketing of products, vary considerably among these industries.

INTERNATIONAL COLLABORATIVE VENTURES

Definition

Collaboration between U.S. and foreign firms assumes many forms. Although a number of the collaborations discussed in this collection fit a narrow definition of a joint venture, including separate incorporation as an entity in which equity holdings are divided among the partners, others, such as partnerships between "risk-sharing" subcontractors and prime contractors, or the purchase by one firm of an equity share in another, do not. In some industries, joint ventures and other forms of collaboration are extensions of subcontracting relationships that cover product development and manufacture; others focus on marketing. For ease of exposition, the discussion in this chapter uses the terms *collaboration* and *joint venture* interchangeably, and therefore occasionally denotes as joint ventures organizational structures that do not fit the legal definition of this entity.[1]

An international collaborative venture may be defined as an instance of *interfirm collaboration in product development, manufacture, or marketing that spans national boundaries, is not based on arm's-length market transactions, and includes substantial contributions by partners of capital, technology, or other assets.* This definition excludes other forms of international economic activity, such as export, direct foreign investment (which implies complete intrafirm control of production and product development activities), and the sale of technology through licensing.

Significance

Joint ventures have long been common in extractive industries such as mining and petroleum production (see Stuckey, 1983), and account for a significant share of the total foreign investments made by U.S. manufacturing firms since World War II. Several features of recent collaborative ventures, however, differentiate them from prior cases. The number of collaborations, both those involving only U.S. firms and those between U.S. and foreign enterprises, appears to have increased considerably. Harrigan's data (1984) suggest that domestic joint ventures among U.S. manufacturing firms have grown in number during the past decade and now appear in a much wider range of industries, and Hladik (1985) found a significant increase during 1970-1982 in the number of international joint ventures involving U.S. firms.[2]

Although many of the alliances discussed in this book involve both product development and manufacture or marketing, a number of joint ventures and consortiums involving U.S. and foreign firms, as well as consortiums of U.S. firms, recently have been formed solely for the conduct of research. Increasing domestic and international collaborative activity thus has been accompanied by a more general upsurge in U.S. firms' reliance on external sources of R&D expertise, including such research consortiums as the Semiconductor Research Corporation and the Microelectronics and Computer Technology Corporation, or cooperative university-industry research institutes.[3] Indeed, some scholars (Friar and Horwitch, 1986; Miles and Snow, 1986; see also Chapter 2) argue that U.S. and other firms will in the future rely more heavily on external sources of technology for commercial innovation.

The structure and activities of the international collaborative ventures in which U.S. firms have participated since 1975 also differ significantly from those of the 1950-1975 period. The share of joint ventures in which U.S. firms hold a minority stake has increased. According to Hladik (1985, p. 51), an average of 80 percent of the joint ventures formed each year during 1974-1982 were "nonmajority" joint ventures in which U.S. firms have an ownership share of 50 percent or less. Moreover, Hladik found that an increasing share of recent U.S.-foreign joint ventures involved either production for export, joint conduct of R&D, or both. In both of these dimensions, recent joint ventures contrast with those of the earlier postwar period, during which many U.S.-foreign joint ventures were engaged primarily in production for the market of the nation in which the foreign firm was located or were formed to exploit natural resources within a foreign nation.

Recent international alliances also are appearing in industries and firms that historically have not been characterized by substantial direct foreign investment activity or multinational corporate organization. Commercial aircraft, for example, in which collaboration recently has been extensive (see Chapter 3), was cited by Hirsch (1976) as an industry in which direct foreign investment activity is largely absent. Other U.S. industries in which these ventures have assumed considerable importance in recent years include both mature industries (such as steel and automobiles) and young industries (biotechnology). Many, although not all, collaborations include R&D and product development, and thereby may result in significant technology transfer. In cases such as aircraft most of the technology transfer within international alliances consists of exports of technology from the United States. In other industries, however, such as steel or automobiles, these ventures involve significant U.S. imports of technology.

International collaborative ventures among firms are based on an exchange relationship, but the assets or commodities exchanged often differ from those exchanged via licensing or export. Some collaborations allow U.S. and foreign firms to pool their technologies in a single product or product line, without merging all of their activities into a single corporate entity. In other cases agreements support the combination of one firm's technological capabilities with the marketing or distribution assets of another. Why are collaborative ventures, rather than alternative mechanisms such as licensing employed for this exchange, and why have such alliances multiplied in recent years? The remainder of this chapter addresses these questions.

ALTERNATIVE CHANNELS FOR THE EXPLOITATION OF FIRM-SPECIFIC ASSETS

A large literature has considered the determinants of the firm's choice among export, licensing, and direct foreign investment as channels for the sale of products or the exploitation of other assets. A fundamental insight into this issue was proposed by Hymer (1961) and extended and enriched by a number of scholars (see Vernon, 1966; Dunning, 1981; Teece, 1982; and Rugman, 1981, among others). Hymer argued that the key determinant of a firm's decision to undertake direct foreign investment, rather than serving foreign markets solely through the export of goods, was the possession by the investing firm of some advantage over firms based in the foreign country.[4]

Hymer did not discuss at length the nature or causes of the firm's advantage, but the empirical and theoretical investigations of other scholars (reviewed in Caves, 1982) suggest that firms undertake direct foreign investment to exploit firm-specific, often intangible, assets or capabilities. Export and sale of its products in foreign markets are less effective means for the exploitation of such assets than direct investment, which enables the firm to realize in foreign markets the returns to its combined strengths in marketing, production, and innovation. In this view, firms engage in direct foreign investment rather than export for the same reasons that U.S. manufacturing firms in the late nineteenth century expanded product lines and absorbed functions such as distribution and marketing that extended well beyond simply manufacturing a single product (see Chandler, 1977). The returns in foreign and domestic markets to the combined performance of these functions by a single firm were greater than those realized by firms specializing only in manufacturing.

Several of the chapters in this book, as well as Teece (1986), argue that the reasons for such "synergy" stem from complementarities among the different functions or capabilities that are necessary to appropriate the returns to a new technology. In order to reap a profit from the development of a technology, for example, firms in some industries may require a wholly owned marketing network. Such complementarities may be less compelling in other industries because of differences in market structure, the characteristics of the technology, and other factors. The ability of firms to purchase these complementary assets often is limited by high transactions costs. A firm then is faced with a choice between developing these capabilities internally and trying to gain access to them through licensing, contractual agreements covering marketing or production, or collaboration with a domestic or foreign firm.

Alternatives to direct foreign investment for the exploitation of firm-specific assets include licensing and collaborative ventures. The advantages and disadvantages of each of these methods depend on the characteristics of the asset in question. These characteristics and other factors also influence the types of activities pursued within collaborative ventures.

Licensing

In most of the industries discussed in this book, an important item of exchange within collaborative ventures is corporate assets that are based on a firm's technological capabilities.[5] Exploitation of technology-based assets often requires complementary assets or capabilities. Where these complementary assets cannot be developed internally, the innovating firm may license its technology, gaining access via the market to the complementary assets controlled by other firms. Licensing, however, can be impeded by high transactions costs. Markets for the licensing of advanced technologies that exploit such firm-specific knowledge often are very thin, with few buyers or sellers. The dearth of alternative outlets for sellers or alternative sources for buyers means that opportunistic behavior may hamper the operation of markets for technology licenses.[6]

Much technological knowledge is tacit in nature. Know-how, in addition to blueprints, is critical to understanding technology and therefore to transferring it. In order for the licensee to exploit the technology, this know-how and the individuals who can convey the codified and tacit knowledge must be made available to the licensee without the evisceration of the licensor firm.[7] Relatively new technologies, as well as technologies that need extensive systems integration, are likely to require intensive exchange of information and know-how for their development and will be less amenable to transfer via license.

A further difficulty in licensing technological assets was first noted by Arrow (1962). In order to justify the price of an asset to a potential buyer, the seller must reveal considerable information concerning the nature and capabilities of the technology in question. If this revealed information can be easily absorbed and exploited by the potential buyer, the revelation of the characteristics of a technology that is necessary to complete a licensing transaction removes any incentive on the part of the potential buyer to pay for the license.[8]

Uncertainty about the behavior of licensor and licensee also reduces the efficiency of markets for technology licenses. A firm licensing its technology risks the possibility that its monopoly power over these technological assets will be undercut, as licensees develop their own capabilities and eventually "reverse engineer" or invent around a license or patent.[9] Many licensing agreements require that such improvements be provided by licensees to the licensor, but these provisions are difficult to enforce.

All three of these difficulties—uncertainties about licensee and licensor behavior, problems in ascertaining value, and the lack of codification—often are less severe for technologies for which patents are comprehensive, well enforced, and difficult to circumvent. Strong patent protection reduces somewhat the dangers to the licensor of reverse engineering. The comprehensive disclosure of characteristics that is necessary for a patent application also facilitates the valuation of the technology by a licensor and the agreement on its value in a contract. Finally, the codification of technological information necessary for a patent application should facilitate the drafting of a license or contract that can convey the essential information for exploitation of the technology.

The nature of the innovation processes associated with different technologies also affects the choice between licensing and other mechanisms for their exploitation. Complex capital goods with long production histories, such as commercial aircraft and telecommunications equipment, often require extensive after-sales product support and service. Separating the responsibility for manufacture from that for product support (when a manufacturer contracts with another firm to market and provide after-sales service for a product) establishes a situation ripe for opportunistic behavior.

Even where both manufacture and product support can be carried out by a licensee, however, the role of product support and marketing in providing data for product design and modifications means that these channels of feedback and information should be controlled by the organization responsible for product design and manufacture. Technologies characterized by "user-active" innovation, to use the phrase of von Hippel (1976), are technologies in which user-supplied operating experience and demands are important inputs for research and design groups. Licensing may deprive a producer of this important channel of information for product modification and improvement.[10] Technologies in which product support and user-active innovation are less central may admit more easily of exploitation through licensing.

Licensing is likely to be preferred to either direct foreign investment or collaborative ventures in technologies that are not complex, have strong, well-enforced patents, are relatively mature, and do not rely on user-active innovation, with its requirements for links among marketing, product support, and product development. Industries in which these features are not characteristic of the technology and in which licensing is less important by comparison with other means to realize value from technology include steel, automobiles, commercial aircraft, and telecommunications equipment.

Despite its limitations, technology licensing is widely employed in several of the industries discussed in this book. Technologies and industries in which product cycles are short, such as semiconductors, often rely heavily on international and domestic licensing. If the market for a product is relatively short-lived, a firm may avoid the fixed investment in production capacity necessary to serve the entire market, instead reaping part of the profits from the production and part from the licensing of the innovation. The establishment of de facto standards around a particular design also can be facilitated through rapid expansion of the production of a new design for an integrated circuit, achieved through licensing other producers. Licensing in this industry also reflects the fact that patents held by competitors often overlap; licensing and cross-licensing can reduce patent litigation.

Licensing also is widespread in the pharmaceuticals industry, where patent protection is strong and the necessary information to produce (as opposed to develop) a drug involves relatively little tacit knowledge. The situation in two other industries discussed in this book, robotics and biotechnology, is more complex, reflecting the fact that the structure of these relatively young industries still is changing rapidly. Although licensing is employed by some biotechnology firms to get their products into widespread production and distribution, the uncertain state of patent protection, among other things, discourages its more extensive use. Licensing is extensive in some segments of the robotics industry, however, as a number of foreign firms have licensed U.S. firms to produce, market, provide applications software, and handle after-sales support for mechanical devices in the U.S. market.

Direct Foreign Investment

Direct foreign investment supports the exploitation of firm-specific technological capabilities, but carries with it substantial risks and costs. Industries in which production technologies exhibit a large minimum efficient scale relative to the size of the world market and strong plant-specific learning and cost reduction effects will incur severe cost penalties by establishing multiple production facilities. Direct foreign investment in such industries, which include commercial aircraft (primarily airframes) and steel, generally is modest in the absence of major trade barriers. The high fixed costs of establishing an offshore production, distribution, and marketing network also may deter direct foreign investment—in a world of imperfect capital markets, only the largest firms can undertake such strategies.

Uncertainties over economic and political conditions in many foreign markets may preclude direct foreign investment for many U.S.

firms. Political barriers have impeded the establishment of wholly owned production facilities in high-technology industries in a number of nations; both Japan and the United States have expressed opposition to direct foreign investment, for example, in their domestic semiconductor industries. In the 1980s joint ventures have substituted for, and in some cases have complemented, Japanese and U.S. firms' direct foreign investment. A number of collaborative ventures in the integrated circuit, automobile, and pharmaceuticals industries have been transitional devices to support the eventual establishment of a wholly owned offshore production or marketing capability.[11] Both licensing and direct foreign investment, as well as export, also force the innovating firm to bear all of the costs and risks of product or process research and development, which have grown considerably in such industries as semiconductors, telecommunications equipment, and commercial aircraft.

Advantages of International Collaborative Ventures

Many of the contractual limitations and transactions costs of licensing for the exploitation of technological capabilities can be avoided within a collaborative venture. The noncodified, "inseparable" character of firm-specific assets that makes their exploitation through licensing so difficult need not prevent the pooling of such assets by several firms within a joint venture or the effective sale of such assets by one firm to another within a joint venture.

Collaborative ventures provide a means for avoiding many of the problems of uncertainty and opportunism that complicate international technology licensing agreements. Although the valuation of partners' contributions can be a central issue in these undertakings, as in the 767 and 7J7 aircraft development projects between Boeing and the Japan Commercial Aircraft Corporation, collaborative ventures may reduce the severity of the Arrow revelation problem. Partner firms make financial commitments to a collaborative venture to back up their claims for the value of the assets they are contributing; such financial commitments may substitute for the complete revelation of the value and characteristics of the assets that would be necessary to complete a licensing agreement. The formation of a joint venture also allows for better monitoring by each partner of the behavior of the other(s) and reduces the incentives for opportunistic behavior.[12]

Technology transfer can be controlled more effectively within collaborative ventures than in licensing transactions. Licensing necessitates the sale of a complete package of technological capabilities in many instances. Joint ventures, however, allow partner firms to "unbundle" their portfolios of technological assets and selectively transfer components of this portfolio, which individual components may be worthless in isolation, to a partner. The transfer of technology through a joint venture from a technologically advanced firm to a less advanced enterprise therefore may enable the technologically senior firm to reap some financial returns to portions of its portfolio of technological capabilities. In many cases, such returns cannot be attained through licensing because of the difficulties of unbundling the firm's technological portfolio through a license. The possibility of financial rewards from selective technology transfer has provided a strong cohesive force in joint ventures involving firms with disparate technological capabilities. Moreover, monitoring of the behavior of the recipient of any such assets within a joint venture reduces the risks that the transferor will not benefit from improvements in transferred technologies made by the recipient.

Collaborative ventures offer a cheaper alternative to the complete merger of firms as a means of pooling assets. Such ventures typically fall well short of a complete merger of firms, covering only a limited range of functions or products. Partner firms may well be competitors in other product areas. Collaborative ventures avoid the difficulties of combining large, multiproduct enterprises through mergers. In view of the disappointing performance of many of the large mergers of the 1960s and 1970s, this feature of both domestic and international collaborative ventures may account for some of their recent popularity among U.S. firms. Collaboration also can allow established firms a more rapid means than internal development to gain access to new technologies that are not easily licensed. The costs and risks of a collaborative venture may be lower than those associated with the acquisition of the technology through the purchase of a firm. This "technology access" motive for collaboration between established and young firms has been particularly important in industries based on new technologies, such as biotechnology and robotics.

By comparison with direct foreign investment, licensing, or export, collaborative ventures lower the financial and political risks of innovation and foreign marketing. The products of a collaborative venture between a U.S. and foreign firm encounter fewer political impediments to market access in the domestic market of the foreign firm than would direct exports from the U.S. firm. Collaboration also can reduce other political uncertainties that make direct investment in such a market unattractive.

The potential difficulties of collaborative ventures should not be minimized. Management of these undertakings has proven to be extremely difficult. The amount of technology transfer occurring within collaborations that focus on new product development, for example, may cause conflict, especially when such ventures involve firms of different technological capabilities. The incentives of the partners in such ventures often are opposed, as the senior firm wishes to minimize, and the junior firm to maximize, the amount of technology transfer. These conflicting interests may prevent the formation or contribute to the collapse of a joint venture.

Joint ventures in product development between erstwhile competitors that cover only one product line among the many produced by the partner firms also may be unstable. Technological change can cause independently manufactured products to become competitors with those jointly developed within the partnership. Collaborative ventures that focus on marketing by one partner of the products of another also may not endure, as Porter and Fuller (1986) note, since one partner's knowledge of market conditions and demand may lose its value to the other partner. Finally, the feasibility of joint ventures is limited by the availability of partners. All partners must bring something to the joint venture, be this a contribution of technology, capital, or access to a foreign market.

Factors Affecting the Focus of Collaboration

The characteristics of the key competitive assets (technological, managerial, production, marketing, and others) within an industry, the structure of the industry (new, with a large number of relatively small firms and low entry barriers, or mature, with significant entry barriers), and the characteristics of foreign markets for the products of an industry (is market access hampered by political or other factors?) not only affect the prevalence of international collaborative ventures within an industry but also influence the activities included in collaborations. In relatively mature high-technology industries, such as telecommunications equipment, integrated circuits, and commercial aircraft, the high costs of new product development, demanding requirements for systems integration, the difficulty of licensing key technologies, and the need to circumvent political barriers to market access all mean that recent collaborative ventures focus on product development. Collaborative ventures in robotics that team user and supplier firms have focused on product development because of the need for substantial exchanges of proprietary data between the partners. The need to integrate complex technologies also has led to product development collaborations among robotics suppliers.

In other high-technology industries with a large number of relatively new firms, such as biotechnology, much of the collaboration
focuses on the marketing and distribution by established firms of the
technologies developed by new entrants. This type of collaboration
aids entry into new domestic or foreign markets and does not always
incorporate joint product development. The limited collaborative
activity in pharmaceuticals, which has involved the use by foreign
firms of the established drug testing, certification, and marketing
networks of U.S. firms to enter this market, consists almost entirely
of marketing. The most significant international collaborations in the
automotive and steel industries center on the exchange of foreign
process technology, foreign managerial expertise and production systems for access to U.S. markets. These joint ventures accordingly
focus primarily on production.

This discussion of the focus of collaboration and the characteristics of different mechanisms for the exploitation of technological
and other assets is an essentially static one that does not explain the
recent upsurge in international collaboration in a number of U.S.
industries. Why have international collaborative ventures, which are a
hybrid of interfirm and intrafirm modes for the exchange or sharing
of technological and other assets, assumed such importance recently,
and why do these ventures encompass a wider range of activities?
The answer is simple—changes in the technological and policy environment within which U.S. firms operate have rendered the potential
contributions of foreign firms to collaborative ventures much more
attractive to U.S. firms.

GENERAL CAUSES OF INCREASED
RELIANCE ON JOINT VENTURES

In discussing the factors that have led to increased collaboration between U.S. and foreign firms in recent years, it is useful to consider
Vernon's "product cycle" model of direct foreign investment (1966).
Vernon's model, which drew on Hymer (1961), explained U.S. direct
foreign investment as a mechanism for the exploitation of firm-
specific technological assets. Vernon hypothesized that differences in
consumer demand among various national markets supported the
development of firm-specific capabilities and other assets in the
domestic firms serving these national markets. As demand conditions
developed in foreign markets that resembled those of the home market, these domestic firms utilized direct foreign investment to exploit their unique assets. Within the product cycle model, firms were

passive channels for the expression of differences among the national markets of the world economy.

International collaborative ventures are one of a number of new channels that have developed to support international flows of goods, technology, and capital in response to changes in the factors identified by Vernon as important causes of direct foreign investment by U.S. firms. The collaborative ventures discussed in this book fail to conform in important dimensions with the predictions of the product cycle model. International flows of capital are less significant in these ventures, relative to the exchange of technological information and data, design and marketing capabilities, and managerial expertise. The establishment of wholly owned foreign production facilities within such collaborations also is rare. Furthermore, the characteristics of the domestic markets of the participants frequently have little to do with the character of the firm-specific assets exploited through such agreements; the attributes of the corporate participants in many industries now are less country-bound.

The diminution in the salience of direct foreign investment and the declining significance of firm-specific attributes based solely on national markets reflect changes in the supply of inputs and the nature of product demand that have increased U.S. firms' demand for foreign partners in these ventures.[13] The enhanced technological capabilities of many foreign firms make them more attractive potential partners in joint ventures with U.S. firms.[14] Foreign firms are better able to absorb and exploit advanced technologies from U.S. firms in industries in which there remains a substantial technology gap between U.S. and foreign firms. In other industries, however, foreign firms are either the technological equals of U.S. firms and can make significant contributions of managerial or technological expertise to joint ventures with U.S. firms, or are more advanced. In the automobile and steel industries and in some instances in the semiconductor industry, U.S. firms collaborate with foreign firms to gain access to superior foreign technologies.

Simultaneously, product demand in the world market for many high-technology and other goods has become more homogeneous and less dominated by any single market as the U.S. share of world demand for many high-technology products has declined. This shift in the profile of world demand renders penetration of foreign markets by U.S. firms essential to commercial success in many industries. Joint ventures offer a lower risk and lower cost alternative to direct foreign investment and allow better access to foreign markets than the export of finished products. Nevertheless, the United States remains by far the largest single market in virtually all of the manufacturing industries discussed in this book. Although the European market is potentially larger, incomplete economic integration means that European markets, especially those for high-technology goods, remain fragmented. European or Japanese firms have developed collaborative ventures with U.S. firms to penetrate the vast U.S. market.

Even as the commercial importance of foreign markets to U.S. firms has grown, access to many foreign markets has been reduced by the industrial and trade policies of foreign governments. These policies have increased the incentives of U.S. firms to seek foreign partners in product development and manufacture. In both industrialized and industrializing nations, the development or stabilization of high value-added industries and skilled manufacturing employment are central goals of industrial and trade policies. Purchase decisions of foreign governments play a major role in the export markets for a number of commodities, including commercial aircraft and telecommunications equipment. These decisions frequently are influenced by the availability of offsets, the production (or development and production) of components for a product by domestic firms in the purchaser nation.

Government demands for offsets create strong incentives for U.S. producers to involve foreign firms as risk-sharing subcontractors or equal partners in product development and manufacture. Such government pressure on the parties to the procurement process remains significant, although restricted by the Procurement Code of the Tokyo Round of multilateral trade negotiations, conducted under the auspices of the General Agreement on Tariffs and Trade, as well as by the GATT Agreement on Trade in Civil Aircraft.[15]

Foreign governments also frequently provide development funding and risk capital to domestic firms as part of their industrial development strategies. Combined with high and rapidly increasing product development costs in many U.S. industries, such as semiconductors, commercial aircraft, telecommunications equipment, and robotics, the availability of capital from public sources for foreign firms has enhanced their attractiveness as partners in product development ventures.

Just as foreign government trade and industrial policies have created incentives for U.S. firms to collaborate with foreign firms in export markets, official restrictions on foreign access to the U.S. market have led to increased collaboration between U.S. firms and foreign firms wishing to export to the United States. Such restrictions are most significant in the steel and auto industries. In several instances (the Toyota-General Motors agreement or that between

Nippon Kokan Steel and National Steel), a foreign production presence in the U.S. has been achieved through a joint venture. In the wake of Fujitsu's failure to acquire Fairchild Semiconductor, joint ventures may become a more important means for Japanese semiconductor producers to establish a U.S. production base.

Paradoxically, the pursuit by the United States and other industrialized nations of essentially nationalistic policies of support for domestic industries has encouraged the development of consortiums spanning national boundaries. The growth of multinational firms and direct foreign investment led some analysts to speculate that national boundaries would mean little or nothing to global firms, but much of the current wave of joint venture activity reflects the opposite phenomenon. Global firms in many industries increasingly must be cognizant of and responsive to the policy environment of the nations in which they are producing or marketing goods and services, because of the greater importance of nontariff barriers to trade.

A number of recent analyses of U.S. industrial competitiveness have criticized the role of U.S. antitrust policy. Have U.S. antitrust statutes prevented the nation's firms from combining their research talents to fend off foreign competition?[16] Historically, Justice Department opposition to domestic joint ventures formed to conduct precommercial or fundamental research has been modest (see Crane, 1984), and it has declined further in the wake of the National Cooperative Research Act of 1984. Nevertheless, some scholars have cited antitrust policy as a factor that has contributed to the decision by U.S. firms in a number of industries to seek foreign, rather than domestic, partners in new product development ventures.[17]

Technological factors have influenced recent decisions of U.S. firms to collaborate with domestic or foreign firms. In a number of industries examined in this collection (commercial aircraft being an exception), product cycles are becoming shorter. If a product design dominates its market for only a short time, rapid market penetration at low cost is essential and may require joint production or collaboration with a firm with an established marketing network. The importance of access to new or unfamiliar technologies in a number of industries also has increased because of technological convergence (the example of telecommunications and computer technologies is well known, but there are others, including the increased importance of biotechnology within pharmaceuticals and food processing and the growing role of computer-based machine vision technologies within robotics). Collaboration offers one means for more rapid access to technological capabilities whose development within a firm may require a large investment and considerable time.

Technological developments also may have reduced somewhat the competitive advantages of the large multinational firm and the strategy of direct foreign investment. The growth of such firms was in part a response to technological changes that reduced the costs and enhanced the reliability of information transmission, storage, and processing (Chandler, 1977). In combination with other technological and organizational changes, declines in information costs created considerable economies of scale and scope within the firm. Recent innovations in the technologies of information transmission, storage, and analysis have lowered information costs still further and facilitate interfirm cooperation in product development, manufacture, and marketing. The exchange of technical, testing, and other data between development teams and the use of computer-aided design and manufacturing technologies in both development and production have made easier the "spinning off" to other foreign or domestic firms of numerous tasks in the design and manufacture of complex products.

CONCLUSION

Although international joint ventures and other forms of collaboration have been a long-standing feature of international investment and production, in recent years they appear to have grown in number. These ventures now appear in a wider range of industries and incorporate new activities, particularly in the area of product development and manufacture. Collaborative ventures occupy a status somewhere between market-mediated transactions and wholly intrafirm activities and therefore pose considerable challenges to both managers and scholars. Although transactions costs, "cospecialized assets" (Teece, 1986), and other concepts have contributed to an understanding of these phenomena, much work remains to be done. The studies in this volume are intended in part to provide the material for additional theoretical and empirical analysis.

Collaborative ventures between U.S. and foreign manufacturing firms are one facet of a larger reorganization of the processes of technology development and innovation, as U.S. firms attempt to monitor and exploit external sources of scientific and technological knowledge more aggressively while lowering costs and reducing risk. By no means, however, do all international collaborative ventures focus on the development or acquisition by U.S. firms of new technologies. Moreover, the permanence of this phenomenon is easily overstated; collaborative ventures are difficult to manage, and their usefulness and their importance in some industries may be temporary.

The causes and consequences of international collaboration are best analyzed in a comparative framework that spans a number of different industries. This comparative analysis of collaborative ventures also sheds light on interindustry contrasts in the structure of the innovation process and in the characteristics of competition, factors that affect the structure and behavior of the institutions governing innovation. Inasmuch as empirical analyses of the relationships between industry or firm characteristics and R&D investment suggest that industry-specific differences in technological opportunity, appropriability, and other poorly understood characteristics account for a large share of interindustry differences in these relationships (Scott, 1984; Levin, Cohen, and Mowery, 1985; Cohen, Levin, and Mowery, 1987), the following chapters also should contribute to the efforts of empirical researchers to understand and model these differences.

NOTES

1. The formal structure of collaborative ventures, however, often has little to do with either their management or success, as Gullander (1976, p. 86) has noted: "There are indications that the difference between a contractual and an equity relationship is highly exaggerated; sophisticated 'cooperators' seem to downplay the importance of ownership control as compared to management control or control through other means."

2. During the 1960s, joint ventures were concentrated in the chemicals, primary metals, paper, and stone, clay and glass industries, but they now extend beyond these sectors, according to Harrigan (1984). Hladik's data indicate a considerable increase in the number of joint ventures between U.S. and foreign firms during 1975–1982, a growth trend that almost certainly has continued. Hladik's conclusions disagree with those of Ghemawat, Porter, and Rawlinson (1986, p. 346), who compiled a time series of "international coalition announcements" (joint ventures, license agreements, supply agreements, and "other long-term interfirm accords") covering 1970–1982 that displays no upward trend. The differences are likely to be more apparent than real; the Ghemawat et al. database includes several types of interfirm collaboration that are excluded by Hladik. The possibility thus exists that a shift in the mix of the different forms considered by Ghemawat et al. occurred during 1970–1982, as joint ventures and other collaborative agreements increased in importance relative to such alternatives as licensing.

3. See the National Science Board (1983), as well as Nelkin and Nelson (1985), Friar and Horwitch (1985), and Graham (1985).

4. "Firms are by no means equal in their ability to operate in an industry. Certain firms have considerable advantages in particular activities. The

possession of these advantages may cause them to have extensive international operations of one kind or another." (Hymer, 1961, p. 41)

5. Caves (1982, p. 9) notes that "as indicators of these [firm-specific] assets, economists have seized on the outlays for advertising and research and development (R&D) undertaken by firms classified to an industry. That the share of foreign subsidiary assets in the total assets of U.S. corporations increases significantly with the importance of advertising and R&D outlays in the industry has been confirmed in many studies. . . ."

6. In Williamson's terminology (1975, p. 26), a "small numbers condition" characterizes such markets: "The transactional dilemma that is posed is this: it is in the interest of each party to seek terms most favorable to him, which encourages opportunistic representations and haggling. The interests of the *system*, by contrast, are promoted if the parties can be joined in such a way as to avoid both the bargaining costs and the indirect costs (mainly maladaptation costs) which are generated in the process." (emphasis in original)

7. Teece (1982, p. 45) argues that "The transfer of key individuals may suffice when the knowledge to be transferred relates to the particulars of a separable routine. The individual in such cases becomes a consultant or a teacher with respect to that routine. However, only a limited range of capabilities can be transferred if a transfer activity is focused in this fashion. More often than not, the transfer of productive expertise requires the transfer of organizational as well as individual knowledge. In such cases, external transfer beyond an organization's boundary may be difficult if not impossible, since taken out of context, an individual's knowledge of a routine may be quite useless."

8. The significance of this form of market failure depends on the assumption that the transfer and absorption of technological knowledge are virtually costless, an assumption that receives little support in the discussion above; see also Mowery (1983). Nonetheless, the problem of partial revelation in the course of establishing the value of a technology within a licensing negotiation is a very real one, as the analysis of Caves, Crookell, and Killing (1983) suggests.

9. Caves, Crookell, and Killing's (1983, p. 259) analysis of a small sample of licensing agreements concluded that severe uncertainties over quality and over licensee and licensor behavior prevent licensors from extracting the full potential rents from the technological assets sold through licenses, and prevent joint-maximization outcomes in the transaction: "the uncertain outcomes of licensing transactions interact with the costs of writing 'complete' contracts to impel the frequent inclusion of inefficient terms in the agreements. The terms are inefficient in the sense of causing the licensing agreement to yield a smaller total cash flow to the two parties than would an idealized contract in which the licensor and licensee select policies to maximize the cash flow from the shared technology and then divide the spoils between them. . . . The surveys of licensors and licensees reveal a high incidence of protective terms that potentially reduce cash flows while protecting the rents expected by one or the other party."

10. The discussion of joint ventures in the commercial aircraft industry (Chapter 3) notes that joint ventures in which control of marketing, product support, and design functions was dispersed among partner firms, rather than being controlled by a single entity, have encountered severe problems.

11. This trend is consistent with Porter and Fuller's (1986, p. 334) observation that collaborative ventures centered on marketing "may be particularly unstable, however, because they frequently are formed because of the access motive on one or both sides. For example, one partner needs market access while the other needs access to product. As the foreign partner's market knowledge increases, there is less and less need for a local partner."

12. Brodley (1982, pp. 1528–29) summarizes the advantages of joint ventures, defined as separate corporate entities in which all partners hold equity shares, over mergers or market transactions as follows: "By providing for shared profits and managerial control, joint ventures tend to protect the participants from opportunism and information imbalance. The problem of valuing the respective contributions of the participants is mitigated, because they can await an actual market judgment. The temptation to exploit a favored bargaining position by threatening to withhold infusions of capital or other contributions is reduced by the need for continuous cooperation if the joint venture is to be effective. Moreover, a firm supplying capital to the joint venture can closely monitor the use of its contributed capital and thereby reduce its risk of loss. Common ownership also provides a means of spreading the costs of producing valuable information that could otherwise be protected from appropriation only by difficult-to-enforce contractual undertakings. Finally, joint ventures can effect economies of scale in research not achievable through single-firm action. Because of these advantages, joint ventures are especially likely to provide an optimal enterprise form in undertakings involving high risks, technological innovations, or high information costs."

13. Vernon (1979) presents similar arguments on the changing international economic environment.

14. Jones (1984) notes the convergence among the industrialized nations in the share of gross national product devoted to R&D and a less dramatic convergence in the proportion of R&D personnel in these countries' labor forces.

15. Recent efforts by a number of European governments to sell off publicly owned enterprises, such as the British government's divestiture of British Airways, a portion of British Aerospace, and British Telecom, as well as the discussion of plans by the Dutch, West German, and Swedish governments to sell all or part of their state-owned airlines may prefigure a significant change in the character of some major foreign markets. However, this "trend" is a very modest ripple at present, and will not destroy the informal sources of financial support and pressure that enable governments to exert considerable influence on the purchase decisions of "private" corporations.

16. See Ginsburg (1980) and the National Research Council (1983).

17. Nelson (1984, p. 84) argues that "Although I am less easy about joint design and production ventures than I am about generic research cooperation, it does not seem right that such an international venture would receive totally different treatment from that received by two or more U.S. firms in a design and production venture for which the market is clearly international. . . . It seems odd that we would discriminate against a national partnership if each partner judged this venture more promising economically than an international consortium."

REFERENCES

Arrow, K. J. 1962. "Economic Welfare and the Allocation of Resources for Invention." In *The Rate and Direction of Inventive Activity*. Princeton, N.J.: Princeton University Press for the National Bureau of Economic Research.

Brodley, J. F. 1982. "Joint Ventures and Antitrust Policy." *Harvard Law Review*, 95: 1523-1590.

Business Week. 1986. "Special Report: The Hollow Corporation," No. 2935, March 3, pp. 57-85.

Caves, R. E. 1982. *Multinational Enterprise and Economic Analysis*. Cambridge, England: Cambridge University Press.

Caves, R. E., H. Crookell, and J. P. Killing. 1983. "The Imperfect Market for Technology Licenses." *Oxford Bulletin of Economics and Statistics*, 45: 249-268.

Chandler, A. D., Jr. 1977. *The Visible Hand*. Cambridge, Mass.: Harvard University Press.

Cohen, W. M., R. C. Levin, and D. C. Mowery. 1987. "Firm Size and R&D Intensity: A Re-Examination," *Journal of Industrial Economics*, 35: 543-565.

Crane, D. M. 1984. "Joint Research and Development Ventures and the Antitrust Laws." *Harvard Journal on Legislation*, 21: 405-458.

Dunning, J. H. 1981. *International Production and the Multinational Enterprise*. London: George Allen and Unwin.

Friar, J., and M. Horwitch. 1986. "The Emergence of Technology Strategy." *Technology in Society*, 7: 143-178.

Ghemawat, P., M. E. Porter, and R. A. Rawlinson. 1986. "Patterns of International Coalition Activity." In M. E. Porter, ed., *Competition in Global Industries*. Boston, Mass.: Harvard Business School Press.

Ginsburg, D. J. 1980. *Antitrust, Uncertainty, and Innovation*. Washington, D.C.: National Research Council.

Graham, M. B. W. 1985. "Corporate Research and Development: The Latest Transformation." *Technology in Society*, 7: 179-195.

Gullander, S. 1976. "Joint Ventures in Europe: Determinants of Entry." *International Studies of Management and Organization*, 6: 85-111.

Harrigan, K. R. 1984. "Joint Ventures and Competitive Strategy." Working paper, Columbia University Graduate School of Business.

Hirsch, S. 1976. "An International Trade and Investment Theory of the Firm." *Oxford Economic Papers*, 28: 258-269.

Hladik, K. J. 1985. *International Joint Ventures.* Lexington, Mass.: Lexington Books.

Hymer, S. H. 1961 [1969]. *The International Operations of National Firms: A Study of Direct Foreign Investment.* Ph.D. thesis, Massachusetts Institute of Technology, 1961. Cambridge, Mass.: MIT Press, 1969.

Jones, K. 1984. "The Economic Implications of Restricting Trade in High-Technology Goods." Presented at the National Science Foundation workshop on the Economic Implications of Restrictions on Trade in High-Technology Goods, October 3.

Levin, R. C., W. M. Cohen, and D. C. Mowery. 1985. "R&D, Appropriability, and Market Structure: New Evidence on Some Schumpeterian Hypotheses." *American Economic Review*, 75: 20-24.

Miles, R. E., and C. C. Snow. 1986. "Organizations: New Concepts for New Forms." *California Management Review*, 28: 62-73.

Mowery, D. C. 1983. "Economic Theory and Government Technology Policy." *Policy Sciences*, 16: 27-43.

National Research Council. 1983. *International Competition in Advanced Technology: Decisions for America.* Washington, D.C.: National Research Council.

National Science Board. 1983. *University-Industry Research Relationships.* Washington, D.C.: National Science Foundation.

Nelkin, D., and R. R. Nelson. 1985. "University-Industry Alliances." Presented at the conference on New Alliances and Partnerships in American Science and Engineering, National Academy of Sciences, Washington, D.C., December 5.

Nelson, R. R. 1984. *High-Technology Policies: A Five Nation Comparison.* Washington, D.C.: American Enterprise Institute.

Perlmutter, H. V., and D. A. Heenan. 1986. "Cooperate to Compete Globally." *Harvard Business Review*, pp. 136-152.

Porter, M. E., and M. B. Fuller. 1986. "Coalitions and Global Strategy." In M. E. Porter, ed., *Competition in Global Industries.* Boston: Harvard Business School Press.

Reich, R. B., and E. D. Mankin. 1986. "Joint Ventures with Japan Give Away Our Future." *Harvard Business Review*, pp. 78-86.

Rugman, A. M. 1981. *Inside the Multinationals: The Economics of Internal Markets.* New York: Columbia University Press.

Scott, J. T. 1984. "Firm versus Industry Variability in R&D Intensity." In Z. Griliches, ed., *R&D, Patents, and Productivity.* Chicago: University of Chicago Press.

Stuckey, J. S. 1983. *Vertical Integration and Joint Ventures in the Aluminum Industry.* Cambridge, Mass.: Harvard University Press.

Teece, D. J. 1982. "Towards an Economic Theory of the Multiproduct Firm." *Journal of Economic Behavior and Organization*, 3: 39-63.

_____. 1986. "Profiting from Technological Innovation: Implications for Integration, Collaboration, Licensing, and Public Policy." *Research Policy*, 15: 285-305.

Vernon, R. S. 1966. "International Investment and International Trade in the Product Cycle." *Quarterly Journal of Economics*, 80: 190-207.

_____ . 1979. "The Product Cycle Hypothesis in a New International Environment." *Oxford Bulletin of Economics and Statistics*, 41: 255–267.

Von Hippel, E. 1976. "The Dominant Role of Users in the Scientific Instrument Innovation Process." *Research Policy*, 5: 212–239.

Williamson, O. E. 1975. *Markets and Hierarchies*. New York: Free Press.

2 JOINT VENTURES AND COLLABORATIVE ARRANGEMENTS IN THE TELECOMMUNICATIONS EQUIPMENT INDUSTRY

Gary P. Pisano, Michael V. Russo, and David J. Teece

The modern corporation appears to be undergoing a significant transformation. The early twentieth century was a period of integration and advance, the middle decades were marked by diversification, and the latter decades are characterized by both integration (via merger) and disintegration (via divestiture), coupled with a marked escalation in the frequency and complexity of collaborative arrangements. These arrangements, variously referred to as strategic partnerships, coalitions, and dynamic networks, include joint ventures, subcontracting, licensing, coproduction, cross distribution, and R&D collaboration. They constitute what might be called interorganizational linkages, and they may be changing the way in which commerce, and especially international commerce, takes place. Along with it, the nature and functions of management are changing.

Interorganizational linkages are not new. Joint ventures have been part of the commercial landscape since the modern corporation was born. Licensing and other complex contracts are also commonplace. What seems to be new are the following:

1. The increased frequency of collaborative deals
2. The diversity of age, industry, and nationality of the companies involved

We are grateful to David Mowery for helpful comments on drafts of this chapter and we are especially grateful to Enrico Ricotta for assisting us in obtaining access to the data analyzed in the fourth section. Financial support from the National Science Foundation (Grant No. SRS-8410556) and from the American Enterprise Institute is gratefully appreciated.

23

3. The frequency with which large firms are engaging in joint activities with small, entrepreneurial firms
4. The variety of functions involved, such as research, product development, manufacturing, and distribution

What is disturbing about this new epoch is our lack of understanding of the phenomenon and its long-run implications. There is only the vaguest notion afloat about the appropriate governance structures in which firms ought to embed their joint activities, an issue that we will address later.

Most efforts to explain cooperative agreements end up presenting a very eclectic view of the process. As Kogut (1985, p. 1) points out, "The motives are many, but . . . in order to compete in many industries, coalitions between firms have become obligatory." In this view, coalitions represent areas of cooperation within a larger competitive relationship.

Firms cooperate for a variety of reasons. Host government regulations often force foreign investors to joint venture with domestic firms. Second, there is international competition. In Kogut's (1985, p. 5) words, "in order to compete in global markets, it is necessary to have a presence in all major markets. . . . Frequently, though, market penetration requires substantial investments, such as in distribution or marketing. Few firms can afford the costs of investing in every major product and regional market." Miles and Snow (1986, p. 62) likewise see collaborative arrangements as an innovative organizational form that is both "cause and effect of today's competitive environment." A related environmental factor is the high fixed costs of product development coupled with the fragmentation of customer markets. This requires joint activities to capture "upstream" scope economies and "downstream" product differentiation. Both can be accomplished by collaborative upstream activities coupled with independent downstream adaptation and distribution. Competition thus occurs not at the firm level but at the network level with a pivotal firm anchoring each network.

The lists of rationales for collaboration do not, however, constitute a conceptual framework for making sense of the variety of arrangements that now characterize international business. Such a framework is necessary to enable managers to understand the strategic and organizational choices now confronting them. Building a suitable framework is a worthwhile endeavor, collaboration having become so pervasive as to challenge the basic concepts of the corporation to which we have become accustomed in the postwar years.

The purpose of this chapter is to put forward a general framework for explaining the phenomenon of collaboration and to suggest how collaborative arrangements might be structured to benefit the transacting parties. The framework is then used to explore collaborative arrangements in the telecommunications equipment industry, and, in the following chapter, biotechnology.

TOWARD A THEORY OF COLLABORATION AND THE CORPORATION

Collaborative agreements constitute an extraordinarily broad set of agreements. Many of these arrangements relate in some way to firms' efforts to commercialize new technology. Although in many instances firms collaborate to exchange commodities (an example being crude oil swaps in the petroleum industry), it is collaboration for the development and commercialization of technological knowhow that is the key to technology strategy.

Whereas deciding upon the allocation of R&D (as to levels and projects) was once considered the key issue in the management of technology, we contend that technology sourcing, commercialization, and related organizational choices are the key issues in the management of technology today. Deciding upon whether to develop technology in-house or use external sources and deciding how or with whom to commercialize it are now key issues for corporate and R&D managers. The more the corporation develops linkages with other key players, the more it takes on what Mel Horwitch (forthcoming) has called "postmodern" features. Figure 2-1 summarizes how we see postmodern corporations in relationship to classic corporations, whose development has been described most succinctly by Alfred Chandler (1962). Firms in the telecommunications equipment industry are taking on certain postmodern features through their collaborative activities.

Two key dimensions of corporate strategy are the international configuration of a firm's activities (where should they be located?) and the coordination of activities located in different countries (how should they be organized?). In Teece (1986) these dimensions are called the location decision and the governance decision. The first decision addresses issues such as where production facilities should be located; the second considers whether a firm should form a joint venture, set up a wholly owned subsidiary, or simply contract with a foreign firm for the goods and services in question.

Michael Porter (1985) has tackled this problem with a tool he calls the "value chain." This involves disaggregating economic activity into the discrete activities performed in developing, producing, marketing, selling, and servicing a product. Coalitions and joint ven-

Figure 2-1. Dimensions of Technology Strategy.

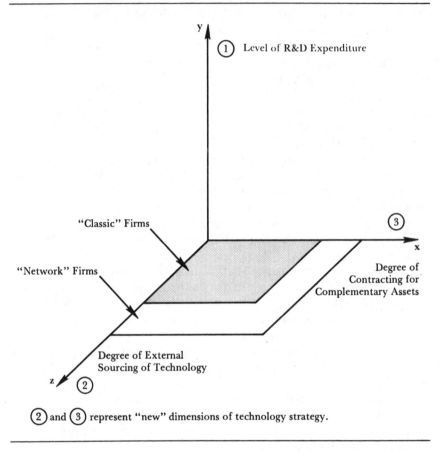

② and ③ represent "new" dimensions of technology strategy.

tures are then seen as being formed to perform any activity or group of activities in the value chain. "Coalitions arise when performing an activity with a partner is less costly than performing it internally on the one hand, and to reliance on arms-length contracts or merger with another firm on the other" (Porter and Fuller, 1986, p. 321).

Within this framework, which is so far quite similar to our own, coalitions are seen as creating four classes of benefits: economies of scale and learning, access to an incumbent's superior capacities, risk reduction, and "shaping" competition. Costs include coordination, competitive position, and rent extraction. Ultimately, however, Porter recognizes that coalitions must be compared to other organizational forms, such as integration or arms-length contracts. Interestingly, integration is viewed as permitting better information disclosures and coalitions are viewed providing better incentives than contracts. Coalitions permit faster repositioning than mergers, and the cash requirements are less than for integration.

Because an important facet of collaboration in our framework is whether the deal does or does not involve equity ownership, we classify collaborative governance structures into two basic categories—those that involve sharing equity and those that do not. Before attempting to develop a theory of the firm that will help to explain why firms will choose one or another of these modes, we need to present some analytical tools.[1]

A fundamental factor conditioning whether an innovator will wish to deal with others is the degree to which its intellectual property is already protected. The two most important factors affecting this are the efficacy of legal protection mechanisms for the technology in question and the nature of the technology itself. Simplistically, we can divide appropriability regimes into the "weak" (innovations are difficult to protect because they can be easily codified and legal protection mechanisms are ineffective) and the "strong" (innovations are easy to protect because knowledge about them is tacit or they are well protected legally). Despite recent efforts to strengthen protection of intellectual property, strong appropriability is the exception rather than the rule.

The best market entry strategies for firms with good, marketable ideas depend not only on the appropriability regime, but also on where the industry is in its development cycle (Dosi, 1982). The existence of a dominant design watershed is of great significance to the strategic positions of the innovator and its competitors or collaborators. Once a dominant design emerges, competition shifts to price and away from design. Competitive success then shifts to a new set of variables. Scale and learning become much more important, and specialized capital displaces generalized capital as incumbents seek to lower unit costs through exploiting economies of scale and learning. Reduced uncertainty over product design provides an opportunity to amortize specialized, long-lived investments.

If an innovator has survived the selection of the dominant design, it faces a new problem—that of securing access to the relevant complementary assets. In almost all cases, the successful commercialization of an innovation requires that the know-how in question be utilized in conjunction with the services of other assets, such as marketing, competitive manufacturing, and after-sales support. These services are often obtained from complementary assets that are specialized.

Figure 2-2. Representative Complementary Assets Needed to Commercialize an Innovation.

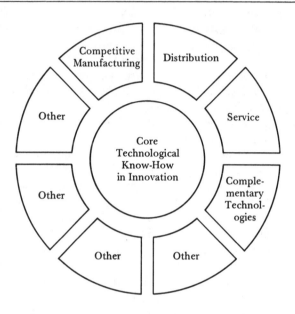

The notion that an innovation requires complementary assets is implicit to Porter's value-chain analysis. Porter has demonstrated the usefulness of disaggregating a firm's business into its constituent functions. Our own version of this—which is more general since it focuses on disaggregating the structure of the required microeconomic activity rather than on the firm itself—is presented in Figure 2-2. The normative question to be addressed is what governance structures to impose over (and between) these elements.

These units of economic activity already are or can be located globally so as to minimize the costs of performing each segment of economic activity. We now ask how the innovator should organize these activities—purely market, purely internal, or through various collaborative (mixed) approaches. The answer depends on the appropriability regime, the nature of the complementary assets (are they specialized or idiosyncratic to the innovation?), and the prior market positioning of the innovator with respect to the crucial complementary assets.

The interdependence between innovators and complementary assets can vary tremendously. At one extreme, the complementary assets may be virtually generic, have many potential suppliers, and be relatively unimportant when compared with technological break-through represented by the innovation. At the other, successful commercialization of the innovation may depend on a crucial asset that has only one possible supplier and is thus a potential bottleneck.

Between these two extremes lies the possibility of "cospecialization," where the innovation and the asset depend on each other. An example is containerized shipping, which requires specialized trucks and terminals that can only work in conjunction with each other.

The main decision facing the innovator once a dominant design has emerged is how to access the relevant complementary assets. Although there are many possible arrangements, two extremes stand out. At one extreme the innovator could build or acquire all of the complementary assets. This is likely to be unnecessary as well as prohibitively expensive. The variety of assets and competencies needed is likely to be quite large, even for only modestly complex technologies. At the other extreme, the innovator could attempt to access these assets through straightforward contractual relationships (for example, component supply contracts, fabrication contracts, distribution contracts). In many instances a contract may suffice, although it does expose the innovator to various hazards and dependencies that it may wish to avoid. An analysis of the properties of the two extremes will be instructive before considering collaborative arrangements, which are mixtures of the two pure cases.

Nonequity, Contractual Modes

The advantages of contractual agreements, whereby the innovator lays down no equity and contracts with unaffiliated suppliers, manufacturers, or distributors, are obvious. The innovator will not have to spend capital to build or buy the assets in question. This reduces the risks associated with a poor market reception as well as cash requirements to bring a product to the market. Moreover, the innovator may gain credibility, especially if the innovator is unknown while the contractual partner is well established.

Such arrangements entail certain hazards, particularly when the innovator is trying to use contracts to access special capabilities. For instance, it may be difficult to induce suppliers to make costly, irreversible commitments whose value depends critically on the success of the innovation. To expect suppliers, manufacturers, and distributors to do so is to invite them to take risks along with the innovator. The problem posed for the innovator is analogous to the problems associated with attracting venture capital. The innovator must persuade its prospective partner that the risk is a good one. The situation is open to opportunistic abuses on both sides. The innovator has incentives to overstate the value of the innovation, while the supplier has incentives to "run with the technology" should it prove successful.

In short, the current euphoria over "strategic partnering" may be partially misplaced. Besides the risk that the partner will not fulfill the contract to the innovator's satisfaction, there is the added danger that the partner may imitate the innovator's technology and attempt to compete with the innovator. The latter danger is more acute if the provider of the complementary asset is uniquely situated with respect to the specialized asset and has the capacity to absorb and imitate the technology.[2]

Full Equity, Integration Modes

Pure integration modes, which by definition involve common ownership, are distinguished from pure contractual modes in that they typically facilitate greater control and greater access to commercial information (Williamson, 1975; Teece, 1976). Owning rather than renting the complementary assets has clear advantages when they are in fixed supply. It is critical, of course, that ownership be obtained before the requirements of the innovation become publicly known, otherwise the price of the assets in question will rise.

Because there may not be time to acquire or to build the complementary assets that ideally it would like to control, an innovator needs to rank complementary assets. The need for ownership is higher for more critical complementary assets.

When imitation is easy, strategic moves to build or to buy specialized complementary assets must occur with due reference to the moves of competitors. There is no point in moving to build a specialized asset if imitators can do it faster. Figure 2-3 summarizes the decisions that ought to be examined before pursuing integration strategies.

If the innovator is already a large enterprise with many of the relevant complementary assets under its control, integration is not likely to be the issue that it might otherwise be. However, in industries experiencing rapid technological change, it is unlikely that a single company has the full range of expertise needed to bring advanced products to market in a timely and cost effective fashion. This is especially true when the boundaries between formerly distinct businesses begin to erode. This is precisely the case in telecommunications, where expertise in computer technology is an essential success factor. In the case of AT&T, integration of these two businesses was

Figure 2-3.   Flowchart for Integration versus Collaboration Decision.

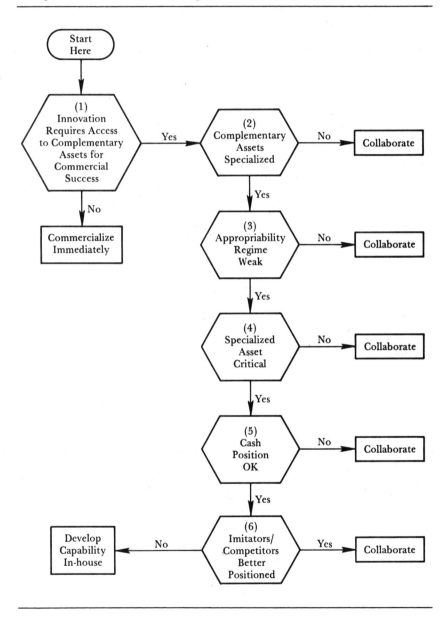

specifically barred by public policy. Hence, integration can be an issue of concern to large as well as small firms.

Mixed Modes: Collaborative Arrangements

Between the extremes of pure contracts and internal organization lies a rich diversity of governance structures that mix elements of both. These attempt to combine judiciously the flexibility of arms-length contracts with the coordination and communication properties of internal organization. Various mechanisms can be used to build such intermediate structures. Two of these are examined below.

Equity Joint Ventures. An equity joint venture, the creation of a new entity jointly owned and operated by the collaborators, is the classic form of organizing collaborative activity. Most studies of jointly organized activities have focused almost exclusively on this legal form. Equity joint ventures have two governance properties that make them ideal for coordinating complex transactions involving specialized assets. First, they create an administrative hierarchy for setting general operational and strategic policies as well as for settling disputes. This structure obviates the need for collaborators to attempt the often impossible task of specifying a complete set of contractual provisions for conducting the collaboration. Instead, the collaborators need only agree on a broad framework of rules for deciding on more specific conditions as more information becomes available. Moreover, the governing body of the venture, usually composed of representatives of both companies, can, if used properly, provide a channel for communicating pertinent information and for coordinating the collaborative roles of the partners.

The second advantage of equity joint ventures is that both parties hold a direct stake in the success of the project. Equity positions align incentives and can lower the risk that one party will behave opportunistically. Partners pay some share of the costs of any actions they take that hurt the viability of the venture. In addition, the formal ownership structure provides each party legal rights with respect to the technology and other strategic assets contributed to or developed by the venture. Parties can agree at the outset about the division of assets in the event of termination of the venture.

Joint ventures entail certain costs. They tend to take longer to negotiate and organize than less hierarchical forms of governance. Given these costs, they are usually appropriate only for longer term projects that involve heavy capital or technological commitment by both parties.

Direct Equity Positions. An alternative to establishing a jointly owned company is for one partner to take a direct equity stake in the other. This is often used where a significant size differential exists between the collaborators and it would be impossible for the smaller party to contribute enough equity into a jointly owned company. The direct equity approach governing features similar to equity joint ventures although they generally provide for less joint control. First, the equity stake again helps to align incentives. It safeguards the smaller partner (or investee) by creating direct costs for the investor to act opportunistically. If the investor takes any action that hurts the investee, it will bear some portion of the resulting costs through its equity stake. Usually the parties to the investment agree on a set of longer run strategic and operational goals of the relationship. The contribution of equity helps to ensure that the investor will have an interest in ensuring that these strategic and operational goals are pursued in good faith.

The direct equity stake can provide some scope for hierarchical governance (as opposed to strictly contractual governance) if it allows the investor a seat on the other company's board of directors. The goal is not to achieve voting power but to gain a channel of direct communication to the highest governing level of the other partner. This ensures that the top management of that partner stays interested in the business relationship. It can help to ensure that critical problems and issues will be brought directly to the top management, rather than having to percolate up from the line managers in charge of the collaborative effort. The board position also helps information to circulate the other way, back to the investor. Often, the corporate investor appoints one of its high level executives to fill the board seat. This provides the recipient of the investment with a channel back to the corporate partner. Like the equity joint venture, direct equity relationships have advantages over nonequity, contractual forms of collaboration when the activities in question involve transaction-specific assets and uncertainty. The use of contractual, equity, and internal forms of organization in the telecommunications equipment industry is discussed in the following section.

JOINT VENTURES IN THE TELECOMMUNICATIONS EQUIPMENT INDUSTRY

Joint ventures in the telecommunications equipment industry reflect broader changes in the structure of the telecommunications industry. Since the early 1970s, a combination of technological, economic, and regulatory changes has changed the structure of the world's markets for telecommunications equipment, simultaneously creating new market opportunities and competitive threats for suppliers. Joint ventures represent an adaptive response by equipment suppliers to the new competitive environment.

Until recently the telecommunications equipment industry was organized around domestic markets where a single buyer (a government owned or regulated telephone service monopoly) purchased most of its equipment from a few, usually domestic, suppliers. In the case of the U.S. market, American Telephone and Telegraph, the major service provider, owned its own equipment manufacturing subsidiary, Western Electric, which supplied approximately 65 percent of its equipment. While vertical integration between equipment suppliers and service providers was not the norm around the world, the effect on procurement was similar. In Japan, the national service monopoly, Nippon Telegraph and Telephone, purchased approximately two-thirds of its equipment from four domestic suppliers (NEC [Nippon Electric Company], Oki, Fujitsu, Hitachi) (U.S. Department of Commerce, 1983, p. 24). The French market was dominated by Thompson, the German market by Siemens, and the British market by the General Electric Company of Great Britain and Plessey. As a consequence, very few equipment suppliers (with the exception of Ericsson, International Telephone and Telegraph, and Philips) ventured beyond their domestic equipment markets. In fact, AT&T was legally prohibited from selling equipment outside the United States.

A second element of this market structure was that the main equipment producers supplied a full range of components for a telecommunications system (phones, switching equipment, transmission equipment). This equipment was *rented* and not sold. One rationale for this structure was to ensure technical compatibility among various components in the telecommunications network. This policy was sometimes referred to as maintaining the integrity of the network.

Since the early 1970s two major forces have driven changes in the structure of the telecommunications equipment industry. First, regulatory changes in the United States opened the world's largest equipment market to new sources of supply and created new sources of demand. Second, technological changes have created new product market opportunities, generated new sources of innovation in telecommunications equipment, forged new market boundaries, and changed the cost structure of the equipment industry.

Regulatory Changes and a New Structure of Demand

The American market, the world's largest, changed dramatically with changes in the U.S. regulatory regime. The 1968 "Carterphone" decision and subsequent decisions of the Federal Communications Commission during the 1970s increasingly opened the equipment market and AT&T's procurement market to outside suppliers. These decisions affected the customer-premises market and opened the door to Rolm, a U.S. supplier of private branch exchanges (PBXs), Northern Telecom and Mitel (of Canada), and NEC, Fujitsu, Oki, and Iwatsu (of Japan). Even before the 1984 AT&T divestiture, Western Electric's share of the U.S. telecommunications market was declining rapidly, especially in the PBX area.

The U.S. Justice Department's antitrust suit against AT&T originally set out to split AT&T from its manufacturing subsidiary as a way of opening competition in the U.S. equipment market. In 1982 AT&T settled the case by agreeing to divest itself of its twenty-two local operating companies. In return, AT&T was freed from a 1956 consent decree that prohibited it from entering businesses outside of telecommunications. The twenty-two local operating companies were reorganized into seven regional operating companies. These regional operating companies are forbidden by the Modified Final Judgment from manufacturing their own equipment. However, they are free to purchase equipment from any suppliers (domestic or foreign) that they choose. The U.S. local operating company equipment market, valued at $20.1 billion in 1987 (by Inan and Lannon, 1987), has created a major opportunity for potential domestic and foreign equipment suppliers.

A second factor expanding opportunities in the U.S. market has been the rise of interconnect companies (which provide "private" communications systems), new common carriers for long-distance (including MCI, US Sprint, Southern Pacific), domestic satellite firms, and value-added carriers. Together, these firms generated approximately 25 percent of the U.S. demand for telecommunications equipment in 1983. This segment was also one of the most dynamic, with a rate of growth of demand in 1983 of 43 percent (U.S. Department of Commerce, 1983, p. 16). The value-added carriers purchase some of the most sophisticated telecommunications equipment available today. This includes equipment for transmitting real-time pictures (used in teleconferencing), still pictures (facsimile), data, text (videotex), and voice (radio phones).

No other country has matched the United States in the extent of telecommunications deregulation and the resulting creation of new market opportunities. Political barriers as well as a lack of common technical standards have prevented any significant opening of the major European markets. They remain structured largely around domestic suppliers who sell to the national postal telephone and telegraph (PTT) agency. The Japanese equipment markets, while protected by numerous trade barriers, have opened slightly in the past few years. The improved access to Japan's interconnect market has allowed U.S. firms such as Rolm to make some inroads into the Japanese markets. Whether foreign markets undergo the radical structural changes witnessed in the United States will depend largely on political decisions within countries and agreements among them.

The Convergence of Computers and Communications

The trajectory of technical change in telecommunications equipment has seen the increasing application of microelectronic circuitry and software-controlled automation. This trajectory has had two consequences for telecommunications markets and suppliers. First, the use of electronic switching has altered the economics of telecommunications networks in a way that has radically restructured the customer-premises equipment (CPE) market. Second, these technical changes have altered the set of R&D skills necessary to innovate and thus compete in telecommunications equipment.

The New Markets for Customer-Premises Equipment. Historically, the high costs and slow speed of switching equipment dictated that telecommunication network design minimize the number of switches relative to phone lines. Huber (1987, p. 1.2) described the Bell System network as a pyramid whereby:

> Customer-premises equipment was primitive, and occupied a correspondingly humble position at the very lowest level of the network pyramid. Arrayed above in a rigid hierarchy lay the five tiers of the AT&T switching system. Thousands of Class 5 switches were located at the apex, providing the highest levels of national coordination and control. Three intermediate tiers of switching lay in between.

The advent of microelectronics and digital circuitry increased the speed of switching while dramatically decreasing switching costs per line. This has permitted the use of more switches, farther down the network hierarchy (closer to the end user) and has thus shifted the distribution of intelligence within the network from central office switching centers toward the customer premises. The cost reductions from microelectronics that have enabled this shift have had a similar effect on the locus of computer processing power. The decreasing costs and size of central processing units have redistributed the locus of computer processing power from centralized mainframes toward mini- and microcomputers on the user's premises (or desk). The lower costs of switching and computer equipment have allowed business computer users to create their own on-premises networks of personal and minicomputers. This has created massive new demand for customer-premises switching and transmission equipment that can handle data (which is carried in digital form). Over the past several years, the PBX and local area networks (LAN) have been introduced for the customer-premises data communications market.

As technological changes have driven down the costs of distributed computer and communications intelligence, private end users themselves have become important customers in the market for telecommunications equipment. They account for 40 percent of the switching equipment sales in the United States, 20 percent of microwave transmission equipment sales, and 20 percent of fiber optic cable and electronics sales (Huber, 1987, p. 1.11). This shift in the locus of purchases is reflected in the rapid growth of the market for PBXs, which are generally used by private customers. PBX sales revenues are now greater than those of new central office equipment (used by common carriers) (Huber, 1987, p. 1.11, fn. 13). An important factor behind the demand for PBXs in the United States lies in the flat rate per line pricing schemes mandated by state regulatory commissions. When an end user is charged a flat rate per line into the common carrier network, there is a strong incentive to minimize the number of external lines. PBXs reduce the number of lines needed for outside access by allowing customers to route their internal traffic entirely on their own, bypassing the local common carrier's central office switch.

Because of the regulatory changes in the United States discussed above, the revival of the CPE market has been most pronounced in the United States. The trend toward CPE-controlled computing and switching, however, is also a technological phenomenon that is international in scope. The emerging office automation and factory automation markets are an outgrowth of this trend. The development of these markets outside the United States will depend largely on whether foreign regulatory policies are reformed in ways similar to the initiatives undertaken in the United States. The current posture in many countries supports the status quo, which in turn suppresses restructuring of the markets for CPE.

New R&D Skills and New Costs of Development. Technical change in switching has also had direct effects on the equipment suppliers themselves. Switching equipment suppliers must have access to state-of-the-art microelectronics and software engineering capabilities to stay competitive. The pace and complexity of new technology have created new sources of innovation outside the boundaries of established equipment producers. For example, merchant semiconductor firms now play an important role in developing electronic components for communications applications. Other potential contributors to telecommunications equipment innovation include the computer firms that have technical know-how and engineering skills to apply elements of computer design to equipment systems.

The pace of technical change in microelectronics and computer technology has shortened the life cycles of switching products while increasing their costs of development. Electronic switches for public carrier central offices can cost from $500 million to $1 billion to develop and become obsolete within five years of introduction. These increased fixed costs have made it imperative that firms achieve a relatively large threshold of sales revenues and thus have increased pressures to market on a global scale. Industry experts generally acknowledge that a supplier needs a minimum of 10–15 percent of the world's $13.5 billion central office switch market to survive. This has increased the importance for foreign firms to enter the U.S. market, which represents 40 percent of that total (*Northern Business Information*, 1986, pp. 36, 39).

The regulatory and technological changes have altered the bundle of strategic competencies and assets necessary to compete in various segments of the telecommunications equipment industry. One result has been substantial entry into the U.S. market by both domestic and foreign firms. In 1978 there were 380 firms producing telecommunication equipment in the United States; by 1983 the number had grown to approximately 550 (U.S. International Trade Commission, 1984, p. 49). Nevertheless, most segments of the telecommunications equipment market remained highly concentrated by 1983. The five firm concentration ratio for transmission equipment was 0.92, for switching 1.0, for customer-premises equipment 0.88, for cable, wire, and lightguide 1.0. To gain access to the requisite competencies and assets, firms in this industry have frequently turned to joint ventures and other forms of cooperation. In summary, we can distinguish two general strategic assets to which firms seek access in the telecommunications equipment industry: (1) access to product and geographic markets and (2) access to technology.

The Governance of Telecommunications Equipment Joint Ventures

The structural changes outlined have created a *market for strategic assets* among firms supplying various types of telecommunications equipment. Both strategic assets providing access to new product and geographic markets and those providing access to complementary or critical input technologies are traded through various governance arrangements, including arms-length contracts, internal organization, and joint ventures.

The Market for Strategic Assets in Telecommunications Equipment

Both market access and technology access may be involved in any given relationship. Distribution arrangements often involve technology transfer or joint development and production of new products. The following discussion is therefore organized around three types of functional arrangements: (1) distribution or marketing only, (2) distribution or marketing coupled with other functions (manufacturing, R&D, product integration), (3) technology access only (joint R&D, technology transfer, licensing).

Distribution or Marketing. The opening of new geographic markets (the United States in particular) and the creation of new product markets have generated demand for distribution and marketing channels into specific geographic and product markets. Data compiled from the business press on joint ventures and collaborative contracts in telecommunications equipment[3] indicates the following: of the 117 arrangements announced, 50 included marketing or distribution as at least one of the motives for one partner; of these 50, marketing or distribution was the sole motive in 35 cases.

A telecommunications equipment supplier that wishes to tap a new geographic or product market has three broad options: (1) it can build the requisite distribution channels itself, (2) it can license existing firms in the market to distribute and market its product(s), (3) it can acquire the relevant distribution channels through some type of joint venture agreement with an existing firm in the market.

The first option, de novo entry, can be prohibitively costly for several reasons. First, many equipment suppliers lack experience marketing their products in competitive markets. An excellent example is AT&T, which will be examined in more detail later. Second, acquiring knowledge of the customers' needs and procurement process in new product and geographic markets requires experience with the customer, which by definition, the new entrant lacks. Procurement in European markets is often a political as well as economic process. New foreign entrants lack the political contacts and hands-on experience to navigate proposals through the proper channels. Third, creating telecommunications equipment distribution channels requires costly specialized investments. A sales and maintenance force must be trained; time and considerable effort must be expended to establish contacts with customers and to learn the market; in some cases additional manufacturing facilities must be built to supply the new market. Before making such specialized investments, the entrant may want to test the waters with a smaller, less risky effort.

Given the costs and risks of investing in de novo distribution, a seemingly attractive alternative is to access the distribution channels of an established firm. This allows the entrant to tap marketing experience and knowledge that would be too costly and time consuming for it to develop on its own. At the same time, the entrant can test the market without investing in durable and specialized assets. Such an arrangement would be more efficient than de novo entry—that is, the established firm can provide distribution services for the entrant at a lower cost than the entrant could provide them for itself. However, given the nature of distribution and marketing in telecommunications equipment, transaction costs will affect the feasibility and form of such an arrangement.

An entrant wanting to access an incumbent's distribution network has two basic alternatives. One alternative is an arms-length contract whereby the incumbent agrees to provide a set of distribution and marketing services on behalf of the supplier. There are numerous variations of this contractual scheme, one of which is the *original equipment manufacturing* (OEM) deal. However, these contractual schemes share certain basic characteristics. The distributor either purchases the equipment and resells it or sells the equipment for the supplier in return for a commission. The arrangements are generally cancellable on short notice, and they vest considerable marketing or distribution control in the hands of the designated distributor. An example is the 1985 Toshiba-Tandy agreement whereby Tandy will market Toshiba's office telephones in the United States under Tandy's label.

The second distribution alternative is for the entrant and the incumbent to form some type of joint venture whereby they share the financial, managerial, and strategic responsibilities of distribution and marketing. Such joint ventures are commonly organized around equity investments, either through the formation of a jointly owned company—the classical joint venture—or through a direct equity investment by one partner into the other. In some cases the equity route is preferred because both parties have existing assets that can be pooled. For example, Fujitsu and GTE formed a joint venture to market PBXs and related business communication systems in the United States that combines the separate operations of Fujitsu America and the business systems division of GTE.

The choice between arms-length distribution contracts and distribution joint ventures should be strongly influenced by the nature of requisite distribution investments and activities. There are three conditions under which arms-length distribution contracts will suffer transactional inefficiencies. First, when the distributor acquires specialized knowledge of the customers and the product during execution of the contract, switching distributors becomes costly because a new distributor would lack the knowledge accumulated by the first. Such switching costs provide the distributor with bargaining leverage to negotiate a better contract with the supplier (acquiring higher commissions, more advertising support, and so forth). The extent of the problem will be greater if the product is unique and customers have idiosyncratic needs. The business communications market is an example where systems are often tailored to the needs of specific clients around nonstandardized components.

The second situation where transactional problems arise is in markets where products that are not standard require after-sales service and upgrading. The supplier takes the chance that the distributor may not train sales and service personnel adequately as to the product's idiosyncrasies. As a result, sales and after-sales service could suffer. The distributor, on the other hand, may be hesitant to invest in such training if it is costly and not applicable to the firm's own or other suppliers' product lines. Such a transaction-specific investment would be lost if the supplier were to cancel the contract.

In most telecommunications markets, sales of equipment to upgrade or improve existing systems generate a stream of revenues. Where technical standards exist, the distributor faces little uncertainty over securing a future supply of compatible equipment. If the distributor cancels a distribution agreement with one firm, it can sell another supplier's product(s) to its customers. However, many customer-premises markets, especially the business systems market, lack such standards, and uncertainty prevails over how future standards will evolve. The risk is that if a distribution contract is canceled, the distributor will not be able to secure a new source of equipment to upgrade its customers' equipment. Forgone upgrade sales are one cost. Perhaps just as important is the cost to the distributor's reputation when customers find themselves stranded with a system that cannot be upgraded.

A final condition under which arms-length distribution agreements are likely to fail is when the pace of product innovation is rapid. Rapid product innovation increases the burden of communication flows between the supplier and distributor. The supplier needs information from the distributor about customers' needs. In fact, research on the likelihood of the commercial success of innovation has shown that understanding user's needs is critical to successful innovation (see Freeman, 1982). For most large-scale systems, the supplier will need the distributor's help in finding a test site. On the other end, the distributor needs to be kept informed about changes in the project's status and the product's design in order to prepare its marketing program. It may be unclear whether the new product is covered under the distribution contract. Product boundaries and definitions in various equipment segments also change. Disputes may arise if the supplier wants to distribute the product through a different channel. Specifying the future product scope of the agreement is difficult when innovation blurs the boundaries between previously well-defined market segments.

The transaction costs rationale for going beyond arms-length contracts compound when the distribution and marketing agreement is part of a broader relationship involving technology transfer, joint R&D, product-line integration, and manufacturing.

Distribution or Marketing Coupled with Other Functions. Our database shows that out of fifty arrangements involving distribution, fifteen also involved some combination of R&D and production. There are many reasons for such multifunction agreements. One rationale is actually a response to some of the transactional difficulties. In analyzing the details of several arrangements, we found that access to technology was granted in exchange for the provision of other services (such as distribution). The AT&T-Philips and AT&T-Olivetti joint ventures are cases where technology transfer was granted in exchange for other services. Barter involving technology may help to support the exchange of other services.

Consider the predicament of the firm that makes idiosyncratic investment to distribute another firm's products. The firm has transaction-specific capital at risk should the supplier stop delivering the specified products. One way to protect the distributor, and thus encourage it to make the necessary transaction-specific investments, is to grant it a license to manufacture and market the product. In Honeywell's agreement with Ericsson to distribute a PBX line in the United States, Honeywell was granted a license to manufacture the system in the event that Ericsson stopped supplying the product (around which Honeywell was developing compatible complementary products). Agreements that incorporate ongoing technology exchanges can also prevent opportunism by raising the benefits of continued cooperation. Technology as a form of payment can also be used to diffuse adoption of a firm-specific standard among as many customers as possible. We should note that technology barter to support exchanges is used in other industries. In pharmaceuticals and semiconductors, it takes the form of cross-licensing; new biotechnology firms often grant licenses as partial compensation to partners providing manufacturing and marketing services (see Chapter 6).

In many cases technology access is packaged with other distribution because technology is central to the strategic goals of the relationship. There are three common cases in telecommunications equipment where technology access and distribution form a single package. First, distribution and technology are commonly coupled when two companies agree to integrate their product lines to form a system. For example, Plessey (United Kingdom) and Mitsubishi formed a joint venture to market cellular mobile phone systems in the United States; the systems would use Plessey's digital switching equipment and Mitsubishi's radio frequency equipment, mobile phone transceivers, and data links. AT&T and Electronic Data Systems (EDS) (a General Motors subsidiary) have a similar agreement to develop and market specially designed computer and communications systems; teams of EDS and AT&T engineers are working together to design and assemble customer hardware and software systems. A contributing factor is the convergence of previously distinct technologies and markets that creates interdependencies between the development and marketing of various products. As we would expect, these arrangements often bring together PBX or LAN vendors with firms making computers and other peripheral equipment.

A second case in which R&D and technology exchange are part of a broader distribution agreement occurs when a product must be modified for use in a particular market. In telecommunications equipment, this often results from the lack of standards among different geographic markets. This is especially common when companies sell their central office switches and transmission equipment in foreign markets. Such modifications can be a complicated and costly endeavor, which requires the technical expertise of a manufacturer familiar with local specifications. Ericsson is reported to have invested $100 million to modify one of its switching systems for the American market; ITT invested $200 million (20 percent of its worldwide R&D) to adapt a central office switch to the *Lata Switching Generic Requirements* of the American market (Done, 1986). Ericsson has only recently sold systems in the United States; ITT wrote off the entire investment when it dropped out of the U.S. equipment market.

A third case in which technology transfer forms part of the package occurs when production economics or political barriers dictate that the product be manufactured locally or by a particular firm. Corning, for example, has its optical fibers manufactured in France (via Fibre Optiques Industries, 40 percent owned by Corning), in Wales (via Optical Fibres, 50 percent), Australia (via Optical Waveguides Australia Pty. 50 percent), in West Germany (via Siecor, 50 percent), and in the United States for a combination of economic and political reasons.

When distribution arrangements involve R&D and technology transfer as basic strategic functions, there are transactional difficulties in addition to those examined earlier for the case of straight distribution. Briefly, these include the costs and difficulties of transferring complex and tacit technology (Teece, 1981), the organizational burdens of coordinating the development of complementary systems, the risks of investing in know-how or manufacturing facilities that are transaction-specific.

These increased transactional burdens should be reflected in the choice of governance structures. We hypothesize that the relative frequency of joint-venture arrangements (as compared to arms-length contracts) should be higher for distribution agreements that include some combination of R&D and manufacturing. This hypothesis is tested in the data analysis section of this chapter.

Technology Access Arrangements.   Of the 117 arrangements in the database, 36 comprise strictly technology transfer or R&D integration. Collaborative technology agreements can take several forms.

One form is the R&D joint venture where two or more firms pool their R&D resources and existing technology over some set of product development efforts. Achieving minimum scale economies in R&D is the usual rationale attributed to such relationships. While the costs of developing certain types of telecommunications equipment have soared since the mid-1970s, we find little evidence that cost alone is driving joint R&D in this industry. There are two basic reasons why R&D scale economies do not drive R&D joint ventures in telecommunications equipment. First, the central office and transmission equipment markets (where product development is most costly) are dominated by large firms. Firms such as AT&T, Northern Telecom, GTE, Philips, Siemens, and NEC do not lack the financial resources to fund the necessary levels of R&D. Second, many firms have made the strategic decision to expand their geographic coverage rather than to pool R&D with other firms in order to cover the high fixed costs of product development. The opening of the U.S. market has made this alternative feasible, although its ultimate success remains to be seen; AT&T, Northern Telecom, and GTE control approximately 85 percent, of the U.S. market for digital central office equipment market (measured by lines shipped). The degree to which other national markets will be liberalized and standardized depends on political factors and is highly uncertain.

Various European government initiative and European Economic Community programs have brought together Europe's leading telecommunications equipment firms in various joint projects (ESPRIT, for example). One of the claimed motives behind these joint programs is to help European equipment firms achieve necessary economies of scale in R&D. The projects, however, do not generally aim to develop particular products. Instead, they are focused on developing and diffusing generic technological know-how among Europe's manufacturers.

It is the nature of R&D and the innovation process in telecommunications equipment, rather than the sheer costs, that are driving the incidence of cooperative technology agreements. As innovation in telecommunications equipment has become more tightly coupled to computer and microelectronic technologies, the resulting interdependence in design paths has had two effects. First, innovation has become far more systemic in the sense that a new product may require changes in the configuration or operating characteristics of the system to which it is connected. For example, advances in LAN and PBX technology must be consistent with the communications protocols of computers and other peripherals that have become part of telecommunications networks. Similarly, the design of computer systems must take into account existing as well as future communications protocols. The second effect of the convergence of telecommunication, computers, and microelectronics has been the creation of new sources of innovation in the form of start-ups and new entrants in PBXs, LANs, communications software, integrated circuits for communications applications, and terminal equipment.

The overall effect of this trend has been to make it more difficult and inefficient for the major equipment firms to track all the relevant technological fronts themselves. Hence they collaborate in various ways to gain access to *complementary* technologies. The relationship sometimes consists of nothing more than a license granting one firm the right to use a certain technology, such as a proprietary communications protocol or operating system.

Another form consists of an R&D contract. Straight R&D contracts are not common in this industry. R&D contracts are generally bundled with supply agreements and perhaps other technology exchange provisions over a some period of time. Thus, when an equipment supplier contracts with a semiconductor merchant to develop a communications chip, the agreement often includes a supply contract and provisions for continued technological cooperation. The resulting technology is often jointly owned by both the contractor and the contractee. Such provisions are designed to protect both parties from opportunistic recontracting.

Another reason that classical R&D contracting is not common in telecommunications equipment again relates to the systemic nature of innovation. Complex systems designs are rarely stable throughout the development process. As unexpected technical problems arise, the design of the entire system or particular components may need to change. To facilitate the requisite communication and coordination, the systems firms and the component contractor often bring their engineering teams together in a joint effort. For example, engineers from AT&T and EDS are working together to develop special communications systems. Engineers from Texas Instruments and IBM have been working together to develop integrated circuits for IBM's token-ring LAN.

Thus the form of a collaborative technology arrangement seems to depend on its function. Arms-length contracts seem adequate if permission to use a certain protocol is the only function of the agreement. In contrast, joint development of complex systems requires a degree of coordination not attainable through arms-length contracts. Joint R&D arrangements can emulate many of the coordination capabilities of internal organization. However, whether such joint R&D needs to be organized through more hierarchical arrangements (such as an equity joint venture) depends on the nature of the project and the goals of the relationship. Where joint R&D creates durable, transaction-specific assets, it is efficient for both parties to continue cooperation for the life of those assets. In these cases more hierarchical forms of collaboration that can better solve disputes and operational problems are warranted.

Joint R&D creates transaction-specific capital but the durability and value of such capital is low compared with that required in the production and distribution of telecommunication equipment. It is probably not worth establishing a joint company solely to cooperate in R&D. One alternative is to form collaborative relationships through partial equity investments. These may provide enough governance to overcome the transactional difficulties of arms-length contracts without creating the rigid hierarchies of acquisitions or joint venture companies.

Before testing the hypotheses about the relationship between governance form and function, we illustrate a few points in more detail through some short case studies.

AT&T and Olivetti

In December 1983 AT&T and Olivetti reached an agreement in which AT&T took an equity position in the Italian office automation company. This agreement formed a bridge between AT&T, with $12 billion in 1983 telecommunications sales, and Olivetti, with $1.3 billion in information processing sales, second in Europe to IBM. The contract was one in a series of cooperative agreements engineered by AT&T to broaden its horizon and position itself to compete in evolving markets for several important products. The agreement called for Olivetti to produce computer equipment for AT&T and to market AT&T's System 85, a PBX communications controller for voice, data, and networking applications. Under the terms of the agreement, AT&T purchased 25 percent of Olivetti for $260 million, and gained an option to raise its Olivetti stake to 40 percent after four years (*Electronic News*, 1983).

For Olivetti the deal represented another move in its thrust to incorporate new communications expertise in its office products and survive the shake-out it anticipates in the computer industry. A major element of its overall strategic plan is the use of alliances to protect and enhance its market position. A recent partnership with Toshiba will allow Olivetti entry to Japan's office automation market and the potential to combine forces with Toshiba in other worldwide markets. It also has spent $60 million to purchase minority interests in twenty-two small firms in high-technology sectors, assuring itself of early access to new ideas (*Business Week*, 1983).

AT&T was not without reasons to collaborate with Olivetti. The consent decree under which it had labored for decades had prevented it from building critical cospecialized assets around its core capabilities in electronic data processing. These regulations prevented AT&T from entering computer markets, even though the rationale for such a separation was not based on technological or economic reasoning (Brock, 1981). Because of these restrictions, AT&T, though it possessed expertise in computer design and manufacturing, had developed no skills in distribution, marketing, and customer service in that field. With the settlement of the Justice Department antitrust case, AT&T had to move quickly to position itself in existing and emerging markets.

An interesting sidelight to the AT&T-Olivetti alliance is the impact on Northern Telecom, which had a long-standing relationship with Olivetti to distribute and market its SL-1 PBX, a system that competes directly with AT&T's System 85 in the United States. The agreement, which expired in late 1985, was not renewed. Thus, AT&T was at once able to enter the European market and deal a major competitor there a severe blow.

AT&T may also see the Olivetti relationship as allowing it to spread the risk of its still-struggling computer sales business. Possibly it is trying to use Olivetti in the same way that IBM used Teledyne to produce its PCjr personal computer. Because IBM was concerned that the product might be a failure commercially, it did not want to commit its own production lines to the product. Thus, the PCjr's ultimate fate had little financial impact on IBM.

However, AT&T is purchasing an enormous number of computers from Olivetti, representing more than half of Olivetti's production in 1986. Some of these are PC-compatible computers, introduced by AT&T in mid-1984 as a bid for a share of the "IBM clone" market. Another offspring of the partnership is a joint company created to sell AT&T's UNIX software in Europe. The adoption of UNIX is seen by both as a vital element in mounting a challenge to IBM there. In March 1986 six of the continent's major computer producers— among them Olivetti, Philips, and Siemens—adopted the UNIX standard, a move seen as an attack on IBM hegemony in Europe (*Business Week*, 1985).

Other competition in office automation will revolve around the holistic systems known as local area networks (LANs). These systems, which are on the verge of major penetration into workplaces, tie together computing, and voice and data transmission, using digital PBX technology. AT&T and Olivetti launched into this market in mid-1984, well over a year before IBM released its system. The computer terminals, produced by Olivetti, can run many IBM PC programs and can also converse with the System 85 PBX, which the two companies have been marketing in Europe since 1984. Thus machines for telecommunications and data processing can be interconnected. The global market for these networking devices; which consist of the hardware and software to connect office machinery, was expected to reach $500 million in 1985. The AT&T-Olivetti coalition appears well positioned to succeed in this market. It may provide AT&T's first victory against IBM in markets shared by both.

As an investment, AT&T's position in Olivetti has been highly profitable. In addition to receiving substantial dividends from its equity in the company, the value of its stock holding quadrupled by May 1987 (Petre, 1987). This appreciation came primarily from the surprising success of the Olivetti-produced PC 6300, an IBM-compatible machine that gained a 5 percent market share almost immediately. But although Olivetti benefited greatly from this rapid market acceptance, AT&T, which discounted away most of its returns to increase sales, earned very little on the 6300. AT&T's well-documented problems in managing its greater Data Systems Division (originally named the Computer Systems Division) have led to Olivetti attaining an ever greater role in computer sales. In late 1986 AT&T brought in its third manager in three years to head the Data Systems Division, Vittorio Cassoni, who came directly from Olivetti. The move was seen as an admission that AT&T was failing in its attempt to gain respectability (and profitability) in computer sales (Guyon, 1986b). *Fortune* reported unofficial divisional losses for 1985 and 1986 were $500 million and $1.2 billion, respectively, with breakeven conditions projected into the future (Petre, 1987). *Business Week* (1987) placed the later figure at $800 million. Regardless of which 1986 figure is more accurate, AT&T's computer business is floundering. The loss figures are striking when one considers that a third of computer sales are made to AT&T's telecommunications divisions.

AT&T extended its agreement with Olivetti through 1996, promising not to raise its stock holdings beyond 25 percent until 1990. Though this move was extolled as a strengthening of the alliance between the two companies, it may represent a cautious response to further integration. Wary of AT&T's lack of agility (and success) in competitive markets, Olivetti probably wishes to maintain its distance from that company. The delay of further integration also means that the distribution of rents from the joint venture may continue to accrue in Olivetti's favor. One lesson that obtains from this case is that in joint ventures that are organized along a vertical stream, returns are open to capture by either party. This underscores the somewhat paradoxical nature of such agreements. Although both parties desire success in the ultimate markets, their interests do not coincide in crucial upstream transactions.

AT&T-Philips

In early 1983 AT&T and Philips NV, an electronics conglomerate based in the Netherlands, announced an agreement to form a joint venture for the purpose of producing and selling telecommunications equipment in international markets. The project, named AT&T-Philips Telecommunications, joins two enormous companies. AT&T had 1982 sales of $12 billion; Philips had 1982 sales of $17 billion, of which $2 billion was in telecommunications. The main thrust of the agreement will be to sell AT&T central office switches in Europe and other global markets. Of all cooperative agreements, the reasons for this alliance seemed particularly clear. In terms of strengths and weaknesses, the combination appears to be highly complementary.

For AT&T, whose marketing style has been criticized as naive and overly cautious, the partnership brings Philips' commercial savvy to bear on international markets where such experience is invaluable. Philips was an AT&T acquaintance for years prior to this joint venture—AT&T and Philips share a long history of cross-licensing. Since AT&T was prevented by law from selling telecommunications equipment abroad until the antitrust case settlement, it lacked experience outside the United States. Given that protected markets constituted the great majority of the world's markets at the time of the agreement, gaining entry alongside an established vendor is a major strategic accomplishment.

Philips, on the other hand, had distribution channels, but lacked a viable product. Its digital switch, the PRX-D, showed little promise in international markets, being years behind schedule in development and having a number of reliability problems (Earnshaw, 1984). The AT&T 5ESS digital switch was a proven product, with a large installed base to provide the partners with substantial working knowledge. For Philips, AT&T was not the sole candidate. Talks with L. M. Ericsson of Sweden, which also had a reliable digital switch, were unsuccessful for two reasons. Ericsson is outside of the European common market, so an agreement with it would not have fully satisfied calls for a "European solution" voiced by several countries, notably France. Furthermore, the Philips workers council voted down an agreement with Ericsson (Earnshaw, 1984).

But the contract with AT&T, practical as it may seem, prompted retaliation by European nations. France, which had been trying for years to forge a link between Philips and its nationalized telecommunications companies, threatened to adopt a standard for videocassette recorders based on the Japanese model rather than that of

Philips (*Business Week*, 1982). More important, a politically charged decision concerning to whom to award a portion of the French market resulted in a reversal of a prior commitment to AT&T-Philips. This decision process amply demonstrates the often hazy line between politics and markets in foreign countries.

Previous segments of this chapter have hinted to the reader that economic efficiency alone does not fully explain the motives for forming international joint ventures. In fact, as a number of observers have noted, the rule rather than the exception is for governments to play crucial roles in international trade. Most countries still have telecommunications monopolies that are public enterprises rather than regulated private utilities, conferring great discretionary powers to their governments. Not surprisingly, these conditions have acted to close many borders to trade in telecommunications goods. The OECD recently estimated that of the $12 billion global switching gear market, only $2-3 billion was truly open to trade (Organization for Economic Cooperation and Development, 1983). As might be expected, by the early 1980s some European telecommunications companies were paying 60–100 percent premiums for their equipment compared to American firms (*Economist*, 1985).

The recent attempt of AT&T-Philips to enter the French market vividly illustrates the level of high politics endemic to a significant portion of telecommunications trade. In mid-1985, AT&T-Philips reached a tentative agreement to purchase the public switching operations of France's Compagnie Generale de Constructions Telephoniques (CGCT). CGCT was the former ITT French subsidiary, nationalized in 1982 and highly unprofitable at the time of the agreement. Compagnie Generale d'Electricité (CGE), France's supplier for the remaining 85 percent of the switchgear (no switch gear is purchased from foreign sources) had a hand in shaping the contract, which called for AT&T to assist CGE in U.S. markets. AT&T also agreed to purchase directly $200 million of CGE gear annually for four years (Kamm and Bray, 1985).

However, the agreement was never executed. A number of European governments strongly opposed an AT&T beachhead in Europe. The German government involved itself most heavily in the debate after CGE moved to take control of ITT's German subsidiary, which has about 40 percent of the switch gear market there. The German government, which controls procurement through its telecommunications monopoly, threatened to curtail purchases of equipment from the subsidiary if CGE finalized its plan, because Siemens, the giant German firm, has been blocked from the French market for a number of years (*Business Week*, 1986). In return for allowing the CGE purchase, it wanted Siemens, not AT&T-Philips, to buy CGCT. Siemens, for its part, offered three times the AT&T price for CGCT. The heads of state of both countries discussed the matter directly at one point (Rezvin and Pine, 1986).

Meanwhile, American trade authorities began to try to negotiate a solution to the stalemated situation. However, the Federal Communications Commission immersed itself in the controversy by threatening retaliation against Siemens in American markets, a move neither expected nor desired by AT&T (Guyon, 1986a). The FCC in early 1987 began to solicit comments on its ability to exercise authority over telecommunications trade issues. Certainly not steeped in international diplomacy, the FCC found itself involved in a process in which it had little aptitude. As if these events did not confuse matters enough, France then decided to limit foreign ownership in CGCT to 20 percent, assuring French majority ownership of the firm (Kamm, 1986). All parties interested in the minority share of CGCT reformulated their bids, while the French government tried to arrange for a group of domestic firms to purchase the remaining 80 percent share. Complicating the matter, both Northern Telecom and L. M. Ericsson joined the contest.

In April 1987 the French government finally acted, awarding the right to purchase 20 percent of CGCT to L. M. Ericsson. The political intensity against choosing either AT&T or Siemens was enormous, resulting in what was generally conceded to be a compromise. The French government, however, claimed that the superior technical performance of the Ericsson test switch made its choice easier (*Wall Street Journal*, 1987). These events suggest that if Philips cannot assist AT&T in entering new markets, the joint venture may be short-lived.

The AT&T-Philips agreement itself stipulates the transfer of technology from AT&T to Philips. In order to implement this portion of the agreement, 140 Dutch employees have been stationed in Illinois for six to eighteen months, where they are gaining experience in AT&T software, the heart of the operating system of the 5ESS (Earnshaw, 1984). Software flexibility will allow the joint venture to adapt the switch to new demands, while retaining installed hardware. This is especially important during the evolution of the integrated systems digital network (ISDN), which is capable of further uniting voice and data transmission and bringing enhanced services to customers. While technology transfer takes place, AT&T will set up a new laboratory at the joint venture's headquarters in Hilversum, the Netherlands, which will employ 200. There are plans to cooperate on transmission equipment and other enhanced services, but the central focus of the joint venture is switching.

Although both AT&T and Philips claimed that their venture would not produce profits for some time, initial results have been encouraging. The joint venture received a long-term contract to supply the Dutch telephone company with a large number of 5ESS switches for twenty years, a contract worth approximately $1.6 billion (*Electronic News*, 1985). It has also received contracts to supply telephone companies in Colombia, the United Kingdom, and Saudi Arabia. Additionally, the joint venture was awarded a small contract for fiber optical transmission from British Telecom. The long-term viability of the partnership will depend on winning bids against rival companies and combinations.

Corning Glass and Siemens

This case demonstrates how a collaborative arrangement can evolve over time as products are brought to the market and as it becomes a logical outgrowth of previous cooperation. In 1977 Corning and Siemens formed Siecor Optical Cables in order to develop and market fiber cable. Corning contributed its large number of patented processes for producing glass fibers of the purity necessary for telecommunications; Siemens brought its expertise in the encabling technology necessary to commercialize the product. Siemens also had expertise in supporting technologies, such as splicers and transmitters, allowing Siecor to act as a single source for fiber optic systems. In 1980 Siecor Optical merged with Superior Cable Corporation, a successful manufacturer and marketer of copper wire cable. The new entity, known as Siecor Corporation, joined in one company the various skills and technologies necessary to bring fiber cables from laboratory to field. Siecor has attained a growing presence within the United States. According to Siemens, Siecor's Hickory, North Carolina plant (finished in 1981) produced the equivalent of 40 percent of the fiber cable requirements of the U.S. market in 1985. The company also is looking for overseas markets, where it anticipates great growth.

Corning is an American business institution. A 136-year-old company, it has used glass and ceramics know-how to branch into a number of important, growing sectors. One of these, fiber optic technology, has received major research and development funding since the mid-1960s. By the early 1970s Corning held a large number of generic patents for the design of fibers and had licensed the technology to a number of firms. But it ran into trouble on a number of fronts. In Japan an effort to register its patents was administratively stalled for ten years while Japanese manufacturers embarked on a crash course of development (Borrus, 1986). One of the eventual global competitors that ascended from this program, Sumitomo, was subsequently sued by Corning for patent infringement (*Chemical Week*, 1984). Sumitomo had previously refused to obtain a license for the technology from Corning, who claims that the process eventually developed by Sumitomo violates Corning's U.S. patents. In late 1987, the U.S. District Court of New York ruled that Sumitomo "willfully infringed" on Corning's patents to produce optical fibers for the U.S. market.[4]

Even within relationships where Corning has licensed its technology, it has had trouble preventing unwanted consequences. Because of AT&T's vertically integrated structure prior to the divestiture, Corning preferred to license its technology to that company. However, AT&T's ability under the 1975 license agreement to sublicense those patents to associated companies eventually led to unforeseen circumstances and legal action (*Wall Street Journal*, 1986). After AT&T sold its 24 percent interest in Southern New England Telephone in 1984, SNET claimed that it could form a joint venture with SpecTran, a fiber manufacturer, and use the AT&T sublicense. Corning contends that the AT&T sale terminated SNET's sublicense rights. The case is still in litigation.

The problems that Corning had in controlling its technology through patents and licenses demonstrate the dangers of operating in a regime of weak appropriability. Corning recognized fairly early in the product life cycle that it had to find a way to manufacture and sell fiber cables itself. This was the driving force behind the development of a relationship that began as joint research and evolved into a joint manufacturing operation.

Siemens, one of the world's largest companies, has been an established force in electronics and telecommunications for many years. Its 1985 sales, $27.3 billion, dwarf Corning's $1.5 billion, showing the great resources it could bring to a joint venture. Though Corning has an increasingly global marketing outlook, Siemens has a practiced hand in the art of worldwide selling. The majority of its sales are made in foreign markets. In most cases these sales are made through foreign subsidiaries or partially owned companies; the 1985 Siemens annual report lists some seventy-five such consolidated and associated companies.

With recent plant expansions, Siecor's Hickory plant has become one of the largest optical cable manufacturing facilities in the United

States. It is well positioned to supply a market that has experienced rapid growth. However, there is evidence that this expansion will not be sustained in the future. Although a recent Siemens estimate had the American market for cable growing from 625,000 miles in 1985 to 2,800,000 miles in 1992, the industry has attracted many new entrants. A 1986 report by *Electronic Business* listed 153 companies supplying fiber optic cable (up from 103 in 1984). Under these conditions even if sales growth is rapid, profits are not ensured. Siecor's fully integrated position may assist the defense of its market share, by ensuring that process and product innovations are quickly exploited and keep it on the market's leading edge.

U.S. antitrust policy has indirectly cultivated the venture's success by making Siecor a beneficiary of the AT&T divestiture. It is a major supplier to both of AT&T's principal competitors in the long distance industry, GTE-Sprint and MCI. But more important, it is establishing itself as a prime supplier to the Regional Operating Companies, which see AT&T as a future competitor and wish to support strong competition among their suppliers. In this respect, Siecor in fiber optics plays a role similar to that of Canada's Northern Telecom in digital switching gear. Both have established themselves as leading "non-AT&T" companies in their respective fields, a position that has been highly profitable in the postdivestiture environment.

Siecor appears to be a well-conceived effort, the culmination of previous efforts by Corning and Siemens. It is similar to the AT&T-Philips venture, wherein one firm's production capacity was linked to another's marketing skill. However, in the case of the original venture, Siecor Optical Cables, research competence was linked to manufacturing expertise. Perhaps because marketing skills were not present, the third party, Superior Cable, was purchased by Siecor. The venture makes sense for Corning by producing the return it needs to support continued fiber optics research. For Siemens the venture offers a foothold in the U.S. market. One would suspect that as the technology underlying fiber optic cables continues to develop, cooperative ventures such as Siecor will be a preferred option for utilizing innovations. They also may prove a wise organizational strategy as competition in the industry becomes more vigorous.

AN EMPIRICAL ANALYSIS OF COOPERATIVE ARRANGEMENTS IN TELECOMMUNICATIONS EQUIPMENT

The strategic theory of collaborative arrangements outlined earlier and more fully developed in Teece (1986) indicates that the functions undertaken collaboratively will affect the nature of the investments made by each party and thus the optimal structure of the arrangement. In the previous section, we examined various strategic functions of collaboration in telecommunications equipment and made some predictions about the type of governance structures that would be appropriate for each. In this section, we test some of these hypotheses with data on collaborative deals struck between 1982 and 1985 in the telecommunications equipment industry.

The data were collected by researchers at Futuro Organizzazione Risorse (FOR) in Rome through an extensive review of the business press. A total of 974 collaborative arrangements were recorded over the period 1982–1985, 117 of which were in telecommunications equipment. Among the information recorded for each arrangement was the legal form, function (or motive), respective nationalities of the collaborators. Under legal form, arrangements were classified as follows:

1. Nonequity agreements. Agreements that do not include equity ties or the creation of new, jointly owned companies. Examples included contracts involving various activities and licensing agreements.
2. Equity agreements. One party acquires a minority equity interest in another for some industrial purpose (excluding purely financial investments).
3. Joint ventures. A new legal entity is created and jointly owned by the partners.
4. Consortiums. Agreements under which two or more companies create a joint organization to perform and coordinate specific activities.

Functional purposes of arrangements were classified into nine categories:

1. Technology-transfer—unilateral assignment of licenses which may also be accompanied by technical assistance
2. R&D integration—cross-licensing, the provision of R&D services and joint R&D for the development of new products
3. Supply arrangements—agreements for the provision of equipment, on either a short-term or long-term basis
4. Production integration—joint production of intermediate or finished goods
5. Distribution/marketing integration—sales and marketing by one party for another or jointly by both parties

6. Integration of R&D and production—a combination of categories 2 and 4
7. Integration of R&D and distribution/marketing—a combination of categories 2 and 5
8. Integration of production and distribution/marketing—a combination of categories 4 and 5
9. Integration of R&D, production, and distribution/marketing—combination of 2, 4, and 5

The raw data on function and form are summarized in Table 2-1. These data reflect the rich diversity of functions and forms of collaboration.

To examine the hypothesis that there are tendencies to one form of governance over others in given functional relationships, several chi-square tests for homogeneity were conducted.[5] The null hypothesis in these tests is that a function will be organized under one form with roughly the same relative frequency with which other functions are organized under the same form. For example, under the null hypothesis, if a given form occurs for 20 percent of all functions in aggregate, we would expect it to occur in about 20 percent of each separate function. The null hypothesis represents a view, contrary to our own, that there is no systematic relationships between the legal form of governance and the functions of collaboration.

To be consistent with the theory outlined in earlier in this chapter, we grouped governance forms into two categories: (1) nonequity arrangements and (2) direct equity, equity joint ventures, and consortium. We felt this classification scheme best captured the delineation between contractually governed versus organizationally governed forms of collaboration. We then tested whether particular functions either alone or in combination with certain others were statistically more (or less) likely to be organized through one mode or the other. For the purposes of the analysis, we will refer to the first category as "nonequity arrangements" and second as "organizationally governed arrangements."

Before proceeding, the reader should be aware of the following caveats. First, while we have been fortunate enough to have access to an extensive database of collaborative arrangements, the data undoubtedly contain some biases based on the primary source (the business press) from which they were gathered. The business press probably has a greater tendency to report collaborations struck between the major players in the marketplace. In addition, the press can cover only those arrangements that are not purposely kept secret

Table 2-1.   Frequency of Form and Function: Telecommunications Cooperative Agreements.

Function	Nonequity	Equity	Joint Venture	Consortium	Total
1. Technology transfer	5	4	0	0	9
2. R&D integration	23	2	1	1	27
3. Supply arrangements	9	0	0	0	9
4. Production integration	2	0	6	7	15
5. Distribution marketing integration	26	1	8	0	35
6. R&D, production integration	2	0	5	0	7
7. R&D, distribution/ marketing integration	5	1	2	1	9
8. Production, distribution/ marketing integration	2	0	1	0	3
9. R&D, production, distribution/ marketing integration	1	0	2	0	3
Total	75	8	25	9	117

by the collaborators. Generalizations based on our results should be limited to the relevant sampling frame (cases where an arrangement was publicly announced and involved a firm or project that was considered "newsworthy").

Second, data limitations prevent us from rigorously testing the extent to which our results are unique to the telecommunications equipment industry or generally applicable across industries producing complex capital goods. In the absence of such information, we recommend the narrower interpretation of our results.

Third, we must stress another, more serious, form of sample selection bias inherent in this type of analysis. Our data include only those cases where some form of collaboration actually took place; we do not (and cannot) observe those cases where it did not. In statistical terms, we have censored cases. The sample distribution is biased because it does not include those unobservable cases where firms chose internal organization over collaboration. This is especially relevant to our analysis if a firm chose to organize a project internally to avoid the high transaction costs of collaboration. Unfortunately, the structure of our data does not permit us to apply any of the available statistical techniques to correct the problem (see Maddala, 1983, ch. 6).

Finally, we must note that the information available on each arrangement permits us to make judgments neither about the uncertainty nor about the transaction-specific investments involved in each. In lieu of such detailed information, we have relied on our knowledge about the nature of technology transfer, R&D, production, and distribution in for telecommunications equipment. This approach obviously limits the degree to which we can make predictive statements about the relationship between form and function.

Despite these limitations, we believe that our analysis is an important step forward in the study of collaborative organizations. It is one of the first attempts to statistically analyze the relationship between the form and function of collaborative arrangements within a transaction costs framework (see also Pisano 1988). The results are intended to stimulate further analysis along these lines.

R&D and Technology Transfer

We ran a series of tests on arrangements involving R&D integration and technology transfer. In Test 1, we combined technology transfer (category 1 in Table 2-2) and R&D integration (category 2) and tested whether the aggregate of these two was less likely to be organized under a nonequity mode when compared to the organization of all other types of arrangements. Together these categories constitute what we referred to earlier as *straight technology access* arrangements.

The results indicate that, taken together, straight technology-access arrangements are more likely than other functional type arrangements to be structured around *contractual forms of governance*. This is not surprising given that technological collaborations can often be carried out project by project, in turn reducing the need to create a specialized governing mechanism to conduct such proj-

Table 2-2. Test 1.

R&D + Technology Transfer vs. All Others[a]

	Observed Frequency		
	R&D + T.T.	Others	Total
Contract	28	47	75
Organizational governance	8	34	42
Total	36	81	117

a. Chi square = 4.23 ($p < .05$).

ects. Also, the risks of opportunism, which we expect to drive transactions from contractual to organizational forms of governance, are attenuated when both parties are contributing technology or technological capabilities and are not deploying any other capital to the collaborative effort.

We were able to test this hypothesis by disaggregating technology transfer and R&D integration arrangements. One-way technology flows were categorized under technology transfer while two-way flows were put under the R&D integration category. It is therefore more likely that technology transfer agreements would be organized under the *organizational governance* category while R&D integration would be more likely to occur through *contractual governance*. The results of Test 2 are presented in Table 2-3.

Our hypothesis is confirmed by these results, with respect to R&D integration. Relative to the entire sample distribution of governance forms, R&D integration was significantly more likely to be structured through contractual modes (Test 2A). Technology transfer was more likely than predicted by the sample distribution to be structured through some type of equity or consortium mode (that is, organizational governance), although our test statistic did not reach a significant level (Test 2B).

As a follow-up, we disaggregated the second governance category into *direct equity* structures and *joint venture* or *consortium* structures. We then tested the hypothesis that technology transfer agreements would have a greater probability of falling under *direct equity* governance than under either joint venture or consortium. The rationale is that direct equity modes are more appropriate than joint ventures or consortiums when one party is contributing technology. The results appear in Test 2C in Table 2-3.

The summary statistic allows us to reject the null hypothesis that the distribution of governance structures for technology transfer is

Table 2-3. Test 2.

Test 2A: R&D Alone vs. All Other Functions
(Including Technology Transfer)[a]

| | Observed Frequency | | |
	R&D	Others	Total
Contract	23	52	75
Organizational governance	4	38	42
Total	27	90	117

Test 2B: Technology Transfer vs. All
Other Functions[b]

| | Observed Frequency | | |
	Technology Transfer	Others	Total
Contract	5	70	75
Organizational governance	4	38	42
Total	9	108	117

Test 2C: Technology Transfer vs. All Others[c]

| | Observed Frequency | | |
	Technology Transfer	Others	Total
Direct equity	4	4	8
Nonequity	5	70	75
Joint ventures or consortiums	0	34	34
Total	9	108	117

a. Chi square = 6.78 ($p < .01$).
b. Chi square = 0.31 (N.S.).
c. Chi square = 23.11 ($p < 01$).

statistically similar to the distribution of governance structures for all other functional arrangements. In confirmation of our hypothesis, an equiprobability model overpredicts the assignment of technology transfer agreements to both nonequity and joint venture or consortium modes while underpredicting its assignment to direct equity modes. Therefore we can conclude that technology transfer agreements are more likely to be organized under direct equity modes than could be predicted by the sample distribution of governance structures.

The high propensity of "R&D integration only" collaborations to be organized through nonequity (or purely contractual) governance was not surprising. We speculated that most joint R&D projects could be effectively organized through complex contractual forms that emulated the communication and coordination properties of quasi-internal organization. We also speculated that transaction-specific investments were relatively small for R&D only collaborations but that such investments would become much more significant when collaboration coupled R&D to other downstream functions such as production or marketing. These multifunction collaborations involving R&D also create greater communication and coordination burdens that may be better dealt with through more hierarchical or formal channels. Thus collaborations tying R&D to either production or marketing will probably tend to be structured around organizationally governed arrangements (direct equity participation, joint ventures, and consortium). The results of Test 3 are presented in Table 2-4.

The test results confirm the hypothesis that R&D collaboration, when combined with other functional objectives, is more likely to be organized through the second category of governance structures than when it is the sole purpose the agreement. We next ran a series of tests to determine if there was a type of equity or consortium mode that was preferred when collaboration involved R&D in combination with other functions.

The results of Test 4 (Table 2-5) show that joint ventures or consortium are the preferred mode when collaboration combines R&D integration with other functional motives (see Test 4A). Test 4B shows that production integration, alone, often drives collaboration to the joint venture or consortium form. This suggested that in an R&D or production collaboration, it was production that was driving the choice of joint venture or consortium forms and not the organizational problems of coupling R&D with other production or other functions. To test this alternative hypothesis, we compared the organization of collaborations that involved R&D and distribution with those that involved R&D and production. If the production aspect of collaboration is driving the form of governance, then we would expect to see a significant difference in the ways these two types of arrangements are organized. The results of Test 4C indicate that there is no significant difference in the ways that these two are organized. Thus it is unlikely that production alone is driving the use of

Table 2-4.   Test 3.

Test 3A: R&D/Production vs. R&D Alone[a]

	Observed Frequency		
	R&D/Prod.	*R&D*	*Total*
Contract	2	23	25
Organizational governance	5	4	9
Total	7	27	34

Test 3B: R&D + Production or R&D + Distribution
or R&D + Production + Distribution[b]

	Observed Frequency		
	R&D+	*Others*	*Total*
Contract	8	67	75
Organizational governance	11	31	42
Total	19	98	117

Test 3C: R&D + Other vs. R&D Alone[c]

	Observed Frequency		
	R&D+	*R&D*	*Total*
Contract	8	23	31
Organizational governance	11	4	15
Total	19	27	46

a. Chi square = 9.15 ($p < .01$).
b. Chi square = 4.77 ($p < .05$).
c. Chi square = 9.42 ($p < .01$).

joint venture or consortium forms in collaboration that link R&D to other functions.

Distribution and Marketing

Access to new product and geographic markets is a major motive for collaborative arrangements in telecommunications equipment. We argued earlier in the chapter that there were a number of circumstances under which marketing and distribution channels represented firm-specific assets. Unfortunately, we do not have enough detailed information about each distribution arrangement to determine the magnitude of transaction-specific investments. It was not surprising,

Table 2-5. Test 4.

Test 4A: R&D + vs. All Others[a]

	Observed Frequency		
	R&D+	*Others*	*Total*
Nonequity	8	67	75
Direct equity	1	7	8
Joint ventures or consortiums	10	24	34
Total	19	98	117

Test 4B: Production vs. All Others[b]

	Observed Frequency		
	Production	*Others*	*Total*
Nonequity	2	73	75
Direct equity	0	8	8
Joint ventures or consortiums	13	21	34
Total	15	102	117

Test 4C: R&D/Production vs. R&D/Distribution[c]

	Observed Frequency		
	R&D/Prod.	*R&D/Distr.*	*Total*
Nonequity	2	5	7
Direct equity	0	1	1
Joint ventures or consortiums	5	3	8
Total	7	9	16

a. Chi square = 6.13 ($p < .05$).
b. Chi square = 27.74 ($p < .01$).
c. Chi square = 2.58 (N.S.).

therefore, that we found no statistically significant trend in the assignment of distribution-and-marketing-only agreements to any one type of governance arrangement. The results of Test 5 are shown in Table 2–6.

However, we did expect the degree of transaction-specific investment for market access arrangements to increase when they also included technology access. We ran a series of homogeneity tests to determine the validity of this hypothesis. The test results are shown in Table 2–7, Tests 6A through 6D.

Table 2-6. Test 5.

Distribution Alone vs. All Others[a]

	Observed Frequency		
	Distr.	*Others*	*Total*
Contract	26	49	75
Organizational governance	9	33	42
Total	35	82	117

a. Chi square = 2.25 (N.S.).

The results of these tests do not allow us to reject the null hypothesis in any of the four cases. That is, the organization of complex distribution agreements is not significantly different than the overall pattern of organization for other types of functional arrangements. If there are higher transaction costs associated with complex distribution agreements, they do not seem to be driving the mode of governance.

CONCLUSION

This chapter has shown that the telecommunications equipment industry, following some abrupt changes in its strategic environment, has taken on certain features of postmodern industry structures. Firms in this industry conduct international commerce and compete through a rich diversity of organizational forms. We have argued and provided some qualitative and quantitative evidence that the choice among alternative organizational reflects the nature of the assets involved in the collaboration. We think our data analysis, albeit limited, suggests a fruitful line for further empirical research. We would also hope that future empirical research examines the normative implications of these arguments, both from the viewpoint of managers who must make these organizational decisions and manage collaboration and from the viewpoint of policymakers, whose initiatives, as we have seen, have a strong impact on the structure and organization of the industry.

From both a managerial and public-policy perspective, a major question of importance is whether the collaborative organization of telecommunications equipment commerce is simply a transitory

Table 2-7. Test 6.

Test 6A: Distribution Alone vs.
Distribution/R&D/Production[a]

	Observed Frequency		
	Distr.	Distr. +	Total
Contract	26	8	34
Organizational governance	9	7	16
Total	35	15	50

Test 6B: Distribution+ vs. Others[b]

	Observed Frequency		
	Distr.	Others	Total
Contract	8	67	75
Organizational governance	7	35	42
Total	15	102	117

Test 6C: Distribution Alone vs. R&D Distribution[c]

	Observed Frequency		
	Distr.	R&D/Distr.	Total
Contract	26	5	31
Organizational governance	9	4	13
Total	35	9	44

Test 6D: Distribution Alone vs. R&D/Distribution
and R&D/Production/Distribution[d]

	Observed Frequency		
	Distr.	Distr. +	Total
Contract	26	6	32
Organizational governance	9	6	15
Total	35	12	47

a. Chi square = 2.12 (N.S.).
b. Chi square = 0.87 (N.S.).
c. Chi square = 1.21 (N.S.).
d. Chi square = 2.42 (N.S.).

phase in the structural evolution of the industry. Few would doubt that the industry is far from any organizational equilibrium, but the direction of change is difficult to ascertain. The framework developed in this chapter suggests that technical standards will play a critical role. In those markets where technical standards stabilize, the incidence of transaction-specific and uncertain investments will decline and thus reduce the need for hierarchically organized forms of governance. Witness what has happened in the personal computer market: IBM's open architecture and out-source strategy set the stage for an industry structure characterized by arms-length supply contracts for accessing standardized components and software. It is also clear that the manner in which standards are set will also have a great influence. If standardization is achieved, for example, because a large firm is able to penetrate all the relevant markets through direct investment or through acquisitions of firms providing complementary products, a by-product of this strategy would be an industry structure characterized by hierarchy. Politics, which are always difficult to predict, will also figure prominently in the evolution of standards.

Finally, we must go back to our original observation about the effect of the telecommunications *service* industry on the equipment supply sector. Fundamental changes in the structure of the service industry played a major role in changing the structure of the equipment supply sector. The future direction of the telecommunications service industry around the world will continue to exert a powerful force on the equipment sector. A trend worth watching is the degree to which service and equipment supply sectors become vertically integrated or disintegrated. Most European markets continue to be organized around the tight links between the PTT and a small core of domestic suppliers. Whether this will change depends on political decisions.

Even the structure of the American telecommunications sector, which has already undergone fundamental change, bears close watching. Will American telecommunications service providers once again become vertically integrated into equipment? Outside the regulated Bell operating companies (BOC) sector, there seems to be a strong trend in this direction. Service providers already have or are accumulating internal equipment supply capabilities; many of the regulated BOC's are arguing that they too should be allowed to manufacture their own equipment if they choose. Vertical integration from the other direction, from equipment manufacturer into services, may also be a factor. We want to stress once again the importance that standards will play in determining structure. If to differentiate their services, telecommunications networks companies must use different equipment, vertical integration and tight links with suppliers (similar to what one finds in the Japanese automobile industry) will become the rule. If, in contrast, differentiated services are not a function of different equipment, then service suppliers will have an incentive to shop among a broad set of equipment vendors.

NOTES

1. These analytical tools are more fully developed in Teece (1986).
2. Apple's agreement with Canon to develop and supply Apple's laser writer is an example of this possibility. Canon introduced its own version of the laser printer by 1987.
3. The data were compiled by researchers at F.O.R.–Montedison in Rome, Italy. We are deeply indebted to Enrico Ricotta for providing us with access to these data.
4. This ruling, however, should not be construed as evidence of a strong appropriability regime; courts in two other countries have ruled in favor of Sumitomo in similar suits.
5. See Feinberg (1977) for a rigorous treatment of contingency table analysis.

REFERENCES

Borrus, M. 1986. "Japanese Telecommunications: Reforms and Trade Implications." *California Management Review* (Spring).

Brock, G. 1981. *The Telecommunications Industry: The Dynamics of Market Structure.* Cambridge, Mass.: Harvard University Press.

Business Week. 1982. "France Is Disconnected in an AT&T-Philips Link." October 11, p. 47.

_____. 1983. "Olivetti Aiming to Become a Global Competitor by Making a U.S. Connection." November 7, p. 139.

_____. 1985. "Olivetti and AT&T: An Odd Couple That's Flourishing." March 4, p. 44.

_____. 1986. "Europe Tries to Break Up AT&T's Affair with France." November 3, p. 49.

_____. 1987. "Dealmaker DeBenedetti: Olivetti's CEO Doubles as an Entrepreneur." August 24, 1987.

Chandler, A. 1962. *Strategy and Structure.* Cambridge, Mass.: MIT Press.

Chemical Week. 1984. "A Fiber Optics Patent Squabble." April 18, p. 17.

Done, K. 1986. "Ericsson Poised for Deal with Bell." *Financial Times,* June 10.

Dosi, G. 1982. "Technological Paradigms and Technological Trajectories." *Research Policy,* 11, pp. 147–162.

Earnshaw, M. 1984. "AT&T and Philips Telecommunications: A Company with Formidable Potential?" *Telecommunications,* May, p. 108.

Economist. "The World on the Line." November 23, 1985, p. 5.

Electronic Business. 1986. "Fiber Optics: Not Just a Niche Market Anymore." February, p. 28.

Electronic News. 1983. "AT&T to Acquire 25% of Olivetti for $260 million: Product Reciprocity Seen." December 26, p. 1.

_____. 1985. "AT&T-Philips, ITT to Supply Dutch Telecom Switch Gear." March 18, p. 4.

Feinberg, S. 1977. *The Analysis of Cross-Classified Categorical Data.* Cambridge, Mass.: MIT Press.

Freeman, C. 1982. *The Economics of Industrial Innovation,* 2nd ed. London: Frances Pinter.

Guyon, J. 1986a. "U.S. Adds to AT&T Problems in Contest over French Market." *Wall Street Journal,* October 10, p. 16.

_____. 1986b. "AT&T Expands Olivetti's Role on Computers." *Wall Street Journal,* October 30, p. 2.

Horwitch, M. Forthcoming. *Post Modern Management.* New York: Free Press.

Huber, P. 1987. *The Geodesic Network: 1987 Report on Competition in the Telephone Industry.* U.S. Department of Justice.

Inan, C., and L. Lannon. 1987. "Carrier Spending Hits a $24 Billion Plateau." *Telephony,* January 12, p. 40.

Kamm, T. 1986. "France Will Limit Foreign Ownership in Telecommunications Firm to 20%." *Wall Street Journal,* December 2, p. 37.

_____, and N. Bray. 1985. "AT&T, GCE Set Draft Agreement on Cooperation." *Wall Street Journal,* September 6, p. 22.

Kogut, B. 1985. "Competing Through International Cooperative Ventures and Strategic Networks." Working Paper 85-10, The Wharton School, University of Pennsylvania, August.

Maddala, G. S. 1983. *Limited Dependent and Qualitative Variables in Econometrics,* Cambridge, U.K.: Cambridge University Press.

Miles, R., and C. Snow. 1986. "Network Organizations: New Concepts for New Forms." *California Management Review,* Spring, pp. 62–73.

Northern Business Information. 1986. *Central Office Equipment Market.*

Organization for Economic Cooperation and Development. 1983. *Telecommunications: Pressures and Policies for Change.* Paris: OECD.

Petre, P. 1987. "AT&T's Epic Push into Computers." *Fortune,* May 25, p. 42.

Pisano, G. 1988. *Innovation Through Markets, Hierarchies, and Joint Ventures: Technology Strategy and Collaborative Arrangements in the Biotechnology Industry.* Unpublished Ph.D. Thesis (University of California, Berkeley, School of Business Administration).

Porter, M. 1985. *Competitive Advantage.* New York: Free Press.

_____. and M. Fuller. 1985. "Coalitions and Global Strategy." In Michael Porter, *Competition in Global Industries.* Cambridge, Mass.: Harvard Business School Press.

Revzin, P., and A. Pine. 1986. "Germany's Kohl Intervenes for Siemens in Bid for French Switch Maker, CGCT." *Wall Street Journal,* October 29, p. 33.

Ricotta, E., et al. 1985. "Joint Ventures and Inter-Company Agreements." Unpublished Report, Futuro Organizazione Risorse. Rome.

Teece, D. 1976. *The Multinational Corporation and the Resource Cost of International Technology Transfer.* Cambridge, Mass.: Ballinger.

_____. 1981. "The Market for Know-how and the Efficient International Transfer of Technology." *Annals of the American Academy of Political and Social Science* (November): 81–96.

_____. 1986. "Profiting from Technological Innovation: Implications for Integration, Collaboration, Licensing, and Public Policy." *Research Policy*, 15, No. 6 (December): 285–305.

U.S. Department of Commerce, International Trade Administration. 1983. *The Telecommunications Industry*, April.

U.S. International Trade Commission. 1984. *Changes in the U.S. Telecommunications Industry and the Impact on U.S. Telecommunications Trade.* June, USITC. Publication No. 1542.

Wall Street Journal. 1986. "Corning Glass Asks Court to Deny Firm's Use of Optics Patents." January 15, p. 2.

_____. 1987. "France Confirms Award of CGCT to L. M. Ericsson: U.S. Officials Leave Open Possibility of Retaliation." April 24, p. 10.

Williamson, O. 1975. *Markets and Hierarchies.* New York: Free Press.

3 JOINT VENTURES IN THE U.S. COMMERCIAL AIRCRAFT INDUSTRY

David C. Mowery

The international commercial aircraft industry now contains a complex system of collaborative agreements involving links among the major "prime contractor" firms and an extensive set of cooperative relationships between these firms and suppliers and subcontractors. The innovation process was different prior to the early 1970s, when both airframe and engine producers largely developed and manufactured their products independently of other firms. Since then, however, virtually no large commercial transport or engine has been developed and produced by a U.S. firm without significant foreign involvement. This chapter analyzes international collaboration between U.S. and foreign firms in the commercial aircraft industry, focusing on the following successful and unsuccessful collaborations:[1]

- Boeing and the Japan Commercial Aircraft Corporation (JCAC, a consortium of Mitsubishi Heavy Industries, Kawasaki Heavy Industries, and Fuji Heavy Industries), a venture that is producing the Boeing 767 in collaboration with Aeritalia and has begun the development of the 7J7

- McDonnell Douglas and Fokker, a venture that failed to produce the MDF100

The research underlying this chapter was supported by the American Enterprise Institute's Competing in a Changing World Economy project, the Center for Economic Policy Research at Stanford University, and the National Science Foundation (PRA 83-10664). I am grateful to the contributors to this volume and the members of the Council on Foreign Relations Study Group on Corporate Alliances for useful comments and discussions.

71

- McDonnell Douglas, Aerospatiale, and Dassault-Breguet, partners in the unsuccessful Mercure 200 venture
- General Electric and the Société Nationale d'Etude et de Construction de Moteurs d'Aviation (SNECMA), producers of the CFM56 engine
- Saab-Scania and Fairchild Aviation, a venture that introduced the SF340 prior to Fairchild's withdrawal
- International Aero Engines, a venture that involves Pratt and Whitney, Rolls Royce, Fiat, MTU, Ishikawajima-Harima Heavy Industries, Mitsubishi Heavy Industries, and Kawasaki Heavy Industries in the development of the V2500 engine

THE STRUCTURE AND PERFORMANCE OF THE U.S. COMMERCIAL AIRCRAFT INDUSTRY

The U.S. commercial aircraft industry has been both innovative and internationally competitive since World War II.[2] In 1986 total shipments of the aerospace industry (aircraft, missiles, and spacecraft) amounted to nearly $97 billion, more than 2 percent of the U.S. gross national product. Within this total, sales of military and civilian aircraft, engines and parts, and aircraft equipment were valued at $72.4 billion (U.S. Department of Commerce, 1987). Exports of aircraft, engines, and parts equaled $18.6 billion in 1986. The industry also is a major investor in research and development. R&D expenditures in the aerospace industry amounted to nearly 17 percent of the value of 1986 sales, a level exceeded only by the electronics industry (federal funds accounted for 75 percent of these R&D expenditures). The industry has important linkages (through its demand for electronic components, advanced materials, and parts) with other high-technology sectors.

The manufacture of aircraft engines requires considerable expertise in aeronautical engineering and airframe design and the converse is true of airframe manufacture. Nevertheless, U.S. engine producers do not manufacture airframes, and vice versa, due in part to differences in the cost structure and minimum efficient volume of production of these goods. Despite the absence of corporate links between these two parts of the commercial aircraft industry, the structure and technological characteristics of engine and airframe design and manufacture are quite similar.

Throughout the recent history of the commercial aircraft industry, the introduction of new aircraft has been paced by the development of new, fuel-efficient engines. Selective withdrawal during the 1970s by each of the three engine manufacturers, General Electric, Pratt and Whitney, and Rolls Royce, from one or more market segments means that only one segment of the engine market now has more than two producers. This withdrawal was aided in one case (the V2500 venture between Rolls Royce and Pratt and Whitney) and attempted in another (a collaborative agreement between General Electric and Rolls Royce concerning the CF6-80 and the RB211-535 was dissolved in late 1986) through collaboration between two of the three firms.

General Electric, Pratt and Whitney, and Rolls Royce currently compete in the upper end (50,000–60,000 pounds of thrust) of the engine market (the PW4000 for Pratt and Whitney, the CF6-80 for General Electric, and the RB211-524 for Rolls Royce), and Pratt and Whitney and Rolls Royce compete in the middle segment (30,000–40,000 pounds of thrust) with the PW2037 and the RB211-535. CFM International, the General Electric-SNECMA joint venture, competes in the lower end of the engine market (20,000–30,000 pounds of thrust) against the consortium teaming Pratt and Whitney with Rolls Royce (the V2500, managed by International Aero Engines), and derivatives of Pratt and Whitney's older engine, the JT8D. Despite the decline in the number of firms active in each segment, competition in the engine market remains intense, in part because airframes now are designed to accommodate several different engine types.

A number of airframe producers also have exited from the industry. Lockheed, Martin, and Convair (a division of General Dynamics and the producer of the CV-880 and CV-990) all went into eclipse following the introduction of commercial jet transports in the late 1950s. Lockheed reentered the commercial airframe industry in the 1970s as the producer of the L-1011, and exited once again in the early 1980s. Boeing now dominates the commercial aircraft market as thoroughly as Douglas dominated the market of the 1930s. By 1983 nearly 55 percent of all commercial jet aircraft produced since 1952 had been manufactured by Boeing. The only other major U.S. producer of large commercial aircraft is McDonnell Douglas, presently manufacturing one aircraft design (the MD-80 and its various derivatives), although the MD-11, a derivative of the DC-10, now is being developed for introduction in 1990.

Both the commercial aircraft and engine industries also contain a large population of vendor and subcontractor firms, engaged in the production of assemblies and components for the much smaller group of major contractors. This group of supplier firms within the United States includes as many as 15,000 firms, many of which produce components for both military and civilian aircraft. These firms now are exposed to greater competition from foreign producers as a result of international collaborative ventures in commercial aircraft and increased foreign involvement in the production of U.S. military aircraft.

Product development in aircraft and engines is a design-intensive process (see Steiner, 1982). Firms produce dozens of "paper airplanes" prior to the decision to launch the development of a specific design, in an effort to accommodate the varied requirements and desires of airline customers.[3] Although the design phase is lengthy, once the decision is made to introduce an airframe or engine, it is essential to bring the product to market rapidly. U.S. producers historically have been able to move from design commitment to production more rapidly than European firms.[4] Design capabilities, as well as the ability to manage the transition from design to production, are among the most important influences on commercial success and failure in this industry.

Another important competitive asset is a worldwide product support and service network. Following the introduction of a new aircraft or engine, incremental modifications are made throughout the life of the design, relying on information gained from close monitoring of operating experience. This monitoring function, as well as the importance of worldwide spare parts supplies and field service, mean that a global marketing and product support organization is critical to the commercial success of a new aircraft or engine design. The requirement for product support and marketing networks acts as a major barrier to entry into the aircraft industry. The high fixed costs of supporting these networks also create a strong incentive for producers to market a number of different aircraft or engine models. The ability to supply a full line, covering all segments of the aircraft or engine market for a given customer class, enables producers to utilize their marketing network more effectively. The need to produce and market a full line of products has played a major role in the decisions of U.S. manufacturers of airframes and engines to seek alliances with other firms.

The high cost of new product development within the aircraft industry is another source of entry barriers. Development of the Boeing 767 is estimated to have cost nearly $1.5 billion, while estimates of the development costs for a 150-seat transport range up to and beyond $2 billion. The V2500, a high-bypass engine scheduled for commercial introduction in 1989, will require at least $1.5 billion for development. Rising development costs have increased the risks of new product development in the aircraft industry. Many of the multinational collaborations in this industry have been motivated in part by the desire of U.S. firms to reduce the financial risks of new product development.

In addition to their sheer magnitude, which is best appreciated by comparison to total stockholders' equity in a firm such as Boeing (in 1984, roughly $2.7 billion), the high fixed costs that characterize commercial aircraft development result in a falling short-run average cost curve. Learning also contributes to cost reduction as a function of production volume and time, making production experience an important competitive asset. Although the learning curve plays an important role in aircraft industry costs, the airframe industry is not a high-volume industry. Since the introduction of the commercial jet transport in the early 1950s, only *four airframe designs* (the DC-9/MD-80, Boeing 707, 727, and 737) *out of twenty-three produced have sold more than 600 units.* Moreover, the total production history for a specific aircraft design may extend over 10–20 years. Average annual production rates for airframes typically are low, but they are subject to wide fluctuations—the peak production rate may be as much as eight times that of the trough output rate.

SOURCES OF TECHNICAL CHANGE

The U.S. commercial aircraft industry has benefited from at least three important external sources of innovation and research funding. Innovations in other industries, such as metallurgy or electronics, government-supported research in civil aviation, and military procurement and research support all have contributed to innovation in commercial aircraft.[5]

Cumulative R&D expenditures from all sources in the aircraft industry (both military and commercial aircraft) during 1945–1984 amounted to roughly $109 billion in 1972 dollars. Of this total, almost 75 percent, $81 billion, was provided by the U.S. military. Industry-financed R&D during the period amounted to $18 billion, more than 16 percent of the total. Federal nonmilitary funding of research in this industry accounted for a small portion of the total investment of federal funds, totaling slightly more than $9 billion. Federal investments in military aircraft technology have had a significant impact on innovation in commercial aircraft, through technological spillovers that resulted in the application of military avionics, airframe, or engine innovations and research findings in commercial aircraft.

While government research funding contributed to the supply of potential innovations, federal policies also affected the demand for innovation by the commercial aircraft industry. Civil Aeronautics Board regulation during 1938-1978 supported the rapid adoption of innovations in commercial aircraft (see Jordan, 1970; Mowery and Rosenberg, 1985). Indeed, federal policy toward the commercial aircraft industry during the postwar period is unusual in that it expanded both the supply of technical knowledge and the demand for application of this knowledge in innovation within the civilian sector.[6]

RECENT CHANGES IN THE POLICY AND TECHNOLOGICAL ENVIRONMENT

Sweeping changes in this federal policy structure and other aspects of the domestic and international environment affected the U.S. aircraft industry during and after the 1960s. These changes included deregulation of domestic air transportation in 1978, a decline in the commonality of military and civilian aircraft technology, and some erosion in the aeronautics research and technology budget within NASA. Combined with steady growth in development costs, these changes made market demand more uncertain and increased the financial risks borne by U.S. airframe and engine producers.

Deregulation of domestic air transport reduced the importance of service quality competition within the airline industry, making U.S. airlines less eager to adopt new aircraft without significant improvements in operating costs. Deregulation also unleashed price competition within the industry and supported entry by numerous firms, transforming the structure of the airline industry. A shakeout period appears to be ending, following a wave of mergers and bankruptcies. Nonetheless, the market for large commercial aircraft now is more uncertain, while the ability of producers to share this risk with major customers has been reduced.

Increasing divergence between civilian and military aircraft technologies and the absence of major defense programs in large transports since the late 1960s have reduced the amount and significance of military-civilian technological spillover. The relationship between military and civilian technological developments has changed considerably; in some cases, technological spillovers now flow from civilian to military applications. Whereas the Boeing 707 and the military KC-135 tanker were developed from a common prototype, the current military tanker design (the KC-10) is a derivative of the DC-10, originally designed for commercial passenger transportation. Both aircraft and engine producers now finance more of the research and development for technological advances. The assumption of a greater share of the financial burden of development by private firms has increased their risks.

The reduction in the indirect contribution of military R&D and procurement to the development of civilian aircraft technology was parallelled by declines in NASA support of aeronautics research during the 1970s and 1980s. Aeronautics research was a less important component of NASA's mission, by comparison with its predecessor agency (the National Advisory Committee on Aeronautics, NACA). The transformation of NACA into NASA in 1958 reduced the agency's commitment of engineering and scientific manpower to aeronautics R&D. Modest growth in real spending for NASA aeronautics programs during the 1970s and 1980s masks an apparent decline in the R&D component of NASA's aeronautics research program.[7] This reduction in federal civilian research funding and manpower increased the share of the costs of R&D that U.S. commercial aircraft firms must assume.

The U.S. aircraft industry also was affected during the 1970s and 1980s by developments in foreign markets, one of the most important of which was a reduction in the U.S. share of world airline traffic. Although the U.S. market for commercial aircraft still represents the largest single market in the world, it no longer constitutes an absolute majority of world demand. The National Research Council's U.S. Civil Aviation Manufacturing Industry Panel projected that the U.S. share of world air traffic would decline to roughly 36 percent by 1990 from 57 percent in 1971 (see National Research Council, U.S. Civil Aviation Manufacturing Industry Panel, 1985).

This decline in the relative size of the U.S. market for commercial aircraft and steady growth of development costs mean that penetration of foreign markets, always important to U.S. aircraft firms, now is essential. Access to foreign markets by U.S. firms often is facilitated by enlisting a foreign firm as a partner in the development and production of an airframe or engine. The large size of the U.S. market also means that penetration of this market is important to the commercial success of foreign aircraft.

Foreign markets also have become more important for firms in the second tier of the U.S. aircraft industry. U.S. exports of components and other parts grew from roughly $2 billion to more than $4 billion during 1977–1982 and reached $6 billion in 1986 (U.S. Department of Commerce, 1987). Reflecting this expansion in international trade in aircraft components, many foreign aircraft now have a substantial U.S. content. U.S. components accounted for as much as 35 percent of the value of the early versions of the Airbus A300, for example,[8] and estimates of the U.S. content of the Embraer Bandeirante, produced in Brazil, range above 40 percent. Producers of components and other firms in the second tier have a stake in open international markets for aircraft and components that is no less significant than that of the major U.S. firms.

EXPLAINING THE FORM AND LOCUS OF INTERNATIONAL COLLABORATION

Changes in the competitive and policy environment of the U.S. commercial aircraft industry supported growth in international collaboration in aircraft development and production, as was noted above. The reasons for the structure of this collaboration and its focus on product development, however, require additional attention.

The principal motives for U.S. firms in seeking out foreign partners in aircraft development projects are access to foreign markets, access to lower cost capital, and risk-sharing. Government ownership or control of the customers for aircraft in many foreign markets means that market access often is improved by providing foreign firms with a share of the development or production of an airframe or engine. Such partnerships also spread risk and can lower the cost of capital, since many foreign governments provide loans or other subsidies for a portion of the development costs incurred by their domestic aircraft firms. Improvements in the technologies of computer-aided design, engineering, and manufacture, as well as information transmission, storage and analysis, also have made multinational cooperation in complex development and production projects more feasible and effective. The stronger technological capabilities of many foreign aerospace firms now make them much more attractive partners for U.S. firms in joint development and manufacturing projects. In addition, the desires of European and Japanese governments to improve or maintain an indigenous aircraft industry (perceived to be a source of high-skill, high-wage employment) favor collaboration over licensing.

The nature of the corporate assets that are essential to success in this industry means that licensing is an ineffective means for transferring them. Design and system integration capabilities, as well as the capacity to manage the transition from paper design to actual aircraft, on schedule, are important competitive assets. The ability to manage wide swings in production volume without incurring major cost penalties is crucial, given the fluctuations in demand that typify this industry. Marketing and product support networks, which facilitate the incorporation of information from aircraft operations into design modifications, are other key competitive assets.

The difficulty of transferring these intangible assets through licensing agreements, as well as the essential contribution that they make to competitiveness, may be inferred from the experiences of Japanese and European licensed coproduction of U.S. military aircraft. Nearly thirty-five years' experience in manufacturing U.S. military aircraft designs under license from U.S. producers and the Pentagon has yet to result in the entry into production of large commercial transports or engines by foreign licensees who did not have considerable prior design and production experience in commercial aircraft.[9]

Direct foreign investment, one alternative strategy to achieve market access, provides little possibility for reductions in the size of the capital investment necessary for product development and no reduction in the risks faced by investing firms. Moreover, the cost structure of airframe production and, to a lesser extent, engine production, makes multiplant production undesirable.

The characteristics of technological competition and market structure in this industry also explain why collaboration focuses on product development and production rather than research or marketing activities. The importance of intensive interaction with potential buyers during the course of aircraft or engine design and strong linkages between product support, engineering, and design, means that the establishment of partnerships in which one partner designs and another produces an aircraft or engine, or one produces and another markets and provides product support for the aircraft, is inadvisable. Since research alone generally does not yield easily appropriable returns (reflected in the limited use of patenting or licensing of innovations) and therefore is not among the key competitive assets in this industry, collaboration focusing solely on research also is rare.

CASE STUDIES IN INTERNATIONAL COLLABORATION

Boeing-JCAC

During the past twenty years, the Boeing Company has responded to the higher costs and risks of commercial aircraft development through more intensive use of subcontractors, frequently requiring that these firms assume a significant share of the costs and risks of launching a new aircraft. Roughly 70 percent of the value of the first versions of the 747 was subcontracted, and a number of subcontractors contributed funds to support nonrecurring costs for the first 200 aircraft produced.[10]

The Boeing 767 joint venture with Aeritalia and the Japan Commercial Aircraft Corporation differed from the 747 program primarily in its increased reliance on foreign subcontractors; these subcontractors also shared a greater portion of the risk. The involvement of Boeing's Japanese partners in the 767 is likely to expand in the development of the 7J7, an aircraft scheduled to be introduced in the 1990s. Japanese firms are expected to have significant roles in product design and development, marketing, and product support, in addition to manufacturing, in the 7J7 project.

During the 1970s Boeing began the development of successor aircraft to the 727 and 707. Simultaneous development of successors to each of these aircraft was necessary for Boeing to remain a producer of a full line of aircraft. The costs of such an ambitious development program, however, were \$1.5–2.5 billion. The participation of risk-sharing partners would provide capital and reduce the firm's financial risk. Foreign aircraft firms were attractive candidates for some form of collaboration with Boeing because of the availability of government funds to support development and production start-up costs for these firms. The importance of foreign markets for the commercial success of the 757 and 767 further enhanced the attractiveness of foreign firms as partners in the development and production of these aircraft. Nonetheless, Boeing discussed participation as risk-sharing subcontractors in the 757 and 767 projects with several U.S. firms during this period, without success.[11]

Negotiations between Boeing and the Japan Commercial Transport Development Corporation (JCTDC, the predecessor of the Japan Commercial Aircraft Corporation, JCAC, a consortium made up of Mitsubishi, Kawasaki, and Fuji Heavy Industries) and Aeritalia, an Italian producer, were concluded in 1978 with the signature of a memorandum of understanding for the production of the Boeing 767. As "risk-sharing subcontractors," Aeritalia and the JCTDC each assumed the costs of development and production tooling for 15 percent of the total value of the aircraft, the overall design of which was largely fixed at that point, for the first 500 aircraft.[12] The JCTDC was responsible for several sections of the fuselage and wing, as well as rudder flaps, a component employing new composite (nonmetallic) materials. The Italian participants were responsible for wing flaps. Both the Japanese and Italian groups received government grants or loans for up to 50 percent of the development costs of their components. Boeing retained sole responsibility for the development of the cockpit and the avionics package, as well as wing design and fabrication and final assembly of the airframe. Project management, marketing, and product support remained the responsibility of Boeing. Since Boeing retained overall control of design, production, and marketing, the 767 venture was not organized as a separate corporate entity.

Although the major design decisions on the 767 had been made by Boeing by the time the consortium was formed in 1978, considerable development and design work remained on many components for the aircraft. A number of these design and development tasks were assigned to Boeing's Japanese partner firms. Japanese engineering personnel were transferred to Boeing headquarters for up to a year, which aided the transfer of component design skills and technologies to the Japanese firms.

The technological and financial benefits for the Japanese and Italian participants in the 767 project have been modest thus far, due to the relatively slow sales of the aircraft. Boeing, however, appears to have benefited from the joint venture in a number of ways. By selectively transferring component design and production technologies to Japanese firms, Boeing has reaped a return on its more mature technological capacities, a return that would have been unattainable through licensing.[13] Boeing's access to the Japanese market, and possibly to rapidly growing Southeast Asian markets, may have been enhanced by its partnership with Japanese firms.[14] The partnership with Japanese and Italian firms has reduced the size, cost, and risks of Boeing's financial commitment to the development of these aircraft. Boeing also has benefited by supporting entry or expanded participation by Japanese firms in the aircraft components industry, thereby increasing competition among component suppliers and subcontractors.[15] Finally, the potentially valuable contributions of capital, production expertise, and market access that the Japanese consortium could offer Airbus Industrie, a major competitor, have been preempted by the link between Boeing and the consortium.

In March 1984 Boeing announced a collaborative development project involving the Japan Aircraft Development Corporation (JADC, which is a consortium of the firms involved in the JCAC, is charged with managing new aircraft development projects) to design and produce a 150-seat aircraft, then expected to be introduced in 1990. The memorandum of understanding between Boeing and the JADC that was signed in March 1984 committed the Japanese group to a share of 25 percent in the "7-7" project (now the 7J7, an aircraft that will employ "unducted fan" engines). As outlined in the memorandum of understanding, Japanese participation in the

7J7 project differs qualitatively from the 767 venture. Rather than participating as a risk-sharing subcontractor, with responsibilities limited to design and production of a modest number of components to meet Boeing specifications, the JADC will participate in all phases of the project, ranging from fundamental design to marketing, finance of aircraft sales, and product support. Boeing remains the senior partner in this joint venture, however, a status reinforced by the U.S. firm's insistence on a higher return on its investment as an acknowledgment of its superior design, project management, marketing, and product support experience.[16] In March 1986 Boeing announced that Saab-Scania of Sweden and Short Brothers of the United Kingdom had agreed to participate in the 7J7 project as risk-sharing associates. Short Brothers' share of the development program was expected to amount to roughly 5 percent, while that of Saab-Scania would be comparable or slightly greater (see Brown, 1986).[17]

The 7J7 venture extends the alliance of Boeing and Japanese firms in commercial aircraft, but this alliance remains one in which Boeing is the senior partner. The strength of this alliance has been tested severely, as the date of introduction of the new aircraft was postponed from 1990 to 1992 in 1985 and to 1993 in 1987, and the decision made not to employ the V2500 engine, produced in part by Japanese firms, on the aircraft. In November 1987 Boeing reduced the staff of the 7J7 project from 1,000 to 200, suggesting that the aircraft may be delayed still further (*Aviation Week and Space Technology*, 1987d and 1987e). All these decisions favor Boeing's near-term interests over those of the Japanese participants in the 7J7 project. If it proceeds, however, the 7J7 project is likely to increase foreign competition for U.S. supplier firms in the aerospace industry. Boeing managers have acknowledged that components suppliers are excluded from full partnership in the 7J7 venture to encourage competition among these firms.[18]

McDonnell Douglas: The Mercure 200 and the MDF100

McDonnell Douglas Aircraft entered into two joint ventures during the 1970s and early 1980s, both of which failed to produce an aircraft. Neither failure can be attributed to a lack of demand for the proposed aircraft, which would have served the market for a 150-seat aircraft several years earlier than the Airbus A320 or the Boeing 7J7. In the case of the MDF100, the venture between McDonnell Douglas and Fokker, the inability to synchronize the airframe development program with the introduction of new engines contributed to uncertainties and delays that led to Fokker's withdrawal. Managerial factors also contributed to the demise of this venture, however, as McDonnell Douglas did not make the financial commitment that could have supported the participation of a European partner with fewer engineering resources. The McDonnell Douglas-Fokker venture also reveals the difficulties of product development collaboration between established firms in technologically dynamic industries. As the technologies of materials, airframes, and engines developed during the early 1980s, the existing McDonnell Douglas product line began to encroach on the market for which the MDF100 was intended.

The Mercure 200, to be designed and produced by a group teaming McDonnell Douglas with Dassault-Breguet and Aerospatiale of France, also failed to reach the market. The demise of this venture was due in part to the unwillingness of McDonnell Douglas to commit the resources to modify the aircraft design to make it more attractive to potential purchasers.

Both the MDF 100 and Mercure 200 ventures were efforts by McDonnell Douglas to develop a new aircraft at roughly the same time that Boeing was evaluating the 757 and 767. Corporate management at McDonnell Douglas was loath to commit large sums of money to the development of a new aircraft in the 1970s, however, in part because of the poor financial performance of its Douglas Aircraft division. Although other aircraft firms, notably Boeing, also were unwilling to undertake new development programs without participation by one or more other firms, Boeing refused to accept anything less than a leadership position in such a consortium. For Boeing, joint ventures were a means for new product development. McDonnell Douglas's joint venture strategy, however, was driven in part by the firm's desire to utilize its extensive product support and marketing network more fully, acting as a marketing and servicing agent for products designed and produced largely by other firms. McDonnell Douglas also employed the Mercure 200 venture as a means to win additional sales of DC-9s and DC-10s to European airlines. Reflecting its motives for collaboration, McDonnell Douglas did not insist on a controlling share in its joint ventures.

The first major joint venture between McDonnell Douglas and foreign firms was the Mercure 200. The Mercure 200 was designed to seat 170 passengers and was a derivative of the commercially unsuccessful Mercure 100, produced by Dassault-Breguet of France. Talks sponsored by the French government among Aerospatiale, Dassault-Breguet, Boeing, and McDonnell Douglas during 1975 and 1976 led to the announcement in August 1976 of an agreement between McDonnell Douglas and the two French firms to develop the Mercure 200. The Mercure 200 airframe was intended to utilize the CFM56 engine then being developed by General Electric and SNECMA of France.

Under the terms of the Mercure 200 agreement, McDonnell Douglas would have a minor role in the development and production of the aircraft. The firm's production share of the Mercure 200 amounted to only 15 percent, although the U.S. firm was to design some of the components of the aircraft. Aerospatiale, which faced continuing financial losses due to the slow sales of the Airbus A300 and the termination of several military aircraft programs, was responsible for the assembly of 40 percent of the aircraft, including final assembly. Dassault-Breguet was in charge of the overall design effort, as well as production of about 15 percent of the aircraft. Although McDonnell Douglas had a secondary role in the design and production of the Mercure 200, the firm was responsible for marketing and product support for the aircraft—the marketing and design efforts of this collaboration thus were not tightly linked. In exchange for giving up the majority of the assembly work for the Mercure, McDonnell Douglas was informally assured of orders from French and Swiss airlines for as many as 75 DC-9s and 8 DC-10s (see Ropelewski, 1976, p. 12).

The Mercure 200's wing design was identical to that of the Mercure 100, which constrained the range and other operating characteristics of the proposed aircraft and limited its potential market.[19] Despite strong support from McDonnell Douglas and a number of airlines for a new wing design, the costs of such a redesign made this alternative unattractive to the French participants.[20] McDonnell Douglas viewed a new wing design as necessary to gain sales in the U.S. market, which was critical to the financial success of the Mercure 200. The U.S. firm was unsuccessful in its efforts to alter the design, however, and the Mercure 200 finally was abandoned. The weak market for the Mercure 200 reflected much more than just the aircraft's wing design, but this flawed design clearly reduced the appeal of the aircraft. Although McDonnell Douglas personnel were concerned about these problems in the Mercure 200 design, the U.S. firm apparently was unwilling to invest in a larger role within the more costly development program that would have been necessary to produce a commercially successful aircraft.

A similar lack of financial commitment to match the firm's considerable technological assets characterized McDonnell Douglas's collaboration with Fokker of the Netherlands in the MDF100 project. McDonnell Douglas and Fokker began joint design and engineering work on a 150-seat aircraft, the MDF100, in May 1981. A serious difficulty with the project from the outset was its timing—there was no all-new engine available for the MDF100, the project having begun prior to the announcement of the V2500 engine venture (see below) and after the introduction of the CFM56. Prospective purchasers of the MDF100 were faced with a choice between two derivative engines, the CFM56 or the JT8D.[21]

Timing problems of this sort frequently require that aircraft producers extend the design definition phase, developing numerous variations on a few basic design concepts and consulting with airlines and engine manufacturers on the evolution of both propulsion technology and customer demand. The uncertain market for the MDF100 dictated a prolonged period of design definition. The length of this gestation period and its demands on Fokker's limited pool of engineering and design talent were critical factors in the demise of this joint venture.

Fokker was producing two successful aircraft, the F27 commuter turboprop and the F28 short-range passenger jet. Product support, production engineering, and design modifications for these products required considerable engineering resources, and a substantial commitment by Fokker of its engineering staff to the joint venture could jeopardize these profitable programs. Any expansion of Fokker's engineering staff to support the joint venture would be temporary and eventually would require costly layoffs. Faced with the likelihood of an indefinite period of preliminary design activity, uncertainty concerning the commercial prospects for the MDF100, and growing risks to the firm's successful product line from continued work on the MDF100, senior management of Fokker elected to withdraw from the MDF100 venture in May 1982.

Although Fokker's withdrawal stemmed from the uncertain market for the MDF100, McDonnell Douglas's interest in the venture also diminished over time, because of the remarkable potential of the DC-9 for additional stretching and re-engining. The basic design of the DC-9 fuselage seemed capable of accommodating fuselage stretches sufficient to accommodate as many as 150 passengers, with a new, fuel-efficient engine. Moreover, a stretched DC-9 could be sold profitably for less than the MDF100. Engine developments and technical possibilities unforeseen at the outset of the joint venture thus contributed to its demise, as McDonnell Douglas's existing product line encroached on the market that would be served by the jointly developed product.

The fact that both firms were involved in the preliminary design of the MDF100 means that considerable exchange of proprietary data and design skills took place. Although the original memorandum of understanding between the firms stipulated that all design data were to be returned to the original provider in the event of termination, the MDF100 project almost certainly resulted in one of the most extensive transfers of design concepts and data of any of the ventures discussed in this chapter. According to senior McDonnell Douglas personnel, for example, the wing design of the MDF100 was a hybrid of Fokker and McDonnell Douglas concepts.[22] Fokker also brought expertise in metal bonding to the joint venture. While substantial technology transfer did occur within the venture, neither participant was motivated by a desire to maximize the amount of learning that took place within the venture, in contrast to the Japanese participants in the 7J7 venture with Boeing.

The MDF venture was managed by a small project office staffed by employees of both firms, reflecting the fact that Fokker and McDonnell Douglas were equal partners in the MDF100 venture. This management structure proved to be unwieldy. While the bulk of the design work and all production management, marketing, and product support activities were carried out by the firms, rather than an independent entity, the small size of the management staff in the project office meant that decisions on design and other issues had to be made by very senior personnel from both firms. Each partner effectively held a veto in all matters of design and management, complicating the resolution of disagreements.

The experiences of McDonnell Douglas in both the Mercure 200 and MDF100 joint ventures suggest some of the difficulties inherent in ventures in which a technologically or financially "senior" firm does not take a controlling role within a joint venture. Had McDonnell Douglas been willing to adopt this more costly role in either joint venture, a technically and commercially successful aircraft might have been produced.[23] The unwillingness of the French participants to address McDonnell Douglas's design concerns in the Mercure 200 project contributed to its failure; however, McDonnell Douglas's modest role meant that the U.S. firm could not make its wishes and design philosophy prevail. In the case of the MDF100, a larger commitment of McDonnell Douglas funds and personnel might have supported Fokker's continued participation. The prospect of a lengthy development period, after all, was not the primary cause of the failure—it was the unwillingness of Fokker to absorb the drain on its engineering resources associated with a lengthy period of design definition.[24]

General Electric-SNECMA

The joint venture between General Electric and the Société Nationale d'Etude et de Construction de Moteurs d'Aviation (SNECMA) is centered on the production of the CFM56, a high-bypass engine of 20,000–30,000 pounds thrust. The collaboration of these two firms is formally managed by a separate entity (CFM International) in which each partner owns 50 percent of the equity. In contrast to the McDonnell Douglas-Fokker joint venture, which operated as an alliance of financial and technological equals, the technological and managerial senior partner within CFM International is General Electric. CFM International also has operated successfully under Defense Department controls that restrict the transfer of engine technology from General Electric to SNECMA through the joint venture.

The CFM joint venture originated in the early 1970s, when engine producers on both sides of the Atlantic recognized the market possibilities for a high-bypass engine of 20,000–30,000 pounds' thrust, to be employed on medium- and short-range aircraft. A major market for such an engine was Europe, with its dense short-haul route structure. Both General Electric and Pratt and Whitney accordingly sought European participation in the development and production of this engine, so as to enhance market access. Simultaneously, SNECMA, 90 percent of the equity in which is owned by the French government (the remaining 10 percent is owned by Pratt and Whitney) had developed a design concept for such an engine.

Following talks with both General Electric and Pratt and Whitney, SNECMA chose General Electric as a partner in the development and production of the so-called ten-ton engine. SNECMA's choice of General Electric built on a relationship that included SNECMA's major subcontracting role in the production of the CF6-50 and CF6-80 engines, employed on the Airbus A300 and A310. Pratt and Whitney's interest in a joint venture with SNECMA also may have been tempered by the fact that the U.S. firm was producing a successful engine in this size class—the JT8D, which was employed on the DC9 and 727.

General Electric's design for the CFM56 utilized the engine core compressor developed by the firm for the military F101 engine. Senior U.S. Air Force officials argued that this engine core compressor represented a considerable technological advance and national security asset, developed with public funds. As a result, the Defense Department expressed strong opposition to any transfer of this technology from General Electric to a foreign firm. After lengthy negotiations that reached the highest levels of the French and U.S. governments (the issue was raised in a letter from French President Pompidou to President Nixon in 1972), approval was granted by the Pentagon for the use of the F101 compressor technology in the CFM56 under restrictive conditions. These included the shipment of the compressor by General Electric in a sealed "black box" module for installation by SNECMA on its CFM56 assembly line, a delay of eighteen months before the compressor could be shipped to France for testing, and the payment to the U.S. government of a royalty on each engine. These negotiations delayed the introduction of the CFM56 by at least one year.

Although such a delay normally would have a disastrous impact on the commercial prospects for an engine, the CFM56 was if anything aided by this hiatus, its market having been quite bleak for several years. Sales of the engine were slow until the early 1980s, when the replacement of older engines on the DC-8 and the KC-135 military tanker with CFM56 engines, as well as the introduction of the Boeing 737-300 and the development of the Airbus A320, both of which employ versions of the CFM56, expanded demand for the engine considerably.

Several aspects of this joint venture are noteworthy. Although the efforts of the Defense Department to restrict technology transfer through CFM International clearly complicated the development of the engine and contributed to higher costs, the imposition of restrictions on technology transfer ultimately did not jeopardize the development program. The relative ease with which the central compressor could be manufactured separately and shipped to SNECMA from General Electric in a sealed black box reflected the fact that General Electric's design for the CFM56 exploited modular design principles, in order to reduce maintenance costs. In addition, General Electric did most of the development and systems integration for the engine, reducing somewhat the requirements for information and data exchange between the two partners. Nonetheless, some observers suggest that the CFM56 incurred performance penalties, due to restrictions on sharing of technology and design data between the parties responsible for the compressor and the rear sections of the engine.[25]

The slow pace of development of the CFM56 also reduced somewhat the complexity of project management. Had the CFM56 been a tightly time-constrained program, project management might have been more difficult. Management of the CFM56 project was further simplified by the fact that General Electric was the acknowledged technological and managerial senior partner within the venture, receiving a fee from SNECMA for project management. Major design decisions typically were made by General Electric personnel, with input from SNECMA. General Electric also provides virtually all of the product support for the engine.

The CFM International has been a commercial success—SNECMA now is a leading French exporter of aerospace products, and the

CFM56 engine is one of the best selling commercial aircraft engines, having been ordered for more than 50 percent of the commercial transports ordered in 1986. General Electric also has benefited from SNECMA's contribution of 50 percent of the development costs of the CFM56, which totaled more than $1 billion. The importance of SNECMA's financial contribution, however, goes beyond its magnitude. In the view of senior managers at General Electric's Aircraft Engine Group, SNECMA's financial contribution prevented the termination by General Electric of the CFM56 program in the mid-1970s. Moreover, the adoption of the CFM56-5 for the Airbus A320 undoubtedly was aided by the engine's substantial French content, providing a good example of enhanced market access through the strategic choice of joint venture partners. Estimates of the French government's share of the SNECMA contribution to the development of the CFM56 are unreliable, but they suggest that the government contribution, much of which took the form of low-interest or no-interest loans, has amounted to several hundred million dollars over the life of the project.[26]

Although the CFM venture has proven financially rewarding for SNECMA, the technological benefits for the French firm are less visible. SNECMA gives no signs of undertaking the development of a commercial engine without General Electric's participation, either independently or in cooperation with other European producers. SNECMA's participation as a prime contractor in the engine business is unlikely, but the firm may well have become more competitive as a supplier of spare parts. Spare parts sales for the CFM56 are regulated by the GE-SNECMA agreement, but SNECMA could produce spare parts for other military or civilian engines.

The agreement between General Electric and SNECMA covers only the CFM56 engine. Recently, however, General Electric and SNECMA have extended their alliance to include the development of an unducted fan (UDF) engine, proposed by Boeing for its 7J7 aircraft. The financial burdens of the UDF project will exceed those of the CFM56, a possibility that makes joint development more attractive to General Electric. The amount of technology transfer that is likely to occur between the partners in the UDF project is difficult to determine because the project is still in its early stages. Thus far in the UDF program, General Electric has assumed primary responsibility for development and testing, although SNECMA also has tested engine components. The UDF project suggests that the SNECMA-General Electric alliance is likely to continue, like the Boeing-JCAC collaboration. Nonetheless, General Electric will remain the senior partner.

The Saab-Fairchild 340

The Saab-Fairchild SF340 is a commuter aircraft introduced in 1984 by a joint venture between Saab-Scania of Sweden and Fairchild Aircraft of the United States. This joint venture collapsed in 1985 with the withdrawal of Fairchild from the partnership, due largely to the U.S. firm's inability to bear the financial and technological burdens of partnership. Saab-Scania now has sole control of the production and marketing of the SF340.

The SF340 venture was initiated by Saab-Scania Aircraft in the late 1970s, as part of the firm's efforts to diversify its production of aircraft beyond military products. Saab-Scania's design and manufacture of military aircraft for the Swedish Air Force during the previous four decades had developed strong design and production capabilities within the firm. For a number of reasons, however, the Swedish military aircraft market in the late 1970s presented limited prospects for future growth and stability, creating strong incentives for Saab-Scania to diversify out of the production of military aircraft.

Production of components for other commercial aircraft afforded one means for Saab-Scania to preserve its employment, production capacity, and design skills. Saab-Scania's role as a subcontractor expanded during the early 1980s as the firm manufactured components for the McDonnell Douglas MD-80 and the British Aerospace BAe 146. Subcontracting alone, however, would not preserve Saab-Scania's design and systems integration capabilities. These could be maintained only through the development and production of a commercial aircraft for which Saab-Scania was a leader in overall design and systems integration. The commuter aircraft market combined less daunting financial requirements than large commercial aircraft with bright prospects for future growth.[27]

Saab-Scania's interest in a U.S. partner for the development, production, and marketing of the aircraft was motivated by several considerations. Penetration of the U.S. market was essential to the commercial success of any commuter aircraft. Access to this market would be aided greatly by the presence of a U.S. partner. In addition, Saab-Scania had no marketing or product support network in the United States or Europe. Teaming with an established U.S. producer could provide such a network for Saab-Scania in the largest single market for the aircraft. Finally, the financial and engineering requirements for development of the SF340 meant that a partner would lower financial risks and costs. Significantly, access to advanced technological capabilities was not a central concern for the Swedish firm in evaluating potential U.S. partners.

A number of U.S. producers of general aviation and business aircraft, including Beech, Cessna, and Piper, were unwilling to participate in the proposed joint venture when approached by Saab-Scania in the late 1970s. Fairchild Aircraft was an attractive partner because of its ownership of Swearingen Aircraft, producers of the nineteen-passenger Metro. In the course of producing and marketing the Metro, Fairchild-Swearingen had developed an extensive U.S. marketing and product support network, the key corporate asset of interest to Saab-Scania.

The terms of the agreement signed by the two firms in 1980 required that each partner contribute 50 percent of the costs of developing the aircraft, which was to be assembled in Sweden by Saab-Scania. Fairchild's primary production responsibility was the wing, fabricated at Fairchild-Republic Aviation, a producer of military aircraft and a subcontractor on Boeing aircraft. Marketing and product support for the aircraft within the United States were the responsibility of Fairchild–Swearingen. A jointly owned entity, Saab Fairchild International, was created, but its responsibilities were limited to marketing and product support outside the United States. Management of the development and production phases of the project was controlled by a special board, with equal representation from senior management of both partner firms. In its financial and technological composition, then, the SF340 venture was a partnership of equals, and had no project management office that was independent of the partner firms.

As in the case of the MDF100, the small management staff associated with the SF340 meant that the project suffered from the frequent necessity to take minor design and technical issues to senior management in both firms for resolution. Both major and trivial decisions on design and technological issues were made at the most senior levels of both firms, and consumed considerable time. Saab-Scania's lack of experience in the civil aircraft market also contributed to the Swedish firm's acceptance of several key design features proposed by Fairchild, including the three-seat cross-section and the thirty-four-seat capacity of the final design. Undertaken in order to make the aircraft attractive to corporate aviation customers, these decisions situated the SF340 in a relatively crowded segment of the commuter aircraft market, one served by products manufactured by both de Havilland of Canada (the DHC-8) and Embraer of Brazil. Although the SF340 fuselage can be stretched, this operation will be costly and may reduce sales of the smaller version of the aircraft.

The protracted discussions and disputes over design features, as well as technical difficulties in mastering the new bonding technologies and wing design incorporated in the aircraft, also contributed to delays in the development of the SF340. As a result, the SF340's lead time over competing commuter aircraft was reduced considerably, while development costs for the aircraft increased to over $400 million (see *Aviation Week and Space Technology*, 1985, p. 23).

Several of the important technological advances in the SF340 were contributed by neither firm. The aircraft wing, for example, is based on a design developed by NASA. Saab-Scania's access to the wing design and performance data was facilitated by its partnership with Fairchild. As a U.S. firm, Fairchild Aircraft had immediate access to any data released by NASA; access to these data for Saab-Scania was prohibited for one year after the date of their domestic release. The construction of the SF340 fuselage also employs high-temperature bonding technologies, which were developed by Lockheed and Boeing and utilized by Fairchild Aircraft in its role as a subcontractor for Boeing. The technological parity of the partners in the SF340 venture meant that the net "outflow" of U.S. aircraft technology within this joint venture was modest. While the aircraft is assembled in Sweden, the U.S. content of the final product, which utilizes General Electric engines, is high—the landing gear and the propeller were the only non-U.S. components in the early versions of the SF340. This joint venture does not appear to have had a detrimental impact on U.S. supplier firms.

The SF340 was introduced in 1984, and has sold well. Unexpectedly high development costs for the SF340, however, imposed great burdens on the U.S. partner. Severe financial difficulties during 1984 and 1985 led Fairchild Industries, corporate parent of the aircraft firm, to withdraw from its partnership with Saab-Scania in September 1985. The firm's withdrawal from the SF340 venture followed a succession of managerial and technical problems, ranging from wing assembly to marketing of the aircraft within the United States, that Fairchild had encountered.[28] Under the terms of the dissolution agreement negotiated with Saab-Scania, Fairchild manufactured wings for the SF340 as a subcontractor through the first half of 1987 (see *Aviation Week and Space Technology*, 1985, p. 23). During 1986–1987, Fairchild transferred manufacturing tooling and design data for the SF340 wing to Saab-Scania, which assumed full responsibility for wing production in 1987. Fairchild also withdrew completely from marketing and product support for the SF340.

In contrast to Fairchild Industries, the corporate parent of Saab-Scania Aircraft has not suffered financial losses as a result of the SF340—the costs of the venture have been partially defrayed by public funds (in the form of loans) and the profits of Saab-Scania's automotive operations. Withdrawal of Fairchild from the joint venture does not mean the end of the SF340. Fairchild's technical and financial weaknesses had for some time forced the Swedish firm to play a more substantial role within the joint venture than originally planned—the U.S. marketing network was reorganized in 1985 and responsibility for U.S. sales and support for the SF340 was transferred to Saab Fairchild International from Fairchild.

Nevertheless, if Saab-Scania is to remain profitably involved in civil aircraft production, the firm may have to introduce additional products in the commuter or business aircraft markets, so as to utilize fully the marketing and product support network established for the SF340. Saab-Scania almost certainly will have to seek other partners in any future product development venture because of the high costs of independent development. Saab-Scania's participation in the Boeing 7J7 venture will provide work for its design staff. The 7J7 project will not utilize the marketing and product support network developed for the SF340, nor will it sustain Saab-Scania's design integration or project management capabilities.

Despite initially promising sales, the financial returns from the SF340 are likely to be modest. Saab-Scania now faces a large additional investment in sustaining the market for an aircraft that will have to be produced in considerable quantity before it returns a profit. Fairchild provided development funding, but ultimately proved to be a weak partner. Although the financial benefits of Saab-Scania's alliance strategy have been mixed at best, the partnership with an American firm does appear to have aided the SF340's penetration of the U.S. market.

The International Aero Engines V2500

The V2500 joint venture involves Pratt and Whitney, Rolls Royce, Fiat, MTU, and Japan Aero Engines Corporation (JAEC, itself a consortium of Kawasaki Heavy Industries, Mitsubishi Heavy Industries, and Ishikawajima-Harima Heavy Industries), in one of the most complex joint ventures in the commercial aircraft industry. Announced in 1983, the joint venture has as its goal the development and production of a new 25,000-pound thrust engine by 1989, for employment in the 150-seat aircraft entering service at that time (currently, the Airbus A320 and McDonnell Douglas MD-89). International Aero Engines, an entity incorporated in Switzerland, has been formed to coordinate development, production, marketing, and product support for the V2500. Ownership of IAE equity is divided as follows: Pratt and Whitney 30 percent, Rolls Royce 30 percent,

Japan Aero Engines 19.9 percent, MTU 12.1 percent, and Fiat 8 percent.[29] While the formal structure of the V2500 venture is complex, the venture in fact appears to be an alliance of two multifirm groups, centered respectively around Rolls Royce (partners with Japan Aero Engines) and Pratt and Whitney (partners with MTU and Fiat). Prior experience in the joint development or production of aircraft engines is reflected in the division of production and design activities among the participants.

The decision by Rolls Royce and Pratt and Whitney to join forces in the development of a new engine followed by several years the demise of a joint venture between these firms. The JT10D project had as its goal the development of a high-bypass engine generating 28,000 pounds of thrust for the Boeing 757. The JT10D partnership lasted less than a year, breaking up "amicably," according to the participants, in the spring of 1977 (*Aviation Week and Space Technology*, 1977a, p. 17).

Several factors contributed to the dissolution of the JT10D collaboration. The most important of these was the growth of the Boeing 757 from 150 seats to 180 seats—as a result, the aircraft needed a larger engine, with a thrust rating well in excess of 30,000 pounds. Growth in the 757's engine thrust requirements diminished the attractiveness for Rolls Royce of participation in the development of a new engine, since the British firm was developing independently an engine of 38,000 pounds' thrust, the RB211-535. Rolls Royce proposed to Pratt and Whitney that the venture be reorganized, with Pratt and Whitney operating as a junior partner in a venture that would develop and optimize a version of the RB211-535 for the 757, but the U.S. firm was not interested. In addition, several observers (notably Steiner, 1982; see also the statement of David Pickerell cited above) have suggested that transatlantic cooperation in the development of this engine was complicated by restrictions on the transfer of engine technology that were imposed on Pratt and Whitney by the U.S. Defense Department.

Before its discussions with Pratt and Whitney on the JT10D, Rolls Royce had joined Japan Aero Engines in the early 1970s in the development of the RJ500, a high-bypass engine producing 20,000 pounds of thrust. The Rolls-Japanese consortium built on the previous efforts of the JAEC in developing the smaller FJR710, which was funded by the Japan National Aeronautics Laboratory as a research project. Lacking high-altitude engine testing facilities within Japan, the JAEC utilized those of Rolls Royce, which led to the decision to cooperate in the development of the larger RJ500. Although test versions of the RJ500 were running successfully in early 1982, airframe manufacturers did not exhibit great interest in the engine. It became apparent that any engine for a 150-seat aircraft would have to generate more than 20,000 pounds' thrust and incorporate new technologies in materials and controls, in order to increase fuel efficiency. Faced with these costly requirements, the RJ500 group in 1982 began exploring the possibilities for cooperation with either General Electric or Pratt and Whitney.

The other group within the V2500 venture consists of Pratt and Whitney and the two European firms with whom Pratt and Whitney worked closely on the PW2037, an engine developed for the Boeing 757 after the termination of the JT10D project. Pratt and Whitney during the late 1970s undertook the development of two new engines, the PW4000 (used on the Boeing 747 and the Airbus A310 and A300–600) and the PW2037, from a "clean sheet of paper"— neither engine had a military antecedent, and neither was a derivative of a previous civil engine design. The technological and financial burdens of these development projects were and remain immense, particularly in view of the modest sales of the Boeing 757. Fiat and MTU account respectively for 4 percent and 11 percent of the value of the PW2037 (Fiat also produces 3 percent of the value of the PW4000). Reflecting an emerging pattern of specialization, Fiat developed and produced the gearbox for the PW2037, while MTU developed and produced the low-pressure turbine section at the rear of the engine.

Although Pratt and Whitney recognized the potential market for an all-new engine in the 25,000-pound-thrust class, the firm's ambitious development agenda precluded the unaided launch of yet another multibillion-dollar engine development program. The U.S. firm accordingly reentered negotiations with Rolls Royce.[30] In 1982 the Rolls Royce and Pratt and Whitney groups agreed to collaborate in the development of an all-new 25,000-pound-thrust engine.

Significant technological contributions to the V2500 will be made by both of the senior partners. Rolls Royce and JAEC are responsible for the forward section of the engine (the low- and high-pressure compressors), utilizing the advanced technology for fan blade fabrication developed by Rolls Royce for its RB211 family of engines. The Pratt and Whitney group is responsible for the rear sections of the engine, employing technologies developed and applied in the PW2037. Pratt and Whitney is responsible for the core section of the engine, while MTU and Fiat respectively will develop and produce the low-pressure turbine and the gearbox, the same components that these firms developed and produced for the PW2037. Assembly of the engine will take place in both the United States and Great Britain. Marketing is to be carried out by International Aero Engines, which also has responsibility for systems integration and project management.

IAE's autonomous control of project management and marketing is important, due in part to the numerous possibilities for conflicts of interest if either Rolls Royce or Pratt and Whitney were given primary responsibility for marketing the engine.[31] Such conflicts between jointly and independently developed products, after all, undermined the JT10D venture. Product support will be delegated by IAE to the member firms best able to provide such support. These firms are likely to be Pratt and Whitney and Rolls Royce. The governments of the nations in which the foreign participants in the V2500 venture are based all have provided significant financial assistance.

The senior partners in the V2500 venture (Pratt and Whitney and Rolls Royce) have devoted considerable effort to minimizing technology transfer in the development of this engine. Some of these efforts were motivated by U.S. government scrutiny of Pratt and Whitney's role within the consortium and the desire of the Pentagon to prevent transfer of the U.S. firm's high-pressure engine core technology to foreign firms. Much of the concern over technology transfer within the V2500 consortium, however, reflects the senior firms' commercial interests. In order to minimize technology transfer, the engine program emphasizes the separate development of engine components by member firms, with limited exchange of technical data among the partners; like the CFM56 engine, the V2500 relies on modular design and construction principles.[32] Interfaces among these components are designed to facilitate the assembly and testing of the entire engine without extensive knowledge about the internal design specifications of the individual components.

Although this development strategy may reduce technology transfer among the participants, it appears to have complicated the testing and integration of the components of the V2500. Development and testing of the V2500 were proceeding ahead of schedule until late 1986, but serious problems have arisen since then, necessitating a significant redesign of the engine's compressor by Rolls Royce. Rather than continuing as an equal partner with Rolls Royce, Pratt and Whitney has been forced to assume overall leadership of the engineering and systems integration for the project (see Kandebo, 1987a). The strict divisions of responsibility between the senior partners thus appear to be blurring somewhat as a result of the requirements for systems integration and testing (see *Aviation Week and Space Technology*, 1987b, pp. 32–33; 1987c, p. 31).

The desire of both Pratt and Whitney and Rolls Royce to minimize technology transfer within the venture also conflicts with the desires of other participants to improve their technological and marketing skills. Japanese participants in the V2500 project, for example, are unlikely to gain a broad knowledge of marketing, product support and development engineering.[33] Nonetheless, the ability of individual participants to exploit their specialized capabilities in the development and manufacture of specific components (for example, Fiat and the gearbox) should yield efficiency gains. The gains from such learning in the design process are likely to be greatest in a collaboration that spans several projects, since design skills acquired in one project can be applied to subsequent projects.

A final aspect of the V2500 venture that is noteworthy is the review and approval of this venture (in September 1983) by the U.S. Department of Justice. It is difficult to think of another U.S. industry with a comparably concentrated market structure (three firms account for virtually 100 percent of sales of large transport engines in the noncommunist world market) in which a joint product development venture between two of the three major competitors would be approved. Moreover, one of the two groups that have joined forces in the V2500 project (Rolls Royce and the JAEC) had a product, the RJ500 engine, that might have supported separate entry into this segment of the engine market. The approval of the IAE proposal by the Department of Justice lends some support to the view that joint ventures between U.S. and foreign firms receive less thorough scrutiny than those involving only U.S. firms.

Like CFM International, the IAE consortium announced in late 1986 that a successor to its initial product, the so-called Super Fan engine, would be developed for the Airbus A340. In April 1987, however, IAE announced the indefinite postponement of the Super Fan project. Combined with the recent development and testing problems in the V2500 project, the Super Fan engine episode has raised serious questions about the long-term viability of the IAE consortium. The ability of IAE to manage the activities of its independent partners in an extraordinarily complex development project thus far raises serious questions.

CONCLUSION

Combined with the declining importance of the U.S. aircraft market and other shifts in the global market for commercial aircraft, changes in the domestic environment of the U.S. commercial aircraft industry have served as powerful incentives for U.S. firms to seek foreign partners in the development of new products. The nature of the technological and competitive assets within this industry, as well as the motives for collaboration between U.S. and foreign firms, have made collaboration far more important than licensing or direct foreign investment in the global strategies of U.S. and foreign firms. These factors also mean that collaboration has focused on product development and manufacture.

The multinational joint ventures and collaborations described in this chapter form a diverse collection, about which generalizations are hazardous. The structure of these ventures, the amount of technology transfer occurring within them, and the relative importance of U.S. and foreign firms as participants within each venture, all differ greatly. Nonetheless, some general themes are clearly discernible within this collection of contrasts.

One obvious conclusion from the discussion of these six collaborative ventures is that collaboration does not guarantee commercial success. At the same time, however, the failure rate of joint ventures does not appear to exceed significantly that of independent product development programs in an industry known for high risk (recall the data cited above indicating that no more than four of twenty-three aircraft designs introduced since 1950 were produced in large quantity).

The composition of the glue binding together the partners in these collaborative ventures is complex. One of the most important bonding agents, observed in the Boeing 767 and General Electric-SNECMA ventures and in the participation of Japan Aero Engines, Fiat, and MTU in the V2500 project, is a technological disparity among the participant firms.[34] The presence of such a disparity creates the basis for an exchange of technology, provided by the technologically advanced partner, for capital or market access, provided by the less advanced firm.

The structure of joint ventures of this variety does not seem to be a serious issue when the more advanced firm assumes responsibility for overall management and design. Ventures founded on the existence of such technological disparities have operated reasonably well as an equity partnership of financial equals (CFM International) or as a partnership between a prime contractor and a risk-sharing subcontractor (the 767 and JCAC, or Japan Aero Engines, Fiat and MTU within the V2500 project).

An important source of tension within ventures between technologically "junior" and "senior" partners, however, concerns the amount of technology transfer acceptable to the participants. Technology transfer within these joint ventures has thus far involved few if any of the key components of the senior firms' most advanced technologies. In other words the quality and quantity of technology transfer within these ventures has been insufficient to enable the junior partners to become serious competitive threats to the senior firms in the near future. The internal barriers to technology transfer erected by the senior partners, however, appear to have hampered seriously the performance of at least one venture, the V2500.

Restrictions on technology transfer imposed by the technologically advanced firms within collaborative ventures mean that the aspirations of technologically "junior" firms for extensive learning and technology acquisition may be disappointed. Firms interested in establishing a specialized subcontracting capability or in stabilizing their workforce and capacity utilization through a subordinate role in a joint venture are more likely to achieve their goals than are firms that use this role to obtain high-level capabilities in management, design, and systems integration. Prospective junior partners in collaborative ventures also must choose between a long-term alliance with a single major firm that spans several development projects, similar to those between Boeing and its Japanese partners or General Electric and SNECMA, and a strategy of successive one-project collaborations, which resembles the current approach of Saab-Scania and Aeritalia to ventures with McDonnell Douglas and Boeing.

Ventures involving firms of comparable technological endowments require greater attention to organization and management. The cases discussed above suggest several sources of difficulty within such partnerships. In both the MDF100 and Saab-Fairchild ventures, the resolution of design disputes between the partner firms proved to be difficult and time-consuming, operating as these ventures did without a strong design staff that was independent of the partner firms. In the absence of such a staff, such issues were resolved only at senior levels of the partner firms. The structure of the V2500 venture, in which the high-level systems integration and overall design activities are the responsibility of an independent staff that works with the participant firms as subcontractors and suppliers seems to have advantages in this regard, although recent events suggest that even this structure can be difficult to manage.

Despite its other problems, an organizational structure like IAE, in which systems integration responsibilities are combined with those of marketing and the management of product support, reestablishes an essential link that was severed or weakened in the MDF100, Mercure 200, and SF340 ventures. As the history of such projects as the Boeing 757 and 767 or the Airbus Industrie A310 and A320 demonstrate, close consultation between potential customers and both the marketing and design personnel of the airframe producer is critical to successful introduction of a new product. Joint venture organizations in which the links between marketing, product support, and design are not preserved may make inappropriate design compromises and decisions.

An additional problem in joint ventures among technological equals is the emergence of competition between the product being developed within the joint venture and those produced independently by participant firms. This problem was particularly important in the unsuccessful JT10D venture between Pratt and Whitney and Rolls Royce, and contributed to the demise of the MDF100 project. Since the degree to which aircraft and engines may substitute for one another varies greatly across customers and markets, uncertainty about such product encroachment is likely to be present in many such ventures.[35]

Some degree of competition between independently manufactured products and those developed and produced jointly therefore is almost always present and may create conflicts of interest for participant firms if marketing is not handled by an independent organization. There are no obvious solutions to this problem, inasmuch as its prevalence stems from the technologically dynamic character of this industry and the capabilities of participants in joint ventures of technological equals. The frequency with which this and other problems have occurred within collaborations between firms of comparable technological capabilities, however, suggests that firms seeking financial support or market access are ill advised to enter such a joint venture. Certainly, the results of such collaborations (the SF340, MDF100, and Mercure 200 projects, as well as the short-lived cooperative agreement between General Electric and Rolls Royce in large engines) suggest low rates of successful product introduction or venture survival.

Other issues that must be resolved for collaborative product development ventures to succeed include the management of project costs and contracting, and the specification in advance of procedures for the dissolution of a venture. The importance of cost controls reflects the need to prevent cost-sharing from reducing the incentives of partner firms to minimize costs. A number of collaborative ventures, including Airbus Industrie and International Aero Engines, have addressed this problem by dividing the ownership of the management organization among the partners and signing fixed-price contracts with partner firms for specific services. Ventures in which cost-sharing has been the rule, like the Anglo-French Concorde, have experienced dramatic cost escalation (in the case of the Concorde, costs rose from $450 million to $4 billion in sixteen years). The Concorde project, which survived in part because of the lack of an exit mechanism for the partners, also underlines the importance of specifying procedures for dissolution of a venture at its inception (see Henderson, 1977; Feldman, 1985; Mowery, 1987).

Are joint ventures between U.S. and foreign commercial aircraft firms eroding the competitiveness of the U.S. commercial aircraft industry? Despite some claims that these ventures result in the wholesale transfer of U.S. technology and eventually, jobs to foreign firms (see Reich, 1986), the evidence thus far does not support such a pessimistic assessment. Joint ventures are not likely to result in significant near-term foreign threats to the supremacy of established U.S. "prime contractor" firms in commercial aircraft. The costs and risks of independent entry into this industry are very high, and maintenance of the research infrastructure necessary for an internationally competitive industry requires a level of public and private investment that exceeds the resources or political tolerance of most foreign governments. Moreover, the flow of technology through joint ventures and multinational collaboration within this industry does not consist solely of technology "exports" by U.S. firms. In a number of the cases discussed in this chapter, foreign partner firms have made or are making significant technological contributions.

Any evaluation of these ventures also must consider the counter-factual case. Although offshore production of aircraft components and assemblies may reduce the U.S. content of each aircraft or engine sold, if such teaming increases total sales the number of U.S. jobs created or preserved through collaborative ventures may in fact exceed those associated with independent development and production. Preemption also plays an important role in the collaborative strategies of U.S. and foreign firms. If the financial and other contributions of the Japanese airframe consortium can be denied to Airbus Industrie through an alliance with Boeing, market access and project finance for Boeing are enhanced, and the U.S. firm's commercial capabilities strengthened in the near term, regardless of the amount of technology transfer taking place.

Recent international collaborative ventures nevertheless may be eroding the competitiveness of one group of U.S. aerospace firms—supplier firms. Many of the collaborative ventures examined in this chapter (Boeing-JCAC-Aeritalia; GE-SNECMA; the collaborations within the V2500 venture between Rolls Royce and JAEC, and among Pratt and Whitney, Fiat, and MTU) involve supplier and "prime contractor" firms, and therefore will enhance the production and competitive capabilities of foreign suppliers of parts, assemblies, and components. Indeed, in some cases, improvement in the capabilities of foreign component suppliers is a goal of U.S. prime contractors.

U.S. supplier firms appear to have been slow to respond to increased competitive pressures and have been reluctant to team on a risk-sharing basis with domestic prime contractors. These supplier firms also are major beneficiaries of liberalized trade in aircraft components and parts, exports of which have grown dramatically during the 1980s. Restrictions on international collaboration or the international trade in components that results from collaboration therefore will do little to assist, and may in fact harm, these firms. Instead, a more effective policy response to the competitive difficulties of this segment of the aircraft industry would enhance technological assistance for these firms, which have reaped little benefit from the Department of Defense and NASA aeronautics and manufacturing technology research programs.[36] Research aimed at strengthening the innovative and manufacturing capabilities of these firms could improve their competitiveness. International collaboration among supplier firms also is likely to grow in the near future, in order to gain market access and capital.[37] As in the automotive industry, increased international collaboration among first-tier firms is expanding collaborative ventures among suppliers.

Should U.S. antitrust policies be revised to restrict international collaboration in this industry? There is some evidence that antitrust policy enforcement, in distinguishing inappropriately between the U.S. and world markets for aircraft engines, may have affected the incentives of U.S. engine producers to collaborate with foreign firms in at least one instance. Antitrust policy, however, is relevant to very few collaborative programs. Antitrust restrictions affect only horizontal joint ventures between prime contractors, but a good deal of the international collaboration in commercial aircraft consists of risk-sharing partnerships between prime contractor and supplier firms. "Vertical" collaborations of this sort are not affected by current U.S. antitrust policies. Moreover, domestic collaboration does not provide the access to foreign markets that is crucial to commercial success in this industry and in most cases is not a viable alternative to international collaboration. U.S. antitrust policy does not appear to be a central factor in motivating the bulk of current international collaboration within the commercial aircraft industry, and revisions are unlikely to affect international collaboration.

In view of the complexity and two-way flow characteristic of much of the technology transfer operating within joint ventures in this industry, the imposition of additional controls or other federal regulations on such collaborations, or on technology transfer within these alliances, does not appear to be desirable. Not only are such controls rarely effective (Harris, 1986, discusses the complex history of English controls on the export of industrial technologies during the eighteenth century), but controls already exist, in the form of federal restrictions on the transfer of so-called dual use technologies (civilian technologies with potential military applications). These restrictions are applied to collaborations and to proposals for joint ventures between U.S. and foreign firms. Rather than expanding the coverage of these restrictions, the logic, speed, and consistency with which they are developed and applied require additional scrutiny and improvement (see the report of the Committee on Science, Engineering, and Public Policy's Panel on the Impact of National Security Controls on International Technology Transfer, 1987). Restrictions on export or data exchange for specific components of aircraft that fly throughout the world, for example, are limited in their effectiveness.

Trade policy plays a central role in motivating international collaboration within the commercial aircraft industry. Foreign government financial subsidies or restrictions on market access by U.S. firms affect the choice of partners for U.S. aircraft firms contemplating development projects. To the extent that foreign trade-distorting policies leave U.S. firms with no choice but to seek out a foreign partner for product development and manufacture, these policies must be resisted by the U.S. government, and multilateral codes of conduct (the GATT Procurement and Subsidy Codes, as well as the Agreement on Trade in Civil Aircraft) must be strengthened and enforced more vigorously. Nevertheless, the perceived importance of the aircraft industry for the industrial and technological development of foreign economies, as well as the belief by the U.S. and foreign governments that a strong domestic aircraft industry is an important national security asset, mean that government involvement and trade-distorting policies are likely to remain permanent features of the international commercial aircraft industry. As a result, international collaboration in this industry is likely to flourish for the foreseeable future.

NOTES

1. This chapter is based on the detailed discussion in Mowery (1987).
2. This section draws on the discussion in Mowery and Rosenberg (1982, 1985), as well as Mowery (1985).

3. In the design of the Boeing 727, Steiner (1982) noted that this process consumed two and one-half years and produced at least nine complete aircraft designs. More recently, the "design definition" phase of the development of the Boeing 767 lasted for nearly six years.

4. "Although the time between design and service release of civil and military aircraft increased over the years in the United States as it did in Europe, data for the late 1960s showed the United States well ahead of the United Kingdom and France. The average development time for civil aircraft was 52 months in the United Kingdom and 62 months in France, but it was 43 months in the United States." (Hochmuth, 1974a, p. 149)

5. The role of innovation in other industries is discussed in Mowery and Rosenberg (1982).

6. This policy structure bears a striking resemblance to Japanese industrial policy, which in many industries combined formal or informal protection of domestic markets with the development of strong interfirm competition and the eventual entry by these firms into international markets. This argument is developed further in Mowery and Rosenberg (1985).

7. See the National Research Council (1982) study, which argues that NASA's "Aeronautics Research and Technology Program" budget has declined in real terms during the past decade. The other components of the NASA aeronautics budget are "Construction of Facilities" and "Research and Program Management."

8. Airbus Industrie, however, appears to be reducing the U.S. content in its new aircraft designs:

    > To ensure that the European partners obtain a bigger share on the A320, the past reliance on U.S. manufacturers will be reduced. There are two other reasons for this trend: with the experience of the A300 and A310 behind it, Europe now feels more technically able to produce its own equipment. Second, the Europeans believe that they have lost aircraft sales due to the amount of U.S. equipment which the aircraft contained. They cite a potential contract for ten A300s with Libya which was blocked because Libya is on the U.S. embargo list. (Reed, 1984, p. 33)

    Current estimates of the U.S. content of the A320, for example, are as low as 20 percent, and federal officials have projected that no more than 13–17 percent of the A330 and A340 will be U.S. components. See *Aviation Week and Space Technology*, 1986, p. 36; 1987a, p. 18.

9. Coproduction programs are discussed in greater detail in Mowery (1987) and in Rich et al. (1981).

10. "This trend toward subcontracting for services and renting or borrowing talent also is part of the [Boeing Company's] desire to avoid the huge buildup of manpower that marked the late 1960s and the subsequent wholesale layoffs that rocked the entire state of Washington. . . . An interesting trend is revealed by a chart comparing Boeing sales in constant dollars with total manpower. From 1957 through the late 1960s the curves traveled closely together. Since then, a wide gap has opened, indicating the company is achieving more total sales with considerably fewer employees." (O'Lone, 1978, pp. 48–49)

11. "According to Boeing, Japan was considered for the 'risk-sharing subcontract' only after U.S. companies had been approached and showed no interest in the program. The U.S. companies were either unable or unwilling to risk the investment." (U.S. General Accounting Office, 1982, p. 16, note)

12. The terms of the Boeing contract with the JCAC were described as "severe" by officials at MITI and the participating firms, requiring considerable efficiency and productivity improvements. Moreover, "a Mitsubishi Heavy Industries executive said openly early in the program that the 767 is 'not an effective program—because the investment is too large and the profit is small.'" (Aviation Week and Space Technology 1978, p. 31)

13. The Japanese partners in the 767 project are making an extra payment of $143 million to Boeing as a royalty for the U.S. firm's production and design experience, as well as its global sales and product support network. See Aviation Week and Space Technology, 1977c, p. 201.

14. Aeritalia's participation in the 767 project has not enhanced Boeing's access to the European market, due to the superior political saliency and strength of Airbus Industrie, whose A310 competes directly with the 767.

15. A similar argument may be found in Moxon et al. (1985), pp. 53–54.

16. The JADC also insisted that Boeing provide at least 51 percent of the equity in the 7J7 project, so as to ensure the U.S. firm's participation as project manager.

17. Interestingly, Short Brothers and Saab-Scania currently are participating only in the design of the 7J7, with no explicit commitment to produce portions of the aircraft. According to senior Boeing management, "The associates [Saab-Scania and Short Brothers] must be able to produce the components they design in a cost-competitive manner, however, if they are to get the production business . . ." (Brown, 1986, p. 32).

18. According to Brown (1986, p. 32), Thomas Albrecht, executive vice president of Boeing Commercial Airplane Company, "ruled out equipment and subsystem suppliers as associate members of the [7J7] group, however, saying that Boeing wanted to retain the advantages of competition in the selection of component suppliers."

19. Among other problems, the original wing design was not well suited to the high-bypass CFM56 engines, the diameter of which was larger than the Mercure 100's engines.

20. According to one estimate, the development costs for the Mercure 200, estimated to be $250 million, would double or even triple if the wing was redesigned. See Ropelewski (1976, p. 12).

21. Commenting on the demise of the MDF 100 venture, one contemporary account noted the " . . . lack of a new fuel-efficient engine in the 23,400-lb. range to power the MDF 100. Economic difficulties have forced engine manufacturers to delay launching new engines, and Fokker had little expectation a new engine would have been certificated by late 1985 to meet an in-service schedule requirement of 1987 for the 150-seat aircraft." (Aviation Week and Space Technology, 1982a, p. 34). Frans Swarttouw,

managing director of Fokker, commented in retrospect; "It should have gotten better as the months went by, but it got worse. The market crumbled, and we ended up by just talking to Delta. United made it clear that they were not in a position to order. The engine was not available. If the market had been there, all these problems could have been solved; but it was not there, and we soon wondered what the heck we were doing." (Reed, 1983, pp. 20–25)

22. The launch by Fokker of the F100 jet aircraft in 1983 drew on some of the design advances developed in the MDF100 joint venture, as well as unexpended government development funds. See *Aviation Week and Space Technology*, 1982b, p. 172.

23. The current agreements between McDonnell Douglas and foreign firms for the development of derivatives of the MD-80 or the MD-11, agreements that include technical cooperation with Saab-Scania and Aeritalia, appear to give the dominant technological and managerial role to McDonnell Douglas, in contrast to these earlier ventures.

24. Balanced against the reluctance of McDonnell Douglas to undertake such a commitment, however, is the evident unwillingness of Fokker to assume a junior role in the MDF100 joint venture. Similar resistance to a subordinate role probably would have been voiced by the French partners in the Mercure 200 project, judging from the statements of French aerospace industry managers and policymakers. Indeed, Hayward (1986) emphasizes such resistance to the modest McDonnell Douglas role in the Mercure 200 project as a factor that contributed to the demise of the venture.

25. One account of the subsequent negotiations between the U.S. government and Pratt and Whitney over technology transfer within the JT10D venture with Rolls Royce cited David Pickerell, a Pratt and Whitney executive: "If the restriction [on technology transfer] is not lifted and the European partners are forced to operate under the same conditions as Snecma on the CFM56—SNECMA is not permitted access to GE core engine technology on the program—'you can be certain the JT10D will not be as good an engine as it could be,' Pickerell said." (*Aviation Week and Space Technology*, 1976, p. 109.

26. Estimates of French government support for SNECMA's CFM56 program may be found in the National Academy of Engineering *Background Paper* for the NAE Roundtable Discussion on the U.S. Civil Aviation Manufacturing Industry, as well as the study by the Aerospace Industries Association (1976). These estimates run to as much as $500 million.

27. Demand for commuter aircraft was expected to grow rapidly in the late 1970s in both the United States, due to the deregulation of domestic air transport, and the industrializing nations, as a result of economic growth and limited substitutes for aircraft transportation.

28. U.S. marketing and product support activities, originally the sole responsibility of Fairchild, were reorganized in 1984 and placed under the control of Saab Fairchild International.

29. The allocation of work on the V2500 engine differs slightly from the equity shares. As of late 1986, Pratt and Whitney and Rolls Royce were

each responsible for production of 30 percent of the value of the engine, while Japan Aero Engines had 23 percent, MTU 11 percent, and Fiat 6 percent. Some revision of these work shares may occur as a result of the expanded role in the project assumed by Pratt and Whitney in 1987.

30. CFM International's participation in this segment of the market (the CFM56) reduced General Electric's interest in teaming with the Rolls Royce/JAEC group in the development of a competing engine.

31. According to one account, "IAE already is facing potential conflicts of interest among its members, Keen [J. M. S. Keen, executive vice president of International Aero Engines] said. There could be a 'clear conflict of interest for a manufacturer,' he said, if an airline were trying to decide between a Boeing 757 equipped with Rolls-Royce RB. 211–535 engines and a 150-passenger aircraft equipped with the IAE V2500, for example. 'That is one reason we believe we have to have our own marketing organization,' Keen said." (Feazel, 1984, p. 108) Despite these efforts to insulate the V2500 from conflicts of interest, recent accounts suggest that middle-level executives at both Pratt and Whitney and Rolls Royce continue to view IAE as a competitor with existing and prospective products (Kandebo, 1987).

32. "'Technology transfer questions were raised by both Pratt and Whitney and Rolls-Royce early in the consortium negotiations,' according to Samuel L. Higginbottom, chairman and president of Rolls-Royce. Both companies feel there will be a minimum of exchange of proprietary data in the final assembly process. 'We will have to know the interfaces, and there obviously will be some exchange of data involved in that,' Higginbottom said. 'But we will not have to get into the details of technology. . . .' It took a lot of work to match the technology split to the work-sharing formula, one official said. But now that it is completed, final assembly essentially will involve bolting together the separate modules." (Fink, 1983, p. 29)

33. "Some consortium partners remain dissatisfied with that, however, because they develop expertise in only one area of engine design. Keen said the Japanese, for example, may be unwilling to participate in future consortiums because they want to develop the ability to design and produce entire engines." (Feazel, 1984, p. 108)

34. Killing (1983, p. 28) also found that collaborations of equals were more difficult to manage in a study of joint ventures in a number of different industries: "shared management joint ventures have a dramatically higher failure rate than dominant parent ventures. I have concluded that this is because shared management ventures are more difficult to manage."

35. Referring to the marketing efforts of Airbus Industrie for the A300, the managing director of Airbus Industrie noted that "'It's misleading to believe that an aircraft is just right for a certain market slot,' Airbus Industrie Chairman Bernard Lathiere conceded recently. 'Our principal competitor for the Indian Airways order was the Boeing 737, and in South Africa it was the 747.'" (*Aviation Week and Space Technology*, 1977b, p. 241).

36. See the report of the National Research Council's Committee on the Machine Tool Industry (1983a) for a critical discussion of technology transfer to small machine tool firms from the Defense Department programs.

37. Donne (1987) discusses a recent joint venture between the Bendix aircraft brake division of Allied-Signal Aerospace of the United States and Dunlop Aerospace of Great Britain that was formed to supply wheels and carbon brakes to the Airbus A330 and A340 aircraft now being developed.

REFERENCES

Aerospace Industries Association, Foreign Competition Project Group, Commercial Transport Aircraft Committee. 1976. *The Challenge of Foreign Competition.* Washington, D.C.: Aerospace Research Center.

Aviation Week and Space Technology. 1976. "Rolls Confident of Major JT10D Task." September 6, p. 109.

_____. 1977a. "Rolls-Royce Leaves JT10D Turbofan Development Program." May 16, p. 17.

_____. 1977b. "Eastern Lease, New Sales Bolster Airbus Prospects." June 6, pp. 234–241.

_____. 1978. "New Efforts Task Japanese Firms." October 2, pp. 31–33.

_____. 1982a. "McDonnell Douglas/Fokker Cancel 150-Seat Aircraft." February 15, p. 34.

_____. 1982b. "Dutch, Swedes Use Innovative Financing." September 6, pp. 171–173.

_____. 1985. "Fairchild Withdrawing From 340 Aircraft Project." October 21, p. 23.

_____. 1986. "U.S.-European Trade Talks Focus on Subsidy Issues." March 31, p. 36.

_____. 1987a. "U.S., Europeans Clash Over Airbus Subsidies." February 9, pp. 18–20.

_____. 1987b. "Pratt and Whitney Expands Role in V2500 Compressor Work." March 16, pp. 32–33.

_____. 1987c. "IAE Delays V2500 Certification to Develop New Components." May 25, p. 31.

_____. 1987d. "Airline Observer." November 23, p. 43.

_____. 1987e. "News Digest." December 14, p. 30.

Brown, D.A. 1986. "Short Brothers, Saab-Scania Join Boeing 7J7 Program." *Aviation Week and Space Technology*, March 31, 1986, pp. 32–33.

Donne, M. 1987. "Dunlop Joins U.S. Group in Airbus Contract Bid." *Financial Times*, September 17, p. 6.

Feazel, M. 1984. "Large Engine Design Costs Dictate Consortium Efforts." *Aviation Week and Space Technology.* June 18, pp. 108–109.

Fink, D. E. 1983. "Pratt, Rolls Launch New Turbofan." *Aviation Week and Space Technology.* November 7, pp. 28–29.

Harris, J. 1986. "Spies Who Sparked the Industrial Revolution." *New Scientist*, May 22, 1986, pp. 42-47.

Hayward, K. 1986. *International Collaboration in Civil Aerospace.* London: Frances Pinter.

Henderson, D. 1977. "Two British Errors: Their Probable Size and Some Possible Lessons." *Oxford Economic Papers*, 29: 159-205.

Hochmuth, M. S. 1974a. "Aerospace." In R. S. Vernon, ed., *Big Business and the State.* Cambridge, Mass.: Harvard University Press.

———. 1974b. *Organizing the Transnational: The Experience with Transnational Enterprise in Advanced Technology.* Cambridge, Mass.: Harvard University Press.

Jordan, W. A. 1970. *Airline Regulation in America.* Baltimore: Johns Hopkins University Press.

Kandebo, S. W. 1987. "International Aero Engines Seeks Solutions to V2500 Development Problems." *Aviation Week and Space Technology*, April 13, pp. 88-89.

———. 1987. "Engine Makers Examine IAE to Avoid Pitfalls in Collaborative Efforts." *Aviation Week and Space Technology*, June 15, pp. 245-246.

Killing, J. P. 1983. *Strategies for Joint Venture Success.* New York: Praeger.

Mowery, D. C. 1987. *Alliance Politics and Economics: Multinational Joint Ventures in Commercial Aircraft.* Cambridge: Ballinger.

———. 1985. "Federal Funding of R&D in Transportation: The Case of Aviation." Presented at the National Academy of Sciences Symposium on the Impact of Federal R&D Funding, Washington, D.C., November 21-22.

Mowery, D. C., and N. Rosenberg. 1982. "The Commercial Aircraft Industry." In R. R. Nelson (ed.), *Government and Technical Progress: A Cross-Industry Analysis.* New York: Pergamon Press.

———. 1985. "Competition and Cooperation: The U.S. and Japanese Commercial Aircraft Industries." *California Management Review*, 27: 70-92.

Moxon, R. W., T. W. Roehl, J. R. Truitt, and J. M. Geringer. 1985. *Emerging Sources of Foreign Competition in the Commercial Aircraft Manufacturing Industry.* Washington, D.C.: U.S. Department of Transportation.

National Research Council, Committee on NASA Scientific and Technological Program Reviews. 1982. *Aeronautics Research and Technology: A Review of Proposed Reductions in the FY1983 NASA Program.* Washington, D.C.: National Academy Press.

———. 1983a. Manufacturing Studies Board, Committee on the Machine Tool Industry. *The Machine Tool Industry and the Defense Industrial Base.* Washington, D.C.: National Academy Press.

———. 1985. U.S. Civil Aviation Manufacturing Industry Panel, *The Competitive Status of the U.S. Civil Aircraft Manufacturing Industry.* Washington, D.C.: National Academy Press.

O'Lone, R. G. 1978. "Boeing Facing New Set of Challenges." *Aviation Week and Space Technology*, November 12, pp. 43-55.

Reed, A. 1983. "Fokker Moving Ahead with New P&W-Powered F27." *Air Transport World*, August, pp. 19-25.

_____. 1984. "Airbus Talks About A320, Future Projects." *Air Transport World*, May 1984, pp. 33-37.

Ropelewski, R. 1976. "Mercure 200 Pact Sparks Uproar." *Aviation Week and Space Technology*, August 23, pp. 12-13.

Steiner, J. E. 1982. "How Decisions Are Made." AIAA Wright Brothers Lectureship in Aeronautics, Seattle, Wash.

U.S. Department of Commerce, International Trade Administration. 1987. *U.S. Industrial Outlook: 1987*. Washington, D.C.: U.S. Government Printing Office.

U.S. General Accounting Office. 1982. *U.S. Military Co-production Agreements Assist Japan in Developing Its Civil Aircraft Industry*. Washington, D.C.: U.S. Government Printing Office.

4 INTERNATIONAL JOINT VENTURES IN THE INTEGRATED CIRCUIT INDUSTRY

W. Edward Steinmueller

International joint ventures in the integrated circuit (IC) industry are part of a complex pattern of intercompany agreements aimed at technology transfer, market access, and cost sharing.[1] In the IC industry, joint ventures have historically played a subsidiary role to interfirm licensing agreements for technology access and to direct investment for market access. And effective methods for sharing R&D costs among U.S. IC producers have only recently been developed through research consortiums such as Microelectronics and Computer Technology Corporation (MCC) and the Semiconductor Research Corporation (SRC) rather than joint ventures (Gerstenfeld and Berger, 1984). The number and relative importance of domestic and international joint ventures in the IC industry may increase as a result of four relatively recent developments:

1. Attainment of technological parity between U.S. and Japanese IC producers
2. Emergence of severe financial constraints in developing new IC process technologies and product innovations
3. Evolution of new technical relationships between IC and electronic system design

Research for this chapter was supported by the American Enterprise Institute's Competing in a Changing World Economy project. Additional support was provided by the High Technology Impact Program of Stanford University's Center for Economic Policy Research and the National Science Foundation (IST 85-07536). I am grateful to David C. Mowery for several close readings of drafts and valuable comments; remaining errors are my responsibility.

111

4. Growth of protectionist sentiment and regulation in the United
   States

The first three of these four developments are examined in a discussion of recent changes in the technology and economics of IC
production, the first section of this chapter.[2] Consideration of the
recent developments in U.S. trade policy is deferred until the discussion of emerging issues and prospects for international joint ventures.
While many industrialized nations developed IC industries following
the commercialization of the integrated circuit in the early 1960s,
for nearly twenty years the U.S. IC industry technologically dominated these entrants. Since the mid-1970s, increases in the technological sophistication of IC devices have been accompanied by a
technological "catch-up" of these entrants and a growing intensity
in competition for international markets. The U.S. IC industry no
longer is the sole source of product and process innovations in integrated circuits. The growing intensity of international competition
has severely strained the financial capabilities of U.S. firms at a time
when the costs of developing new process technologies and product
designs are soaring. Technological changes have also had an impact
on the relation between IC producers and their customers, electronic
system designers. Improvements in product design technologies have
blurred the distinctions between component and system design,
transforming the economic relationships between component and
system producers.
   The second section of this chapter provides an overview of past
international joint venture and other interfirm agreements. Specific
agreements have been made for technology exchange, product licensing, and distributorship arrangements as well as more broadly based
agreements for joint product development aimed at specific technologies and markets. These agreements have been structured in several
different ways. The most common arrangement has been explicit
arms-length contracts. Other agreements include equity purchase,
joint ventures, and looser partnering in joint research activities including specific intent to share advances in knowledge. The number
of all such agreements is on the rise and the breadth of recent agreements exceeds that of earlier agreements. Joint ventures between
firms, narrowly defined as joint equity participation in a third entity,
have rarely been the mechanism for these agreements. Elements of
joint venturing including cost and profit sharing, establishment of
separate facilities, and transfer of personnel have, however, become
more common in recent agreements.
   The assessment of motives for future joint venture activities later
in this chapter requires a degree of speculation. Competitive struggle
between U.S. and Japanese IC producers has been rancorous, yet a

recent joint venture between Motorola and Toshiba is perhaps the broadest agreement ever made between a U.S. and Japanese IC firm. The role of U.S. system producers in financing the R&D costs for new generations of process equipment is uncertain, as is the future nature of technical development agreements between U.S. IC and system producers. In either area significant changes in domestic U.S. patterns of exchange between IC and system producers would have major impacts on international agreements. These exchanges, including planned research consortiums such as Sematech, are examined for insights into changing motives for interfirm agreements.

International IC firms are, however, not alone in their struggle for competitive dominance. National governments from Tokyo to Paris are intent on preserving and expanding their domestic IC industries. The U.S. government is not an exception. At the behest of the industry, the U.S. government has sought to regulate international trade in IC products with actions including setting prices for the import of memory products produced in Japan and seeking Japanese government assurances of future imports of U.S. IC products. Increasing international competition, the rising cost of technical progress, shifts in the relationships between IC and system producers, and the regulation of international competition by the U.S. government provide the setting for examining changes in the motives for international agreements among firms including joint ventures.

Actions of the U.S. government including the discouragement of Fujitsu's attempted purchase of Fairchild Semiconductor are certain to reflect future changes in the political environment. An expansion in protectionist sentiment and action will influence the course of international agreements. Nationalistic policies of European governments toward their IC industries are also subject to reforms that would improve the feasibility and desirability of international agreements. The Japanese government may also launch new initiatives in response to U.S. and European policies. While these factors pose major uncertainties over the future course of international agreements in the IC industry, the four factors mentioned in this introduction and examined in this chapter are the most likely candidates for influencing the course of such agreements.

TECHNOLOGICAL, STRUCTURAL, AND HISTORICAL FOUNDATIONS OF INTERFIRM AGREEMENTS IN THE IC INDUSTRY

Integrated circuits are miniaturized transistor circuits that are used as components in electronic systems. Technical improvement in IC manufacturing technology has been very rapid. The first ICs produced in the early 1960s contained only about two dozen transistors and consequently only performed simple electronic functions. As a result, complex electronic systems constructed from early ICs required hundreds or even thousands of components. During the late 1960s, process improvements in IC manufacturing processes made it possible to increase dramatically the number of transistors that could be placed on each IC. These improvements, collectively referred to as large-scale integration (LSI), reduced the number of components needed in complex electronic systems such as computers.

LSI circuits also created new system design opportunities for electronic systems including computers, telecommunication equipment, and scientific instruments. By the early 1970s, ICs with 4,000 transistors were being manufactured. With this number of transistors, electronic calculators and semiconductor memory subsystems for computers were commercially attractive and mass markets for ICs emerged.[3] Increases in the number of transistors on each IC also led to a major IC product innovation, the microprocessor, that has been the source of many innovative electronic systems products including the personal computer.

Rapid increases in the number of transistors in each IC and the reduction of the number of components in IC-based systems are responsible for continuing major performance improvements and cost reductions in electronic system products. IC devices with over one million transistors, referred to as very large scale integration (VLSI), are now commercially feasible. VLSI circuits make it possible to create desktop systems for thousands of dollars that rival the information processing capabilities of major computer systems that a decade ago cost millions of dollars.

Major economic changes in the IC industry have accompanied the process improvements responsible for the nearly millionfold increase in transistor count in the shift from early ICs to VLSI. The U.S. IC industry technologically dominated other nations' semiconductor industries from the commercialization of the IC to the about 1980. During the 1970s, Japanese firms launched a program of development aimed at achieving technological parity with or superiority to U.S. IC producers. (For a more detailed accounting of Japanese efforts, see Okimoto, Sugano, and Weinstein (1984) and Steinmueller (forthcoming).) The eventual success of this effort has most recently been chronicled by the Defense Science Board of the United States. The Defense Science Board Task Force on Defense Semiconductor Dependency (1987, p. 58) presents a collection of twenty-five technologies related to IC production and finds the U.S. industry only retains a lead in five technologies. The technologies chosen are broadly defined although the rankings themselves are subjective. Nevertheless, it is reasonable to conclude that, at minimum, Japanese IC producers have succeeded in attaining their aim of parity across a broad range of IC technologies.

The emergence of technological parity and direct competition between Japanese IC producers and U.S. merchant IC companies is among the most important developments in the international IC industry's history. In addition to being a major example of technological convergence between a follower and leader, Japanese competition with U.S. merchant IC firms is a major force for structural change in the U.S. electronics industry (Steinmueller, forthcoming). And it is uncertain what long term effects this competition will have. The U.S. IC industry cannot be regarded as a technologically laggard or uncompetitive industry. Its performance compares favorably with other sectors of the U.S. economy. Nevertheless, it is apparent that this industry has suffered dramatic reversals in financial strength and morale during the 1980s as a consequence of the growth of Japanese competition.

The vulnerability of U.S. IC companies to competition from a technologically strong international rival is directly traceable to the conditions under which the domestic U.S. IC industry developed. From the outset, U.S. IC producers have either been specialized IC producers producing for the system companies or systems companies producing for their own use. The world's largest IC producer is IBM, which until recently produced solely for internal use. The existence of specialized or "merchant" IC producers has been effective in stimulating technological competition and encouraging the entry of both new electronic system producers and innovative IC manufacturers. It has been a model of the virtues of competition; profits in the industry are at or below the average rate of return for manufacturing as a whole and no firm has succeeded in attaining a dominant market position. But as investment costs for new facilities and R&D rapidly increase, return on investments in this industry have declined. Economic adjustment to these changes would normally drive the price of ICs upward or at least slow their decline, but sustained capacity expansion by Japanese IC producers have led to precipitous declines in prices for new generations of mass marketed products such as memory ICs. The motives for Japanese firms' behavior and the ability to sustain this competitive battle are less important for present purposes than the effect of this battle. What was once an effective industrial organization for both U.S. IC and system producers is no longer as advantageous for IC producers.

A crisis in the U.S. merchant IC industry has grown out of the increasing costs of pursuing the technological trajectories these companies pioneered. In the competitive struggle to improve product performance and complexity, IC companies have sought reductions in the size of semiconductor components and exhausted the inexpensive methods for making further technological progress. As a consequence, semiconductor processing facilities have become much more sophisticated and costly. During the late 1970s, it was possible to construct a state-of-the-art fabrication facility for approximately $4 million (Dataquest, 1980, p. 3.4-3). By 1986 facility costs for state of the art plants were $50–100 million depending upon extent of automation and "throughput" capacity (McClean, 1986, p. 52). Rapid increases in facility costs have led to dramatic increases in capital expenditures among the world's IC producers. Whereas in 1979 worldwide capital expenditures were $1.8 billion on $11.2 billion of sales (16 percent), in 1985, a recession year for the industry, expenditures had increased to $5.1 billion on $22.9 billion of sales (22 percent) (McClean, 1986, p. 41).

Financing the investment necessary for achieving state of the art production has placed a major strain on IC producers worldwide. In the United States, financing has been made more difficult by the relatively small size of the U.S. companies producing ICs for sale. The sales volume of merchant IC producers is lower and more variable than electronics industry system producers that produce ICs for their own use. This dependence on IC component sales of merchant IC producers means that internal resources for capital investment by merchant IC firms are quite limited. Despite the value of ICs to system producers, the merchant IC industry has earned very modest average returns on equity, making it difficult to attract outside financing for new investment (McClean, 1986, p. 70). The modest levels of profitability of U.S. IC producers have also made them less attractive as acquisition targets for system producers.

Increases in capital investment allow IC producers to manufacture ICs with greater numbers of transistors. But the costs and risks of designing these more complex IC products are growing at least as rapidly as manufacturing facility costs. Both capital investment and product design expenditures are fixed costs that must be spread over large quantities of output. The product design challenge facing IC producers can be thought of either in terms of producing very large numbers of products, each of which has modest sales but high value, or a smaller number of "standard" products that can be mass produced and sold for more modest prices. Merchant IC producers have pursued both alternatives in their efforts to utilize productive capacity. This problem emerged in the 1970s (Moore, 1979; Rosenberg and Steinmueller, 1982). The problem of spreading fixed costs of productive capacity and product design highlights the importance of the relationship between IC producers and electronic system manufacturers.

Each system manufacturer would like IC products that meet their individual system design needs, perform their electronic functions at blinding speed, and sell for pennies. The problem that this set of demands presents is that system design needs have historically differed among electronic system producers. IC producers are able to define some mass produced products that are used in many system products. Competition for these mass markets is fierce, driving prices downward toward the marginal costs of production. As a result, revenues from these mass produced products only partly support the costs of product and process R&D and capacity investment.

For less standard products, where price competition is less severe, fragmentation of user demands forces higher product design costs and risks on IC producers. The large number of transistors in VLSI circuits impose high design costs, so the fixed costs of launching a fleet of different designs have increased with the onset of the VLSI era. Since the entire rationale for diversity in IC designs is to address system producers divergent design needs, competition among IC producers occurs through differentiation of product features, speed of operation, and reliability as well as price. Competition in these product characteristics has been almost as severe as price competition, and hence as destructive of profitability.

System producers' pursuit of specialized components that will create rents in the sale of system products has sustained growth of captive IC manufacturing capability among leading electronic system producers such as computer producers.[4] Specialized components allow system producers to foreclose direct imitation and may delay the entry of firms offering similar system products. They also permit system designers to integrate the design of components and systems. Despite rising costs of captive facilities, output in this sector has been increasing rapidly since 1977 and did not fall during the 1985 recession despite the nearly 30 percent contraction of the "merchant" market. In 1985 captive production value was estimated by ICE at 33 percent of total U.S. IC production. (McClean, 1986, p. 50).[5]

The rising costs of captive facilities suggest that there are growing potential gains from trade between electronic system producers and merchant IC producers. One barrier to moving more IC production capability upstream from system producers to merchant IC companies is the difficulty of integrating component and system design efforts between different firms. Another is the assurance that system companies will have proprietary access to circuit designs. Captive IC producers have historically been willing to pay a large premium on individual ICs in order to integrate the component and system design processes and maintain proprietary knowledge about circuit design.

This willingness to make rather than buy reduces the revenues available to IC producers for investment in manufacturing capability and product design. As a consequence, U.S. merchant IC firms face a continuing reliance on mass produced standard ICs, the area of greatest international competition.

Emergence of technologically sophisticated international rivals, growth of facility and product design investment costs, and the structure of producer-user relationships underlie the development of international agreements among firms in the IC industry. A prerequisite for joint ventures is the existence of firm-specific assets that can profitably be exchanged. Such assets clearly exist in the IC industry. In addition, interfirm agreements have been influenced by the experience of firms during the growth of the industry.

The history of intercompany agreements in the IC industry was strongly influenced by the origins of the semiconductor industry in the United States where an antitrust consent decree was signed by AT&T in 1956, limiting its ability to appropriate economic benefits from the invention of the transistor. Because AT&T agreed to license its patents at reasonable rates to all future entrants in the IC industry, AT&T's direct economic returns from this major innovation were severely limited. However, the consent decree did not forbid AT&T from requiring reciprocal licenses when it licensed transistor patents. As a consequence, AT&T negotiated licenses to manufacture (for its own use) the technological innovations of the licensee of basic AT&T transistor patents. Moreover, AT&T played an active role in disseminating the technical know-how to practically implement transistor technology. As a consequence, a number of entrants began at a similar level of technical knowledge.[6]

Since many U.S. semiconductor companies began with the same level of technical knowledge, many similar innovations were closely spaced, creating the possibility of protracted patent litigations. Because many of the innovators were new entrants, the market for ICs was initially small. The eventual commercial importance of individual innovations was highly uncertain, contributing to the signing of cross-licenses between most of the early semiconductor industry participants. This pattern was reinforced by the lengthy and equivocal results of patent dispute over the IC concept and its implementation

(Braun and MacDonald, 1978). The rough technological parity of companies also meant that firm-specific assets were similar, reducing the motive for joint ventures among IC producers. It is surprising, however, that system companies did not seek joint ventures early in the development of the industry.[7]

A second carryover from the transistor era influencing the IC industry was the institution of "second sourcing." Mandating the existence of a second source for transistor types was a means for the military to assure product delivery, reliability, and that the price would have a competitive character. Military demand played an important role in the origins of both the transistor and IC industry and hence second sourcing was a familiar institution in the early history of these industries.

While military semiconductor requirements are very different than civilian, second sources proved desirable in commercial markets as well. Second sources are desirable to commercial purchasers because purchasers are reassured that the product design is commercially viable when more than one company has committed to its production. In addition, competition among sources is likely to reduce the price for the product and the product design is likely to be available for a longer time.[8] Second sourcing practices may, however, make it more difficult for system companies to develop unique relationships with their suppliers.

The commitment of more than one company to the production of a transistor or IC design was significant in the transistor era because of the very large number of product types that came into existence. According to Jerry Eimbinder, 6,000 different transistor types were placed on the market between 1956 and 1962, but by 1963, 1,500 of these types had been discontinued (Eimbinder, 1963). System producers who used one or more of these 1,500 discontinued types faced significant maintenance problems for their products. For this reason, the commercial viability of transistor designs became established as a criterion in the choices of system producers.

Each of the reasons supporting second sourcing favors looser arrangements than a joint venture between companies for the production of the product. Creating a joint venture to manufacture a product is less likely to signal that the product is technologically viable than separate production by two firms. If a joint venture is a substitute for two firm production, users will expect less price competition. When the joint venture withdraws the product or is dissolved, purchasers may have no recourse to other product suppliers for replacement parts or continuing manufacture of system product designs employing the withdrawn IC. For these reasons, in choosing between cross-licensing and joint venture, the IC producer is likely to favor cross-licensing, other things being equal.

Intercompany agreements for technical exchange are one method to assure that the second source firm can reliably reproduce device design and operating characteristics. Technology exchange agreements of this sort are clear alternatives to joint ventures and a direct means to create second sources for IC product designs. For example, such technology exchange agreements have included the lithography "masters" or computer tapes to produce such masters, minimizing the extent of variation of second source products. The use of common production equipment in the IC industry including automated "mask makers" permit the direct exchange of product design information among firms. In contrast to other industries such as automobile or jet aircraft manufacture, specific product designs can be closely replicated by many firms due to the use of common manufacturing technology in IC fabrication. Licensing of a product design permits the licensee to directly duplicate the physical design of a component and manufacturing that physical design is more straightforward in the IC industry than in other manufacturing industries due to common fabrication technology.

Technology exchange agreements have also been used for the transfer of process technology. These agreements also preserve firm-specific assets related to product design. Process exchanges have similar objectives to second source product design technology exchanges and are often complementary to such arrangements. The collection of process technologies employed by firms has changed over time and incremental improvement of process technologies is uneven across firms. Hence, some firms become relatively advanced in one process while their know-how in other processes lags behind that of rivals. Because the pattern of technical advance across these processes is uneven, periodic exchanges of process knowledge permit leading firms to economize on the R&D necessary to stay current across a broad front of technologies. One of the most active areas of exchange in recent years has been CMOS technology. Japanese firms development of CMOS was driven by their needs for low-power ICs for consumer goods. As circuits with smaller "feature size" are sought, the low-power consumption of CMOS circuits has impelled U.S. firms to acquire and further develop CMOS technology.[9] Such process agreements are often a prelude or complement to product license exchanges or joint ventures, as was the Sharp-RCA joint venture discussed later in the chapter.

The feasibility of technology exchange agreements for transferring product designs or process knowledge depends upon the capabilities of the partners. In cases where one firm has a major technological lag, feasibility is reduced and other arrangements may prove desirable. In such cases joint ventures may be favored where the technologically "junior" partner offers other assets such as well-established distribution channels or a product set that is complementary to the technology to be employed in the joint venture.

In each of these cases of technology exchange, the very rapid rate of technical progress in the IC industry plays an important role. Firm-specific assets depreciate very rapidly as a consequence of this rapid technical change. Licensing today's know-how may often be desirable since it leads to short-term returns on assets that will quickly become worthless. Moreover, frequent exchanges of technology among leading firms insulates them from uncertainties about future developments of technology.

Since technology exchange agreements have proven to be a relatively efficient method of interfirm agreement in the IC industry, joint ventures between IC producers aimed solely at technology exchange have historically been uncommon. Joint ventures aimed solely at technology exchange may arise from the inability of firms to evaluate, prior to extensive experience, the value of a particular technology. Until recently, marked divergence in technological capabilities have been rare among major U.S. IC producers. The success of Japanese and European firms in technological catch-up efforts have increased the stocks of technological knowledge and may create uncertainties about specific process technologies or product designs. In addition, further technological improvements may require pioneering major and expensive new process innovations. These developments may reduce the historical tendency toward instability in technology exchange joint ventures. In the past, once specific aims of such joint ventures were accomplished the venture would be disassembled. Historical joint ventures have rarely survived more than one technological generation (three to five years).

Arrival of non-U.S. IC producers at the IC technological frontier has intensified international competition. But it has also altered the environment for interfirm agreements. Technological agreements among U.S. firms that grew to maturity in the 1970s have been facilitated by common business practices, parallel relationships with equipment suppliers, and a common view of markets for products. These broad similarities are less applicable in agreements spanning national boundaries. The evolution of IC producers in both Europe and Japan reflect different relationships to system customers and priorities in technological development. The more recent efforts of European firms to overtake U.S. and Japanese firms in mass produced devices as well as continuing strength in specialized markets have also created unique technological assets. In Japan investment in capital intensive facilities to attain a dominant position in mass produced ICs as well as the significance of ICs for technologically advanced consumer products have created a knowledge base that differs from that of U.S. firms. These developments are partially reflected in the general studies of interfirm agreements examined in the next section.

INTERNATIONAL JOINT VENTURES IN THE IC INDUSTRY

International joint ventures in the IC industry are one form among many of intercompany agreements spanning the history of the semiconductor industry. Other intercompany agreements include technology or "know-how" exchange agreements and more limited product cross-license agreements. Two recent studies, one by Carmela Haklisch (1986) and the other by the Organization for Economic Cooperation and Development (1985), have examined a large number of technical agreements in the semiconductor industry, focusing on the international dimensions of these agreements. Neither of these studies provides a detailed explanation for the motives for joint venture agreements or descriptions of their management and organization. The Haklisch study provides limited information on the functions of joint ventures; its sections 3 and 4 examine the motives, functions, and organization of some specific joint ventures between U.S. and foreign firms. Nevertheless, considerable work remains to be done in this area.

The OECD study (1985, p. 50) provides an overview of 69 agreements formed between June 1979 and June 1983 and classified 23 of these agreements as joint ventures. Of these 69 agreements, 30 were made between two U.S. firms. While compiled from public sources, the agreements enumerated in this summary were not identified. The appendix to this study, by contrast to the text, enumerates 57 international joint ventures and an additional 26 domestic joint ventures among U.S. firms. Of the 57 international joint ventures identified in the appendix, 17 are joint ventures. Reporting of these agreements was also compiled from the business press. Hence, between one-quarter and one-third of *reported* interfirm agreements in the period 1979–1983 may be joint ventures. It is likely that the business press underreports interfirm agreements not involving joint ventures. Since joint ventures normally require equity participation, public corporations are obliged to provide some information about them. Disclosure of other interfirm agreements is unlikely to be as complete. For example, the fact of a technology agreement may be strategically important to third parties who are competitors providing an incentive for the parties to make an agreement to prevent its disclosure.[10]

The Haklisch study (1986) reports on 121 interfirm agreements, all of which are between partners of different nationalities. Of these agreements, about 20 percent involved joint venture agreements of some sort. While survey research was conducted in the course of Haklisch's research, the reported results are strictly from public sources (p. 25). The lower incidence of joint ventures in this sample is partly accounted for by the addition of 1984 to the years covered. In 1984, 42 agreements were reported, or more than one-third of the sample, while only seven joint ventures were listed. Whether the greater number of technology exchange agreements in 1984 reflects an unusually high number for that year or improving coverage of such developments by the press remains uncertain.

It is significant that agreements among IC producers have been much more common in the IC industry than agreements between IC and system producers. In addition, agreements among IC producers appear to be favored regardless of the type of arrangement, whether product licensing, joint venture, or joint development accord. The reasons for this pattern are not at all apparent but appear to be related to the structure of the U.S. IC industry. Many system producers have developed their own IC production facilities and look to the merchant industry to produce inexpensive standard products. Merchant IC producers have developed circuits that new entrants as well as existing companies can utilize. The innovativeness of IC producers is therefore a mixed blessing to system producers. On the one hand, these new companies have pioneered new design opportunities and created inexpensive mass produced designs. On the other hand, these same innovations have provoked entry and intensified competition in system markets.

Drawing meaningful quantitative conclusions from the OECD and Haklisch studies is difficult. However, the following conclusions appear warranted:

1. A majority of international interfirm agreements in the IC component industry are for licensing, cross-licensing, or technical exchange.

2. Of the minority of agreements that are joint ventures, alliances are between U.S. and European firms are significantly more common than between U.S. and Japanese firms. But agreements between European and Japanese firms are rare.

3. Reported interfirm agreements are increasing rapidly, but joint ventures are being reported at a fairly constant rate.

4. U.S. firms are the most common partners in agreements of all types. In examining domestic joint ventures, U.S. companies are quite active in nonjoint venture activities. By comparison, very few agreements and no joint ventures were identified where both partners were Japanese firms.[11]

While these conclusions do indicate the relative incidence and probable partners in joint ventures, a more detailed examination of specific joint ventures is necessary to understand motives and determinants of joint venture activity.

U.S.-EUROPEAN JOINT IC VENTURES

Intercompany agreements between U.S. and European producers also have favored technology exchange agreements over joint ventures. Unlike Japan, European nations did not bar U.S. direct investment during the early development of the semiconductor industry. As a consequence, U.S. firms have been active in the European market since the transistor era. As Franco Malerba observes in his history of the European semiconductor industry, the initial impact of U.S. direct investment was complementary to the growth of the European industry during the transistor era (Malerba, 1985, Ch. 4). Subsequently, the existence of IC production facilities in Europe owned and operated by U.S. IC firms has allowed close ties with European system producers. Local manufacturing facilities are significant for the credibility of promised delivery schedules and for assuring technical support in using IC components. Malerba observes (pp. 45–46) that European IC production has been dominated by the vertically integrated European electronic system producers including the Netherlands' Philips, Germany's Siemens, France's Thomson-CSF, and Great Britain's GEC. The role of U.S. companies in European markets is therefore somewhat similar to their role in U.S. markets, as complements to system companies' own capabilities.[12]

In 1960 Fairchild decided to enter the European market by purchasing a one-third interest in the Italian firm SGS (Malerba, 1985, p. 109). This purchase had many of the characteristics of a joint venture including technology transfer of Fairchild's planar process for silicon transistor production. SGS-Fairchild increased its share of the European market compared with that achieved by SGS alone. However, European markets focus on consumer electronics, leading to divergence in the outputs and research directions of the two companies. Malerba summarizes the consequences:

> the management of SGS-Fairchild realized that the European semiconductor market was consumer-orientated and that there was a growing demand for custom and specialty devices. These were neither the markets nor the types of products that their American partner was addressing; Fairchild's R&D was done in the United States and was aimed at the development of standard devices for the computer and industrial markets. The divergence of targets (custom-specialty devices and consumer market for SGS, standard devices and computer market for Fairchild) led the Italian SGS-Fairchild management to create a separate R&D group in Europe during the mid-1960s. This new group was assigned to do basic and applied research on digital and analog devices. This independent R&D effort gradually separated SGS-Fairchild from Fairchild's strategies, both in terms of final markets and in terms of the types of products that were being developed.
>
> In 1968 Fairchild divested itself from SGS for two reasons. First, Fairchild was experiencing both technological and financial difficulties in the United States. Second, it was unable to compel SGS-Fairchild to produce specific types of devices (digital integrated circuits) for specific final markets (the computer market). (p. 118)

Joint ventures were not attempted again until mid-1970s when European system producers became concerned with the technological gaps between their capabilities and those of U.S. merchant producers and the rapidly emerging Japanese IC producers.

The boldest move addressing this problem was a 1975–1979 acquisition drive by European companies. In 1975 Philips purchased Signetics that was at the time the United States' ninth largest merchant IC producer. (Malerba, 1985, p. 164).[13] In 1977 Siemens purchased 17 percent of AMD, a company that also ranked among the top ten U.S. merchant IC producers (p. 166). And in 1979 Schlumberger purchased Fairchild, which was then the fifth largest U.S. merchant IC producer. These three major acquisitions by European companies reduced the stock of available joint venture partners and provided some remedy for gaps between U.S. and European technological capabilities.

Joint ventures were also a means of addressing technology gaps between European system companies and U.S. IC producers. In 1978 a joint venture between Matra (51 percent), a French company that has been supported by the French government, and Harris Instruments (49 percent) was capitalized at $40 million. In 1981 Matra-Harris formed a joint venture with Intel called Cimatel. This particular joint venture had to be explicitly approved by the French government. It began a pattern of government involvement that has marked subsequent U.S.-European joint ventures and reflects a more general growth in European government involvement in the IC industry.

A similar joint venture, also in 1978, between National and Saint-Gobain was established with French government support (Malerba, 1985, p. 169). In 1983 this joint venture, called Eurotechnique, was purchased by Thomson-CSF in a major merger movement that consolidated Eurotechnique, Sescosem, and EFCIS. Thomson-CSF's moves were supported by the French government which encouraged Thomson-CSF to enter the merchant IC market. This move has proven reasonably successful, Thomson is now the fourth largest European IC producer.

In Germany AEG-Telefunken restructured its semiconductor activities in 1982 and 1983 and launched two joint ventures with United Technologies. The first of these, Telefunken Electronics, was a 1982 partnership among AEG-Telefunken (49 percent), United Technologies (49 percent), and the Sueddeutsche Ind-Beteiligungs GmbH (2 percent). In the following year Eurosil Electronics GmbH was formed as a joint venture between Telefunken Electronics (43.6 percent) and the Diehl Gruppe (13 percent). According to Malerba (1985, p. 168), these joint ventures "focussed on the production of custom NMOS and CMOS ICs and of gate arrays." The custom and semicustom focus of this joint venture differentiates it from the French strategies in search of a more active position in Europe's merchant IC market.

A U.S.-British joint venture was formed in August 1978 between Fairchild and GEC for merchant IC production. The start-up capital of $38.8 million, equally contributed by the two companies, was used to construct a 16K memory facility at Neston in Cheshire County, England (*Electronic News*, 1978). In 1980 one year after Schlumberger's acquisition of Fairchild, the companies dissolved the joint venture and GEC retained the facility (*Electronic News*, 1980). Although this venture was heralded as more commercially viable than INMOS, which was financed by the National Enterprise Board, its product choice was ill timed and was unlikely to have been successful in the price cutting that accompanied the maturation of the 16K memory market.

Two final joint ventures are Philips and Siemens links to produce advanced ICs launched in 1984 and AT&T's joint venture with Telefonica, Spain's telecommunications company. The Philips-Siemens link is an attempt to catch up with U.S. and Japanese leads in memory ICs. A four-megabit memory chip is the focus of this venture's efforts. This venture is being heavily supported by the governments of Germany and the Netherlands with $140 million for the research phase of the project (*Electronic News*, 1984b). AT&T's venture with Telefonica also appears to be a move into merchant markets; AT&T has agreed to export 81 percent of production (*Business Week*, 1984). The Spanish government has undertaken a $60 million immediate commitment to the project and has made commitments for a future $75 million loan. The Telefonica deal was concluded after AT&T's attempts to purchase a 60 percent interest in the British IC company, Inmos, were rebuffed by that company, which has close ties to the government.

There appears to be no clear direction in the U.S.-European joint ventures. Some have focused on vertical markets in which the firm-specific assets of European companies involved in system production sought technology infusions from U.S. companies. Others appear to mainly be the result of European government's desire for a domestic industry that could keep pace with the U.S. and Japanese IC producers. There is a notable absence of agreements focusing on the early development of products and processes. The single exception, the Siemens-Philips joint venture, while international, confined participation to European firms. This suggests that a primary motive of European firms is technological parity with U.S. and Japanese firms. If this is true, agreements aimed at "catch up" may be forthcoming, a possibility that gains some support from the details of two joint ventures between European and Japanese firms.

Joint ventures between European and Japanese firms include ties between Fujitsu and ICL as well as Toshiba and SGS-Ates (Haklisch, 1986, pp. 188–197). The Fujitsu-ICL tie involves gate array technology, a principal method of achieving customizable ICs. Fujitsu is the world's largest gate array producer. This agreement focused on current Fujitsu technology rather than development of new capabilities. The agreement between SGS-Ates appears somewhat broader and is focused on CMOS technology. CMOS techniques are likely to be important for extending current trajectories toward higher transistor counts in each IC.

European electronic companies in the IC industry apparently continue to concentrate on keeping pace with IC developments in order to develop competitive system products. Because of government-industry ties in telecommunication and computer equipment industries, it is difficult to evaluate the commercial efficiency of this strategy. The increasing costs of keeping pace with state-of-the-art technology may lead to further efforts such as the Siemens-Philips joint venture. Direct investment by U.S. IC companies in European production facilities is, however, likely to remain an effective method for European system companies to gain access to advances in IC technology. If bilateral competition between U.S. and Japanese companies weakens U.S. subsidiaries in Europe, it is likely that other methods for technology transfer will have to be devised, including increases in Japanese direct investment and joint ventures between European and U.S. or Japanese firms.

U.S.-JAPANESE JOINT VENTURES

Joint ventures between U.S. and Japanese firms fall into two distinct periods. During the first, prior to 1980, foreign trade and investment policies of the Japanese government and the technological backwardness of Japanese IC producers dictated joint ventures where U.S. firms provided technological assets for the more direct access to the Japanese domestic market. Participants in these ventures were "second tier" Japanese electronics companies and these arrangements were discontinued prior to 1980. Japanese trade liberalization in the late 1970s and the attainment by Japanese companies of technological parity by 1980 has created a second period of joint venture activity. In this new period, beginning in 1980, larger electronic firms have sought direct and bilateral technology exchanges with U.S. firms. In addition small Japanese companies seeking entry in electronics markets have also agreed to finance Japanese facilities based on U.S. technology rather than concluding domestic joint ventures. This latter development highlights the growing importance of capital spending for achieving a significant position in the international IC industry.

Japanese IC producers have been investing at a faster rate than U.S. firms despite their smaller current share of the world IC production (McClean, 1986). In 1985 Japanese IC output accounted for 30 percent of world IC production, but their capital expenditures were 46 percent of worldwide IC industry capital expenditures. In the same year North American production was estimated at $14 billion or 47 percent of world production but capital expenditures were only 36 percent of the worldwide total.[14] While international capacity races in the IC industry are a recent phenomenon, temporary excess capacity has been common in the U.S. industry and a major contributor to severe recessions in 1971, 1975, and 1985. Growth in demand and alleviation of capacity utilization problems requires an expansion in market demand by system producers, often accompanied by new generations of IC products. Attainment of technological parity by Japanese IC producers has created a deep foreboding over future U.S. IC industry prospects, a development that may reduce U.S. companies' ability to restore capital spending during a future recovery. The history of joint ventures between U.S. and Japanese firms reveals a pattern of evolution toward increasing exchange and agreements of broader scope. These changes contrast with the period before Japanese firms attained technological parity and launched the capacity expansion efforts.

Joint ventures solely to gain access to the Japanese market were the first interfirm agreements between U.S. and Japanese IC firms. The first international semiconductor joint venture of consequence accompanied Texas Instruments (TI) attempt to gain access to the Japanese market. Japan had prohibited direct investment by firms in a number of industries including electronics, a policy that was not reversed until the 1970s. John Tilton (1971, p. 146) summarizes the consequences:

> The [Japanese] government's determination to resist the formation of semiconductor firms controlled by foreign interests was tested in the late 1960s by Texas Instruments. The American firm petitioned the Japanese government for a wholly owned subsidiary in the early 1960s, and was offered instead a minority interest in a joint venture with a Japanese company. Texas Instruments rejected this offer and continued to press for a wholly owned subsidiary. To strengthen its bargaining position, it refused to license its strategic integrated-circuit patents to Japanese firms.

Tilton (p. 147) summarizes the result:

> TI subsequently petitioned the U.S. government for trade protection based on patent infringement of Japanese system products. The resolution of this impasse was an international joint venture between Sony and TI established in 1958 with each owning 50% of the equity.

This was an inauspicious beginning for international joint ventures between U.S. and Japanese firms. Four years later Sony sold out to TI. (Office of Technology Assessment, 1983).

Similar arrangements were made with Fairchild, which had established a wholly owned subsidiary on Okinawa in 1969. When Okinawa reverted to Japanese control in 1972, Fairchild established a 50 percent joint venture with TDK, a smaller Japanese firms best known for consumer magnetic tapes (Boardman, 1972).[15] During the same period of direct Japan's Ministry of International Trade and Industry (MITI) control of foreign investment, Motorola began a joint venture with Alps. This arrangement was terminated with liberalization of Japanese trade policies in the 1970s. During the late 1970s, Motorola had a direct marketing subsidiary in Japan. In 1980 Motorola formed a joint venture with Toko to manufacture ICs. Toko was a very small electronics components company with sales of $120 million in 1979. In 1982 Motorola purchased Toko's 50 percent share of the joint venture and became the second firm (following TI) to have a wholly owned manufacturing facility in Japan.

These international joint ventures are representative of a "first stage" in such agreements between U.S. and Japanese firms ended prior to 1980. Japanese government control of direct foreign investment in Japan forced U.S. firms who desired Japanese manufacturing facilities to form joint ventures. U.S. firms chose minor electronics companies as partners and the results were quite unstable.[16] The primary motives for these ventures was market access since, in the absence of manufacturing and design facilities in Japan, U.S. IC companies experienced difficulties in assuring Japanese system producers of IC availability and support. U.S. firms operated the ventures with a mixture of expatriate personnel and U.S. trained engineers and sold the output internationally complementing the output of U.S. facilities while servicing the domestic Japanese market. The relatively low wages of Japanese engineers and high-quality assembly labor motivated the establishment of the facilities in Japan. The 1970s were also a period of direct investment in other Asian nations based on creation of assembly operations (Grunwald and Flamm, 1985). Existence of wafer fabrication facilities in Japan complemented these overseas assembly operations.

During the early 1980s, new international joint ventures between U.S. and Japanese firms began to be formed. By 1980 Japanese firms had achieved technical parity with U.S. firms in several areas and the large domestic demand for ICs in Japan became a source of interest to new Japanese entrants and to U.S. firms seeking marketing channels. Examples of joint ventures with these new motivations include AMI's joint venture with Asahi Chemical in 1983, National and Oki's 1983 joint development venture, LSI Logic's joint venture with Toshiba in 1982, RCA and Sharp's 1984 joint venture for CMOS IC design and fabrication in the United States (an agreement that was subsequently abandoned when General Electric purchased RCA), and Motorola's recent Japan-based joint venture with Toshiba.

AMI, a subsidiary of Gould Electronics since 1981, has strongly emphasized vertical ties to system producers and the production of system designer "solutions" for specific niche markets. Its joint venture with Asahi Chemical Industry Company, a large ($3.1 billion annual revenue) Japanese chemical and textile producer was a direct transfer of technological assets. The joint venture included a $9 million sale of AMI's Japanese distributing subsidiary.[17]

The motive for this joint venture focus was the construction of a medium volume manufacturing facility in Japan for which AMI's contribution is process technology and engineering support (*Electronic News*, 1983). The partners were engaged in a relatively straightforward exchange of Japanese capital and market ties for AMI's technological contribution. Asahi's contribution for plant construction and equipment for the facility was very large compared with earlier U.S.-Japanese joint ventures. AMI's Japanese market sales in 1982 were estimated at less than $6 million by *Electronic News* (1983), yet Asahi paid $7 million to purchase this distributorship. Moreover, although the structure and equipment expenditures for the facility are not publicly available, the type of facility planned suggests they were likely to exceed $50 million. AMI's cash commitments to the venture were limited to loans for "other funding requirements." In short, this arrangement reflects a major departure from past U.S.-Japanese IC industry joint ventures, an exchange based on major contributions by the Japanese partner.[18]

The National-Oki agreement reflects the changing set of motives for new U.S.-Japanese joint venture arrangements created by technological parity between U.S. and Japanese IC producers. National, which built a reputation of low-cost mass production of standard IC types, licensed Oki's 64K dynamic memory technology and scrapped its own development efforts (Bagamery, 1984). The agreement commits National to a supply arrangement for Oki requirements and includes joint development efforts for future products (*Wall Street Journal*, 1983). The agreement calls for joint technology development and in this respect sharply differs from prior agreements. It is the first of several agreements concluded in recent years that reverses the historical U.S.-to-Japan flow of technology transfer.[19] The reversal in flow of technology reflects the success made of Japanese firms in gaining technological parity with their U.S. competitors and is noteworthy since it involves process technology (memory technology) in which international gains of Japanese firms have been concentrated.

LSI Logic's formation of a Japanese venture is another model for the new climate in U.S.-Japanese cooperation. The Japanese company, Nihon LSI Logic Corporation, was funded primarily from Japanese capital sources. A one-third ownership share of the venture was purchased by Japanese venture capitalists for $18.8 million while LSI Logic Corporation's initial capital contribution was set at $1.5 million (*Electronic News*, 1984a). This venture's initial activity was the formation of a semicustom design center in Tokyo with plans for manufacturing facilities at a later time. Subsequently, the joint venture was expanded to include financing by Kawasaki Steel for a major Japanese manufacturing facility.

Sharp and RCA agreed in 1984 to form a joint venture for CMOS IC technology (*Wall Street Journal*, 1984). CMOS is now believed to be the leading technology for sustaining technical improvement in transistor count and functional complexity of IC technology. The joint venture subsequently selected a site in the state of Washington, at Camas (*Electronic News*, 1985).

This complex venture was the high point in international joint ventures in the IC industry prior to the major worldwide recession in 1985. Neither company is a leading IC producer. However, both are in the top ten in their national IC industries and hence have considerable firm-specific technology. While Sharp has had more experience in CMOS because of the consumer electronics focus of the company, RCA is also an experienced IC producer. Both companies have well-developed marketing channels and planned to divide the output of the joint venture evenly. A principal motive for the formation of this venture was that both companies wanted to expand their merchant position and diversify risks in the development of new CMOS products and processes. The joint venture was canceled after General Electric purchased RCA. The significant problems of merging RCA and General Electric's efforts as well as the diminished importance of Sharp's role in financing the project appear to be responsible for the cancellation.

In 1985 the IC industry plunged into a major recession and bilateral relationships between U.S. and Japanese IC producers worsened. The recession has had a major impact on expectations regarding the industry's future. The precipitous decline in demand from the high levels of 1983 and 1984 created worldwide overcapacity in the industry and imposed very large financial losses and forced major layoffs for U.S. merchant producers. The 1985 recession provoked the U.S. industry to take a very aggressive stance toward Japanese competitors who, in less than a decade, had achieved a strong competitive position in several markets for mass produced ICs. The common perception in the U.S. industry was that U.S. merchant firms losses were exacerbated by the loss of these markets to Japanese competitors.[20] U.S. firms made the case that competitive losses of U.S. merchant producers were the result of deliberate targeting practices of the

Japanese government and concerted actions of Japanese firms in two areas, capital investment and Japanese domestic market restrictions on the entry of U.S. firms and products (Semiconductor Industry Association, 1983). Actions against the major Japanese firms were filed at the U.S. International Trade Commission by U.S. producers leading to major penalties on several mass produced memory products. A bilateral trade agreement was signed between the U.S. and Japanese governments and dumping penalties were suspended in favor of a price maintenance arrangement.

Two major events occurred during this international crisis in the IC industry. In October 1986 Fujitsu announced plans to acquire Fairchild Semiconductor from Schlumberger Ltd. (*Electronics*, 1986). A major motive for this purchase was the acquisition of Fairchild's well-established distribution channels in the United States. While Fairchild has several unique technologies, the predominant direction of technology exchange in this merger is expected to be from Fujitsu to Fairchild (Malone, 1987). The planned purchase was withdrawn following objections by the U.S. Department of Commerce and Defense. Subsequent efforts have aimed at Fujitsu participation in a leveraged buy out by Fairchild management. The extent of Fujitsu investment, originally to be $400 million over a two-year period in the purchase agreement, is uncertain. Arrangements for marketing access are also uncertain. In the original agreement Fujitsu planned to give Fairchild responsibility for marketing its IC products in both the United States and Europe. Had this agreement succeeded, it would have opened a major new era in international ties between the Japanese and U.S. IC industries involving joint production.

Another model for major joint ventures between U.S. and Japanese firms was established in 1986 between Motorola and Toshiba. Both companies are major IC producers. The joint venture is aimed at giving Toshiba access to Motorola technology in the area of microprocessors, where Motorola has a 57 percent of the 32 bit market (*Wall Street Journal*, 1986b). In exchange Motorola will gain access to Toshiba's major investment in technology for one megabit memory. In addition the venture includes plans for a joint development of future products, reciprocal marketing of ICs, and a $215 million plant in Japan (*Wall Street Journal*, 1986b). This joint venture is by far the most important joint agreement existing between U.S. and Japanese firms.

The scale and complexity of U.S.-Japanese joint ventures have increased remarkably since their inception. The active successful effort by Japanese firms to attain technological parity its U.S. competitors is a major factor in these developments. There are now several models for future U.S.-Japanese interfirm agreements. Firm-specific assets are a clear motive in more recent agreements such as National-Oki and Motorola-Toshiba joint ventures. Capital availability appears responsible for the AMI-National and LSI Logic-Kawasaki Steel pacts. And market access appears a central motive for the attempted Fujitsu purchase of Fairchild Semiconductor. Which of these models are reproduced in future arrangements is likely to depend on experience with their success or failure.[21]

PROSPECTS FOR FUTURE INTERNATIONAL IC JOINT VENTURES

Evaluating the prospects for future international joint ventures involves comparing trends whose ultimate resolution is uncertain. Nevertheless, three such factors are examined in this section: technologically driven changes in industry relationships, government protectionist policies, and cooperative research activities. Each of these factors is likely to have a major impact on the likelihood and structure of future international joint ventures.

Changes in IC Industry Relationships

The leading indicator of the changing market relationships between IC and system producers is in markets for ICs that can be customized to specific design needs, or application-specific ICs (ASICs) that began to emerge in the early 1980s. The most straightforward of these products permit the user to specify a combination of electronic functions for a single device that will substitute for a larger number of less complex ICs. More complex ASICs permit the user to combine functional blocks of greater complexity, creating entire electronic subsystems that are customized to specific design requirements. ASICs can be grouped in four categories: programmable logic, gate array, standard cell devices, and devices designed using "silicon compilers." For economic analysis, the first and last two categories can be grouped together.[22]

Programmable logic and gate array devices allow users to specify connections among a large number of memory cells or simple digital logic functions. The pattern of connections chosen by a user reflects that user's unique approach to a system design. Many different system designs can utilize a single programmable logic or gate array device design, each design incorporating a different pattern of interconnections. The function of these connections in each system design will differ depending on the system in which it is embedded.

Programmable logic and gate array devices perform the same functions on a single IC as those performed by a collection of simpler logic and memory ICs that must be connected on a printed circuit board. As a consequence, programmable logic and gate array devices are effective substitutes for large numbers of simpler ICs and offer substantial economic advantages to the system designer because reducing the "parts count" or number of ICs in an electronic system reduces cost and increases reliability.

Effective use of these devices in system design requires the development of computer assisted design and engineering (CAD and CAE) systems. CAD/CAE systems are used to simulate the performance and debug designs of systems employing these devices. For standard cell and silicon compiler devices the design of individual ICs is made using CAD/CAE systems. Manufacture of CAD/CAE systems provides opportunities for IC manufacturers in selling design tools to system companies and data about device characteristics to third-party producers of such systems.

Over time, however, the variety of products in programmable logic and gate array designs is likely to fall as designs are standardized and, unless U.S. IC firms develop unique process advantages or proprietary implementations of popular designs, Japanese firms will retain their competitive lead in these markets. In 1986 three of the top five gate array producers were Japanese companies (Waller, 1987). The other two LSI Logic (the second largest) is a relatively new entrant to the U.S. IC industry and a specialist in ASICs. The fourth largest is Ferranti, a British firm. The fall in the number of types of customizable products will be accompanied by growth in the number of application specific uses of these circuits. Since each IC can be customized for any one of many end use applications, a significant amount of value added to these products will be in the design of these applications using CAD/CAE systems. CAD and CAE systems are offered by both IC manufacturers and third-party producers. It seems unlikely that IC firms will succeed in tying CAD/CAE system use to particular products or that they will have unique advantages in this system market. Nevertheless, gains from trade between IC producers and CAD/CAE system producers may lead to interfirm agreements including joint ventures based upon exchange of firm-specific assets.

The third category of ASICs, standard cell devices, offer considerably greater opportunities for appropriating the returns from IC design innovation. At present U.S. firms are leaders in this segment; nine of the top ten firms in 1986 were U.S. companies (Waller, 1987, p. 61). Unlike programmable logic and gate array devices, standard cells incorporate functional units whose alternative implementation may be difficult or impossible for other firms. For example, a standard cell IC may include an array of microprocessors and memory cells. The microprocessor may be of a type that is familiar to system designers and employ a proprietary circuit implementation. With more complex and potentially proprietary elements, standard cell ICs may permit IC firms to achieve higher IC prices from system producers. System producers may be motivated to adopt these devices for the same reasons they adopt other ASICs, to reduce the parts count of systems, and for the additional reason of employing circuit elements, such as microprocessors, where they have invested in design expertise.

Standard cell ICs also require highly sophisticated CAD/CAE design tools.[23] The greater complexity of standard cell ICs make independent design of third-party "compatible" CAD/CAE systems more costly and increase the gains from trade between IC and CAD/CAE system producers. To date, however, standard cell ICs are in their infancy and are generating only modest levels of sales. Their complexity is a major challenge to system designers indicating that there may be a limit, at least in the short run, to the amount of complexity that can be successfully employed in the quest for reduced parts counts in systems. Nevertheless, the history of the IC industry is one of employing ever greater levels of complexity to increase the performance and reduce costs of system products. Both U.S. and Japanese firms have launched vigorous development efforts and Japanese companies have increased direct investment in the United States to gain access to customers for such devices. For example, Fujitsu has established five U.S. design centers to "make it easier for our customers to access Fujitsu," according to Hirofumi Takeda, manager of the ASIC engineering-support (Cohen, 1987).

Innovations in the design tools for creating ASIC circuits are a wild card in the future of the IC industry and interfirm agreements. At one extreme, system and IC design may become inseparable activities with a vestigial role for mass produced ICs such as memories in system designs. At the other, ASIC designs may play a minor role in markets dominated by new types of mass produced standard ICs. Which alternative emerges, or whether either will exclusively prevail, will depend upon the effectiveness of joint design and manufacturing models for customized IC design versus design innovations and software techniques for utilizing standard ICs. Carver Mead, one of the proponents of the former alternative has stated "the chip is software. The medium is not the value; information is the value" (Barney and Walker, 1987, p. 61).[24] If this statement is true, it still leaves the question of which method will lead to economically superior system implementations. Systems based on purely custom ICs may incur higher test and maintenance costs to assure reliability given the inability to modify the system without modifying the hardware.[25] If the value added is information, the economic contest is between embodying that information in customized chips or in software for systems employing standardized IC components.

This technological context will be tested in IC and system markets. If this market test favors highly customized ICs, interfirm agreements will tilt toward links between IC and system producers. If standard devices are favored, proprietary rights in successful designs are a likely source of interfirm agreements among IC producers. Marked dominance of standard devices is likely to sustain past patterns of technology exchange agreements rather than encouraging joint venture formation. Which of these two alternatives will prevail will remain uncertain until both have been further developed. During this development period, cost and risk sharing arrangements including joint ventures are likely. Joint ventures aimed at developing highly customized ICs may be stable if that technique is successful. If standard approaches fail or *prevail*, joint ventures to develop them are likely to be unstable. In the case of success, races to appropriate technology for parent companies are likely to destabilize ventures. Failure, of course, will remove incentives to support such ventures.[26]

This international diversification of process technology and product design knowledge will challenge the efficacy of technology exchange agreements as vehicles for trading and developing technological assets. The U.S. history of firms having similar technological capabilities and experience with the value and meaning of a specific technological asset has less applicability in a world of rapidly diversifying technical capability. Diversity of capability creates uncertainty and increases the costs of evaluation of potential international technological exchange agreements. These problems favor interfirm agreements such as joint ventures where partners can share in benefits and costs of further developments of particular technologies or efforts to combine expertise. This motive for joint ventures, identified by David Mowery in Chapter 1, has only recently been a factor in the IC industry and is one consequence of growing international capabilities in IC technology.

U.S. Government Trade Policy

To consummate a joint venture, two firms must believe that neither partner will achieve an advantage at the expense of the other. U.S. firm market losses to Japanese IC firms and difficulties in selling ICs to Japanese electronic system users who are IC producers and direct competitors in merchant IC markets are an important issue in U.S. IC industry appeals for government assistance in gaining "access" to the Japanese market. The sharp readjustment in IC market shares in a short time were a factor in industry efforts to gain U.S. government protection of domestic merchant IC producers.

A common perception in the U.S. IC industry is that the weakening of U.S. merchant IC producers' positions is the consequence of a deliberate drive by Japanese IC producers, who are also large system producers, to weaken the financial position of U.S. merchant IC producers. This view gained the support of the U.S. government when the U.S. International Trade Commission (ITC) sustained U.S. industry claims that Japanese firms' pricing of several types of memory ICs met the "dumping" standard of price predation. The ITC finding was subsequently used as leverage in obtaining a bilateral accord setting Fair Market Values (FMVs) for Japanese memory ICs and extracting a promise from the Japanese government to seek dramatic increases in importation of U.S. IC products. As recognition of these concessions, the U.S. government suspended the "dumping" penalties in the ITC action.

FMV regulation of Japanese memory pricing quickly developed characteristics common to administered price systems. The initial shock of the agreement led to price quotations far in excess of FMV values. This was followed by a period of rapid growth in third country and gray markets for new production and existing inventories. Pressures to curtail these practices were applied by the U.S. government while several U.S. system producer organizations announced their opposition to the accord. The Japanese government apparently issued requests to major producers to *restrain* production to force prices upward.[27] Demand for memory by U.S. producers increased during 1987, creating shortages and thereafter, requests by the Japanese government for Japanese IC firms to *increase* production. Aside from illustrating the problems of government price administration, these events suggest that the U.S. government is willing to implement regulation of trade in IC products despite resulting market confusion and protest by segments of the U.S. electronic system industry.

U.S. government interventionist intent is also illustrated by efforts to obtain a larger share for U.S. IC producers in domestic Japanese markets. Gaining greater access to the Japanese domestic market is a twofold problem. First, the continuing effects of historical restrictions on U.S. direct investment in the Japanese market, cannot be ignored. Interfirm arrangements that might have grown out of a strong U.S. presence in the Japanese domestic market, such as that attained in the European market, did not have opportunity for a market test because of early restriction on direct foreign investment in the Japanese semiconductor industry. The success of Texas Instruments and IBM, who forced early admission, in attaining a strong position in the Japanese market and strengthening their international position through involvement in the Japanese market suggest major losses were imposed on the U.S. merchant IC industry by Japanese restrictions. This experience did not lead to substantial joint ventures, in part, because Japanese firms elected to develop technological capabilities independently during the 1970s. The second issue in access to the Japanese domestic market involves the historical and present extent of nontariff barriers on importation of U.S. ICs. Aside from the modest share of U.S. imports in the market, little systematic evidence of nontariff barriers has been offered. Nevertheless, the perception of these barriers is widespread in the U.S. industry and may itself be a barrier to making substantial investments in gaining access.

U.S. government policy in regulating the international price of memory ICs and seeking increased access for U.S. IC production in Japan is likely to have several consequences. If these policies are continued or extended, several consequences appear likely. The most obvious is an increase in direct investment by Japanese IC producers in the United States. But these policies may also stimulate increased joint venture activities aimed at gaining market access to an increasingly restricted U.S. market.

The bilateral trade agreement discussed above is only one of several actions that suggest the U.S. is moving toward a protectionist stance in IC industry issues.[28] These policies may be a transitory response to industry crisis. If they are continued or extended, the issue of U.S. market access will become a motive for increases in direct investment and interfirm agreements. The precedent of Fujitsu's attempted purchase of Fairchild Semiconductor, scuttled by the U.S. government, makes Japanese purchase of U.S. IC producers an uncertain arrangement for gaining market access in a climate of protectionism. The most likely consequence of such policies is increased Japanese and European direct investment for their own facilities in the United States.

Agreements aimed at penetrating the Japanese market under threat of U.S. sanctions may be organized as joint ventures. Success in this policy objective, if endorsed by the Japanese government, will require greater cooperation between U.S. IC producers and Japanese customers than has been attained to date. Protectionist U.S. policies are still young and have not yet been a significant motive for joint ventures, although they are clearly an alternative to direct investment pending future tests of mechanisms for interfirm agreements between U.S. and Japanese firms.

Cooperative Research Activities

Discussions of international technology and joint ventures ultimately confront the issue of whether such agreements undermine the long-term competitiveness of a particular company or a nation's industry. One view is essentially neomercantalist: technological exchanges including joint ventures inexorably undermine a "home" nation's industry to the advantage of a industry in a "foreign" nation. But, if such exchanges are voluntary, leakage of advantage should be reciprocal; the value of outflows and inflows should be roughly equal. Exchanges of U.S. knowledge for Japanese or European knowledge should strengthen both parties and narrow gaps in capabilities. To make such exchanges, firms must be able package knowledge in ways that will be appropriable and transferrable. If this cannot be done, commercial exchanges will not occur and other methods for knowledge transfer will be developed. These other methods include acquisitions, joint ventures, and direct investment accompanied by recruitment of employees that have useful knowledge.

One means to a stronger competitive position for U.S. firms may be cooperative research efforts. The process advances necessary for sustaining trends toward higher levels of integration and the fixed costs of product design of very complex devices are the principal source of these costs increases. Interfirm agreements have become more important as the size of these costs have become apparent. The size of these costs have not yet reached a point where international cost sharing is the only means to generate new technologies. It may have exceeded the capabilities of current U.S. firms, except perhaps IBM.

U.S. domestic cost-sharing arrangements have, until recently, been modest. Research consortia such as MCC and SRC mentioned in the introduction are relatively small by comparison with overall industry R&D expenditures. A proposal to create a major U.S. consortium, Sematech, seeks substantial U.S. government support (Pollack, 1987). Private agreements among U.S. firms for cost sharing have been actively pursued in developing markets including ASICs (Barney, 1987). More general domestic domestic U.S. cost-sharing arrangements await resolution of Sematech's funding from the U.S. government. Sematech is planned as a joint research effort in production technology with strong support by IBM and other system houses.

The support for Sematech by the U.S. government and private industry will have a major impact on the future of interfirm process development accords. If Sematech falters, a wave of process technology agreements, acquisitions, and joint ventures appears likely. Even if Sematech is funded, many opportunities will exist for structural change in the U.S. IC industry to allow cost sharing since Sematech will ultimately need to focus on a collection of specific technologies. Although the Sematech initiative is large, its technological efforts will not be comprehensive.[29] As a consequence, evolution in ASIC markets and the relationships between system and IC producers are likely to be complementary to agreements confined to IC producers, both domestic and international.

NOTES

1. For comprehensive descriptive reviews of these arguments, see Hacklisch (1986) and United Nations Centre on Transnational Corporations (1986).
2. Comprehensive treatments of the technological and economic developments in the IC industry include those of Golding (1971), Tilton (1971), and Braun and MacDonald (1982).
3. Hand-held calculators also played an important role in this early market growth. See Moore (1979).
4. Captive facilities also produce fairly standard products ensuring product availability and keeping up with current process technology.
5. Several large firms, including IBM, are responsible for the majority of captive production.
6. As is often the case in the IC industry, technology diffusion accelerated by the hiring of key personnel. For example, Gordon Teal, an expert on silicon material was hired by Texas Instruments in 1953 and helped TI become an early leader in silicon-based transistors the forerunner of silicon-based ICs. See Levin (1982).
7. Early transistor and IC products had broad application and therefore system companies may not have seen any particular advantage to joint ventures for these commodities.
8. A product is likely to remain available for a longer time with more than one firm because as firms drop out of production, the demand for remaining firm's output increases.
9. CMOS was not developed earlier because of a specific technical problem called "latch up." Subsequent development of the technology by both U.S. and Japanese firms has partially ameliorated this problem.
10. Announcement of second source agreements and product licensing is also unnecessary, although it may prove beneficial to the licensee in promoting the "compatibility" of products.
11. This conclusion is based on independent examination of the English language business press for the years 1978–1986.

12. European IC producers are, however, more likely to sell ICs in direct competition than their counterparts in the United States, the captive IC producers.
13. Philips subsequently increased its stake to 20 percent.
14. For rates of investment, see McClean, 1986, pp. 38–40, or Semiconductor Industry Association, "Japanese Market Barriers in Microelectronics," San Jose, California: June 14, 1985): 6–8.
15. Boardman (1972) also mentions a National direct investment in Okinawa whose future was uncertain.
16. Sony was an exception to the size of joint venture partners, although short-lived. Its sales in 1969 were 94 billion yen.
17. This marketing subsidiary was a joint venture with Rikei Corporation, a trading company, during the restricted foreign investment period (*Electronic News*, 1972).
18. In the same week AMI signed a second-sourcing agreement with NEC in which the two companies agreed to exchange database tapes for a number of specific products. This agreement indicates the continuing technology exchange agreements between U.S. and Japanese firms outside of the joint venture structure (*Electronic News*, 1983, p. 27).
19. For a summary of recent U.S.-Japanese and U.S.-Korean technology exchange agreements, see McClean, 1986, p. 32.
20. The pricing of Japanese ICs led to several "dumping" complaints before the U.S. International Trade Commission with findings against the major Japanese IC producers. Subsequent bilateral agreements on pricing are currently in place. These actions may make U.S. market access an important criterion for future Japanese joint ventures with U.S. firms.
21. Texas Instruments has appointed an Executive Vice President to develop new joint ventures in Asia (*Wall Street Journal*, 1986a). Advanced Micro Devices has established ties with Sony Corporation for joint development of ICs (*Business Week*, 1986).
22. The economics of the last two categories may diverge in the future if standard cells become proprietary physical designs and silicon compiler design systems become proprietary software designs. Currently both markets are nascent and the future focus of intellectual property is uncertain.
23. An extension of the standard cell is the notion of a silicon compiler, a CAD/CAE system that allows a system designer to specify the functional characteristics and performance of an IC but ignore implementation details such as the placement of transistors within the IC. The CAD/CAE system translates these specifications into a manufacturable IC and produces a data tape with full manufacturing specifications. See Mead and Conway (1980).
24. Moore maintains that standard products will continue to dominate and that proprietary circuit designs will be the basis for standard ASIC subsystems. The April 2, 1987 number of *Electronics* presents a comprehensive and useful collection of industry views on these issues.
25. This simplifies the issue since custom systems can be designed using electrically alterable components such as electrically erasable nonvolatile memory that permit modifications without changing components.

26. Partners in such ventures will have different capabilities for appropriating knowledge and are likely to be direct competitors meaning that when one firm pulls ahead the loser is likely to seek termination of the joint venture.
27. It is somewhat perplexing that this request had to be made if Japanese firms were producing memory at low or no profit. One explanation consistent with economic rationality is that overcapacity considerations forced continued production. Another is that the FMV prices were significantly above target returns of Japanese IC producers.
28. Others include the abortion of Fujitsu's acquisition of Fairchild, unprecedented sanctions against Toshiba for technology transfer to the Soviet Union, and proposals for sanctions against nations where U.S. imports have been stalled. These early indicators may prove false in time, a possibility entertained in the text.
29. This conclusion is drawn from public documents and statements. At this writing, Sematech is seeking funding at the $300 million level, one half of which is being sought from the U.S. government.

REFERENCES

Bagamery, Anne. 1984. "Good-By, Animal House." *Forbes*, November 19, pp. 232-233.

Barney, Clifford. 1987. "Winds of Change Sweep the Industry." *Electronics*, April 2, p. 62f.

_____, and Larry Walker. 1987. "Moore vs. Mead: Is Silicon Valley Obsolete?" *Electronics*, April 2.

Boardman, George. 1972. "TDK, Fairchild in Venture as Japan Regains Okinawa." *Electronic News*, May 15, 1ff.

Braun, Ernest and Stuart MacDonald. 1978. *Revolution in Miniature*. London: Cambridge University Press.

_____. 1982. *Revolution in Miniature: The History and Impact of Semiconductor Electronics*, 2nd ed. Cambridge, England: Cambridge University Press.

Business Week. 1984. "AT&T's Route into European Chipmaking." July 23, pp. 83-84.

_____. 1986. "Now Japan Is Where It's At for U.S. Chipmakers." November 24, p. 108.

Cohen, Charles L. 1987. "Fujitsu's Problem Is How to Stay on Top." *Electronics*, August 6, pp. 71-72.

Dataquest. 1980. *Integrated Circuit Manufacturing Model*. San Jose, Calif.: November 15.

Defense Science Board Task Force on Defense Semiconductor Dependency. 1987. Washington, D.C.: Office of the Under Secretary of Defense for Acquisition, February.

Eimbinder, Jerry. 1963. "Transistor Industry Growth Patterns." *Solid State Design*, 4 (January): 57-59.

Electronic Business. 1980. September, p. 106.

Electronic News. 1972. "AMI Japan Goes into Operation." July 3.

_____. 1978. "GEC (U.K.), Fairchild Confirm Joint Venture Plans." August 14, p. 43.

_____. 1983. "AMI, Asahi Plan Venture for IC Manufacturing/Sales in Asia." July 4, pp. 27–28.

_____. 1984a. "LSI Logic Opens Gate Array Firm, Nihon, in Tokyo." April 9.

_____. 1984b. "Philips, Siemens Ink 5-Year IC R&D Accord." October.

_____. 1985. "RCA, Sharp Pick Washington State for Joint-Venture Chip Plant." June 24, p. 17.

Electronics. 1986. "Is the Fairchild-Fujitsu Deal A Vision of the Future?" November 13.

Gerstenfeld, Arthur, and Berger, Paul D. 1984. "Joint Research—A Wave of the Future." *Research Management*, 27, no. 6 (November-December): 9–11.

Golding, A.M. 1971. The Semiconductor Industry in Britain and the United States, Unpublished Ph.D. Thesis, University of Sussex.

Grunwald, Joseph and Kenneth Flamm. 1985. *The Global Factory—Foreign Assembly in International Trade.* Washington, D.C.: The Brookings Institution.

Haklisch, Carmela. 1986. *Technical Alliances in the Semiconductor Industry.* New York: Center for Science and Technology at the Graduate School of Business, New York University.

Levin, Richard. 1982. "The Semiconductor Industry." In Richard Nelson, ed., *Government and Technical Progress.* New York: Pergamon Press.

Malerba, Franco. 1985. *The Semiconductor Business: The Economics of Rapid Growth and Decline.* Madison: University of Wisconsin Press.

Malone, Michael S. 1987. "Fear and Xenophobia in Silicon Valley." *Wall Street Journal*, February 23.

McClean, William J. 1986. *Status 1986—A Report on the Integrated Circuit Industry.* Scottsdale, Ariz.

Mead, Carver, and Lynn Conway. 1980. *Introduction to VLSI Systems.* Reading, Mass.: Addison-Wesley.

Moore, Gordon. 1979. "VLSI: Some Fundamental Challenges." *IEEE Spectrum* (April): 30–37.

Office of Technology Assessment. 1983. *International Competitiveness in Electronics.* OTA-ISC-200. Washington, D.C.: Congress of the United States. November, p. 194.

Okimoto, Daniel I., Takuo Sugano, and Franklin B. Weinstein, ed. 1984. *Competitive Edge: The Semiconductor Industry in the U.S. and Japan.* Stanford, Calif.: Stanford University Press.

The Semiconductor Industry-Trade Related Issues. 1985. Paris: OECD. Organization for Economic Cooperation and Development.

Pollack, Andrew. 1987. "U.S. Chip Makers Plan Huge Venture." *New York Times*, January 6, p. 31f.

Rosenberg, Nathan, and W. Edward Steinmueller. 1982. "The Economic Implications of the VLSI Revolution." In Nathan Rosenberg, ed., *Inside the Black Box: Technology and Economics.* London: Cambridge University Press, pp. 178–192.

Semiconductor Industry Association. 1983. *The Effect of Government Targeting on World Semiconductor Competition*, Cupertino, Calif.

_____ . 1985. "Japanese Market Barriers in Microelectronics." San Jose, Calif., June 14, pp. 6–8.

Steinmueller, W. Edward. Forthcoming. "Industry Structure and Government Policies in the U.S. and Japanese Integrated Circuit Industries." In John B. Shoven (ed.), *Government Policies Toward Industry in the U.S. and Japan.* Cambridge, England: Cambridge University Press.

Tilton, John. 1971. *International Diffusion of Technology: The Case of Semiconductors.* Washington, D.C.: The Brookings Institution.

United Nations Centre on Transnational Corporations. 1986. *Transnational Corporations in the Semiconductor Industry.* New York: United Nations.

Waller, Larry. 1987. "Can Big Chip Houses Make It in ASICs?" *Electronics*, August 5, pp. 60–64.

Wall Street Journal. 1983. "National Semiconductor Sets Venture with Japanese Firm." January 26.

_____ . 1984. "RCA and Sharp Plan U.S. Venture Firm in Electronic Parts." November 30, p. 7.

_____ . 1986a. "Texas Instruments to Pursue Asian, Other Ventures." December 3.

_____ . 1986b. "Toshiba's Motorola Tie-up Is Latest Bid to Bolster Its Semiconductor Business." December 5, p. 30.

5 MULTIFIRM STRATEGIES IN THE U.S. PHARMACEUTICAL INDUSTRY

Lacy Glenn Thomas

In recent years increased attention has been drawn to corporate strategies that require for their execution the administrative linkage of two or more firms. Joint ventures are perhaps the most conspicuous of these *multifirm strategies*, but they are hardly the only form. Indeed, in the pharmaceutical industry joint ventures are dwarfed in frequency and significance by a variety of other multifirm linkages. This chapter seeks to elucidate the nature, origins, and importance of these multifirm strategies in the research sector of the U.S. domestic pharmaceutical industry.

The focus of this study is narrowed in two important ways. First, attention is largely restricted to operations located in the United States, regardless of the nationality of ultimate ownership of these operations. Thus the U.S. research, manufacturing, and marketing activities of the German firm Hoechst, the Swiss firm Ciba-Geigy, and the British firm Burroughs Wellcome (as examples) will be considered U.S. located operations, even though they are foreign-owned. Similarly, the European activities of the firms Merck, Lilly, and Pfizer (for example) will be considered foreign-located even though they are U.S. owned. To avoid confusion, any discussion of nationality in this study will explicitly state the terms of national identification as either by location or by ownership.

The author is indebted to Rocki DeWitt for research assistance and to John Kober, Kathryn Rudie Harrigan, David Mowery, Richard Nelson, and Ed Steimueller for comments on earlier versions of this chapter. Views expressed in the current version are those of the author alone. Portions of this chapter draw from an earlier study by the author (Thomas, 1983).

147

Table 5-1. Market Divisions of the Domestic U.S. Pharmaceutical Industry, Various Years ($ millions).

Year	Prescription Drugs	All Medicines	Prescription Drugs as a Percentage of All Medicines
1929	190	600	32
1949	940	1,640	57
1969	5,395	6,480	83

Source: Temin, Peter. 1980. *Taking Your Medicine: Drug Regulation in the United States.* Cambridge, Mass.: Harvard University Press. Reprinted by permission of the publisher.

The focus of this study is additionally restricted largely to the research-oriented or *patented drugs* sector of the pharmaceutical industry. Patented drugs represent the driving force of the modern pharmaceutical industry and are responsible for the spectacular growth in sales since 1940 (see Table 5-1). In the United States, about 150 firms conduct research for and produce patented drugs, though the 20 largest of these U.S. located firms account for 80 percent of sales and 98 percent of new patented drug sales. Most of these 150 research operations are U.S. owned as well as U.S. located, and about two dozen of the U.S. owned firms maintain significant multinational operations outside the United States. About another two dozen of the U.S. located operations are foreign-owned, capturing about 15 percent of domestic U.S. sales. The remaining 105 or so patented drug firms have largely domestic sales, and some have only very small research facilities. Competition in this segment of the pharmaceutical industry is quite distinctive and occurs through corporate development of new patented therapies. These new products are sold by prescription through doctors to their ultimate consumers.

A second division of the U.S. domestic industry, *generic products* or multisource drugs, exhibits the classical form of price competition. Generic drug products are well-established compounds no longer under patent that are produced as standardized commodities by more than one firm. Generic products are generally unadvertised and subject to price competition among the various producers with the result of low profit margins for generic producers. Multisource drugs accounted for about 45 percent of prescription drug sales within the United States in 1979, though only 7 percent of these sales (or 3 percent of all drug sales) were achieved by the smaller, non-research-intensive firms. The bulk of generic sales are provided as a secondary line of business by the dominant research-oriented pharmaceutical firms. About 600 nonresearch-oriented firms produce generic drugs in the United States. Almost all of these 600 firms have exclusively domestic distribution, and many sell only to regional markets. Most purely generic drug houses have annual sales of less than $10 million.

The third and final industry division, *proprietary drugs*, or over-the counter (OTC) medicines as they are also called, encompasses products sold directly to consumers without prescription and heavily advertised. Competition in this segment of the pharmaceutical industry depends largely on marketing of established brands with occasional new product development. New proprietary drugs rarely represent breakthroughs in treatment and often are simple reformulations of existing therapies that facilitate consumer convenience or are products switched from prescription to OTC status. Proprietary drugs are thus characterized by high advertising intensity but a very low research intensity. Sales of proprietary drugs have grown at a markedly slower rate than other pharmaceutical sales and currently comprise less than 15 percent of total industry sales, as can be seen in Table 5-1. About 550 firms in the U.S. produce and distribute exclusively OTC medicines.

MULTIFIRM STRATEGIES

The world's largest pharmaceutical firms are listed by nationality of ownership in Table 5-2. While each of these firms has access by itself to significant resources for research, production, and marketing of patented drugs, there are nonetheless a high frequency and wide variety of multifirm strategies among these firms (and their smaller counterparts). Patterns and trends for the most important of these linkages are described in the following paragraphs.

Mergers. Over ninety mergers involving U.S. pharmaceutical firms have occurred since 1950 (see Table 5-3). The vast majority of these mergers have involved a small, national drug firm as target, most usually with a large, multinational firm as parent. These mergers have occurred in waves. U.S. multinational pharmaceutical acquisitions abroad centered on the 1960s and tapered off in the 1970s, with targets almost entirely in Europe. In contrast, acquisitions of targeted smaller U.S. pharmaceutical firms did not begin in earnest until after 1965, with a slow steady pace of acquisitions by U.S. parents and a much larger wave of European-parented acquisitions centered on the 1970s. Conspicuous by their absence are mergers between U.S. and Japanese firms, despite the fact that Japan persistently offered the second largest domestic market for pharmaceuticals in the world (with the U.S. the largest).

Table 5-2.   Worldwide Pharmaceutical Sales of Major Corporations, 1975 and 1980 in $ Millions, by Nationality of Ownership.

Firm	1975		1980	
Hoechst	1,269		2,645	
Bayer	939		2,371	
Boehringer-Ingelheim	629		907	
Schering AG	437		763	
Germany		3,274		6,686
Roche/SAPAC	1,105		1,552	
Ciba-Giegy	993		1,923	
Sandoz Group	759		1,422	
Switzerland		2,857		4,897
Merck	1,028		1,896	
American Home Products	881		1,486	
Bristol-Myers	768		1,357	
Eli Lilly	690		1,156	
Pfizer	683		1,291	
Warner-Lambert	652		753	
Abbott	614		1,379	
Schering-Plough	484		852	
Squibb	554		822	
Upjohn	532		951	
Johnson and Johnson	400		869	
American Cyanimid	400		695	
Dow	356		481	
Searle	319		590	
Sterling Drug	299		702	
Smith Kline	283		1,175	
United States		8,943		16,455
Glaxo Group	508		926	
Wellcome Foundation	492		996	
Beechem Group	385		705	
ICI	289		805	
United Kingdom		1,674		3,432
Takeda	591		1,084	
Japan				
Rhone-Poulenc	620		1,066	
Sanofi	154		589	
France		774		1,655
Akzo	308		665	
Netherlands				
Montedison	301		529	
Italy				

Source: National Academy of Sciences. 1983. *The Competitive Status of the U.S. Pharmaceutical Industry.* Washington, D.C.: National Academy Press. © 1983 by the National Academy of Sciences.

Table 5-3. Mergers Involving U.S. Owned Pharmaceutical Firms, 1950-1985.

U.S.-U.S.

Parent	Target	Year
Mathiewson Chemical	E. R. Squibb and Sons	1952
Merck	Sharpe and Dome	1953
Warner-Hudnut	Lambert	1955
Warner-Lambert	Emerson Drug	1956
Dow Chemical	Allied Labs	1960
Atlas Chemical	Stuart Pharmaceuticals	1961
Bristol-Myers	Mead Johnson	1967
Morton	Norwich	1969
Bristol-Myers	Westwood	1969
Dupont	Endo	1969
Mallickrodt	Neisler	1969
Warner-Lambert	Parke-Davis	1970
3M	Riker	1970
Rorer	Dermik	1971
Schering	Plough	1971
Richardson-Merrell	Lakeside	1975
Revlon	Armour	1978
Revlon	Biotherax	1979
Smith Kline	Allergan	1980
Squibb	Advanced Technology	1979
Abbott	Sorenson Research	1980
K-V Pharmaceutical	Heun-Nurwood	1981
Dow	Richardson-Merrell	1981
American Hospital Supply	Bio-Sciences	1982
Procter and Gamble	Norwich-Eaton	1982
Forest Labs	O'Neal, Jones, and Felman	1984
ICN	Frossman Lab.	1984
Baxter Travenol	American Hospital Supply	1985
Carter Wallace	Youngs Drug Products	1985
Procter and Gamble	Richardson-Vicks	1985
Reid-Provident	Rowell Labs	1985
Monsanto	Searle	1985
Forest Labs	Gilbert Labs	1985

U.S.-Foreign

Parent	Target	Year	Target Country
Johnson and Johnson	Janssen	1961	Belgium
Lilly	Dista	1962	United Kingdom
Dow	Lepetit	1965	Italy
Merck	Frosst	1965	Canada
Robins	Martinet	1966	France
Searle	Sintetico	1967	Brazil
Warner-Lambert	DIWAG	1967	West Germany

(Table 5-3. continued overleaf)

Table 5-3. continued

U.S.-Foreign (cont.)

Parent	Target	Year	Parent Country
Richardson-Merrell	Tonrade	1967	France
SKF	RIT	1968	Belgium
Merck	Chibret	1969	France
AHP	ORFI	1969	Spain
ICN	Arco	1970	Switzerland
Pfizer	Mack	1971	West Germany
Schering-Plough	AESCA	1972	Austria
SKF	Gremy-Longuet	1975	France
Revlon	Biotherax	1979	France
Rorer	Kyoritsu	1979	Japan
Schering-Plough	Kirby	1979	United Kingdom
Schering-Plough	Unita	1979	Argentina
Syntex	Laroche Navarron	1979	France
Upjohn	Duphar	1979	Spain
Schering-Plough	Unita	1979	Argentina
Abbott	Pravaz Recordati	1980	Brazil
Rorer	Radial Chemicals	1980	United Kingdom
Dow	Astra (local only)	1980	Brazil
Robins	Eurand	1981	Italy
Syntex	Sarva	1981	Belgium
Marion	Omnimedic	1982	Canada
Searle	Labs Adromaco	1983	Brazil
Searle	Labs Exa	1983	Italy
Rorer	Roedler	1983	West Germany
Smith Kline	Labs Dulcis	1984	West Germany
Colgate-Palmolive	Reckitt and Coleman (local only)	1984	Indonesia
Merck	Neophamed	1984	Italy
Rorer	Pharbil	1984	Belgium
Searle	Endopharm Arz.	1984	Belgium
Smith Kline	ISF	1984	Italy
Johnson and Johnson	Janssen-Leo	1985	Sweden

Foreign-U.S.

Parent	Target	Year	Parent Country
Beecham	Massingill	1971	United Kingdom
ICI	Atlas/Stuart	1971	United Kingdom
Bayer	Cutter	1973	West Germany
Montedison	Adria	1974	Italy
Boehringer-Ingelheim	Hexagon	1975	West Germany
Sanofi	Towne Paulson	1975	France
Sanofi	Generic Pharmaceuticals	1976	France
Sanofi	Western Research	1976	France
Hoechst	Calbiochem	1977	West Germany
Montedison	Warren-Teed	1977	Italy

Table 5-3. continued

Foreign-U.S. (cont.)

Parent	Target	Year	Parent Country
Boots	Riker	1977	United Kingdom
Glaxo	Meyer Labs	1977	United Kingdom
Nestlé	Alcon	1977	Switzerland
Ciba-Geigy	Alza	1977	Switzerland
Bayer	Miles Labs	1978	West Germany
Bayer	Dome Labs	1978	West Germany
Nestlé	Lafayette Pharmaceuticals	1978	Switzerland
Connaught	Swiftwater Bio.	1978	United Kingdom
Green Cross	Alpha Therapeutics	1978	Japan
Ciba-Geigy	Tutag	1978	Switzerland
Boehringer-Ingelheim	Philips Roxane	1979	West Germany
Schering	Berlex	1979	West Germany
Kali-Chemie	Purepac	1979	West Germany
Bayer	Cooper	1980	West Germany
Natterman	Lemmon	1981	
Beechman	J. B. Williams	1982	United Kingdom
Natterman	Federal Pharmaceuticals	1982	
Fisons	United Diagnostics	1984	United Kingdom

Sources:
1950–1979: U.S. Federal Trade Commission. 1981. *Statistical Report on Mergers and Acquisitions*, July.
1980–1985: Predicast. Various years. *F&S Index: United States.*

Patent Licensing. During the last two decades, almost one third of new drug introductions into the U.S. market have been sold under a patent license (see Table 5-4). For the majority of new drugs, the firm that discovers the drug and holds its patent, also develops and markets it. In other words, innovators vertically integrate downstream into distribution. These compounds sold by vertically integrated firms in the U.S. market are labeled "self-originated" in Table 5-4. Frequently, however, the firm marketing a drug is not the innovator, but rather has acquired domestic rights in exchange for compensation to the patent holder. Some of the best-selling drugs in the U.S. market are in fact sold under patent licenses (see Table 5-4). A minority of these patent licenses are made with U.S. innovators (including universities and government institutions); the majority of patent licensors are foreign multinational drug firms that lack extensive marketing presence in the United States. It should be noted that many of the drugs falling into the self-originated category in Table 5-4 are also foreign owned, but are sold through the established domestic subsidiaries of foreign multinationals (see Table 5-5).

Table 5-4. Patent Licensing, U.S. Domestic Pharmaceutical Market.

A. *Bestselling Licensed Drugs, 1980*

Drug	Marketer	Patenter	Sales ($ millions)	Sales Rank
Inderal	AHP (Ayerst)	ICI (U.K.)	179	3
Motrin	Upjohn	Boots (U.K.)	135	4
Hygroton	Revlon (USV)	Ciba-Geigy (Swiss)	50	26

B. *Licensed vs. Self-Oriented Drugs Sold by Domestic Firms, Stratified by Firm Size*

	1963-1968	1969-1974	1975-1980
% Self-originated			
Small	50.00	51.72	41.67
Middle-sized	55.56	26.67	52.63
Large	77.27	80.00	83.33
% Licensed from U.S. Sources			
Small	20.59	17.24	22.22
Middle-sized	0.00	26.67	21.05
Large	4.55	0.00	0.00
% Licensed from Foreign Sources			
Small	29.41	31.03	36.11
Middle-sized	44.44	46.67	26.32
Large	18.18	20.00	16.67

Source: National Academy of Sciences. 1983. *The Competitive Status of the U.S. Pharmaceutical Industry.* Washington, D.C.: National Academy Press. © 1983 by the National Academy of Sciences.

Marketing Agreements. Strategic linkages between marketing and innovative drug firms with considerations extending beyond a single product will be called marketing agreements for purposes of this chapter. Prior to the commercialization of biotechnology, these agreements were relatively rare, and they remain transitional in the sense that only quite infrequently do they last more than a decade (see Table 5-6). Nonetheless, such agreements may be quite successful for both parties. The innovative firm is capable of offering a stream of products, usually in a specific therapeutic area but lacks domestic marketing strength either because it is foreign, small (Alza), or nonpharmaceutical (Pennwalt, a chemical company). For many innovative firms (notably Syntex and Bayer), marketing agreements were a prelude to direct investment in the United States—Syntex by

Table 5-5.   Foreign Direct Investment and Marketing of Pharmaceuticals in
the United States.

A. *Bestselling Foreign Self-originated Drugs,*
   U.S. Pharmaceutical Market, 1980

Drug	Marketer and Patent Holder	Sales ($ millions)	Sales Rank
Valium	Roche (Swiss)	221	2
Lasix	Hoechst (FRG)	108	9
Persantine	Boehringher-Ingelheim (FRG)	59	20
Slow-K	Ciba-Geigy (Swiss)	52	24
Melloril	Sandoz (Swiss)	51	25
Zyloprim	Wellcome (U.K.)	49	28
Dalmine	Roche (Swiss)	47	30

B. *Foreign Direct Investment in the United States*

Firm (Nationality of Ownership)	Year
Hoffman LaRoche (FRG)	1905
Burroughs Wellcome (U.K.)	1906
Dorsey (Swiss, merged with Sandoz)	1908
CIBA (Swiss)	1920
Sandoz (Swiss)	1925
Geigy (Swiss, merged with CIBA)	1949
Astra (Sweden)	1949
Beecham (U.K.) (but see 1971 acquisition—Table 5-3)	1970
Boehringer-Ingelheim (FRG) (but see 1975 and 1979 acquisitions—Table 5-3)	1971
Fisons (U.K.) (but see 1984 acquisition—Table 5-3)	1973

Sources:
A. National Academy of Sciences. 1983. *The Competitive Status of the U.S. Pharmaceutical Industry.* Washington, D.C.: National Academy Press. © 1983 by the National Academy of Sciences.
B. Corporate inquiries.

relocation to Palo Alto in 1960, and Bayer through purchase of Miles Labs in 1978 (see Table 5-3).

Joint Ventures. Joint ventures require the creation of a free-standing subsidiary jointly owned by its parent firms. Each parent contributes significant assets to the child firm, but nonetheless grants at least some measure of autonomy to its executives. Joint ventures are rare in the pharmaceutical industry, do not have profound competitive implications for other firms, and are usually transitional in nature (see Table 5-7). Recent joint ventures have exclusively represented

Table 5-6. Marketing Agreements, U.S. Domestic Pharmaceutical Market,
1960-1984.

Year	Marketer	Developer	Description
1962	Lilly	Syntex (Mexico)	Sell full range of Syntex's drugs in U.S. market
1966	Schering-Plough	Bayer (FRG)	Sell full range of Bayer's drugs in U.S. market
1976	Merck	Alza (U.S.)	Worldwide marketing of Alza's cardiovascular and anti-inflammatory drugs
1977	Norwich-Eaton	Rhone-Poulenc (France)	Cross-marketing in U.S. and France of new drugs
1978	Searle	Knoll (FRG)	U.S. marketing of cardiovascular drugs
1978	Searle	Pennwalt (U.S.)	U.S. marketing of anti-inflammatory drugs
1980	Key	Mitsubishi (Japan)	Cross licensing of drugs for U.S. and Japanese markets
1982	Roche (Switzerland)	Glaxo (U.K.)	Zantac sold under Glaxo name by Roche in the United States
1982	Lederle	Toyoma (Japan)	U.S. marketing of cephalosporin products

a sharing of marketing expertise by established pharmaceutical firms
either with foreign pharmaceutical firms lacking a U.S. presence or
with small generic engineering firms.

Minority Interests. The acquisition of noncontrolling equity positions in competing firms is especially rare between pharmaceutical
firms but rather common between pharmaceutical firms and small
genetic engineering firms (see Table 5-8).

The goal of this study is to explain these patterns of multicorporate strategies, and to evaluate their competitive implications. Briefly, the fundamental perspective underwriting the analysis of this
chapter is that each firm represents a hierarchically administered

Table 5-7.   Joint Ventures, U.S. Domestic Pharmaceutical Market, 1960–1985.

Year	Child	Parent	Parent	Description
1974	Adria	Hercules	Montedison (Italy)	U.S. marketing of Montedison products
1976	Newport-Eaton	Norwich	Newport	Development and marketing of Newport drugs
1977	Takeda-Abbott	Abbott	Takeda (Japan)	U.S. marketing of Takeda products
1977	Eaton-Recoll	Norwich	Reckett and Coleman (U.K.)	U.S. marketing of Reckett and Coleman products
1977	Eaton–Merz	Norwich	Merz (FRG)	U.S. marketing of Merz contraceptive
1977	Cutter-Vitrium	Bayer[a] (FRG)	Kabi Vitrium (FRG)	U.S. marketing of Intralipid
1981	Otsuka-Merrell	Otsuka	DOW (Japan)	U.S. marketing of Otsuka products
1981	b	American Home Products	Sanofi (France)	U.S. marketing of Sanofi cardiovascular products
1982	b	Merck	Astra (Sweden)	U.S. marketing for selected product lines of Astra products[c]
1982	Lorex Pharmaceuticals	Searle	Nestlé (Switzerland)	U.S. and U.K. marketing of Synthelabo (subsidiary of Nestlé products
1983	d	Lilly	Yamonouchi	U.S. and Canadian marketing of Yamonouchi products
1983	Oncogen	Syntex	Genetic Systems	Genetic Engineering (anticancer drugs)

(Table 5-7. continued overleaf)

Table 5-7. continued

Year	Child	Parent	Parent	Description
1985	NARI	ICN	Eastman-Kodak	Genetic Engineering (antiviral and antidrugs)
1985	Tanabe-Marion	Marion	Tanabe (Japan)	U.S. and Canadian marketing of Tanabe products

a. Cutter is now a U.S. subsidiary of Bayer. For acquisition, see Table 5-3.
b. Separate sales office only, not a free-standing company.
c. Astra's long-standing U.S. subsidiary (of the same name) markets remaining product lines. For direct investment, see Table 5-5.
d. Initially only a marketing agreement; to develop over time into a joint venture.

portfolio of strategic operations; multifirm linkages thus occur between firms that need some but not all of the strategic operations of each other, with the specific form of linkages chosen to minimize all types of costs including transactions and adjustment costs. From this perspective, the antique Marshallian conception of the firm as merely a production function is wholly inadequate for analysis of the modern corporation, precisely because it assumes that transactions costs (underlying hierarchy) and adjustment costs (underlying strategic operations) are zero so that only production costs matter.

ADJUSTMENT COSTS AND STRATEGIC OPERATIONS

Adjustment costs are the excess of costs incurred by the expansion (or contraction) of operations. More technically, adjustment costs are present whenever the investment rate is a separate argument of the cost function, alongside simple levels of capital and other production inputs (with positive and increasing marginal costs of investment). When adjustment costs are important, established operations of a given size will have lower costs of operation than new operations functioning for the first time at this size. Gradually over time, the cost of new operations will fall toward those of established firms, but in the interim established firms will enjoy competitive advantage. The most prominent sources of adjustment costs are provided by experience effects (as in AT&T's difficult entry into the computer industry) and by brand loyalty (as in Procter & Gamble's difficult entry into the citrus juice industry).

Table 5-8.   Minority Interests, U.S. Domestic Pharmaceutical Industry,
1965-1985.

A. *Pharmaceutical Targets*

Year	Suitor	Target	Interest (%)
1976	Merck	Alza	3.5
1978	Rhone-Poulenc	Norwich-Eaton	20.3
1979	Mitsubishi	Key	10.0
1984	Eastman Kodak	ICN Pharmaceutical	5.0
1985	Cooper Labs	Rorer	5.0

B. *Genetic Engineering Targets*

Year	Suitor	Target	Interest (%)
1981	Green Cross (Japan)	Collaborative Research	1.1
1982	Baxter Travenol	Genetics Institute	NA
1983	Abbott	Boston Scientific	NA
1984	Abbott	Fuller Research	NA
1984	Fujisawa (Japan)	Lypho-Med	22.5
1984	Eastman Kodak	Viratek	10.0
1984	Warner-Lambert	Luther Medical Products	2.0
1984	Syntex	American BioNuclear	17.0
1985	Pharmacia (Sweden)	Biotechnology General	4.5
1985	Boehringer-Ingelheim (Germany)	Genentech	4.9
1985	Bristol-Myers	Oncogen (see Table 5-7)	33.0
1985	Johnson and Johnson	Thoratec Labs	10.0
1985	Eastman Kodak	Elan (Ireland)	10.0
1985	American Home Products	California Biotechnology	15.5
1985	Syntex	Genetic Systems	18.0
1985	Syntex	T-Cell Sciences	15.0

NA = Not available.

When the underlying conditions of technology and demand are
stable in an industry, the presence of significant adjustment costs
leads to a dynamic equilibrium in which all operations grow at roughly the same proportional rate, hence the relative sizes of operations
are constant over time. Such equilibria have been discussed in the
popular writings of the Boston Consulting Group and the technical
studies of several scholars.[1] The two key features of such dynamic
equilibria are that increases in demand are met predominantly by existing firms rather than new firms, and that the percentage rate of
firm growth is independent of firm size. The latter stylized fact on
proportional growth is called Gibrat's law. Under such dynamic

equilibria, ongoing operations become largely induplicable, hence scarce. For the purposes of this study, significant scarce functions of an industry will be called *strategic operations.*

Industrial disequilibria may of course alter the configuration of strategic operations. Unanticipated booms of demand may yield temporary windfall profits that sufficiently offset adjustment costs so that new firms enter and established firms expand, while unanticipated busts lead to exit and contraction (for example, recent restructurings in the petroleum industry). Major changes in technology or regulation may blur the boundaries between specific industries by radically lowering the adjustment costs so that firms traditionally outside an industry can successfully enter (for example, the entries of General Electric, Sears, and Ford into the financial services industry). Under these new circumstances, adjustment cost analysis predicts that entering firms will be those with the most closely related technical experience or consumer loyalty—in other words, those firms facing the smallest adjustment costs will take advantage of changes in demand, technology, or regulation to enter. Further, at the early phase of industry development, adjustment costs are relatively minor so that effectively no strategic operations exist. Thus, over the course of the industry life cycle, operations become progressively more costly to duplicate, hence progressively more strategic and the relative sizes of these operations rigidify.

Only rarely are more than one or two of the major operations of an industry (research, manufacturing, marketing, service) truly strategic. In some industries no operations at all are strategic so that entry into the industry and (more important) rapid mobility for corporate size and success is possible. In general for operations to be strategic they must entail strong customer loyalty or involve complex corporate tasks performed by large highly interdependent groups. In short, strategic operations are relatively induplicable, firm-specific assets.

To identify strategic operations in the U.S. pharmaceutical industry, it is useful to survey the historical development of the modern pharmaceutical firm, examining first innovation and second, marketing. As regards innovation, the drug industry before 1950 was profoundly different from that of today. New drug discoveries were infrequent and externally derived, and firms manufactured a limited number of unpatented products that were largely marketed without prescription directly to consumers. The mix of products available to consumers has been described by a pharmaceutical executive, Henry Gadsden of Merck, when he outlined the nature of the market in the 1930s:

You could count the basic medicines on the fingers of your two hands. Morphine, quinine, digitalis, insulin, codeine, aspirin, arsenicals, nitroglycerin, mercurials, and a few biologicals. Our own Sharp and Dohme catalog did not carry a single exclusive prescription medicine. We had a broad range of fluids, ointments, and extracts, as did other firms, but we placed heavy emphasis on biological medicines as well. Most of our products were sold without a prescription. And 43 percent of the prescription medicines were compounded by the pharmacist, as compared with 1 percent today. (Cited in Temin, 1980, p. 59.)

None of these products mentioned by Gadsden had resulted from research efforts of the pharmaceutical industry. Only a handful of drug discoveries from any source had been made by 1930 (principally salversan in 1908 for treatment of syphilis and insulin in 1922 for treatment of diabetes) and these discoveries were infrequent, unrelated, and unanticipated, and resulted from prolonged and tedious research. Nothing about these discoveries suggested a method of research or a mechanism of disease prevention that could be economically exploited for development of new pharmacological agents.

This noninnovative technological environment changed rapidly just before and during World War II, in a "therapeutic revolution" that transformed the industry. First, during the period 1930–1950, a series of natural products, particularly the vitamins and hormones, were discovered, developed, and commercialized. These discoveries led to the conquest of scurvy, pernicious anemia, beri-beri, and pellagra as well as significant endocrine therapies. Second, the foundation was laid for modern research in anti-infectives. The discovery of the therapeutic properties of sulfanilamide by I. G. Farbenindustrie in 1935 and of penicillin by Oxford scientists in 1940 indicated the possibilities for *systematic* research in finding new sulfa drugs and new antibiotics. Neither sulfanilamide nor penicillin were patentable at the time; sulfanilamide was a known discovery with belated demonstration of therapeutic properties; and the discoverer of penicillin declined to patent the drug, generously giving the discovery to the world. Nonetheless, the tremendous demand for anti-infective agents by allied military forces during wartime made the manufacture of these scarce substances a national priority. The U.S. government spent almost $3 million to subsidize wartime penicillin research and encouraged private construction of penicillin manufacturing plants by allowing accelerated depreciation. The returns from sales of these and other drugs were subject to wartime "excess profits" taxes, but at the conclusion of World War II, federal penicillin plants were sold to private firms at half cost.

The simultaneous demonstration of new technological opportunities and of potential profits combined to change the pharmaceutical industry dramatically. The next step necessary for the emergence of the industry in its modern form was a legal mechanism to allow commercial exploitation of the new technological opportunities for biological products. This step occurred with the 1948 decision of the U.S. Patent Office to grant a patent for streptomycin. A patent, of course, is a legal monopoly for seventeen years over commercial exploitation of a new discovery. During the period before expiration of the patent, the innovative firm may charge prices above manufacturing costs and thus recoup earlier research expenditures that led to the innovation. Rapidly, a new form of competition emerged in the pharamaceutical industry—competition through product development.

Under patent protection, firms that introduce new products are able in principle to earn large returns on their innovations. In practice, however, there are significant constraints on the abilities of firms to generate earnings through innovation. The first constraint is that it is generally technically possible for another firm to produce compounds of similar therapeutic action, though with different and hence also patentable molecular structure. The second constraint is, of course, that pharmaceutical innovation is a highly uncertain process that does not predictably yield therapeutically, let alone commercially, important products. Numerous firms have expended substantial funds for pharmaceutical R&D but failed to develop a commercially successful product. Table 5-9 tabulates U.S. sales in 1972 of all new medicinal chemical compounds introduced into the U.S. market in the mid-1960s. While a very few products enjoyed substantial commercial success, the vast majority of products were relative commercial failures and did not contribute significantly to defraying R&D costs. Given that most pharmaceutical innovations are commercially not very successful, it is clear that modern pharmaceutical firms depend crucially for positive cash flow on a small handful of successful innovations, as is demonstrated for the United States in Table 5-10. Failure to produce new products continuously to replace those that lose market share to imitation or on which patents expire would ultimately be devastating to the financial health of a pharmaceutical company. In short, competitive advantage in sales of patented drugs, by far the most financially lucrative segment of the modern pharmaceutical industry, depends crucially on the ability of the firm to produce occasional but significantly successful new products through industrial innovation.

Table 5-9. New Chemical Entities (NCEs) Introduced in the United States from 1962 to 1968, by 1972 Domestic Sales.

Sales ($000)	Number of Drugs
0-999	33
1,000-1,999	14
2,000-3,999	9
4,000-5,999	5
6,000-7,999	3
8,000-9,999	1
10,000-14,999	4
15,000-19,000	2
20,000-29,999	2
30,000-39,999	2
40,000-49,999	2
50,000-59,999	0
60,000-99,999	1
100,000+	1
Total	70

Source: Schwartzman, David. 1976. *Innovation in the Pharmaceutical Industry.* Baltimore: Johns Hopkins University Press. Reprinted by permission of the publisher.

In an extraordinarily profitable industry where research and development is central to competitive success, a traditional Marshallian analysis would predict extensive entry and expansion of R&D operations. Yet examination of Table 5-11 indicates that no significant new American firm entered the patented medicines sector of this industry from 1960 to 1980, and that during these two decades the relative levels of R&D expenditures among existing firms were remarkably stable. For example, the lowest five major firms in 1960 remained the lowest five in 1980, despite the tremendous profits of the larger firms. Merck and Lilly retained leadership of industry R&D through this period. The handful of significant anomalies to this rule of proportional growth are largely explained by diversifications beyond the pharmaceutical industry. For example, American Cyanamid was throughout this period predominantly a chemical company, so that its base of purely pharmaceutical R&D in 1960 was much smaller than that of total corporate R&D reported in Table 5-11. Similarly Johnson and Johnson during the late 1970s made significant acquisitions of medical technology firms, so that much of its reported explosive growth in R&D is due to this diversification out of ethical drugs.

Table 5-10. Proportion of Total Domestic U.S. Pharmaceutical Sales
Provided by Three Best Selling Products, Selected Pharmaceutical
Corporations, Selected Years (%).

	1970	1975	1979
Abbott	36	33	28
American Home Products			
Ayerst	64	74	84
Wyert	37	44	43
Bristol-Myers			
Bristol	69	46	28
Mead Johnson	40	38	37
Burroughs Wellcome	NA	56	51
Ciba	47	NA	55
Lederle	48	31	32
Lilly	46	60	43
Merck	35	44	44
Pfizer	52	65	65
Robins	43	45	46
Roche	80	80	70
Schering	42	48	40
Searle	45	49	44
Smith Kline	44	42	66
Squibb	28	31	23
Upjohn	47	50	56
Warner-Lambert			
Warner	53	NA	NA
Parke-Davis	25	27	22

NA = Not available.

Source: National Academy of Sciences. 1983. *The Competitive Status of the U.S. Pharmaceutical Industry.* Washington, D.C.: National Academy Press. © 1983 by the National Academy of Sciences.

This absence of entry and presence of proportional growth is caused by the extensive adjustment costs for R&D operations in this industry. Pharmaceutical R&D is highly complex and quite different from simple academic research, as can be seen from how few ethical drugs originate from government or university laboratories. For research that will lead to completely new drugs, the process begins with assemblage of a research team to consider a therapeutic problem, to review the literature, to synthesize and screen hundreds of chemical substances, and to select fewer than 10 percent of these substances for further investigation. The potential toxic and pathological properties of these compounds will be checked through biological (animal) research, and only about 2 percent of these tested compounds will exhibit desirable properties. Next, clinical (human)

Table 5-11. Research and Development Expenditures, Major U.S.
Pharmaceutical Firms ($ millions).

	1960	1965	1970	1975	1980
Merck	21	33	69	125	234
Lilly	20	31	61	104	201
American Cyanamid	33	41	46	67	142
Parke-Davis ⎱	12	14	54	74	102
Warner Lambert ⎰	5	13	Merger	Merger	Merger
American Home Products	18	28	50	56	101
Johnson and Johnson	16	25	42	97	233
Upjohn	18	23	42	78	147
Bristol-Myers ⎱	8	12	37	74	128
Mead Johnson ⎰	4	6	Merger	Merger	Merger
Pfizer	14	20	31	79	160
Smith Kline	14	23	31	52	135
Abbott	9	17	27	50	98
Schering ⎱	8	21	21	47	90
Plough ⎰	2	3	7	Merger	Merger
Squibb	8	14	28	49	77
Searle	7	11	22	56	71
Sterling	10	13	20	31	58
Baxter Tavenol	2	3	10	26	57
Syntex	1	4	11	23	55
Miles	5	6	11	21	Merger
Robins	1	3	6	11	27
Norwich-Eaton		4	8	14	21

Source: Corporate annual reports and corporate inquiries.

testing for efficacy and safety will be conducted, under extensive
and strict guidelines of government regulations. Only about 10 percent of those drugs that are initially included in clinical trials will
ultimately be brought to market. The total period from initiation of
basic research to commercial launch of a new product reached an
average of fourteen years at a cost of $100 million by 1980. Of every
new drug brought to market, on average over 5,000 basic compounds
were synthesized. The conduct of such research demands, in addition to patience and money, a broad range of expertise from commercial knowledge of the market, to advanced research techniques
in medicine, chemistry and biology, to an ever expanding battery
of government regulations. Also required is an extensive array of
contacts with university medical staffs that will conduct much of the
clinical testing so vital for regulatory approval and commercial
success of new drugs. Any effort to amass this formidable body of
expertise de novo will inevitably entail a lengthy and expensive

Table 5-12. Categories of Therapeutic Specialization, Major U.S. Pharmaceutical Firms, 1970s.

Therapeutic Category	Firms
Analgesics	Johnson and Johnson, Lilly, and Sterling
Antibiotics	Lilly, Beecham, Merck, Schering-Plough, Squibb, Pfizer, Bristol, and Upjohn
Cardiovascular agents	Merck, Ciba-Geigy, Ayerst, Squibb, Pfizer, U.S. Vitamin, Searle, Smith Kline, and Hoechst
Hormones	Merck, Schering-Plough, Upjohn, Syntex, and Squibb
Nonsteroidal anti-inflammatory agents	Merck, Upjohn, Lilly, Johnson and Johnson, Syntex, and Ciba-Geigy
Oral contraceptives	Ortho (Johnson and Johnson), Wyeth, Syntex, and Searle
Psychotherapeutics	Merck, Hoffman-LaRoche, Abbott, Squibb, Pfizer, Sandoz, and Ciba-Geigy
Respiratory agents	Key, Ciba-Geigy, Parke-Davis, and Breon
Vitamins (mostly OTC)	Lederle, Squibb, A. H. Robbins, Parke-Davis, and Upjohn

Source: Reprinted by permission of the publisher, from *Strategies from Vertical Integration* by Kathryn Rudie Harrigan (Lexington, Mass.: Lexington Books, D.C. Heath and Company, © 1983, D.C. Heath and Company).

period during which the productivity of the new research staff will be abnormally low. Indeed, so daunting are these adjustment costs that before 1980 almost all firms specialized in a few therapeutic areas and only slowly expand into new areas or abandon old ones (see Table 5-12).

Because pharmaceutical R&D activities are relatively induplicable in dynamic equilibrium for this industry and because these activities contribute vitally to the competitive position of firms in this industry, these activities are strategic operations as defined by this study. If a pharmaceutical firm neither internally owns such strategic operations, nor is linked by multifirm agreements to such operations of another firm, its abilities to compete in the patented medicines sector of ethical drug markets are extremely limited.

A second major category of pharmaceutical strategic operations lies in the marketing of new drugs. U.S. pharmaceutical firms spend about as much to market a new drug as to discover and develop it. These enormous marketing expenditures are caused by the almost unique conditions for sales of ethical drugs. The immediate "consumer" of ethical drugs is of course a doctor, though the patient pays for and directly consumes the product. Three features characterize the environment in which doctors select products for their patients: (1) doctors have an extremely high value of time and thus resist search for alternatives beyond satisfactory therapies, (2) doctors have little price resistance, as they do not pay for the product, and (3) doctors are highly concerned with product quality, as quality is a life-and-death matter for their patients. These three features lead to an extremely high degree of brand loyalty to successful products, and to first mover advantages, whereby the first successful product into a new therapeutic category seizes and maintains high market share regardless of the price of subsequent entrants. These market features radically skew the returns to innovation so that a handful of first movers remain highly successful while most products are relative failures (see again Table 5-9). These features also place a strong premium on prompt, aggressive rollout of new products, and on a high professional quality of marketing staff that retain the confidence of the thousands of individual doctors who prescribe drug products.

In short the basic characteristics of consumer demand make marketing activities a strategic operation for the pharmaceutical industry. Heavy brand and firm loyalty by a dispersed population of consumers makes marketing both critical and relatively induplicable for established drug firms. Indeed, the adjustment costs of establishing pharmaceutical marketing activities are sufficiently strong that most drug firms also specialize their sales efforts in specific therapeutic categories, though this specialization is far less rigid for marketing than for research. Thus firms that neither own internal marketing staffs nor have access through multifirm linkages to other established marketing staffs have dim competitive prospects in the U.S. market.

Three major trends have affected the configuration of strategic operations in the pharmaceutical industry since 1950: (1) the decline of small and medium-sized research operations, (2) the rise of foreign research operations, and (3) the diversification out of pharmaceuticals by U.S. drug firms. The first of these trends dates from 1962 and is indicative of a radical increase in economies of scale for drug research and development. The source of these changing economies is clearly the greatly increased complexity, expense, delay, and regulation of drug development; the average cost per newly introduced drug has risen from $2 million to $100 million since 1960, while the delay from synthesis to marketing has increased from two to fourteen years. The smallest innovative firms ceased self-origination of new drugs by 1962, after Congressional adoption of Amendments to the U.S. Food, Drug, and Cosmetic Act. In the ensuing years, economies of scale continued to mount so that by 1980, the minimum efficient scale of research operations was on the order of $100 million annual expenditures. By this time even midsized pharmaceutical operations were at some competitive disadvantage (compare Table 5-11).

The second pronounced trend in strategic operations has been the rise of multinational drug firms. At the outset of the 1950s, world pharmaceutical competition remained largely national in scope. Economic linkages among the various national pharmaceutical industries were largely confined to trade, and even then were relatively unimportant. Imports amounted to less than 10 percent of domestic consumption in the major industrial nations, with the exception of Switzerland. Beginning in the early 1950s, U.S. and Swiss firms began substantial multinational operations, and these firms largely dominated world markets. These firms were joined in the 1960s by non-Swiss European firms that significantly expanded their research efforts and drug discoveries. The resulting pattern of multinational sales is displayed in Table 5-13.

The most distinctive feature in Table 5-13 is the absence in 1973 of Japanese and non-Swiss European firms from the lucrative U.S. market. This absence is due to the presence of economies of scale in marketing and the limited breadth of product lines for most such firms before 1970. A marketing operation represents a substantial overhead expense. American and Swiss drug firms that enjoyed a surge of successful new patented drugs in the 1950s could afford to spread these overheads over the several drugs distributed by their firms, making the marketing cost per drug affordable. Other firms, recovering from the devastation of World War II, faced the significant adjustment costs of creating research operations almost from nothing. As adjustment cost analysis would predict, the firms that were most successful in pharmaceutical research were those with previous experience in the chemical industry. Thus the German firms, with their illustrious pre-World War II tradition of chemical innovation and production, recovered most quickly, while the Japanese, lacking such a tradition, fared least well. It is a prominent measure of just how strong adjustment costs are in this industry that it took fully three decades for the West German chemical firms to enter the U.S. pharmaceutical market in even moderate strength, and that after four decades Japanese pharmaceutical firms are still struggling to achieve large-scale innovation despite their enormous, lucrative, and protected domestic market.

A third trend in strategic operations for this industry has been diversification beyond pharmaceuticals (in other words, increasing

Table 5-13. Multinational Sales, World Pharmaceutical Industry, 1973.

Nationality (Ownership)	United States	Japan	Germany	France	Italy	Spain	United Kingdom	Brazil	Mexico	Canada
United States	*	12.2	12.6	17.4	15.8	14.4	38.4	35.4	49.6	63.4
Japan	—	*	—	—	—	—	—	—	0.1	—
West Germany	1.0	4.6	*	4.5	7.6	10.4	7.1	13.3	7.4	2.0
France	—	0.3	1.9	*	3.7	3.1	4.6	3.4	3.5	2.2
Italy	—	—	0.2	0.1	*	2.7	0.1	4.6	2.7	—
Switzerland	12.6	3.3	9.3	9.2	10.9	8.9	10.7	10.3	9.4	11.1
United Kingdom	2.2	2.3	1.8	3.5	5.1	1.2	*	1.9	3.5	4.9
Netherlands	0.1	0.4	1.8	1.2	0.3	0.8	1.7	1.1	1.3	—
Sweden	0.1	0.2	0.4	0.3	—	—	0.7	0.3	0.2	0.3
Other foreign	—	0.1	1.7	1.6	1.1	2.1	0.4	—	—	0.8
Total foreign	16.0	23.4	29.7	37.8	44.5	43.6	63.7	70.3	77.7	84.7
Local ownership	84.0	76.6	70.3	62.2	55.5	65.4	36.3	29.7	22.3	15.3
Total	100.0%	100.0%	100.0%	100.0%	100.0%	100.0%	100.0%	100.0%	100.0%	100.0%

Note: Asterisk takes place of local percentages in top half of table. Local percentages are given separately in the bottom half as "local ownership."
Source: James, Barrie. 1977. *The Future of the Multinational Pharmaceutical Industry to 1990.* New York: John Wiley. Reprinted by permission of Associated Business Press, 76 Shoe Lane, London EC4A 3JB.

the number of different strategic operations controlled by a single firm). A listing of the largest U.S. owned drug firms and the extent of diversification is contained in Table 5–14. In general, diversifications, which have steadily increased over time, have focused on industries that are synergistically related to ethical drugs either through marketing or technology, including medical devices, hospital supplies and services, cosmetics, agricultural chemicals, and environmental control. In this diversification, American owned pharmaceutical firms are becoming more like their major foreign owned counterparts, many of which are divisions of very large parent companies (such as Hoechst, Bayer, ICI, Sanofi).

TRANSACTIONS COSTS AND HIERARCHY

One of the most significant developments in economics during the last several decades has been the discovered importance of transactions costs.[2] Traditional Marshallian microeconomics effectively had no explanation for the existence of even simple corporate structures, much less for more complex multicorporate linkages such as joint ventures. From the traditional perspective, markets fully mediate between consumer demand and production supply, so that corporate forms are all but irrelevant. While the Marshallian paradigm may well have been useful for an agricultural economy with its commodity markets, it is in and of itself inadequate for understanding the modern economy. Principal contributors to our recognition of the significance of transactions costs have been Arrow, Demsetz, and Williamson.

Transactions costs are the expenses of conducting business and include

Search costs.	The time needed to identify purchase or sales options, and to verify price and specifications
Monitoring costs.	The time and needed to supervise performance, to diagnose errors, and to remedy such errors
Quality costs.	The risk and expense of poor quality performance
Extortion costs.	The risk and expense of excessive price for buyers or insufficient price for sellers

As anyone who has had an automobile repaired can attest, transactions costs are quite significant in many markets and can rival production costs in magnitude.

Table 5-14. The U.S. Pharmaceutical Industry: Lines of Business, 1978.

Company	Worldwide 1978 Sales ($ millions)	Percentage Ethical Pharmaceuticals	Percentage Ethical and Proprietary Products	Percentage Human Health
1. Johnson & Johnson	3,497	18	62	91
2. American Home Products	3,277	<39 inc/vet. prod. and med. instr.	53	53
3. Warner-Lambert	2,878	<34 inc/diagnostics and surg. prod.	57	57
4. American Cyanamid	2,746	<20 inc/med. equip.	<20	20
5. Bristol-Myers	2,450	<34 inc/surg./dent. products	57	57
6. Pfizer, Inc.	2,362	42	>42	>50
7. Merck & Co., Inc.	1,981	69	69	69
8. Eli Lilly	1,852	49	49	57
9. Squibb Corp.	1,516	<44 inc/ethical OTC	44 inc/diagnostics and vet. products	48
10. Revlon, Inc.	1,452	18	>18	35
11. Abbott Labs	1,445	29	47 inc/nutritionals	89 inc/hosp. solutions
12. Upjohn Co.	1,329	<52 inc/ethical OTC	52	65
13. Sterling Drug	1,315	13 exc/foreign sales	25 exc/foreign sales	25 exc/foreign sales
14. Smith Kline Corp.	1,112	60	71	79
15. Schering-Plough	1,082	<64 inc/ethical OTC	64	64
16. Richardson-Merrell	945	<25 inc/ethical OTC	<89	<89
17. G. D. Searle	848	49	53	89
18. Syntex Corp.	381	73	73	>73
19. A. H. Robins	357	<69 inc/ethical OTC	69	69
20. Rorer Group	220	77 inc/ethical OTC	77	100

The arguments developed by transaction cost theorists consist of a general principle and several subsidiary theorems. The general principle is that corporate structures will be chosen to minimize the *sum* of production, adjustment, and transactions costs. To consider the theorems, note that various possible corporate structures may be arrayed along a one-dimensional continuum of *hierarchy* ranging from most decentralized (spot markets) to most centralized (unidivisional bureaucratic decisions). Between these extremes are intermediate structures such as long-term contracts, franchises, joint ventures, and multidivisional firms. The virtues of executing business through the extreme of spot market transactions are well known, and indeed these virtues are the empirical foundation of the Marshallian perspective. But there are also vices to spot markets, namely transactions costs. The modern perspective thus specifies that business will be conducted in spot markets *unless* specific industry features make the transactions costs of using these markets overly high. The theorems developed by the transaction cost theorists are thus each associated with a specific market feature that when present propels organizational form toward greater centralization of bureaucratic control. Two of the most prominent of these theorems are as follows.

Sunk Cost. Many transactions require one party to invest in assets that are useful only for this specific transaction. For example, the marketer of a new drug may build specific manufacturing facilities, will train sales staff as to specific medical properties, will heavily advertise the new drug, and will conduct the costly clinical trials necessary for regulatory approval. These expenses, once made, cannot be recouped except through sales of the specific drug, and hence are sunk costs. The presence of sunk cost in any transaction exposes the party making them to open extortion in spot markets. For example, marketers making the investments listed above could subsequently find themselves charged royalties by innovators several times larger than initially promised, so as to render worthless their marketing investments. While long-term contracts may well protect marketers, these contracts can potentially be breached, exposing the marketer to the costs of enforcement. The first theorem then is that as sunk costs become more significant in transactions, the appropriate structure for execution of these transactions moves away from markets toward hierarchy.

Uncertainty. The launch of new drugs is marked by the wide range of possible revenue outcomes (see again Table 5–9). This significant risk persists even after launch, as initially promising therapies may develop unexpected side effects and be withdrawn from the market. The transactions between marketers and innovators in the drug industry are thus characterized by significant uncertainty. The use of a predetermined fee for transfer of technology between innovator and marketer is thus difficult to set and raises the likely prospect of breach of contract. The more common use of royalties avoids these problems, but the high costs of innovation and high expected short-term profits force royalty rates to be large in this industry. For successful ethical drugs, the profit markup amounts to as much as 80 percent of sales, compared to less than 5 percent for the simple remedies distributed before the therapeutic revolution of World War II. Note that high royalty rates significantly distort the incentives of marketers to sell new drugs, so that there is an inevitable tradeoff between generation of maximal profits from sales of new drugs and transfer of these profits to the innovator. Complete transfer to the innovator strips the marketer of any incentive to sell. The second theorem then is that as uncertainty surrounding transactions increases, the desirability of conducting these transactions through markets decreases.

CORPORATE STRUCTURES

The most striking feature of corporate structures in the modern pharmaceutical industry is the extensive vertical integration between innovation, manufacture, and marketing of new drugs. All of the larger U.S. firms own internal research, manufacture, and sales operations, and over two-thirds of U.S. new drug sales are made through completely integrated transactions (exclusive of retail; see again Table 5-4). This vertical integration extends across national boundaries with the largest pharmaceutical firms, both U.S. and foreign, owning significant multinational subsidiaries that perform local manufacture and sales. Such integration is a comparatively recent phenomenon, arising with the emergence of the modern industry after 1950. For example, Pfizer and Bristol-Myers integrated forward into marketing (by direct investment) only with the introduction of their proprietary tetracycline derivatives in the early 1950s. Merck integrated forward only in 1953 with the acquisition of Sharp and Dome in that year.

Using the transactions cost theorems presented above, it is straightforward to explain this extensive vertical integration. The tremendous uncertainty and high value added of pharmaceutical sales makes it difficult to rely on decentralized mechanisms for distribution of ethical drugs. The corporate structures that result are thus a trade-

Table 5-15. Adjustment Costs and Strategies for Commercialization Innovations.

Number of Innovations	Magnitude of Adjustment Costs			
	None	Moderate	High/Match Available	High/Match Unavailable
Few	License	License	License	License
Some	Direct Investment	Marketing Agreement	Acquisition	Marketing Agreement
Many	Direct Investment	Marketing Agreement	Acquisition	Joint Venture

off between the high transactions cost of nonintegrated operations and the high production (marketing, really) cost of small-scale distribution. Firms discovering a steady stream of new drugs will integrate forward, while firms that expect to sell only a handful of drugs in the United States over time will suffer the high transactions costs of more decentralized distribution in order to economize on the overhead of a domestic marketing operation (see Table 5-15). Thus smaller foreign firms and nonprofit U.S. sources (such as universities) will license their innovations to established U.S. distributors rather than set up their own distribution operations.

In the absence of adjustment costs, innovators with many new drugs would integrate forward by direct investment. Indeed, in the 1950s, those foreign firms ready and able to enter the U.S. market did so entirely through direct investment (see Table 5-5B). At that time, U.S. innovators were themselves integrating forward into marketing and thus any adjustment cost penalties were few or nonexistent. By the 1960s experience effects and customer loyalty in marketing had grown sufficiently to make foreign direct in U.S. marketing operations difficult, but not inconceivable. While some firms did make direct investments during these years, the last entry of this form occurred in 1973.

Foreign firms with a sufficiently broad product line to merit a U.S. marketing subsidiary faced then three alternatives to direct investment: marketing agreement with, acquisition of, or joint venture with an established U.S. marketing operation (again, see Table 5-15). Marketing agreements were used somewhat in the 1960s as an interim arrangement pending expansion of direct investments. The advantage of these agreements arose from the incentives they provide the marketer. As discussed before, both research and marketing experience effects in pharmaceuticals tend to be specific to therapeutic category. Innovators thus expect the bulk of their new drug discoveries to fall within certain predictable categories and wish their marketer to develop complementary expertise in those categories. Because however this expertise represents a sunk cost for the marketer, there are high transactions costs to inducing the marketer to make these investments on a license-by-license basis. The disadvantage of marketing agreements is of course that they transfer very little in the way of experience effects or customer loyalty to innovating firms. In the 1960s adjustment costs were sufficiently moderate that major firms with some marketing expertise could reasonably make other arrangements to acquire proficiency in U.S. marketing. Firms of this type include Syntex (relocating from Mexico City to Palo Alto) and Bayer (one of the largest chemical and pharmaceutical companies in the world). In the 1980s adjustment costs were sufficiently large that firms with even moderate product lines were unlikely ever to successfully establish their own U.S. marketing operations. For these late-entering firms (see Table 5-6), marketing agreements represented a reasonable and final compromise between the high transactions costs of single licenses and the high adjustment costs of direct investment.

A second alternative to direct investment for foreign firms with broad product lines is acquisition of a local firm. It is important to remember that firms are a portfolio of strategic operations, but that foreign drug firms appropriately sought only a single operation, namely U.S. domestic marketing of ethical drugs. In the early 1960s successful pharmaceutical firms consisted of both research and marketing functions, with even smaller drug houses successful at both functions. Because foreign drug firms did not need these (largely incompatible) research operations and because the research operations could not be spun off as viable independent entities, acquisition of U.S. firms initially represented an expensive method of building U.S. marketing operations. By 1970 however, as discussed earlier, an onslaught of regulation and technical change had drastically reduced the viability of small research operations, just at a time that non-Swiss European drug firms achieved critical mass in their research operations. The newly weakened U.S. firms made excellent matches for the Europeans, with their robust (if small) marketing operations needing sources of new drugs and their residual research operations adaptable for performing final tests required by the FDA for U.S. launch. As a consequence a torrid wave of European acquisitions of small U.S. drug firms occurred after 1970 (partly counterbalanced by U.S. acquisition of small drug firms abroad). By the end of the

1970s, with the pool of smaller U.S. drug firms nearly depleted, the pace of acquisition slowed.

A third and most recent alternative to direct investment is provided by joint ventures. These free-standing units are in the pharmaceutical industry exclusively marketing operations, both in the United States and abroad. The pattern in the United States is for domestic provision of established expertise in development and marketing with foreign provision of patent licenses. These multifirm linkages are transitional with the foreign innovator ultimately gaining direct control of the joint venture child. For example, the 1974 U.S. joint venture between Hercules and Montedison was in 1983 folded into Montedison's worldwide health operations and spun off as a new company, Erbamont, with Hercules owning 15 percent equity in the new firm. All three Norwich-Eaton joint ventures were dissolved by 1981; Newport-Eaton never registered sales; Reckett and Coleman fell back to an untargeted strategy of licensing. Abroad, at least some joint ventures are more balanced and durable.

Explanation for the recent emergence of joint ventures in the pharmaceutical industry is straightforward. By the 1970s, adjustment costs for marketing operations had grown to be large; the acquisition pool of small U.S. marketing operations suitable for development and distribution of major ethical drugs had been depleted; and most mid-sized U.S. firms had significantly diversified beyond simple ethical drugs. For example, Abbott by 1980 had significant business in nutritional products while Searle by the early 1980s drew a significant share of its sales from artificial sweeteners. High adjustment costs thus made direct investment prohibitively expensive and marketing agreements futile (as a substitute for investment), while high transactions costs made foreign acquisition and administration of diversified medium-sized firms unattractive. Despite the complexities of balancing interests among parents and child in joint ventures, foreign pharmaceutical firms, especially Japanese firms developing significant product lines only in the 1980s, were forced into these ventures as a last resort.

The arguments above (summarized in Table 5-15) have outlined the principal multifirm strategies for domestic marketing of new patented drugs in the United States. A remaining multifirm strategy is minority equity interest by one pharmaceutical firm in a second firm (see panel A of Table 5-8). Examination of Table 5-8 indicates that this strategy is rare, recent, and (with the sole exception of the Cooper-Rorer linkage) practiced by an innovative multinational firm acquiring a stake in a domestic marketing firm. Comparison of Tables 5-6 and 5-7 with Table 5-8 indicates that (again with the exception of the Cooper-Rorer link) minority interests in purely pharmaceutical targets are pursued in tandem with marketing agreements or marketing joint ventures. The minority interest is thus in part an asset play. The strategic linkage by the marketing firm to discoveries of the innovative firm increases the asset value of the marketing firm, and by acquiring an equity stake in the marketing firm, the innovator may further appropriate returns from its new drug discoveries. The minority interest is also in part a mechanism of control, to ensure the correct execution of the marketing agreement or joint venture from the perspective of the innovator.

All of these multifirm strategies have linked the research operations of one firm with the marketing operations of a second firm. Conspicuous by their absence are linkages purely in research, with the exception of those in genetic engineering—a handful of recent joint ventures (Table 5-7) and a dozen or so minority interests (Table 5-8). In explanation of the patterns of pharmaceutical multifirm strategies, the nonexistence of pure-research multifirm strategies is as important as the actual research-marketing linkages documented in Tables 5-3 through 5-8.

There would appear two critical reasons for the nonexistence of research multifirm strategies apart from those in genetic engineering. First, pharmaceutical research is primarily conducted for new products, not new processes. The returns from these new products are diminished if they are simultaneously marketed by two or more firms in the same geographic territory. At minimum, the overhead costs of duplicative marketing, advertising, and management efforts would provide a significant offset to rents. At worst, competition between the two different brand names of the same drug would induce price competition and weaken brand loyalty, with the latter facilitating ultimate generic drug competition. Thus, a research joint venture (say) between two marketing operations would be an inefficient means for either marketing operation to provide itself with new products. The extreme uncertainty and high variability of new pharmaceutical products would make an alternate one-for-you, one-for-me sharing of research joing venture outputs impractical and contentious. Further, even if both marketing operations did choose to simultaneously market new drugs from a research joint venture, the significant first mover advantages that accrue to the first marketer of equivalent drugs would make an equal split of the market highly unlikely. The pressures on each marketer to preempt the other through early introduction would further undermine efficacious appropriation of possible returns from any innovations.

A second reason for the nonexistence of traditional pharmaceutical pure-research multifirm strategies outside of genetic engineering is the strength of adjustment costs for strategic operations in research. As discussed at length earlier, pharmaceutical innovation marshals a broad yet interrelated array of highly technical skills in scientific, legal, and managerial areas. Because any one of these skills in isolation is not especially useful, the returns to these skills accrue to the firm as a whole, not to isolated individuals or even isolated departments. Further, the major multinational pharmaceutical firms have developed expertise in all of these areas for over three decades, amassing formidable experience effects in each area. Thus, if two marketing operations were to jointly begin or acquire a research operation, each marketing operation would have considerable difficulty transferring fragments of the research operation to its own corporate domain. An amoebalike splitting of the research operation would be especially implausible. Yet, as discussed at length at the outset of this section, vertical linkage between research and marketing operations is critical for successful appropriation of the returns to innovation in the pharmaceutical industry (and indeed most high-tech industries). At some point in time, the joint research operation would need to be vertically merged with one (and only one) of the marketing operations, and this ultimate prospect provides strong disincentives to initiate the research joint venture in the first place.

While these two reasons provide a powerful damper on purely research multifirm strategies among traditional pharmaceutical firms, it is precisely the diminished force of these two reasons that enables such strategies in genetic engineering (again, see Table 5-7 and panel B of Table 5-8). Genetic engineering, of course, leads to process innovations for the discovery of new products. The simultaneous exploitation of these new processes by two or more firms may actually increase the rents flowing from the discovery, as the new process may be applied to disparate therapeutic areas by each firm. This augmentation of rents is in sharp contrast to the diminution of rents caused by simultaneous marketing of a new product by two or more firms. Additionally, genetic engineering affects only one small part of the entire innovative process for new drugs. Thus technology transfers from one firm to another in genetic engineering are far more easily arranged than for the process of pharmaceutical innovation as a whole. Finally, genetic engineering is a very young technology and experience effects are not yet large. Thus, firms attempting to acquire the new technology from a joint venture child or minority interest will pay only a small adjustment cost penalty in effecting the transfer, relative to the somewhat more established genetic engineering operations of other firms. In summation, research joint ventures and minority interests in research firms for genetic engineering face few of the barriers that confront such multifirm strategies in traditional pharmaceutical research.

Examination of Table 5–8 demonstrates that the typical suitors for small, genetic engineering interests are midsized firms, including both U.S. owned pharmaceutical firms (Abbott, Baxter, Bristol-Myers, Syntex; compare Table 5–11) and foreign owned pharmaceutical firms (Boehringer-Ingelheim, Fujisawa, Green Cross, Pharmacia) or U.S. owned firms outside the pharmaceutical industry (Eastman Kodak) seeking entrance to the industry via this new technology. Thus it is firms weak in competitive advantage in pharmaceutical research that resort to these multifirm strategies.

PUBLIC POLICY

Multifirm strategies pursued in the U.S. pharmaceutical industry are the results of corporate efforts to minimize the production, adjustment, and transactions costs of marketing new drugs. As such, given the existing environment for the regulation and diffusion of pharmaceutical innovation, these strategies are efficiently conducted and should be neither actively promoted or inhibited by public policy. The vast majority of multifirm strategies in this industry represent a transfer of marketing/regulatory expertise from firms with significant U.S. marketing experience to innovators of new drugs seeking to sell their products in the United States. The upshot of these transfers of technology is a wider range of new therapies distributed by a wider range of competitors.

Only in the area of genetic engineering are transfers among firms of fundamental research technologies affected. Yet, here the research efforts of the largest U.S. owned pharmaceutical firms in the genetic engineering area are not currently exposed to multifirm strategies. The most common strategic linkage in genetic engineering is between a small, start-up research firm and a significantly larger pharmaceutical firm combining marketing and traditional research operations. The smaller firm shares process innovations and perhaps licenses products while the larger firm provides financial support and development/marketing expertise. Recently, sensationalist reports in the press have labeled these exchanges "giveaways" of American technology to foreign firms. While the research conducted by these start-up firms is genuinely exciting, it should nonetheless be stressed how implausible this characterization is. The U.S.-foreign multifirm strategies in genetic engineering are quite limited; the U.S. genetic engineering firms joined in these strategies are generally small, start-up operations; and only a fraction of the total process of pharmaceutical innovation (the discovery phase) is affected. Again, current multifirm strategies in and of themselves pose few or no special issues of public policy.

NOTES

1. The clearest theoretical exposition of industry equilibria under adjustment costs is Lucas (1967). While many other economists have examined adjustment costs, their theoretical expositions have almost always considered a single firm in isolation. Lucas (1978) is a related study.

   Lucas has stressed the similarity of his work in this area and that of Herbert Simon, for example (Simon and Bonini 1958). Simon has always emphasized the stochastic features of his models, but it is his imposition of Gibrat's law of proportional growth that generates the log-normal size distributions reported in his work.

   Recently, David Evans (1987) and Brownwyn Hall (1987) have empirically examined Gibrat's law. Their findings are that Gibrat's law is a reasonable approximation of corporate growth rates for larger firms such as those in the patented medicines sector of the pharmaceutical industry examined in this study. They also find, however, that Gibrat's law is violated over the full range of firms in an industry, because the smallest, fringe firms have slightly faster though more volatile growth rates than do large firms.

2. The seminal study of transactions cost as a basis for corporate organization was Coase (1937). Fundamental contributions to theory were provided by Arrow (1974) and Williamson (1975), with important applications given by Chandler (1962, 1977). A survey of the field is provided by Williamson (1981). Specific applications of the transaction cost paradign to industrial innovation are provided by Arrow (1962), Langlois (1987), and Teece (1986a, 1986b).

REFERENCES

Arrow, Kenneth. 1962. "Economic Welfare and the Allocation of Resources to Invention." In National Bureau of Economic Research, ed., *The Rate and Direction of Inventive Activity: Economic and Social Factors.* Princeton: Princeton University Press.

_____ . 1974. *The Limits of Organization.* New York: Norton.

Chandler, Alfred. 1962. *Strategy and Structure: Chapters in the History of Industrial Enterprise.* Cambridge, Mass.: MIT Press.

_____ . 1977. *The Visible Hand: The Managerial Revolution in American Business.* Cambridge, Mass.: Belknap Press.

Coase, Ronald. 1937 "The Nature of the Firm." *Economica.*

Evans, David. 1987. "The Relationship Between Firm Growth, Size, and Age: Estimates for 100 Manufacturing Industries." *Journal of Industrial Economics* (June).

Hall, Brownwyn. 1987. "The Relationship Between Firm Size and Firm Growth in the U.S. Manufacturing Sector." *Journal of Industrial Economics* (June).

Langlois, Richard. 1987. "Disequilibria, Path Dependence, and Organizational Form." Working paper, University of Connecticut.

Lucas, Robert. 1967. "Adjustment Costs and the Theory of Supply." *Journal of Political Economy* (August).

_____. 1978. "On the Size Distribution of Business Firms." *Bell Journal of Economics* (Autumn).

Simon, Herbert, and Charles Bonini. 1958. "The Size Distribution of Firms." *American Economic Review*.

Teece, David. 1986a. "Firm Boundaries, Technological Innovation, and Strategic Management." In. L. G. Thomas, ed., *The Economics of Strategic Planning: Essays in Honor of Joel Dean*. Lexington, Mass.: Lexington Books.

_____. 1986b. "Profiting from Technological Innovation: Implications for Integration, Collaboration, Licensing, and Public Policy." *Research Policy* (December).

Temin, Peter. 1980. *Taking Your Medicine: Drug Regulation in the United States*. Cambridge, Mass.: Harvard University Press.

Thomas, Lacy Glenn. 1983. *The Competitive Status of the US Pharmaceutical Industry: The Influences of Technology in Determining International Competitive Advantage*. Washington, DC: National Academy Press.

Williamson, Oliver. 1975. *Markets and Hierarchies: Analysis and Antitrust Implications: A study in the Economics of Internal Organization*. New York: Free Press.

_____. 1981. "The Modern Corporation: Origins, Evolution, Attributes." *Journal of Economic Literature* (December).

6 JOINT VENTURES AND COLLABORATION IN THE BIOTECHNOLOGY INDUSTRY

Gary P. Pisano, Weijian Shan, and David J. Teece

Biotechnology is not a well-defined industry. It is a set of technologies that have actual and potential applications across a wide range of industries, including pharmaceuticals, disagnostic products, animal and plant agriculture, specialty chemicals, food, industrial processes, energy, and waste treatment. A nascent biotechnology industry has emerged in the form of the approximately 300 new ventures that have been launched since 1976. Various forms of collaboration between these genetic engineering specialists and established firms that will apply the new technologies have pervaded the development and commercialization of biotechnology.

This chapter explores several aspects of collaborative innovation in biotechnology: What are the overall characteristics of and motivation for collaboration in the commercial development of biotechnology? Why is collaboration generally struck between small biotechnology start-ups and established firms from downstream sectors? What factors affect the incidence of collaborative innovation relative to alternative modes? What are the common structural characteristics of these collaborations? And what role will collaboration play, relative to the alternatives, in shaping the emerging industry structure?

The analysis is organized around the conceptual framework developed in Teece (1986) and used in Chapter 2 of this volume to

This chapter draws in part on the doctoral thesis of Gary Pisano and, to a lesser extent, on that of Weijian Shan (see references). We would like to thank David Mowery for helpful comments on earlier versions of this chapter. This research was supported in part by NSF Grant No. SRS–8410556.

examine patterns of collaboration in the telecommunications equipment industry. Unlike other chapters in this volume, this chapter focuses on collaboration per se, rather than on U.S.-foreign alliances. We will, however, examine the subset of international alliances in the context of public policy issues related to international competition. The main source of data used throughout the analysis is a proprietary database compiled by a leading biotechnology firm in the San Francisco bay area.[1]

OVERVIEW OF BIOTECHNOLOGY: THE TECHNOLOGY AND ITS COMMERCIAL DEVELOPMENT[2]

Biotechnology can be broadly defined as the use of biological organisms or biological processes in some industrial or therapeutic application. By this definition, biotechnology is not new. It has been used since the Stone Age when man first began to use selective animal breeding and yeasts, bacteria, enzymes, and fungi in fermentation (Sharp, 1985, p. 11). Beginning in the 1930s, biotechnological innovation focused on improving the efficiency of fermentation through the development of enzyme catalysts and the selective use of mutant and selected strains of bacteria and fungi. These biotechnological innovations, which are sometimes referred to as second generation biotechnology, were applied to the production of pharmaceuticals (mostly antibiotics) and other fermentation products such as beer.

Our analysis examines the most recent phase of biotechnology, sometimes referred to as "the new biotechnology" (see, for example, Sharp, 1985). This regime departs from earlier biotechnology in its focus on engineering specific changes in the genetic structure of microorganisms. The foundation for the new biotechnology was laid by Watson and Crick's 1956 discovery of the double helix structure of DNA and by other research in molecular biology and biochemistry during the 1960s. Two discoveries with the greatest commercial potential were made during the 1970s. In 1973 Herbert Boyer and Stanley Cohen discovered a technique for removing specific genes from one organism and implanting them into the DNA structure of another. This technique, which has since become a basic tool of biotechnology R&D, is known as recombinant DNA (r-DNA). The other basic technology was discovered during the 1970s by Dr. Cesar Milstein and Georges Köhler. They produced monoclonal antibodies (MAb's) by fusing antibody-producing lymphocytes with malignant myeloma cells. The resulting hybrid cell expressed both the lymphocytes' specific antibody production and the myeloma cells' rapid and continuous proliferation properties. This method for fusing two different cells in order to create a hybrid that shares specific attributes of both parents is referred to as cell fusion or "hybridoma" technology.

The goal of both r-DNA and cell fusion is to engineer organisms to produce desired proteins for use in particular therapeutic, diagnostic, or industrial applications. It is now possible to generate a wide range of proteins from genetically altered bacteria and yeasts. In the case of insulin and human growth hormone, r-DNA techniques subsitute for existing methods. For interferons and other proteins, r-DNA represents the only economically feasible method of commercial production. R-DNA techniques can also improve yields from existing fermentation processes by altering the genetics of cells to increase their productive efficiency (Sharp, 1985, p. 17).

Cell fusion can be used to produce large quantities of pure antibodies. Conventional methods of producing antibodies, injecting an antigen into a live animal and collecting the antibody containing blood serum, do not yield pure antibodies. Because a given antibody recognizes (and attaches to) only one type of antigen, monoclonal antibodies (MAb's) are ideal for drug delivery, diagnostics, separation processes, anf purification processes. For example, MAb's are being developed that can deliver toxic substances to specific cancer cells with minimal toxicity to normal cells. While therapeutic applications of MAb's are a potentially large market, early commercial exploitation of the technology has concentrated on in vitro[3] diagnostic products. In the United States, the first in vitro diagnostic product employing MAb's was approved in 1981; by June 1983, twenty-six MAb-based in vitro diagnostic products had been approved (Office of Technology Assessment, 1984, pp. 144–145).

It should be stressed that advances in aseptic operation, reactor design, product recovery, and other second generation biotechnological production techniques will affect the commercial potential of many new genetically engineered products. Margaret Sharp (1985, p. 19) observes:

[M]uch of the technological endeavor needed to "put biotechnology on the map" in areas where it is not already established will of necessity be based on further development of second generation techniques. Genetic engineering is essentially a "design input" into biotechnology—it creates novel genetic combinations. But to make use of these combinations will require the application and development of second generation process technologies both in production and extraction. (p. 19)

This element of continuity plays an important role in shaping the division of labor between new biotechnology firms and established firms in various sectors of application.

THE CHARACTER OF AND MOTIVATION FOR COLLABORATION IN BIOTECHNOLOGY

Collaborative arrangements in biotechnology are primarily concerned with the development and commercial exploitation of new technologies. Significant differences exist between collaborative arrangements in biotechnology and in the telecommunications equipment industry (see Chapter 2). While collaboration in both industries is strongly influenced by the requirements for profitably commercializing new technology, the nature of technological change differs in several ways that affect the motives for and characteristics of collaboration. First, in telecommunications equipment, innovation fundamentally involves systems design and systems engineering. Systems level innovators need access to various component technologies; component level innovators need to ensure that their product designs are compatible with other components in the relevant system. In contrast, biotechnological innovation is generally not systemic in nature. Compatibility among different processes and products is not an issue and therefore not a reason for firms to collaborate.[4] Second, the new biotechnology is basically a process technology. It represents either a new way of making certain substances or the only known way of making others in commercial quantities. As a result the innovation process entails the transfer of know-how from the laboratory to production. While cost competitive manufacturing is important in telecommunications equipment, the link between product and process innovation is not as tight as it is in biotechnology. The locus of manufacturing is thus a critical issue in biotechnology innovation; it is less so in telecommunications equipment innovation. Finally, biotechnology represents a new "technological paradigm" (see Dosi, 1982) that originated from the research efforts of universities and a swarm of new biotechnology companies. Established chemical and pharmaceutical producers were not directly involved in the earliest phases of the technology's emergence. In telecommunications equipment, while there have been new sources of innovation, incumbent equipment firms (particularly AT&T) have often played leading roles in the emergence of the major new technologies.

   To illustrate the character and motivation of collaboration in biotechnology, we will examine the roles and distinctive competencies of three types of organizations involved in biotechnological innovation: (1) universities and other nonprofit research institutions, (2) new biotechnology firms (NBFs), and (3) established firms interested in application of the new technologies.

Universities and Nonprofit Research Institutions

Universities and nonprofit research organizations have shaped the scientific foundations for commercial biotechnological developments. This differs from the semiconductor case where, in the early phases, university basic research lagged behind the work done by industry (OTA, 1984; Daly, 1985, p. 52). University research in molecular biology and biochemistry continues to provide critical inputs into the commercial innovation process. American universities have been among the leading patent holders in the area of genetic manipulation (Office of Technology Assessment Forecasting, 1983). An unusual feature of genetic engineering is the blurry distinction between basic research and applied commercial development. The technical distance between a basic discovery and a commercial product is distinctively shorter in biotechnology than in other technologies. (See for example, Office for Technology Assessment, 1984, and Ruscio, 1983.) Basic biomedical and biochemical research can generate know-how with a direct and identifiable commercial application. For example, in developing r-DNA insulin, Genentech used the nucleic acid sequences synthesized at the City of Hope Medical Center, an academic laboratory. The distinction between basic research and applied development will likely become sharper as the technological paradigm matures and applied development becomes focused on incremental innovation.

The more immediate commercial value of university-generated research has put universities in a novel position in the innovation process relative to their traditional role. While links between universities and industry are not new, the character and motivation of these linkages seems to have changed. Linkages with a major university or research institute (including teaching hospitals) are viewed by industry as necessary to track and exploit a rapidly expanding technological frontier. In addition, the complexity of the technologies and their strong tacit character make direct contact between basic (university) and applied (commercial) researchers necessary for successful technology transfer. For universities, such arrangements provide financial and other advantages; they are the chief mechanisms for universities to capture returns from their research.

In our database, approximately 19.5 percent of all collaborative arrangements involve universities or other nonprofit research institutions (based on a random sample of 200 collaborative arrangements). This suggests that there are several hundred collaborative arrangements between private firms and universities or other nonprofit research institutions. Our data also suggests that nearly 80 percent of these university and research institute relationships are focused on human pharmaceutical applications.

New Biotechnology Firms

New biotechnology firms (NBFs) are defined as firms that were organized specifically to develop and exploit the commercial potential of the new biotechnologies of the 1970s.[5] Since 1976 approximately 280 NBFs have been formed. Figure 6-1 represents the distribution of NBF births across the years 1976-1986.

As indicated, NBF entry peaked in 1981. NBF entry has virtually stopped in the past few years.[6] There have been significant differences in the patterns of NBF entry across sectors of application. According to a survey by the OTA (1984) of 179 NBFs, 44 percent are pursuing applications in pharmaceuticals, 20 percent in animal agri-

Figure 6-1. The Emergence of Biotechnology Firms.

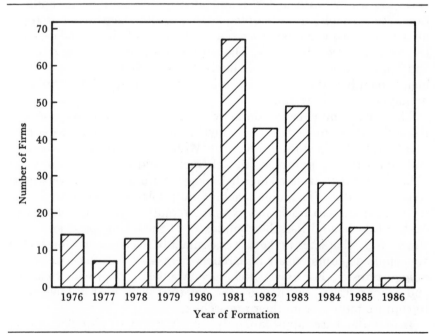

Source: Shan (1987).

culture, 11 percent in plant agriculture, 9 percent in specialty chemicals and food, 9 percent in commodity chemicals and energy, and 8 percent in environment.

NBFs have been an important channel for the commercialization of university research. Most NBFs have been founded by or in conjunction with university scientists. The incentive structures of NBFs have been such to attract the participation of some of the best minds in molecular biology and biochemistry. University researchers have also been attracted by the quasi-academic environments of some NBFs. The combination of these features is not easily replicated by established firms [7] or by academic research institutions.

The distinctive advantage of NBFs clearly lies in R&D. Although a majority of NBFs have already established limited production capabilities and some have integrated into marketing selected product lines, NBFs face capital constraints to complete forward integration. For many applications, the downstream stages of innovation, process development, manufacturing, product testing (or clinical evaluation), promotion, marketing, and distribution can require enormous sums of capital.[8] After investing in R&D and limited production facilities, most NBFs have little capital left over to fund these downstream activities. Those NBFs that plan more extensive integration have had to seek the additional capital from external sources. While capital markets generously funded the initial phase of NBF development, they have been less willing to finance forward integration.[9] This may reflect investors' pessimism about the ability of NBFs to develop manufacturing and marketing capabilities competitive with those of experienced and powerful incumbents in downstream sectors. Whatever the causes, investors are demanding a higher risk premium from NBFs than NBFs think it is worthwhile to pay. Information asymmetry underlies this market failure (see Williamson, 1975). NBFs cannot convince investors that downstream integration investments are a good risk. Whether the NBFs or the investors are correct is difficult to say. The end result is that most NBFs cannot pursue full vertical integration. Those firms that plan to integrate forward into specific sectors are also planning to use joint ventures and licensing arrangements to generate returns on certain segments of their technological portfolios.

There is an important difference between the role of new biotechnology firms and the new semiconductor firms that emerged in the early stages of that industry. The new semiconductor firms of the 1950s did not resort to licensing and joint ventures to commercialize their technology as have the new biotechnology firms. Mowery (1983a) has attributed this to the fact that new semiconductor firms were selling largely to the Department of Defense, a market that had much lower marketing and product introduction costs than the markets for new biotechnology products. The military market provided the new semiconductor firms with the production experience and financial resources necessary to enter commercial markets on their own (Malerba 1985, pp. 84–85).

Established Firms from Downstream Sectors

The established firms from downstream sectors of application have exerted and will continue to exert a strong influence on the rate and direction of biotechnology innovation. In the earliest phases of commercial development, established firms were not *directly* involved to any significant degree in biotechnology R&D. However, they have influenced the process by sponsoring NBFs' R&D and by contracting with NBFs for the development of selected technologies. According to an OTA survey (Office for Technology Assessment, 1984) and our own data, only Monsanto, DuPont, Eli Lilly, Ciba-Geigy, Merck, and Hoechst had in-house biotechnology R&D programs by 1978. Most established firms relied exclusively on R&D contracts and sponsored R&D until 1981. European and Japanese firms generally did not begin to undertake biotechnology R&D until 1981 and 1982. It is interesting to note 1981 marks the year in which the first diagnostics based on MAb's were approved for the market. The clearer commercial prospects of biotechnology (at least in health care) seems to have brought a wave of entry by established firms.

During the past five years, established firms have increasingly shaped the development trajectory of commercial biotechnology through their in-house efforts. As indicated by the following data (Office for Technology Assessment, 1984), some established chemical and pharmaceutical firms have already committed relatively large sums to biotechnology R&D.

Firm	1982 Biotechnology R&D Budget ($M)
DuPont	$120
Monsanto	62
Eli Lilly	60
Schering-Plough	60
Hoffman-LaRoche	59
Genentech	32
Cetus	26
Biogen	9
Genex	8

Unfortunately, this data does not distinguish between spending on in-house R&D and externally sponsored R&D. We do know that the percentage of expenditures for external research can be substantial: Monsanto reports that approximately $40 million (65 percent) of their 1982 biotechnology R&D budget was spent on outside contracts (Office for Technology Assessments, 1984).

Even as established firms build in-house technical capabilities in biotechnology R&D, their relative advantage remains in the downstream complementary stages of manufacturing and distribution. Commercialization of many biotechnology products requires suitable fermentation techniques for large-scale processing. Many pharmaceutical and chemical firms have over forty years experience with large-scale fermentation, a technology that has been described as more of an art than a science. Because many of the technical advances in fermentation and large-scale bioprocessing have occurred through incremental improvements by the in-house production engineering departments of established firms, there is little publicly available knowledge upon which NBFs can draw. NBFs lack the key input necessary for competitive large-scale bioprocessing, namely, *production know-how gained through experience.*

The control by established firms of distribution channels is an additional factor of great importance. In the pharmaceutical area, established companies already have in place large and experienced marketing and sales organizations. These organizations have extensive contacts with oncologists and other medical personnel that will ultimately make the purchasing decisions regarding new therapeutics based on biotechnology. In addition, established pharamceutical firms have extensive experience in the costly and complex process of gaining regulatory approval for new drugs. Their advantage at this stage is bolstered by their existing contacts with experienced clinical researchers as well as by their familiarity with FDA procedures.

An example of how an NBF's lack of experience with the FDA can delay approval is Genentech's experience with its blood-clot-dissolving drug known as tPA. Genentech's clinical studies demonstrated that the drug is safe and effective in dissolving blood clots in heart attack victims. The FDA advisory committee, however, delayed approval of the drug because Genentech had not produced evidence that the drug actually improved the survival rate of these patients. Some experts have argued that Genentech's inexperience with the regulatory approval process and the FDA were responsible for its failure to generate the appropriate data (*Wall Street Journal*, 1986, p. 23).

It may seem that established firms will be able to integrate into the core technical activities of NBFs far more rapidly than the NBFs will be able to integrate into the activities now dominated by established firms. However, while the basic technologies of genetic engineering have diffused widely, established firms face a number of organizational barriers to achieving competitive advantage in biotechnology R&D. First, NBFs are able to offer environments and incentive structures that established firms, for some reason, seem unable to replicate. (See Williamson, 1985, on the incentive limits of firms.) Second, the addition of new R&D organizations within the established firm requires changes in managerial skills and internal organizational structures. This is more likely to be true when the new R&D area represents a break with the dominant technological paradigm in which the firm has traditionally participated.[10] Organizational change is costly. There are often strong political forces at work within the administrative structure which confound the process. Because of bounded rationality, organizational changes occur through a sequential, adaptive process of trial and error. Thus, even though established firms have set up in-house programs, it remains to be seen whether they can adapt their internal organizational structures to achieve the R&D capabilities of the new biotechnology firms.

Some studies have suggested that as established firms have accumulated internal biotechnology skills and experience, they have become less reliant on external sources of technology (see, for example, Office for Technology Assessment, 1984, and Daly, 1985). Unfortunately, there is little data to either substantiate or refute this claim. Our interviews with a small number of NBFs suggest the following: While established firms have increased the size of their in-house biotechnology programs, the NBFs still have an advantage in the early stages of product development.[11] This advantage may be temporary for several reasons. First, many of the basic tools and techniques of biotechnology research have diffused widely. NBFs cannot block established firms with proprietary control over critical basic technologies. Second, while established firms have entered biotechnology R&D behind the NBFs, the lag has not been so great as to leave them very far behind on the R&D experience curve. Those firms that have launched large-scale programs are rapidly accumulating R&D experience. Finally, established firms in the United States can draw from a large supply of Ph.D.s in the biological sciences. In addition to drawing in new Ph.D.s, established firms may also be able to hire experienced scientists from NBFs that fail.

The possibility must also be considered that even as in-house capabilities grow, established firms will maintain their linkages with external technology sources. The firms cited earlier as having been the earliest to establish in-house programs (Eli Lilly, Monsanto, DuPont, Hoechst, Ciba-Geigy, and Merck) have relatively large numbers of links with new biotechnology firms. The data are not sufficient to support any specific conclusions, but it does suggest that there may not be a simple inverse relationship between in-house R&D and external linkages. As Mowery (1983b) has shown, there is often a complementary relationship between in-house and external sources of R&D. The multidisciplinary nature of biotechnology and the breadth of its potential applications may make it extraordinarily difficult for any firm to track all of the relevant technological frontiers through in-house R&D. Firms with stronger in-house capabilities, however, may be better able to identify, absorb, and apply the valuable technology from external sources.

The Characteristics of and Motives for Collaboration

Each of the main organizations involved in biotechnology has an advantage in different functions along the innovation spectrum. For universities, it lies in basic and generic research. The competitive advantage of NBFs is concentrated in product R&D. For established firms, in general, it lies in the downstream activities (manufacturing, marketing) where they have many years of experience. This complementary structure of comparative advantage provides the economic rationale for collaborative arrangements in biotechnology. The following statistics on partner selection patterns reflect this complementarity. In a random sample of 200 relationships from our database, 62 percent were between established firms and NBFs, 10.5 percent were between established firms, and 5 percent were between NBFs (the remaining arrangements involved universities, research institutions, and government agencies).

In virtually all the established firm-NBF relationships, the NBF supplies the technology (or the capability to develop a particular technology) and the established firm commercializes it. These arrangements can take various forms, including R&D contracts, licensing agreements, supply contracts, manufacturing agreements, and marketing agreements. The relative distribution for a sample of 200 arrangements between NBF and established firms is shown in Table 6-1.

Table 6-1. Functional Distribution of Collaborative Arrangements in
Biotechnology.

Function	Relative Frequency (%)	
R&D	36	
R&D marketing	17	
Manufacturing	5	
Marketing	19	
Supply	5	
Technology Transfer	17	
Other	1	Sample Size = 200

A COMPARATIVE ANALYSIS OF
COLLABORATION WITH ALTERNATIVE
FORMS OF INNOVATION

Collaborative innovation in biotechnology is characterized by the
linking of complementary assets of NBFs and established firms. It
must be recognized, however, that there are different types of linkages between NBFs and established firms and that such links are but
one alternative for organizing the innovation process. To understand
fully the rationale for collaboration, and its future role in biotechnology, we must compare the economics of collaborative governance
to that of the alternatives.

Three general types of governance structures can link the source
of R&D with the assets necessary for commercialization. Arms-
length markets for embodied and disembodied know-how are one
channel by which NBFs and established firms can coordinate R&D
and commercialization. An example of this type of arrangement is
where the NBF develops the technology independently and then
licenses it to an established firm (either for further development or
commercialization). Supply contracts for specific biological inputs
(such as antibodies) to be used by the established firm are another
example of arms-length links between the source and user of the
technology. A second mode of organization is vertical integration
between the source of R&D and the owner of the assets. Examples
of this form of organization include cases where an NBF integrates
into manufacturing and marketing or where an established firm develops a technology in-house. Third, NBFs and established firms can
forge some type of joint venture or collaborative linkage for the development and commercialization of particular technologies. In these
relationships, both parties contribute some combination of capital,

management, and technology for developing a specified product or set of products.

On the surface, it can be difficult to distinguish arms-length and collaborative relationships. Detailed information on the nature of the relationship is needed. For example, specific R&D contracts, licensing arrangements, supply agreements, or marketing agreements can be embedded in a longer term relationship. Our data do not allow us to make fine distinctions. We do know, however, that because of the length of the innovation process in biotechnology (and for pharmaceutical applications in particular), most R&D relationships are designed to operate over a three- to five-year time frame.

The form of longer term relationships can vary. Our data show that equity investments are used in approximately 22 percent of all NBF-established firm collaborations. In a relatively small number of cases, we found relationships formed around equity partnerships or joint ventures. However, in many other instances, where no equity ties exist, firms create a set of rules for governing the funding, management, and commercialization of a particular product or set of products. In a relatively common type of agreement, the established firm commits a specified amount of funding for a particular project in return for exclusive commercialization rights. In this type of arrangement, the NBF may retain significant rights to supply the established firm and to commercialize, on its own or in conjunction with others, specific applications of the technology.

The economic advantages of linking R&D and commercialization functions through collaborative (versus arms-length) arrangements stem from the particular conditions associated with the biotechnology innovation process. We divide these conditions into two categories: appropriability problems and transaction costs. These conditions, by hindering the operation of arms-length markets for technology, drive the organization of innovation toward quasi-integrated (collaborative) and vertically integrated forms.

Appropriability in Biotechnology.[12]

For arms-length markets to function efficiently, property rights must be clearly separable. In biotechnology a fundamental uncertainty has been the degree to which patents protect an innovation from imitation. While a landmark Supreme Court decision (*Diamond v. Chakrabarty*, 1980) held that new microorganisms could be patented, much uncertainty remains over their efficacy and in particular, the scope of protection. Because a patent might protect only a particular route to a given substance, innovators are not well protected when rivals (and licensees) can develop a product through alternative avenues. The complexity of biological processes can create disputes over the similarity of different routes to the same substance. There have been numerous patent challenges in those technologies where different firms claim to have developed distinct routes to producing a particular substance or product. While a few important court decisions, such as *Hybritech v. Monoclonal Antibodies* (in the United States) and *Genentech v. Wellcome* (in Britain) have been handed down, the efficacy of biotechnology patents is still to be determined by future court decisions.

The uncertain protection of patent protection in biotechnological products is a common theme in the 10-k and initial public offering prospectuses of new biotechnology companies. The following paragraph from one 1986 disclosure is representative:

> The patent position of biotechnology firms generally is highly uncertain and no consistent policy regarding the breadth of allowed claims has emerged from the actions of the United States Patent Office with respect to biotechnology patents to date. Products and processes important to [COMPANY] are subject to this uncertainty. The technology is developing rapidly; many patent applications have been filed, but the claimed scope of many is unknown. . . . Accordingly, there can be no assurance that the Company's patents will afford protection against competitors with similar technology, nor can there be any assurance that the patents will not be infringed upon or designed around by other. . . . Competitors of the Company may seek patents claiming aspects similar to those covered by patents held by the Company or for which it has applied. (Xoma Corporation, Prospectus, 1986)

The hazy nature of patent protection creates two problems for innovation through arms-length markets. First, when patent protection is weak, firms generally rely on some combination of trade secrets and lead time to appropriate returns on their innovations.[13] Trade secrecy, however, can hinder efforts to market the know-how and thus is more useful for process innovations. For product innovations, sophisticated analytical instruments and techniques can be used to reveal the molecular structures of chemically based products. The other mechanism, lead time, will not be of much use to an innovator that lacks the capabilities to commercialize the product.

Collaborative arrangements generally create a more protective environment for commercializing an innovation outside the firm's own boundaries for several reasons. First, the NBF avoids the problem of having to expose their know-how to a wide range of prospective licensees. Instead, they can deal with a particular partner in a confidential fashion. Safeguards can be built into the relationship that prohibit the partner from abusing confidential access to the NBF's know-how. Confidentiality agreements are common elements of arrangements that involve trade secrets. However, these agreements are more enforceable for product technologies than for process technologies because it is more difficult to detect cheating on process technology.

Second, the appropriability problem can be mitigated by having a prospective licensee pay for some portion of the product research and development costs at the outset. This explains why licensing agreements are often bundled with R&D agreements. Equity investments and equity joint ventures are also mechanisms to prevent an established firm from opportunistically appropriating rents on the technology. Up-front equity investments force the partners to agree ahead of time on the relative value of the technology under development and thus reduce the scope for ex post opportunistic recontracting. Direct equity investment represents a type of performance bond; if the established partner takes any actions that damage the NBF, it is penalized through reductions in the value of the equity held. Williamson (1985) refers to this type of contractual safeguard as an "exchange of hostages."

A third safeguard is the provision for ongoing collaboration that gives the established partner rights to technical improvements in the initial product. This is very important for "first generation" products (and therefore biotechnology in general) because of expectations of important technical improvements over the life cycle of a technology. This type of provision creates strong incentives for the established partner to maintain an ongoing ("good faith") relationship with the NBF partner. It can create a significant cost to the established partner for cheating on the original agreement.[14]

There are a number of organizational boundary adaptations by NBFs that can shield their proprietary know-how. One is to integrate forward into manufacturing. When the NBF does only the R&D and allows the licensee(s) or joint venture partners to manufacture the product, the partner(s) must be shown (and taught about) a significant share of the technical details. This type of technology transfer leaves the NBF vulnerable to appropriability problems. By integrating into manufacturing and by using established partners only for marketing, the NBF needs to disclose far fewer technical details. Even when the established partner will be licenced for marketing only, the NBF can still require the established firm to pay for some portion of the R&D costs up front.

Increasingly, NBFs are integrating into manufacturing to control what they see as a critical complementary asset. As one analyst writes:

> The ability to successfully scale up and purify a product is often the key factor in a competitive R&D race with another company. Many companies have chosen to keep this type of bioengineering knowledge secret and diffusion of

this knowledge will depend on personnel mobility within the industry. Such bioengineering knowledge can take several years to acquire from start-up and the lack of access to this type of information is an important entry barrier. (Daly, 1985, p. 42)

Because proprietary process technology is much more protectable than product technology, NBFs can use it to shield their less protected product technology. This trend is apparent in the MAb segment of the industry. As NBFs gain better protection of their technology by integrating into manufacturing, they will become less reliant on joint ventures as a means of capturing rents.

Transaction Costs in Biotechnology Commercialization

In addition to appropriability problems, there are a number of transactional difficulties in the intermediate market for biotechnology know-how. First, the complexity of decision making, communication, and coordination between R&D, manufacturing, and marketing has been increasing as biotechnology moves toward commercialization.[15] When established firms were interested in acquiring applied know-how and undeveloped technologies through licenses and R&D contracts, there was little need to coordinate major production capacity investments and marketing programs with the R&D contractor. Such coordination problems become relevant when the purpose of the arrangement is to acquire technologies for manufacturing or marketing. Collaborative arrangements can be structured to emulate many of the organizational properties of internal organization by creating specialized communication channels and coordination protocols.

The communication and coordination burdens of product development and launch can be appreciated by examining a typical program plan for pharmaceutical products. The pharmaceutical product development process can be divided into eleven basic stages:

1. Basic research, screening, and early evaluation
2. Initial biochemical, pharmacological, and toxicological evaluation
3. Pharmaceutical development
4. Clinical evaluation
5. Filing an investigation for new drug application
6. Phase I clinical
7. Phase II clinicals
8. Phase III clinicals
9. Preparation and filing of new drug application
10. Production engineering and manufacturing scale-up
11. Marketing

Each one of these phases can be further subdivided into seven to ten subactivities. The process can take from five to ten years. Pharmaceutical companies have developed specialized information and reporting systems to coordinate these interdependent phases efficiently.

A second dimension of biotechnology affecting the organization of innovation is the degree to which it embodies a tacit dimension. According to the OTA: "Because of their complex and unknown nature, many biological inventions, especially organisms, cannot be sufficiently described in writing to allow their predictable reproducibility on the basis of that description alone" (Office for Technology Assessment, 1984, p. 368). When technology embodies a highly tacit dimension, it can be difficult to transfer without face-to-face communication (Teece, 1981). This creates two problems for arms-length R&D contracts and licenses. First, transfer costs make it more difficult to switch R&D sources during a project. Thus there are strong economies in having the same organization carry out all of the sequential phases of R&D. The original contractor gains a first-mover advantage through the experience and know-how it accumulates while executing the first phase of the project. These switching costs prevent competitive bidding across subsequent phases of the research and development process and create the well-known problem of lock-in discussed in the transaction costs literature.

Short of undertaking the R&D project in-house, it may be difficult to avoid the problems associated with switching costs. However, the technology acquiring firm can negotiate a contractual structure that lowers the incentives for the contractor to exploit its first-mover advantage. For example, established firms often commit funding to specified future projects. In addition, they often commit to distribute the products of those projects. The benefits of future joint efforts create incentives for the NBF to maintain the agreement. Another common incentive feature allows the NBF to retain specific rights to the technology under development. In most cases, the NBF retains rights to a specific application. Such a structure provides an incentive to the NBF to complete the original contract.

The second type of difficulty created by the highly tacit nature of biological innovations concerns the difficulty of technology transfer from R&D into the manufacturing stage. When blueprints and other codified medium are insufficient to convey the relevant technical parameters, manufacturing scale-up requires significant face-to-face contact between product developers and process engineers. Communication between R&D and manufacturing flows more easily when the organizations share common experiences and information systems (Teece, 1981). The organizational problems of transferring know-how can be overcome by vertical integration between R&D and manufacturing. As mentioned, there has been a general trend for NBFs to develop some in-house processing capabilities. In addition to the proprietary protection advantages discussed earlier, vertical integration into manufacturing may allow the NBF to achieve more rapid manufacturing scale-up than is possible by transferring know-how to external manufacturing facilities.

When vertical integration into manufacturing is not feasible for the NBF, several types of collaborative structures economize on costs of technology transfer across organizational boundaries. For example, a long-term relationship between a source of R&D and a manufacturer can achieve many of the economies of team-learning that are normally possible within the same firm. By a long-term collaboration, we mean an arrangement that anticipates cooperation over a stream of future projects. There are many examples of such long-term alliances in biotechnology. Recently, Genentech has entered into a marketing agreement with Mitsubishi whereby Mitsubishi will distribute Genentech's future therapeutic products in Japan. Similarly, Cetus has entered into a long-term alliance with Squibb whereby Squibb will fund Cetus's anti-infective and cardiovascular R&D programs in return for exclusive distribution and marketing rights to the resulting products. We would argue that such long-term relationships allow the partners to exploit team-learning effects in the transfer of technology that would not be possible if these firms were to deal with a new partner for each project. The transaction costs per transfer will also decline when the parties can dispense with new rounds of negotiation for each new project.

Another method of reducing transfer costs that is used within biotechnology is to exchange personnel. Transfers of personnel (temporary assignments) are in some cases explicitly specified in the contract. A more extreme version of personnel exchange occurs when the principal technology supplier (usually the NBF) and the manufacturing partner (usually the established firm) undertake research and development jointly. By becoming directly involved in the R&D process, the manufacturing firm can more readily absorb the technology.

A second element of transaction costs in the organization of biotechnology innovation is the degree to which R&D and commercialization require complementary specialized investments. An established firms risks becoming locked into a particular NBF if it invests heavily in production or distribution for technology that is available from only one NBF. Once a technology is developed and transferred, the established firm is no longer dependent on the NBF. However, it is often the case that downstream investments must be made before the R&D cycle is completed. If an established partner is making these investments and these investments are specialized to the product under development, the established firm has transaction-specific investments at risk. The established firm risks that the NBF will not perform as expected. There is also the risk that the NBF could go bankrupt or be purchased by a competitor. Contracts can provide for these contingencies by granting the downstream partner rights to the technology under development. However, the costs of technology transfer discussed above limit the amount of technology that can be salvaged from the deal.

The supplier of technology, the NBF, runs similar problems. Should the established partner pull out of the project, the NBF may be left with a technology but no available commercial partners. Termination penalties are unlikely to offset the economic loss from the foregone opportunity. Similarly, the commercial partner may have developed specialized expertise during the course of collaboration that made it the most preferred partner. For example, the commercial partner may have acquired manufacturing expertise with the NBF's product line or a strong name brand recognition in the market. Its sale force may have developed specialized know-how about the line of products (for example, immunotoxins). These first-mover advantages will provide the commercial partner with bargaining leverage over the NBF for successive rounds of product development.

NBFs are also making a transaction-specific investment when they develop technologies for a specific partner (as did Genex when it developed L-phenylalanine for G. D. Searle) or when they develop products where one firm dominates distribution (as does Eli Lilly in insulin). Generally, the NBF can avoid the risks of opportunistic recontracting by requiring the partner to make significant benchmark (or milestone) payments. This payment scheme is very common for R&D contracting in all industries. However, when projects entail significant levels of uncertainty, it can be difficult, if not futile, to specify a rigid schedule of benchmarks. Under these circumstances, governance structures that rely more on general ground rules than on rigid contractual provisions are necessary to affect the requisite adaptations to unfolding circumstances.

Finally, the novel, unique, complex, and unknown nature of biological organisms can make it extremely difficult to verify and assure the performance of a technology. This creates a situation ripe for opportunism and haggling when technology is developed under contractual arrangements. Consider, as an example, the following dispute between Genex and Bristol-Myers. Bristol-Myers contracted with

Genex to develop microorganisms for the production of alpha interferon. The contract stipulated that Genex would receive a $300,000 bonus if they developed a microorganism that achieved a particular yield of interferon. After developing a microorganism that it believed met the bonus requirement, Genex was unable to collect the bonus payment from Bristol-Myers due to a dispute over how the microorganism's yield should be verified. When the firms could not agree on a testing procedure, they reached an out-of-court settlement whereby Genex retained the high-yield microorganisms (but not others developed under the contract) and was paid no bonus money.

We have examined how transaction costs and appropriability considerations drive the organization of innovation away from arms-length relationships between NBFs and established firms. Arms-length contracting, however, is feasible for R&D activities that do not involve substantial transaction-specific investments or the transfer of tacit and unpatentable know-how. R&D contracting in biotechnology is likely to survive in the form of a technical services segment where specialist firms undertake preliminary research, feasibility studies, and protein analysis for firms with in-house biotechnology R&D. Such a form of R&D contracting allows the firm that eventually commercializes the technology to internalize the critical development functions relatively early in the innovation cycle. Thus external R&D will complement internal R&D activities.[16] Arms-length markets have already evolved for research reagents and other standard physical inputs into the innovation process.

We have viewed collaborative governance structures and integration as responses to the transactions costs and appropriability problems inherent in biotechnology innovation. When the transaction costs and appropriability problems are sufficiently high, vertical integration will be preferred to collaborative innovation on purely *organizational efficiency* grounds. However, the gains in organizational efficiency must be weighed against any losses in *productive efficiency* that result from being less skilled than specialists in the relevant stage of production. Not only do NBFs face high costs of integrating forward into certain markets, but established firms may face high costs of integrating backward into certain areas of biotechnology R&D. We expect the net marginal gains (organizational gains minus productive efficiency losses) of integration to vary across downstream sectors of application. The following section examines these cross-sectoral differences.

Figures 6–2 and 6–3 summarize the organizational issues we have raised. Figure 6–2 represents the perspective of a potential buyer of technology; Figure 6–3 represents the technology provider's per-

Figure 6-2. Know-how Procurement Strategy (Buyer's Perspective).

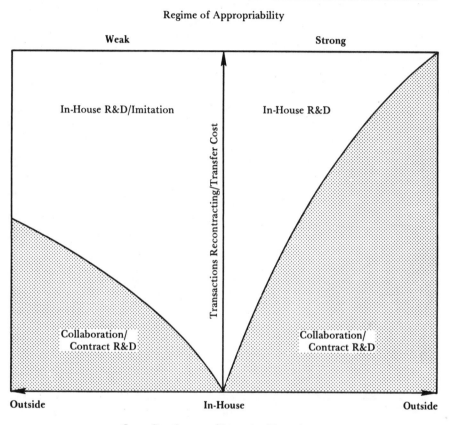

spective. Briefly, since buyers and providers must accommodate each other if collaboration is to occur, it is apparent that licensing or collaboration will be favored by an established firm when the provider has strong intellectual property protection (otherwise, the potential buyer can acquire the technology through imitation) and transaction and technology transfer costs are low. The collaboration may involve the exchange of services when the new business firm cannot build the relevant cospecialized assets competitively, transaction costs are modest, and intellectual property protection is strong enough that the technology provider does not fear competition from its commercial partner.

Figure 6-3. Technology Commercialization Strategy (Technology Provider's Perspective).

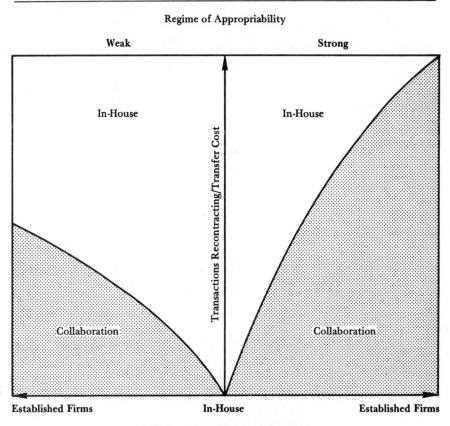

Regime of Appropriability

Location of Most Efficient Capacity in
Manufacturing, Marketing, and Distributing

INTERSECTORAL DIFFERENCES IN THE ORGANIZATION OF BIOTECHNOLOGY

The relative roles of NBFs and established firms in the development and commercialization of biotechnology differ across downstream sectors of application. Table 6-2 provides some indication of these differences.

A significant difference across sectors, which is not revealed in the data above, is the relative frequency with which (1) NBFs market

Table 6-2. Role of New Biotechnology Firms (NBFs) by Sector of
Application.

Sector of Application	NBFs as Percentage of Total Firms
Pharmaceuticals	59
Environment	58
Animal agriculture	57
Commodity chemicals and energy	47
Plant agriculture	39
Specialty chemicals and food	36

Source: OTA (1984).

their own products, (2) established firms develop their own products, and (3) NBFs and established firms cooperate in the development and commercialization of new products. This section analyzes the available evidence and discusses the economic rationale underlying the observed differences.

Salient cross-sectoral differences in the nature and function of collaboration are reflected in Tables 6-3 through 6-5. Table 6-3, showing a weighted cross-sectional distribution of collaborative arrangements, indicates the relatively high propensity for collaboration within the pharmaceutical area. Table 6-4 provides a cross-sectoral comparison of the functions of collaboration. Table 6-5 reveals cross-sectoral differences in forms of collaboration. Worthy of note is the more frequent use of equity forms (either direct or joint) in plant agriculture and specialty chemicals.

Pharmaceutical Products: Human Therapeutics

The high relative frequency of collaboration in human therapeutic products reflects the significant barriers to forward integration facing NBFs. In human therapeutics, NBFs face two major barriers to downstream integration into marketing. First, human therapeutic products require a lengthy and costly process of clinical trials to meet government regulations for safety and efficacy. As discussed earlier, established pharmaceutical firms have forty years of experience in sponsoring clinical trials for new drugs. This experience and their extensive contacts with clinical researchers are assets that are not easy for NBFs to replicate in a cost effective way. In addition, the clinical development process itself is costly; it can take from five to seven years and cost up to $70 million. Most NBFs lack the cash resources or the access to capital markets to undertake such an investment on their own. While a number of NBFs have used R&D

Table 6-3. Distribution of Collaborative Arrangements across Sectors (%).

	Pharmaceuticals	Diagnostics[a]	Animal Health	Plant Agriculture	Specialty Chemicals[c]	All Others[d]	Total
Number of agreements[b]	90	33	14	18	10	35	200
Percentage of total	45.00%	16.50%	7.00%	9.00%	5.00%	17.50%	100.00%
Number of Firms[e]	136	f	61	53	44	g	158
Agreements: Firms	0.66	—	0.23	0.34	0.23	—	1.27

a. Diagnostics category includes three in vivo diagnostic projects and one DNA probe diagnostic project.
b. Based on random sample of 200 collaborative arrangements.
c. Specialty chemicals includes food applications.
d. "Others" category includes reagents, lab equipment, production equipment, and basic scientific research.
e. This figure from Office of Technology Assessment (1984, p. 71).
f. Office of Technology Assessment (1984) included diagnostics with pharmaceuticals.
g. Not comparable with Office of Technology Assessment classification.

Table 6-4. Cross-sectoral Comparison of the Motives for Collaboration (%).

Function	Pharmaceuticals	Diagnostics	Animal Health	Plant Agriculture	Specialty Chemicals
R&D	34	17	36	67	40
R&D and marketing	13	10	21	33	10
Manufacturing	7	10	0	0	10
Marketing	21	31	36	0	20
Supply	2	21	0	0	0
Technology transfer	22	10	7	0	20
Other	1	0	0	0	0
	100	100	100	100	100

Table 6-5. Distribution of Collaborative Forms, Cross-sectoral comparison (%).

Form	Pharmaceuticals	Diagnostics[a]	Animal Health	Plant Agriculture	Specialty Chemicals	All Others
Contractual	73	86	100	56	40	80
Direct equity tie	18	7	0	44	30	14
Equity joint venture	9	7	0	0	30	6
	100	100	100	100	100	100

a. Diagnostics category includes in vitro products only.

limited partnerships to fund clinical development, a majority have teamed up with established pharmaceutical companies to tap their clinical experience and contacts.

The second major barrier to forward integration by NBFs is the high fixed cost of creating distribution channels. Again, pharamaceutical companies have batteries of "detail men" with extensive contacts with physicians and hospital pharmacies. They also have extensive marketing capabilities in overseas markets. Economies of scope in marketing pharmaceuticals means that there are declining marginal marketing costs per new product. Because of their inability to match these marketing economies, most NBFs have relied on established pharmaceutical firms to market and distribute their products.

A few of the larger and more experienced NBFs have begun to push through these barriers. Firms such as Genentech and Cetus have announced their intention to become fully integrated pharmaceutical companies. These firms are targeting selected therapeutic markets where a small specialized sales force can market products directly to specialists in regional medical centers.

The propensity of established pharmaceutical firms to integrate backward into biotechnology R&D has been discussed earlier in this chapter. Because NBFs developed an early lead in biotechnology R&D, most established firms have been content to rely on them as a source of "first generation" products (such as insulin). However, whether these firms can rely on NBFs for longer term products is questionable. Besides the transactional difficulties, the supply side of the market for R&D may become much thinner as NBFs integrate forward, fail, or become acquired by competitors.

The demographic trends in the organization of therapeutic product development are captured in Figure 6-4, which profiles the incidence of NBFs and established firms are acting alone versus the incidence of those in partnership for products in various stages of development and commercialization. The *number* of biotechnology products being developed by NBFs and established firms without partners is higher for products *earlier* in the innovation cycle. This may reflect two patterns in the development of biotechnology-based therapeutics. First, the higher uncertainties associated with earlier stage research and development may be creating transaction costs for joint efforts and thus increasing the number of solo efforts (by both NBFs and established firms). Collaborative organization may become more frequent as these products move into later stages of development. Second, this data may reflect an increasing trend toward more vertical integration in the development and commerciali-

Figure 6–4. Patterns of Collaboration across the Stages of Innovation, Human Therapeutic Products (as of January 1986).

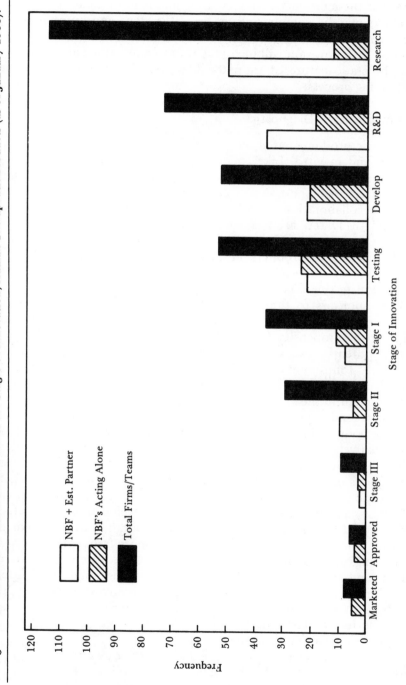

Source: Constructed from information contained in Paine Webber's Biotechnology Fact Book (1986).

zation of these products. An increasing number of human therapeutic products may be commercialized by NBFs alone and by established firms without NBF partners. If this is the case, then collaboration as a mode of innovation will likely fade. Both alternatives are plausible, but the static nature of the data does not allow us to identify the underlying process.

Pharmaceuticals: Diagnostics

Diagnostic products based on biotechnology fall into two categories: in vivo and in vitro. Like therapeutic products, in vivo diagnostics (which are used inside the body) must undergo rigorous safety and efficacy testing. The costs of commercialization might be expected to drive collaboration in this segment. However, our sample uncovered relatively few arrangements in the in vivo segment. There are two reasons for this. First, there are relatively fewer firms pursuing a small number of products in this area.[17] Second, because a large proportion of the product development efforts are in the R&D and preclinical testing phases, NBFs may not have yet needed to turn to outside sponsors to fund the costly clinical development phases. A key transactional difficulty in this area, however, one that may be limiting the propensity for collaboration, is the relatively small number of potential established partners. Paine Webber (1986) reports that only Johnson and Johnson, Medi-Physics (a Hoffman LaRoche subsidiary), and Eli Lilly (via Hybritech) were pursuing product development in the area of in vivo imaging in 1985.

The second type of diagnostic, in vitro diagnostics, are used outside the body and are thus not subject to the same regulatory hurdles. The relatively lower cost of development is the major factor underlying the rapid rate at which in vitro diagnostic products have been developed. As of June 1983 approximately forty-two in vitro MAb diagnostic products had been approved for sale in the United States. Of these approximately 75 percent were developed and manufactured by NBFs. Table 6-4 reveals that collaboration in in vitro diagnostics, compared to that in other sectors, more frequently involved marketing only, supply, or technology transfer. This suggests that NBFs fund and develop products internally and use established firms only for marketing. Supply arrangements often involve the supply by the NBF of a particular antibody that the established firm is licensed to use in its own test kits. This type of supply agreement is functionally akin to a marketing arrangement.

Increasingly, however, NBFs are building their own marketing and distribution channels. At the same time established firms such as Abbott, Becton Dickinson, Johnson and Johnson, and Eli Lilly are accumulating in-house expertise in in vitro MAb diagnostics. In 1985 Eli Lilly made a major move toward in-house self-sufficiency in MAb technology by acquiring Hybritech, which accounted for approximately 30 percent of all in vitro diagnostics developed by NBFs as of 1983.

The relatively short product cycles in in vitro diagnostics (due mainly to the lower regulatory hurdles) also affect the form of collaboration in this segment. As shown in Table 6-5, a relatively low proportion of collaborations in this area involved direct or joint equity ties. These equity forms are preferred for longer term alliances for reasons discussed earlier and in Chapter 2.

Animal Health Care

The organization of biotechnology development in animal health applications is similar to that found in the human health markets. In fact the major producers of animal health products include many of the world's largest human pharmaceutical producers. The extensive international marketing and distribution networks of incumbents represents a major barrier to entry for NBFs. However, similar to the case of human health care, NBFs have generally focused on animal vaccines and diagnostics because these products have relatively small markets and low commercialization costs. In many cases animal vaccines and diagnostic products are being developed by NBFs independently of established companies (Office for Technology Assessment, 1984, p. 80).

In most segments of animal health care (and unlike the human pharmaceutical area), established firms have been relatively slow to develop in-house expertise in biotechnology. They have generally relied on R&D contracts and marketing arrangements with NBFs for specific products. Data compiled by Paine Webber (1986) indicate that none of the research or development stage animal health projects in progress during 1985 were being undertaken solely by an established firm. Established firms have tended to enter the process by sponsoring field trials for products developed by NBFs. The future organization of biotechnology innovation for animal health care, however, may change dramatically as established pharmaceutical firms accumulate in-house expertise from their human health care R&D that can be applied to animal health products.

Plant Agriculture

In plant agriculture, the bulk of R&D is being undertaken by established oil, chemical, food, and pharmaceutical companies (Office for Technology Assessment, 1984, p. 81). These firms are relying on a combination of in-house R&D and R&D contracts with NBFs. In addition to collaborating with NBFs, many U.S. companies have acquired plant and crop seed companies for their distribution systems and for their gene pools (which would require ten to twenty years of R&D to develop on their own).

As indicated in Table 6–4, R&D contracts and R&D and marketing agreements accounted for all the collaborative arrangements in our sample from this sector. The lack of straight marketing, supply, and technology transfer agreements suggests that NBFs are not carrying out R&D on their own. Indeed, of the forty-eight plant agricultural product development projects listed in Paine Webber (1986), NBFs are acting without a commercial partner in only eight cases. The lack of proprietary or self-funded R&D by NBFs is due to the fact that biotechnology in plant agriculture is not as far along the commercial development path as it is in other sectors. To fund the requisite long-term R&D, NBFs, as they did in the earlier stages of pharmaceutical biotechnology, have turned to corporate sponsors. (These corporate sponsorships supplement the funds from venture capital and other financial markets.) The long-term nature of R&D at this early stage of commercial development is reflected in the relatively high proportion (44 percent) of relationships involving direct equity ties (Table 6–5). As the time horizon for commercial development shortens, we would expect NBFs to fund a greater share of product development internally and to link up with various corporate partners on a shorter term basis.

Specialty Chemicals

A number of NBFs are pursuing biotechnology R&D for specialty chemical applications. However, technological and competitive conditions do not favor independent innovation by NBFs. First, biotechnological innovation in specialty chemicals will require many incremental improvements in process technology. Established firms, particularly the leading Japanese food and chemical companies, have an advantage because of their extensive operating experience with bioprocessing. Second, these established companies have experience with designing and implementing the high-quality control systems necessary to produce biotechnology-based specialty chemicals. Third, established firms have the capital and production capabilities to scale-up rapidly and to reap cumulative scale economies. Finally, NBFs are likely to face strong competition from established chemical firms (such as Dow, DuPont, and Monsanto) that are increasingly shifting from bulk to specialty chemicals. As of yet, no NBF has integrated forward into specialty chemicals. Genex originally planned to do so through production of certain amino acids; however, their plans changed after a nearly disastrous problem with L-phenylalanine.[18]

As indicated in Table 6-4, there seems to be a wide variation in the types of arrangements through which NBFs in specialty chemicals capture returns on their technological capabilities. The functional distribution of collaborative arrangements in specialty chemicals and pharmaceuticals are similar. However, the nature of biotechnological innovation in specialty chemicals differs from other sectors in the degree to which it depends fundamentally on processing know-how.

Process R&D involves a number of transactional difficulties that will affect the preferred forms of collaboration. First, tacit knowledge from actual production experience often plays a key role in the development and application of process innovations. The problems of transferring tacit know-how make it difficult to coordinate process development at arms-length. Second, the knowledge of a production process may be firm-specific. As result, the market for know-how may be thin on both the supply and demand sides. Finally, there is an appropriability problem if proprietary process technology is not protected by patents. Firms often prefer to use their factory walls rather than patents to protect their proprietary process know-how. Superior process technology is often the key to defending a product technology where patent protection is weak. Confidentiality agreements, which might otherwise protect a firm's technology from leakages during collaboration, may be difficult to enforce for process technology because the imitator, like the innovator, can hide the technology behind its factory walls.

These transactional and appropriability problems create an incentive to collaborate through more hierarchical and specialized channels than pure contracts. Relationships organized around direct equity investments and equity joint ventures may alleviate some of these difficulties. Table 6-5 reflects the preference that collaborators in specialty chemicals (versus other sectors) have for direct equity and joint equity venture forms of collaboration.

COLLABORATIVE ARRANGEMENTS
WITHIN A GLOBAL CONTEXT:
PUBLIC POLICY IMPLICATIONS

Thus far, the analysis has not distinguished between international and domestic collaborations. As reported in Table 6-6, linkages be-

Table 6-6. International Patterns of Collaboration as a Percentage of All
Collaborations.

Partners	Pharmaceuticals (%)	All Others (%)
U.S. NBF/United States	49	65
U.S. NBF/Europe	31	30
U.S. NBF/Japan	20	5

Note: Table is based on a random sample of 120 links between U.S. NBF's and established
firms. Canada and other parts of world are excluded.

tween U.S. NBFs and foreign firms represent a significant share of
collaborative activity. The economic rationale underlying domestic
and international collaboration is similar. Both provide the NBF with
a critical complementary asset, namely, a channel for accessing specific markets. While the general analytical framework used throughout this chapter can be applied to transactions involving international
technology transfer, there is a critical difference between the assets
commonly traded within domestic collaborations and international
collaborations. NBFs face much higher barriers to entering foreign
markets than they do for domestic markets. The economic reasons
for such differences are relatively clear; domestic-based firms (or
long-standing subsidiaries of multinationals) have experience with the
relevant regulatory authorities, contacts with clinical hospitals, and
strong links with prospective customers in the national market.
Political barriers can also prevent NBFs from direct entry into foreign markets.

As a result of these economic and political barriers, we would
expect NBFs to first integrate forward into marketing within the
United States and to continue to use linkages with foreign firms (or
global scale multinationals) to expand returns on their innovations.
We therefore predict that international marketing alliances will
endure longer than domestic alliances.

From a U.S. public policy perspective, arrangements that transfer
technology from U.S. NBFs to foreign firms create a paradoxical
problem. On the one hand, these arrangements improve the financial
position of NBFs and thus enable them to maintain their high levels
of R&D and to expand their downstream operations in the United
States. On the other hand, these arrangements increase the biotechnological capabilities of foreign firms and thus reduce the future
rent-earning potential of U.S. biotechnology (*Venture*, 1986). From
a public policy perspective, the relevant question is whether the net
discounted social benefits exceed zero and whether the divergence

between private and public returns is significant. Unfortunately, the cost-benefit analysis of this question would be enormously complex and, at best, could provide only a rough estimate of the actual net economic benefits. In any event, regulating the flow of technology abroad has traditionally proven futile (a prime example being England during the Industrial Revolution) and there is no reason to believe that government policies for biotechnology would approach the theoretically optimal point. Meanwhile, U.S. firms might to be able to circumvent restrictions on the export of know-how, while foreign firms obtained technology through "reverse engineering."

We believe that a more fruitful policy approach would be to focus on policies that can improve the relative ability of U.S. factors of production in biotechnology to capture returns from U.S. generated know-how. In addition to the general advantages of open foreign markets, we see two areas that are important for the future competitiveness of U.S. biotechnology. First, rigorous protection and enforcement of intellectual property rights at home and abroad is critical for NBFs to fully appropriate rents when they must license technology to established firms. While U.S. patent protection for biotechnological products is considered to be the strongest in the world (Office for Technology Assessment, 1984), it is still quite uncertain.

In the meantime the uncertain nature of patent protection has two potential consequences for U.S. competitiveness in biotechnology. One is the obvious possibility that patented biological innovations will not ultimately be protected from imitation. This will lower the incentives for NBFs to innovate in the future and will allow foreign firms to catch up in product know-how through imitation. The second problem of uncertain patent protection is that it may be leading NBFs to attempt forward integration (to protect their technology) when their scarce resources might be more efficiently deployed in R&D. At the same time established firms may be diverting resources from downstream functions to develop technologies that would be more efficiently developed by NBFs. The consequences of uncertain patent protection is failure in the markets for know-how with unambiguous welfare losses.

The second policy area concerns U.S. capabilities in biotechnology production. Future competitiveness in biotechnology will likely depend on strong production skills, especially as foreign firms catchup to NBFs in terms of product know-how. The OTA reported that bioprocessing was an area of relative weakness in the U.S. biotechnology industry (Office for Technology Assessment, 1984). Their survey of manpower needs suggested that there is a relative shortage of bioprocessing engineers in the United States. Stronger U.S. bioprocessing skills will be critical to ensuring that U.S. biotechnology can fully appropriate rents on their product innovations. If the critical cospecialized production skills are located outside the United States, then much of the rent streams from product innovations generated in the United States will flow to those foreign factors of production.[19]

One might argue that firms have an incentive to develop the requisite bioprocessing skills and that therefore public policies in support of such skills are not necessary. We argue, however, that the private incentives to develop bioprocessing know-how are undermined by an appropriability problem. There is little private incentive to train bioprocessing engineers when those engineers can carry their newly acquired know-how to competitors. The divergence between private and social returns causes firms to underinvest in the development of bioprocessing know-how.[20] Public policies in support of generic bioprocessing know-how are necessary to redress this market failure.

COLLABORATIVE ARRANGEMENTS WITHIN A GLOBAL CONTEXT: MANAGERIAL ISSUES

In analyzing the proclivity of biotechnology firms, both new and established, to engage in various forms of cooperation, we have built a normative framework that can provide guidance to managers. Although collaboration makes sense in some circumstances, however, the benefits of collaboration may have been oversold in the biotechnology industry. The benefits from integration are increasingly being recognized by NBFs. Firms that continue to rely on partners, for manufacturing and to a lesser extent for marketing, may have difficulty capturing large shares of the rents from the innovations that they were first to commercialize.

The task of managing collaborative arrangements in biotechnology is unusually difficult because the partners generally have entirely different organizational routines and cultures. Protecting one's technological assets in a collaborative arrangement is as much a challenge to the manager responsible for the partnership as it is for the lawyers and managers who structure the arrangement. Line managers who can work within the context of contractual instruments (often necessarily vague and incomplete) are critical to the overall success of the partnership.

So complex and pervasive are the arrangements characterizing this industry that it could well be the case that biotechnology will provide the training ground for managers of strategic alliances. Just as the railroads in the nineteenth century provided the basic training for modern management, so may the biotechnology industry provide the training ground for what Mel Horwitch has called a "post modern management," a paradigm of management that focuses on managing interfirm relations rather than intrafirm coordination. Managers on the technology supplier side must learn to avoid technology leakages while those on the acquisition side must learn to promote it. Other critical skills are the ability to establish and deepen harmonious inter-organizational relationships, to manage with contractual ambiguities and uncertainties, and to integrate activities across firms as though they belonged to just one organization.

COMPARISONS WITH OTHER FORMS
OF INDUSTRIAL ORGANIZATION

Despite the pervasiveness of collaborative arrangements in biotechnology, this form of industrial organization is still quite different from network forms of business alliances which exist in other industries and in Japan. Lest the reader mistake a semantic similarity for an organizational one, some brief points of comparison are in order.

Various forms of network organization are found in the publishing, aircraft, automobile, banking, and telecommunications services industry. In Japan an important form of network organization is the bank centered enterprise group known as *keiretsu*.[21]

Network structures are generally organized around some type of formal or informal hierarchy to integrate members' activities. In Japanese *keiretsu*, high-level executive councils provide a forum for interaction among group firms. In industries such as automobiles and aircraft, the large assemblers (such as General Motors, Ford, Boeing) act as hub for a network of suppliers. The assembler, by virtue of its buying power, sets technical standards and shapes the direction of component level R&D. Such relationships are generally governed through a combination of legal (contracts), financial (quasi-vertical integration), and informal ties.

The alliances that exist in biotechnology (and also in telecommunications equipment) bear only remote similarities to these structures. First, the relationships in these industries are primarily bilateral. There is no group structure. While some relationships might be long-standing, the reciprocity is generally limited to a well-defined set of projects or activities. An NBF can have ties to multiple partners for different projects. It is extremely rare in biotechnology for an NBF to be tied exclusively to a single established firm.

Second, there is no equivalent of the executive councils or other hierarchical structures to integrate the long-term activities of a set of biotechnology firms. However, equity joint ventures have separate boards of directors on which representatives of both firms sit. These boards usually set policy for the partnership and, when they arise, settle disputes.

Third, while one party may be the capital provider, the financial relationship underlying alliances in biotechnology (and telecommunications) typically does not allow the capital providing partner broad rights to intervene in the corporate governance of the other. When large capital stakes are provided, the provider generally obtains representation on the other firm's board of directors. However, such representation is usually limited to a small proportion of available seats. Nor does the capital provider in these relationships have only a banker's interest in the capital-absorbing enterprise; there is almost always an underlying business function (R&D, manufacturing, marketing) interest between the parties.

CONCLUSIONS

The organizational separation of biotechnology R&D from downstream functions reflects the pattern of distinctive advantage among different organizations in different functions of the innovation process. The firms best able to research and develop the technology, the NBFs, have generally not had the resources to commercialize it. Similarly, the firms best positioned to commercialize the technology, established firms from various sectors of application, have lagged behind the NBFs at the leading edge of biotechnology.

Basic principles of economic theory suggest that there would be mutual gains from trade between the two groups of firms, particularly when intellectual property regimes are tight. Indeed, our data showed that trade between NBFs and established firms was more likely than trade within these groups. However, our analysis also suggested that this trade in know-how would not generally be conducted through arms-length markets. Appropriability and transaction costs problems confound standard economic analysis. What we find in the coupling of biotechnology R&D to downstream functions is a complex set of contractual and organizational arrangements that simultaneously mix elements of arms-length contracting and internal organization. These organizational forms include joint ventures and what we have referred to as collaborative relationships.

The organization of biotechnology innovation is not in equilibrium. Pressures seem to be driving the R&D/commercialization linkages away from collaborative arrangements and toward vertical integration. In general, collaborative alliances in biotechnology are a transitory phenomenon. This trend, however, is not constant across sectors because of cross-sectoral differences in the marginal costs of transacting versus the marginal costs of integrating complementary functions.

Public policies to strengthen domestic and foreign patent protection and U.S. capabilities in bioprocessing will be important to ensure that U.S. biotechnology innovators are able to capture a large share of the international distribution of rents from their innovations. Should patent protection remain weak, NBFs must integrate forward to capture value from their innovations. Biotechnology may be on the vanguard of a very different form of industrial organization in America, one that will require a different set of managerial skills. Certainly, organizational developments in this industry bear watching.

NOTES

1. The firm provided the database on the condition that its identity be kept secret. The database contains information on approximately 750 firms worldwide that are involved in commercial biotechnology. For each firm, information is provided about its structure, history, strategy, main product areas (including products in development and on the market), areas of R&D, and, most important for this analysis, its collaborative arrangements. For each collaborative arrangement, information is provided on the partner, the product or technical area covered by the agreement, and the basic content of the agreement. Additional detail on several new biotechnology firms was collected by examining 10-k reports filed with the Securities and Exchange Commission and through interviews with a number of biotechnology firms in the San Francisco bay area.

2. This section provides a very general orientation of biotechnology. The interested reader is referred to OTA (1984) and Elkington (1985) for more detailed discussion of the technologies.

3. *In vitro* means outside the living body. In vitro diagnostics are performed in test tubes and other laboratory apparatus. *In vivo* means inside the living body. In vivo diagnostics refer to techniques where some diagnostic substance is used inside the patient's body to indicate or measure the presence of some type of cell or chemical.

4. An exception is in the area of diagnostic instrumentation which can "read" only certain types of diagnostic tests.

5. Definition from OTA (1984); an exception to this definition is Cetus, which was founded in 1971 as an R&D contractor for classical biotechnology. During the mid-1970s, Cetus shifted its focus to "new" biotechnology.

6. The rapid decline in NBF entry can be attributed to several factors. Perhaps the most powerful restraint on entry has been the hesitancy of venture capitalists to fund new ventures for an already crowded, competitive, and highly uncertain market.

7. For a treatment of the difficult encountered by large enterprises in creating the same incentives of small-scale firms, see Williamson (1985, Chapter 6).

8. Intersectoral differences in the costs of downstream integration and their effects on the organization of innovation are discussed later.

9. Cetus for example failed to raise enough capital from a private offering in Europe to fund the creation of a European clinical development and marketing subsidiary.

10. The difficulties that firms have in adapting to new technological paradigms is discussed by Clark (1985) for the case of the U.S. automobile industry and Malerba (1985) for the semiconductor case.

11. We should note a potential bias from our interviews; they were conducted with managers and scientists from NBFs.

12. This section and the next are adapted from Pisano (1988).

13. See Levin, Klevorick, Nelson, and Winter (1984). Our discussions with industry insiders suggest that their findings are also applicable to the biotechnology industry.

14. Williamson (1985) refers to these types of safeguards as "hostage exchanges."

15. The uncertainty that results from the inability to communicate and coordinate complex decisions is referred to as *secondary uncertainty* (see Teece and Helfat, 1987; Koopmans, 1957).

16. In a historical context, Mowery (1983b) found statistical support for the hypothesis that R&D contracting complements internal R&D activities. Biotechnology, which did not exist during his sampling time frame, was obviously not included in his analysis.

17. Because the OTA did not separate in vivo diagnostic from pharmaceuticals, it was not possible to derive a normalized frequency that would be comparable to the other sectors. However, we know from Paine Webber (1985) that the number of firms and projects is relatively small.

18. Genex had planned to sell large quantities of L-phenylalanine to G. D. Searle, one of the world's largest consumers of the amino acid. When Searle began in-house production, it did not renew its supply contract with Genex. As a result, Genex was left stranded with a specialized production facility.

19. The theoretical underpinnings of this argument are developed in Teece (1986).

20. On the divergence of private and social returns to R&D and the effect on innovation, see Arrow (1962).

21. On the form and role of Japanese business alliances, see Gerlach (1987).

REFERENCES

Arrow, K. 1962. "Economic Welfare and the Allocation of Resources for Invention." In R. Nelson, ed., *The Rate and Direction of Inventive Activity*, Princeton, N.J.: Princeton, University Press.

Buttrick, J. 1952. "The Inside Contracting System." *Journal of Economic History*, 12: 205-221.

Clark, K. 1985. "Managing Technology in International Competition: The Case of Product Development in Response to Foreign Entry." Unpublished paper prepared for NEC/KSG Conference on International Competition.

Daly, P. 1985. *The Biotechnology Business*. London: Frances Pinter.

Dosi, G. 1982. "Technological Paradigms and Technological Trajectories: A Suggested Interpretation of the Determinants and Directions of Technical Change." *Research Policy*.

Elkington, J. 1985. *The Gene Factory*. New York: Carrol and Graf.

Gerlach, M. 1987. "Business Alliances and the Japanese Firm." *California Management Review* 30, no. 1 (Fall).

Helfat, C., and D. Teece. 1987. "Vertical Integration and Risk Reduction." *Journal of Law, Economics, and Organization*, 3, no. 1 (Spring): 47-67.

Horwitch, M. Forthcoming. *Post Modern Management*. New York: Free Press.

Koopmans, T. 1957. *Three Essays on the State of Economic Science*. New York: McGraw-Hill.

Levin, R., et al. 1984. "Survey Research on R&D Appropriability and Technological Opportunity." Unpublished manuscript, Yale University, New Haven, Conn.

Malerba, F. 1985. *The Semiconductor Business*. London: Frances Pinter.

Monoclonal Antibodies Inc. 1986. *10-K Report*.

Mowery, D. 1983a. "Innovation, Market Structure and Government Policy in the American Semiconductor Electronics Industry: A Survey." *Research Policy*, 4.

_____. 1983b. "The Relationship between Contractual and Intrafirm Forms of Industrial Research in American Manufacturing, 1900-1940." *Explorations in Economic History*, 20: 351-374.

Office of Technology Assessment. 1984. *Commercial Biotechnology—An International Analysis*. U.S. Congress. Washington, D.C.: U.S. Government Printing Office.

Office of Technology Assessment and Forecasting. 1983. *Patent Profiles—Biotechnology: 1982 Update*. U.S. Department of Commerce. Washington, D.C.: U.S. Government Printing Office.

Paine Webber Company. 1986. "Biotechnology Industry: 1986 Fact Book." A report prepared by Linda Miller, Paine Webber Company, New York.

Pisano, G. 1988. Innovation Through Markets, Hierarchies, and Joint Ventures: Technology Strategy and Collaborative Arrangement in the Biotechnology Industry. Unpublished Ph.D. dissertation, University of California, Berkeley.

Ruscio, K. 1983. University Industry Relations in Biotechnology: A Study of the Public Policy Issues. Unpublished Ph.D. dissertation, Syracuse University.

Shan, Weijian. 1987. Technology Change and Interfirm Cooperation: Evidence from Commercialization of Biotechnology. Unpublished Ph.D. dissertation, University of California, Berkeley.

Sharp, M. 1985. "The New Biotechnology: European Governments in Search of a Strategy." Sussex European Paper No. 15. Science Policy Research Unit, Sussex, United Kingdom.

Teece, D. 1981. "The Market for Know-How and the Efficient International Transfer of Technology." *Annals of the American Academy of Political and Social Science*, 458 (November): 81-96.

_____. 1986. "Profiting from Technological Innovation: Implications for Integration, Collaboration, Licensing, and Public Policy." *Research Policy*, December, 1986.

Venture. 1986. "Asian Money." November: 34-38.

Wall Street Journal. 1987. "Genentech Inc. Shares Tumble in Response to License Rejection," June 2, pp. 3, 23.

Williamson, O. 1975. *Markets and Hierarchies.* New York: Free Press.

_____. 1985. *The Economic Institutions of Capitalism.* New York: Free Press.

7 COLLABORATIONS IN ROBOTICS

Steven Klepper

The international robotics market is dominated by producers from Japan, the United States, and Europe. It is characterized by numerous international agreements, including marketing agreements, manufacturing and technology licenses, R&D collaborations, limited equity investments, and equity joint ventures. In a recent article (Reich and Mankin, 1986), the general value of U.S. firms' participation in such agreements was questioned, with three international robotics collaborations singled out for criticism. This chapter examines the nature of industrial robotics alliances involving U.S. firms, the motives for the alliances, and the consequences of robotics international equity joint ventures for U.S. welfare.

The paper is organized as follows. In Section 2 the technology of robots is reviewed. The historical development of the market in the United States, Japan, and Europe is traced in Sections 3 and 4. In Section 5 the collaborations engaged in by U.S. firms are reviewed and analyzed. The international equity joint ventures involving U.S. firms are reviewed in depth in Section 6. Speculation about the welfare effects of and future trends in robotics international equity joint ventures are offered in Section 7. Throughout attention is restricted to industrial robots.

ROBOT TECHNOLOGY

The word *robot* first entered the English language in a 1923 translation of the Czech play, "Rossum's Universal Robots," by Karel Capek. In the play robots are biologically grown and human like except for a lack of emotions. Most industrial robots, however, are simply mechanical arms fixed to the floor, ceiling, wall, or another machine. Robots are distinguished from related devices, such as numerically controlled (NC) machines and teleoperators, in that they are multifunctional, programmable, and involve no human interaction.

Robots are powered by electric, hydraulic, or pneumatic means. They are controlled by a controller, which today is typically microprocessor based. The controller operates by adjusting the position of the robot arm in response to feedback from internal and external sensors. End effectors, which can be tools or simply devices to pick up parts, are connected to the arm. Robots can be used to perform numerous functions, including welding, spray painting, machine loading and unloading, assembly, and parts transfer.

Robots come in many different configurations depending upon their purpose. They differ in reach, accuracy, and ability to repeat a programmed path. They are typically powered by electric drives, with hydraulic drives used for robots lifting heavy loads, and occasionally pneumatic drives used for tasks requiring less precision. Controllers vary in their capacity to store and process information and their ability to coordinate information from multiple sources. Different approaches are used to program robots, with some robots programmed via teaching (i.e., recording the movement of the robot as it is moved through a desired path) and others through formal programming languages. Sensors are also used to provide information about the external environment. These can be vision sensors, which use cameras to record images and computer algorithms to identify the images, as well as simpler touch and proximity sensors.

The characteristics of a robot that determine its attractiveness include

- Cost
- Repeatability—how well the robot can repeat a programmed path after repeated use
- Accuracy—the ability of the robot initially to follow a certain path
- Ease of programming

- Maximum lifting capacity
- Reliability
- Ease of integration into a broader system

Each of these characteristics is the subject of a great deal of current research. New materials are being experimented with to increase the stiffness of robot arms in order to improve their accuracy. Vision and other types of sensors are being used to improve both accuracy and reliability. New types of motors are being developed to reduce the cost of robots and to improve their lifting capacity. A great deal of work is being devoted to the development of robot programming languages to facilitate off-line programming of robots—programming that does not require taking the robot off the production line. In addition, considerable research is being devoted to the development of controllers and software to coordinate robots with other programmable devices. A distinctive feature of robot technology, illustrated by current research, is that it draws on many diverse disciplines, including computing, mechanics, electrical engineering, mathematics, fluid engineering, metallurgy, and control engineering.

Installing robots involves a lot more than merely picking a robot. An end effector must be chosen; sensors must be selected and integrated with the robot and its controller; the robot and peripheral devices must be programmed; the robot must be integrated with other devices on the factory floor such as parts feeders, conveyors, and NC machines; user personnel must be trained; and the whole system must be coordinated. These steps, often called *application engineering* or *systems engineering*, can be considerably more costly than the robot itself.

More complicated robot installations involve flexible manufacturing systems (FMS). Such systems consist of workstations composed of machine tools, robots, inspection devices, and related types of machinery linked by materials handling systems such as parts feeders, conveyors, and automatic guided vehicles (AGVs). They are typically used to produce a family of parts. The most complicated applications of robots involve computer integrated manufacturing (CIM), which integrates FMS with computer aided design (CAD), computer aided engineering (CAE), and management information systems (MIS). CAD uses computers and graphics software to design products on a screen. CAE simulates the performance of products to detect defects. Coupled with software to program the FMS to produce the product according to the computer aided design, CAD and CAE are lumped together and called CAD/CAM (computer aided design/computer aided manufacturing). MIS is used to store and process production information for management purposes.

Future advances in robotics and CIM are likely to depend on advances in computers and software. The technological frontiers in robotics will be the areas most related to computers—electronic controls, sensing (especially vision), programming languages, and software to integrate components of CIM.

DEVELOPMENT OF THE U.S. MARKET

The Demand for Robots

The major advantages of robots are savings in labor and materials, improved product quality, and greater flexibility in responding to demand changes. Robots tend to be most advantageous when production occurs in small lots. When large volumes are produced, less flexible, "hard automation" devices are usually more economical. When volume is very small, manual labor is usually cheaper.

The leading robot users in the United States are the automobile and electronics producers. Not only are many of their activities performed in small lots, but they also face severe competition from firms in low-wage countries. The use of robots and other flexible automation devices is an essential part of their strategy to remain competitive in the future. The primary use of robots in the automobile industry is for spot welding. Other important applications include coating, arc welding, and assembly. Electronics firms use robots primarily for small parts assembly. Robots are also used extensively by metal forming firms to load and unload die casting machines.

Most robot adoptions have been by large firms. The use of robots requires large engineering expenses to fit them into the workplace. These costs can be prohibitive for small firms, which tend to use only a few robots. Large firms are also more able to withstand the uncertainty concerning the performance of robots on the work floor.

There has been very rapid growth in the use of robots by U.S. firms. Table 7-1 lists the sales of U.S. based robot firms from 1976 to 1984 with estimates provided for 1985 and 1986. The annual growth rate in robot sales has been very high in the last ten years, in many instances exceeding 50 percent. Although growth has been high in the last few years following the severe recession of the early 1980s, annual growth rates are expected to decline in the near future to around 20 percent. Fueled by advances in vision technology, the big growth areas in robot usage are expected to be assembly and arc welding, with assembly applications growing from 10 percent cur-

Table 7-1.   Sales of U.S. Based Robot Vendors, 1976-1986.

Year	Sales ($ millions)
1976	$ 15
1977	25
1978	30
1979	45
1980	90
1981	155
1982	190
1983	240
1984	395
1985	585 (est.)
1986	690 (est.)

Source: Prudential-Bache Securities, various reports.

rently to as high as 40 percent of all robot applications in the future (Baranson, 1983, p. 49).

Robots are expected to be used increasingly as interface devices in flexible manufacturing systems. By 1992 it is expected that over 30 percent of all robots will be interfaced with CAD/CAM systems (Tech Tran Corporation, 1982, p. 218). While the current users are expected to remain the biggest users of robots, robots are also expected to spread to, among other uses, the production of pharmaceuticals, cosmetics, personal care products, and medical products and to be used for inspection, handling of nuclear/radioactive materials, and in unmanned space vehicles.

The Production of Robots

The development of the robotics industry has closely paralleled the prototypical developmental pattern of new industries.[1] Initially the industry experienced a gestation period in which the number of producers was quite small. These initial producers tended to be highly vertically integrated, producing many of their own components and engaging in substantial efforts to market and service their robots. As sales of the industry grew, component suppliers and application specialists emerged, reducing the vertical requirements to enter the industry. Many new firms, some start-ups and others spinoffs of incumbents or related firms, entered the industry. These entrants often introduced major product innovations or concentrated on producing robots and related devices for specific applications. Market shares were unstable, with new entrants sometimes gaining a substantial share of the market at the expense of established firms. Over time, the rate of growth of output declined, the number of entrants fell, and the number of firms exiting the industry increased. Currently the industry seems poised for a long predicted shakeout in the number of producers.

A more detailed description of the development of the robotics industry is presented below. Four stages are distinguished in the development of the industry. In each stage the principal entrants and exiters are described and major developments in the industry are reviewed. Data on sales shares throughout is from Conigliaro and Chien (1985).

Stage 1.   Stage 1 is composed of the period 1961 to the mid-1970s. Over this period robot sales grew very slowly, reaching $15 million by the end of the period. The industry was composed of just a few vendors and a few major customers, principally the automobile companies. The first entrant into the industry was Unimation. Set up as a subsidiary of Consolidated Diesel Engine, Unimation bought up the early robot patents of George Devol and sold its first robot to General Motors in 1961. This first robot, the Unimate, was a hydraulic robot with a high lifting capacity that was widely used for spot welding. Subsequently Unimation introduced a wide range of robots, including the PUMA robot for assembly. It also developed its own programming language and vision systems as well as producing a number of its own components. After experiencing managerial difficulties, Unimation was acquired by Westinghouse in 1983. Its original leader, Joseph Engleberger, often called the father of robotics, was replaced and the company was reorganized, with Westinghouse's robotics business merged into Unimation's. In the early years of the robotics industry Unimation accounted for over 50 percent of all robot sales. By 1985, however, its combined share with Westinghouse of the sales of U.S. based firms was estimated to be only 9 percent.

A few years after the Unimate was introduced, AMF, a producer of leisure equipment, introduced the Versatran line. For many years the Versatran was the main competitor to the Unimate. In 1979 the Versatran line was acquired by (then) Prab Conveyors, a supplier of scrap handling conveyor and processing systems. Prab had entered the market itself in 1968 with a line of medium-technology robots designed for machine loading and unloading. Prab now produces a wide range of robots for machine loading and unloading and markets a West German robot for process applications. It has also expanded heavily into robotic systems, and it recently introduced a software system linking CAD output to its robots and a new, low-cost vision system. Like Unimation, Prab produces a number of its own components. While its sales have risen, its share of the sales of U.S. based firms has declined over time to around 3 percent in 1985. Prab is one of the few robot firms that has been consistently profitable in recent years.

Stage 2.   Stage 2 is composed of the period from the mid-1970s to 1979. During this period robot sales rose steadily, increasing from $15 million to $45 million, with automobile firms fueling the rise. Besides Unimation and Prab, the industry was composed principally of four other firms: Cincinnati-Milacron (CM), ASEA, DeVilbiss, and Autoplace.

CM is a major producer of NC machine tools. Capitalizing on its NC expertise, it introduced the first minicomputer-controlled robot in 1974. Currently CM markets a broad line of robotics products, including robots supplied by a Japanese firm. Like Prab and Unimation, CM produces a number of its own components. For many years CM was the number two firm in sales in the United States, behind Unimation. It passed Unimation in sales in 1983–1984 and currently ranks second in the industry with about 10 percent of the sales of U.S. based firms. CM has sold a number of robots in Europe and is one of the few U.S. firms that produces and markets its robots in Japan.

ASEA is a leading Swedish electronics company that produces robots worldwide, including in the United States. It produced the first all electric robot in 1974. Its strength is its broad line of robots and numerous robotics service centers throughout the world. Its share of the sales of U.S. based firms has remained steady between 5 and 10 percent and currently is 7 percent. DeVilbiss produces spray painting guns and related equipment. After conducting some of the early research in spray painting robots, it entered the market in 1974 by licensing the hydraulic spray painting robot of Trallfa, a leading Norwegian robotics firm. It began producing the Trallfa robot in 1980. It markets a narrow range of robots, accounting for currently about 23 percent of the sales of finishing and coating robots. Overall it currently has about 4 percent of the sales of U.S. based firms. The last major early producer was Autoplace, which was acquired by Copperweld in 1979. It exited the industry in 1984. Although its market share was never very substantial, hovering around 2 to 3 percent in 1980–1983, Autoplace was considered the largest U.S. producer of small robots when it was acquired. It was also one of the early firms to develop a robot vision system.

Stage 3. Stage 3 is composed of the period 1979–1983. This period is characterized by a great deal of entry by innovative firms. The capabilities of vision systems advanced greatly, much new software to control robots and integrate them into systems was developed, and CIM began to emerge as a reality. Declining prices of robots, coupled with their increasing capabilities, caused demand to surge and sales to grow rapidly. Demand expanded beyond the automobile companies, as the use of robots for assembly and arc welding increased greatly. Sales rose from $45 million in 1979 to $240 million in 1983 despite the severe recession of the 1980s.

During stage 3 firms devoted a large amount of resources toward improving the capabilities of robots and integrating robots with other flexible automation devices. R&D averaged around 19 percent of shipments (U.S. International Trade Commission, 1983, p. 16). A great deal of resources were devoted to customizing robots as parts of systems including vision, tactile, and force sensors, CAD, CAE, AGVs, NC machines, and automated handling systems.

The market began to disintegrate vertically in stage 3. Entrants produced a narrow range of robots relying heavily on the components of other firms. Some entrants specialized in robot controls, others in the software to coordinate the robot with other flexible automation devices, and others in vision systems. Another group of entrants exploited their knowledge of specific applications, such as arc welding, to develop specialized robotic systems. A third group of large electronics/machine tool producers entered by providing a wide range of CIM products, specializing in selling all the flexible automation equipment needed for the factory of the future. All three types of entrants in this period relied heavily on foreign robot firms to provide arms for their robots, causing the number of international collaborations to rise greatly. Robot imports increased sharply, rising from roughly 1 percent of shipments in 1979 to 17 percent of shipments in 1983, with the percentage of imports accounted for by robot subassemblies rising from 3.4 percent in 1979 to 52 percent in 1983 (U.S. International Trade Commission, 1983, p. 35).

The firms that entered during stage 3 based upon expertise in electronic controls and software were primarily new entities financed by venture capital. Many of these firms produced stand-alone vision systems as well as robots. Some specialized in CIM, while others left systems engineering to specialized vendors. The most prominent firms in this group are Automatix, American Cimflex, Adept, Intelledex, International Robomation/Intelligence (IRI), Control Automation, Machine Intelligence Corporation (MIC), and Object Recognition Systems (ORS). Other firms in this category include Nova

Robotics, U.S. Robots, and two machine vision companies, Robot Vision Systems and Machine Vision International, both of which have links to robotics firms. All of these firms specialize in robots for small parts material handling and assembly and some market arc welding robots and systems. Among U.S. based firms selling small parts material handling and assembly robots, Adept is the leader with 16 percent of the market, Automatix ranks seventh with 8 percent of the market, and American Cimflex ranks eighth with 7 percent of the market. Automatix also ranks second in sales of arc welding robots by U.S. based firms with 13 percent of the market. Automatix, Intelledex, and IRI are all leading vendors of stand-alone vision systems and Control Automation supplies CM with vision systems for its robots. Both MIC and ORS are primarily machine vision companies whose involvement with robotics is through collaborations with robotics firms.

Another group of firms entered to capitalize on applications expertise. The most prominent firms in this group are GMF, Kuka, Graco Robotics, IBM, Cybotech, Seiko U.S.A., ESAB, Hobart, Advanced Robotics, Nordson, and Admiral. Of these firms, GMF stands out. It is a joint venture of GM and Fanuc of Japan and currently is the leading U.S. based robot firm and a world leader in robotics. It combines GM's expertise in applications, software, vision, and robotic painting systems with Fanuc's expertise in electronic controls and robots. It produces an extremely broad line of robots and currently accounts for 31 percent of the sales of U.S. based robot vendors and 60 percent of the sales of finishing and coating robots by U.S. based vendors.

Kuka, a leading West German producer of robots, assembles robots in the United States through a U.S. subsidiary. It capitalizes on its background in welding equipment to produce spot and arc welding robot systems. It currently accounts for 5 percent of the sales of U.S. based vendors. Graco Robotics is a joint venture of Graco, a U.S. manufacturer of fluid handling equipment, and Edon Finishing Systems of the U.S. It specializes in spray painting robots, where it currently ranks third behind GMF and DeVilbiss with 14 percent of the sales of U.S. based firms. IBM has been involved in robotics for a long time. It concentrates on robots for the assembly of small parts and extensively uses its robots in its own plants. It currently ranks second behind Adept with about 15 percent of the sales of small parts handling and assembly robots by U.S. based firms. Cybotech is a joint venture of Ransburg of the United States and Renault of France. It combines Renault's expertise in producing and using robots with Ransburg's expertise in resistance welding. It has concentrated on heavy duty hydraulic robots for arc welding, cutting, and heavy part transport, currently ranking fourth in the sale of arc welding robots by U.S. based firms with 10 percent of the market.

Seiko U.S.A. is a leading Japanese watch producer that initially developed robots for its own use. It has a base in the United States, where it specializes in low-priced robots for assembly and small parts material handling. It currently accounts for 10 percent of the sales of U.S. based firms in this submarket. ESAB is a manufacturer of welding equipment based in Sweden with subsidiaries around the world, including the United States. It sells welding robot systems and currently ranks first with 13 percent of the sales of arc welding robots by U.S. based firms. All of its robots are supplied by ASEA, which owns a controlling interest in ESAB. Hobart and Advanced are also welding specialists. Hobart is a welding systems supplier that sells its own welding equipment with the robots of other manufacturers. It currently ranks fourth with about 10 percent of the sales of arc welding robots of U.S. based firms. Advanced began as a leveraged buyout of the automated systems division of Air Products and Chemicals. Before going bankrupt in 1985, it had captured 4 percent of the total sales of U.S. based firms.

Nordson designs, manufactures, and markets industrial equipment for applying paints and adhesives. Before exiting the market, it specialized in finishing and coating robots. It had 2 percent of the market of U.S. based firms in 1982 and 1983 (see Table 7–2). Last, Admiral is a specialist in the design and manufacture of polyurethane processing machinery. It has an agreement with a Japanese firm to use its robots in systems involving reaction injection molding presses. Other robot producers in specialized markets, not necessarily associated with specific applications, include Thermwood, Mobot, and Oedetics.

The last group of entrants in stage 3 is composed of the so-called factory-of-the-future firms. These firms sell robots as just one part of flexible automation systems. They not only produce and sell a wide range of flexible automation equipment, but they are also heavy users of it as well. The leading factory-of-the-future firms include GE, GCA, Westinghouse, and Bendix. GE entered the robotics market through a series of agreements with foreign robot manufacturers. It has also developed its own controller and vision systems for arc welding and bin picking (selecting specific objects from a bin of diverse objects). In 1985 it accounted for a little over 2 percent of the sales of U.S. based robot producers. GCA is a major manufacturer of equipment used to produce semiconductors. It acquired PaR Systems, a robot manufacturer, and licenses the robots of a lead-

Table 7-2. Sales of U.S. Based Robotics Firms, 1980-1985 ($ millions).

Firm	Year					
	1980	1981	1982	1983	1984	1985
GMF	—	—	0.3	22.3	102.8	180.0
Cincinnati Milacron	29.0	50.0	32.0	51.0	52.5	59.0
Westinghouse/						
Unimation	40.0	68.0	63.0	36.0	44.5	45.0
ASEA	2.5	9.0	9.5	15.0	30.0	39.0
GCA	—	—	1.5	6.0	13.5	35.0
DeVilbiss	5.0	6.5	23.7	21.0	30.0	33.0
Kuka	NA	NA	NA	NA	NA	27.0
Automatix	0.4	3.0	8.1	12.7	17.3	25.0
American Cimflex	—	—	—	2.8	8.0	20.0
Graco	—	—	—	5.0	9.3	20.0
IBM	—	—	4.5	9.0	12.0	16.0
Adept	—	—	—	—	1.1	15.0
GE	—	—	1.8	11.0	10.0	13.0
Cybotech	—	—	9.0	2.3	7.0	12.0
Prab Robots	5.5	8.2	12.5	13.5	11.0	12.0
Seiko	—	—	—	4.0	6.5	11.0
Intelledex	—	—	—	2.0	10.0	10.0
ESAB	NA	NA	NA	4.0	4.5	8.0
Hobart	—	—	—	3.5	5.5	6.5
Total	90	155	190	240	395	585

NA = Not available.
Source: Prudential-Bache Securities, various reports.

ing Japanese producer. It uses its own controller and programming language on all of its robots. Currently it accounts for 6 percent of the sales of U.S. based firms. Westinghouse was an early researcher in flexible manufacturing systems, performing some of this work with financial support from the National Science Foundation (*Robotics Today*, 1983). Like GE it has accumulated considerable experience from automating its own plants. Its entry into the robotics market was through a series of agreements with foreign firms. Subsequently it acquired Unimation. Last, Bendix is a specialty tools manufacturer. It discontinued production of its own robot in 1983 but has agreements with two foreign manufacturers to use their robots in automated systems.

Stage 4.   The last stage in the development of the robotics industry began in 1983 and is still going on. This has been a stage of consolidation. Entry has slowed drastically, with venture capital virtually drying up. Exit has increased, with a number of firms, including Copperweld, Advanced, Bendix, and Nordson, ceasing production. For the years 1983–1985 sales growth was high as the U.S. recovered from the deep recession of the early 1980s, but it is predicted to slow considerably in the coming years.

Market shares have been unstable as users have shifted toward recent, innovative entrants. GMF has expanded greatly, especially at the expense of Unimation and CM. Some new firms specializing in controls and software, including Adept, Automatix, American Cimflex, and Intelledex, have grown impressively. Other specialist firms have captured sizable shares of certain submarkets. In arc welding this includes ESAB, Hobart, and Kuka; in finishing and coating Graco; and in small parts material handling and assembly IBM and Seiko. The change in the market shares of U.S. based firms in recent years is illustrated in Table 7–2.

The vertical disintegration of the industry has continued in stage 4. Sizable markets have developed for end effectors, stand-alone vision systems (as well as robot guidance vision systems), CAD, CAE software and hardware, and programmable controllers. Robot rental firms, consultants, systems companies, and factory automation firms have emerged. Imports, especially of robot subassemblies, have also continued to increase. GMF has imported a large number of robots from Fanuc and most of the major robot firms have begun importing robots, especially from Japanese firms. In addition, some major foreign producers, such as Kuka and Seiko, have developed a presence in the U.S. market. Exports have also increased, but not at the pace of imports. GMF and a number of other U.S. based firms sell a substantial amount of robots in Europe. CM now produces and sells robots in Japan, as does ASEA. Some software/electronic control firms, such as Automatix and American Cimflex, also sell in Japan. A number of the stand-alone vision companies have made considerable inroads in Japan and Europe selling vision systems.

R&D continues at a very high percentage of sales. A great deal of R&D by American companies is devoted to vision, advanced control systems, off-line programming, and interfaces between components of flexible automation systems. The buzzword of the industry has become CIM. Some standardization is just beginning to occur in CIM products across users.[2] This may signal a trend toward less customization of products in the future. It also augurs well for the robot producers, many of whom have incurred substantial losses in part because of high costs of custom application engineering. Indeed, it appears that by mid-1986 a number of robot firms will be earning profits for the first time (Conigliaro and Chien, 1985).

Development of the International Market

Japan is the world's leading producer and user of robots. Although the Japanese began producing robots only in 1967 with the importation of the Versatran robot of AMF, the number of producers and the use of robots has expanded much more rapidly in Japan than in the United States in recent years.[3] Japan has concentrated on using and producing less complicated robotic devices than in the United States and has been faster to adopt robots for assembly and arc welding. The strength of Japanese producers has been in motors and mechanical arms. Unlike U.S. producers, many Japanese robotics firms started producing robots for their own use. Robot sales typically account for only a small portion of the total sales of Japanese firms, many of whom are leaders in other industries. The Japanese industry is much more fragmented than the U.S. industry, with anywhere from 150 to 250 sellers, none of whom have more than 17 percent of the market. The leading Japanese firms are listed in Table 7-3 along with some of their characteristics.

West Germany has also become a leading producer and user of robots in recent years. Like the United States, the major users of robots in West Germany are the automobile producers, including Volkswagenwerks, BMW, Daimler-Benz, Ford, and ZF. The West German robotics industry is fairly concentrated, with the top five firms accounting for 70 percent of total robot sales. The leading West German firms and their characteristics are presented in Table 7-4.

Other countries with major robotics producers include Sweden, France, Norway, Italy, and the United Kingdom. The most notable firms in these countries and their characteristics are presented in Table 7-5.

COLLABORATIONS

The robotics industry is characterized by a great deal of collaborations ranging from simple original equipment manufacturer (OEM) deals to equity joint ventures. A number of factors have been conducive to collaborations, especially those transcending national boundaries. First, the robotics industry has developed at a very different pace in different countries. The United States was the first to develop its industry and early on was a source for much robotics technology. Subsequently robotics developed very rapidly in Japan, partly fueled by government efforts. Coupled with the production ex-

Table 7-3. Leading Japanese Robotics Firms: Selected Characteristics.

Firm	Characteristics
Matsushita	Market leader with 17 percent of sales of Japanese firms; specialists in assembly robots; has a U.S. subsidiary
Fanuc	Second biggest Japanese producer with 7 percent of sales of Japanese firms; world leader in computer numerical controls and specialist in motors for NC machines and robots; sells a wide range of robots via international collaborations
Yaskawa	Third leading Japanese producer, specializing in arc welding robots and recently assembly robots; strong export orientation, many international agreements
Dainichi Kiko	Fourth leading Japanese producer; strong export orientation, many international agreements
Hitachi	Fifth leading Japanese producer; leading producer of computer and related electronic control equipment and leader in production of sophisticated robots and flexible manufacturing systems; uses extensive network of U.S. and Canadian firms to market and service its products in North America
Kawasaki	Leader in spot welding robots; licensee of Unimation
Nachi Fujikoshi	Leader in spot and arc welding robots
Toshiba	Specialist in assembly robots and vision
Mitsubishi	Specialist in arc welding robots
Kobe Steel	Licensee of Trallfa and leading Japanese producer of spray painting robots
Mitsubishi Heavy Industries	Specialist in painting and welding robots
Sankyo Seiki	Leader in assembly robots
NEC	Specialist in assembly robots and vision systems
Tokico	Produces major spray painting robot
Aida	Specialist in robots for press working operations
Seiko	Specialist in small assembly robots with major presence in United States
Yamaha	Recent producer of assembly robots

Table 7-4. Leading West German Robotics Firms: Selected Characteristics.

Firm	Characteristics
Volkswagenwerks	Produces material handling and machine loading robots, mostly for own use
Kuka	Leading West German exporter of robots; specialist in welding robots and recently introduced an assembly robot
Nimak Machinen Automation	Sells welding robots through a U.S. licensee
Jungenheinrich	Recent entrant whose robots used principally for welding and machine tool applications
GdA	Recent entrant that specializes in spot welding robots

Table 7-5. Other Leading International Robot Producers.

Firm	Characteristics
ASEA, Sweden	Producer of broad line of robots; has subsidiaries in the United States and Japan
Saab-Scania, Sweden	Leading Swedish developer of CAD/CAM
Renault, France	Leading French robot producer
Trallfa, Norway	Leading worldwide producer of painting robots; markets internationally through a U.S. and a Japanese licensee; ASEA recently acquired a controlling interest
Comau, Italy	Supplies Fiat with flexible manufacturing systems
Osai, Italy	Supplies robots to Olivetti
Basfer, Italy	Specialist in painting robots
DEA, Italy	Producer of assembly robots used in the automotive industry
Meta Machines, United Kingdom	Produces a laser-based arc welding system called the Meta Torch

pertise of Japanese firms, this has made Japanese firms attractive partners in recent years. A similar pattern has contributed to collaborations involving West German firms. Second, firms in different countries have different skills. The U.S. firms specialize in electronic controls and software but tend to be weaker in robot arm technology. Consequently U.S. firms have sought out overseas partners who specialize in robot arm technology while at the same time marketing their technology to foreign firms through various types of collaborations. Third, robotics technology has undergone rapid technological change in recent years. This has contributed to the dispersion of expertise across firms and thus provided an obvious incentive for collaboration.

Another factor that has contributed to collaborations is the importance of users in the robotics industry. Like many young industries, users are an important source of information about market demands and the technological means to satisfy them. Moreover, robots are rarely useful as stand-alone devices. They need to be integrated into systems that often involve a great deal of peripheral equipment, such as in arc welding applications. Firms with specialized application knowledge—that is, specialized users of robots—are well situated to provide these services. However, users frequently lack the technological capacity to design and produce robots. This provides a natural motive for collaborations between users and producers.

A last pertinent factor is that robot production is not yet characterized by substantial economies of scale. Consequently there is not a strong motive to centralize production, thus removing a barrier to certain types of collaborations.

A distinctive characteristic of robotics collaborations involving U.S. firms is that they are not concentrated in just one aspect of robotics. Some of the collaborations involve R&D and product development, some production and marketing, and others product support. This is a reflection of the different types of backgrounds and expertise of the U.S. firms and the different motives for their collaborations. To highlight this, the collaborations involving the U.S. firms are discussed separately for the set of six early producers, the electronic controls/software specialists, the application specialists, and the factory-of-the-future firms. Information concerning the robotics collaborations involving U.S. firms was drawn primarily from the trade press.

Collaborations of the Early Producers

The principal collaborations involving the initial six major U.S. robot producers and the motives for the collaborations are summarized in Table 7–6. Unimation has been the most active collaborator of the initial producers, reflecting its historical position as leader in the industry. It has licensed many firms internationally to sell or produce its products. Its most notable licensee is Kawasaki Heavy Industries of Japan, which used its agreement with Unimation initially to be-

Table 7-6.   Principal Collaborations of the Initial Six Major Producers.

Firm	Partner	Nature of Collaboration	Primary Motives
Unimation	Kawasaki	Manufacturing license, technology transfer, joint technology development	Expand distribution, acquire technology to exploit distribution
"	Linde Division of Union Carbide	Limited marketing license	Expand distribution
"	Nokia	Manufacturing license	Expand distribution
"	Koor Industries Clal Industries	Manufacturing license	Expand distribution
"	GKN	Marketing license	Expand distribution
"	Unimation Europe	Wholly owned subsidiary	Expand distribution
"	Electrolux	Unimation got marketing license	Exploit distribution network
"	Trallfa	Unimation got marketing license	Exploit distribution network
"	Vicarm	Unimation acquired Vicarm	Expand technological capacity
"	ICC	Unimation acquired manufacturing license	Expand technological capacity
"	Komatsu	Unimation acquired marketing license	Exploit distribution network
Prab	Daido Steel	Marketing license	Expand distribution
"	Hawker-Siddeley	Marketing license	Expand distribution
"	Can Eng	Manufacturing license, technology exchange	Expand distribution
"	Murata Machinery	Manufacturing license, technology exchange	Expand distribution
"	Fabrique Nationale	Manufacturing license, technology exchange	Expand distribution network
"	Electro-Matic Inc.	Limited marketing license	Expand distribution network
"	EKE	Prab acquired a manufacturing license	Exploit distribution network
"	Siemens	Prab acquired a manufacturing license	Exploit distribution network
"	Matra Datavision	Joint technological development	Expand technological capacity

(Table 7-6. continued overleaf)

Table 7-6. continued

Firm	Partner	Nature of Collaboration	Primary Motives
Cincinnati-Milacron	Ansaldo Elettronica	Marketing license	Expand distribution
"	Utsumi Kiko	Supplier of Cincinnati-Milacron components	Expand distribution (by lowering cost)
"	Dainichi-Kiko	Dainichi-Kiko supplies robots to Cincinnati-Milacron specifications, technology exchange	Exploit distribution network
"	Control Automation	Purchase of vision systems	Expand technological capacity
"	Hitachi	Cincinnati-Milacron acquired a marketing license	Exploit distribution network
ASEA	Electrolux	Acquisition	Expand technological capacity
"	Nitto Seiko	Nitto Seiko supplies robots to ASEA specifications	Exploit distribution network
"	Trallfa	Acquisition of controlling interest	Expand technological capacity, exploit distribution network
DeVilbiss	Trallfa	DeVilbiss acquires manufacturing license (previously had marketing license)	Exploit technological and market knowledge
"	Matsushita	DeVilbiss gets limited marketing license	Exploit distribution network
"	American Cimflex	DeVilbiss gets limited marketing license	Exploit distribution network
Copperweld	Nachi-Fujikoshi	Copperweld gets marketing license	Exploit distribution network
"	Remek Automation	Copperweld gets marketing license	Exploit distribution network

come the leading producer of robots in Japan. In recent years Kawasaki has provided technology to Unimation and has collaborated with Unimation on research and on the development of robots. Unimation also started a subsidiary in England using financial support from the British government. The subsidiary is now a full-fledged manufacturing and research entity.

Unimation also markets the products of other firms and has engaged in collaborations to expand its technology. Around 1975 it acquired Vicarm, a small, innovative robot firm that produced the robot language VAL, which serves as the basis for Unimation's current programming language. When Unimation was acquired by Westinghouse, Vicarm was spun off as Adept Technology. Unimation retained a 15 percent interest in Adept in order to access technological developments at Adept. More recently, Unimation licensed an advanced control technology from International Cybernetic Corporation (ICC) and got manufacturing rights to an ICC controller.

The other five initial major producers have engaged in similar collaborations to Unimation. Prab licenses its technology and also licenses the technology of other firms. Recently Prab licensed a controller of Siemens of West Germany to use with a robot it licenses from GdA of West Germany. It also recently developed a software system with Matra Datavision of France, which it uses to direct its GdA robots from remote CAD systems. Cincinnati Milacron has set up production of its robots in Japan using Utsumi Koki Machinery Company of Japan to manufacture its robot arms. It has also signed an agreement with Dainichi Kiko (DK) of Japan for DK to develop robot models to its specifications, and it has worked in the United States with Control Automation to develop robot vision systems and with McAuto of McDonnell Douglas on a CAD system. ASEA has a major presence worldwide, which it expanded recently by acquiring a controlling interest in Trallfa of Norway, a leading producer of painting robots, and by agreeing with its Japanese partner Gadelius KK and Trallfa and its licensees to collaborate on the manufacture, marketing, and development of robots. Previously, ASEA acquired the pneumatic robots of Electrolux of Sweden and engaged Nitto Seiko of Japan to produce robots to its specification. DeVilbiss, which originally was not a manufacturer but a licensee of Trallfa, has concentrated on acquiring licenses to market and manufacture the products of other firms. Last, before its exit Copperweld gained the U.S. distribution rights to the robots of two non-U.S. producers.

The principal motivations for the various collaborations of the initial six major producers can be divided into three categories:

1. Expansion of the firm's distribution network by granting other firms marketing, manufacturing, and technology licenses for regions or business segments not served by the firm

2. Exploitation of the firm's distribution network by marketing the robots of other producers that complement the firm's line

3. Expansion of the firm's technological capacity by acquiring a robot line or by having a producer design and supply robots to the firm's specifications

None of the collaborations engaged in by the initial six major producers involved a joint equity arrangement, either between national or foreign firms. Neither of the first two types of collaborations require coordinated joint participation. However, the third type of collaboration could conceivably benefit from a joint equity arrangement. Why wasn't this form of collaboration used? In some instances a simpler arrangement, in which one firm acquired the interests of the other, was possible. Examples include the acquisition of Electrolux's robot division by ASEA and the acquisition of Vicarm by Unimation. In other instances the technology exchange involved only a small part of the acquirer's business and was restricted to a fairly easy to specify set of technologies, thus facilitating contracting. Moreover, by and large these agreements did not involve continuing technological exchanges of diffuse information, thus making an ongoing relationship unnecessary. Examples of contracts in which one firm produced a robot to the buyer's specifications include the agreements between CM and Dainichi Kiko and ASEA and Nitto Seiko. Other contractual relationships include the Unimation-ICC, Prab-Matra Datavision, and CM-Control Automation arrangements.

Collaborations Involving the Electronic Controls/Software Firms

The electronic controls/software firms have introduced a number of software, controls, and vision innovations. At the same time they tend to lack expertise in mechanical arms and, being younger than the initial six major producers, have not developed large international distribution channels. These factors have shaped the collaborations engaged in by these firms. Table 7–7 summarizes the major collaborations of the electronic controls/software firms and the motives for them.

A number of these collaborations are designed to enable the U.S. firms to access or acquire robot technology which complements their specialized expertise. For example, Automatix has combined its controller and vision systems with the robots it licenses from Hitachi and Hirata Industrial Machineries Company of Japan and Jungenheinrich of West Germany. It also started a limited $7.7 million R&D partnership with four other firms to finance computer-aided manufacturing products. American Cimflex has acquired marketing and manufacturing licenses from various firms, purchased IRI's vision technology, and cofinanced Visual Machines and Rediffusion Simulation of Great Britain, firms involved in the development of new robotics technology. Similar agreements have been engaged in by: Intelledex, which is working with Applied Materials of California to develop a clean room robot; IRI, which is participating in a $1.3 billion consortium in West Germany to develop intelligent computers for processing vision information; Machine Intelligence Corporation, which has set up two joint venture companies in the United States and Japan with Yaskawa of Japan to develop vision guided robot systems; and Object Recognition Systems, which agreed with Combitech, a subsidiary of Saab-Scania of Sweden, to exchange technology and collaborate on the development and distribution of vision products.

A second type of agreement engaged in by these firms is designed primarily to market their technology. One way the electronic controls/software firms have done this is by licensing firms in other countries to market or manufacture their products. Another way they have sold their expertise is through R&D funding and equity agreements. In 1985 Automatix finalized a deal in which GM provided it with $3 million in R&D funding for near-term development of certain machine intelligence applications and long-term development of advanced vision and machine intelligence systems. GM was also given the option of purchasing up to 15 percent of Automatix stock, which would give it a seat on the Automatix board. In 1983 when American Cimflex licensed Rediffusion Simulation of Great Britain, Rediffusion purchased 6 percent of American's stock and arranged for another 7 percent to be purchased by a British venture capitalist fund. In 1984 BMW of West Germany increased its share of American's stock to 5 percent and provided R&D funding for a new vision products subsidiary, and Ford provided $20 million in equity and R&D funding for the development of robotics software and systems. Both BMW and Ford acquired seats on American's board. Similarly, Westinghouse and Cummins Engine have made limited equity investments in Adept.

There are some notable differences between the collaborations of the electronic controls/software specialists and the six initial major producers. For one, there are very few agreements engaged in by the electronic controls/software specialists designed to enable them to exploit their distribution networks. One reason is that these firms are later entrants who have not yet built up such networks. Another reason is that these firms have narrow expertise and tend to sell to a narrow segment of users (mostly automotive and electronics firms), which precludes the development of a broad distribution network.

Table 7-7. Principal Collaborations of the Electronic Controls/Software Specialists.

Firm	Partner	Nature of Collaboration	Primary Motives
Automatix	Hitachi	Automatix got a manufacturing license	Expand technological capacity
"	Jungenheinrich	Automatix got an OEM agreement	Expand technological capacity
"	Hirata	Automatix got an OEM agreement	Expand technological capacity
"	Tokyo Electron	Marketing license	Expand distribution
"	GM	R&D funding	Sale of expertise
"	Four unspecified firms	R&D partnership	Expand technological capacity
American Cimflex	Marubeni	Marketing license	Expand distribution
"	Cyclomatic	Limited marketing license	Expand distribution
"	Fairchild Test Systems	Limited marketing license	Expand distribution
"	Rediffusion	Manufacturing license	Expand distribution
"	Daikin Kogyo	Manufacturing license	Expand distribution
"	DeVilbiss	Marketing license	Expand distribution
"	Tecnomatix	Marketing license	Expand distribution
"	Sulzer Brothers	Technology license	Expand distribution
"	Rediffusion	Equity financing	Sale of expertise
"	BMW	R&D and equity financing	Sale of expertise
"	Ford	R&D and equity financing	Sale of expertise
"	Visual Machines	Jointly owned company	Expand technological expertise
"	IRI	American purchased vision systems from IRI	Expand technological expertise
"	Rediffusion Simulation	Jointly owned re-organized company	Expand technological expertise
"	Dynamac, Inc.	American acquired Dynamac	Expand technological expertise
"	Daikin Kogyo	American got OEM marketing rights	Exploit distribution network and also expand technological expertise

Table 7-7. continued

Firm	Partner	Nature of Collaboration	Primary Motives
Adept	Kawasaki	Manufacturing license	Expand distribution
"	Meta Machines	Marketing license	Expand distribution
"	Westinghouse	Equity financing	Sale of expertise
"	Cummins Engine	Equity financing	Sale of expertise
Intelledex	Chartered Electronics	Marketing license	Expand distribution
"	Microsoft	Technology license	Expand technological expertise
"	Applied Materials	Joint technology development project	Expand technological expertise
International Robomation/ Intelligence	GMF	Potential manufacturing license	Sale of expertise
"	American Cimflex	Sells vision systems	Sale of expertise
"	West German Consortium	Joint technology development	Expand technological expertise
Control Automation	Nissho Iwai	Marketing license	Expand distribution
Machine Intelligence Corporation	Tecnomatix	Marketing license	Expand distribution
"	Rietschoten and Houwens	Marketing license	Expand distribution
"	Yaskawa	Two joint companies	Expand distribution and technological capacity
Object Recognition Systems (ORS)	Combitech	Manufacturing license, ORS gets a marketing license, some joint product development	Expand distribution, exploit distribution network, expand technological expertise

These firms engage in one type of collaboration that none of the initial six entrants pursued: R&D/equity funding agreements. Examples include GM's funding of Automatix, Rediffusion, Ford, and BMW's funding of American Cimflex, and Westinghouse's funding of Adept. The robot firms that are involved in this type of collaboration tend to be on the frontier of control, vision, or artificial intelligence technologies. One way for users of these technologies to monitor and influence technological developments in these areas is through such ventures. Not surprisingly, the users most often employing this type of collaboration are the automobile companies.

Like the initial six entrants, these firms also engage in collaborations to expand their technological capacity. However, in contrast to the initial six entrants, a number of these agreements, both those that are national as well as international in scope, involve ongoing joint relationships. Examples include Automatix's R&D partnership, American's participation in Visual Machines and Rediffusion Simulation, Intelledex's joint project with Applied Materials, IRI's involvement with the West German consortium, MIC's venture with Yaskawa, and ORS's tie-up with Combitech. These collaborations typically occur in areas where the technology is changing rapidly and the collaborators have different skills. Unlike the initial six entrants, the firms engaged in this type of agreement generally have comparable stature. As a result, few of these collaborations involve the outright acquisition of one firm's robot business by another. Furthermore, the fact that the technological frontier is moving quickly seems to motivate ongoing as distinct from one-shot collaborations. In many instances it is neither practical nor desirable to specify well-defined projects for collaboration, making licensing unattractive.

Collaborations Involving the Applications Specialists

The collaborations engaged in by the application specialists and the motives for them are summarized in Table 7–8. With a few exceptions, these agreements provide the application specialists either with a technological capability or valuable know-how. There are two equity joint ventures, GMF and Cybotech. In both of these joint ventures the U.S. partner lacked technological expertise. In the case of GMF, Fanuc of Japan supplies technological expertise through the production of GMF's robots. Cybotech produces its own robots but secured much of its technology from Renault of France. Similarly ESAB secures much of its technology from ASEA, which owns a controlling interest in ESAB, while Hobart Brothers and Torsteknik, a Swedish arc welding systems firm coowned by Hobart and Yaskawa of Japan, secure their technology from Yaskawa. A number of the other applications specialists, including Graco Robotics, which is a U.S. joint venture of Graco and Edon Finishing Systems, IBM, Hobart Brothers, Advanced, Nordson, and Admiral, engaged in licensing agreements to secure technology. GMF has also licensed the robotics-related technology of other firms, including Niko GmbH of

West Germany, Robcad of Israel, Applied Robotics of the United States, and Eaton-Kenway of the United States. It also purchased IRI's vision hardware to incorporate into its vision systems and acquired a manufacturing license for the technology once its purchases reach $60 million, and it engaged in joint development projects with AMC and Western Engineering, Intergraph, a U.S. computer graphics company, and Meta Machines of Great Britain, the producer of the Meta Torch. Finally, Caterpillar Tractor purchased 20 percent of the stock of Advanced Robotics and supplied it with an arc-welding data base developed from its experience in arc welding. Before it exited the market, Advanced also licensed the robots of Nachi Fujikoshi of Japan, cosponsored or collaborated on research performed at Carnegie Mellon University and Ohio State, and developed a vision system with Odelft of Holland.

Many of these collaborations are similar to the collaborations of the initial six producers and the electronic controls or software specialists. However, with the exception of GMF, these firms are not licensing others to use their technology. For the most part this reflects the fact that original technology development is not the strength of this group of firms. Its main strength is knowledge of users' desires and the technology available to satisfy them. Its agreements are heavily concentrated in licensing the technology of others or contracting, sometimes through equity joint ventures, to develop technological capacity. Two exceptions to this are IBM and Seiko. Both companies possess not only specialized application expertise but also considerable technological expertise relevant to the production of robots. Control Automation, reviewed earlier as an electronic controls or software specialist, is also similar to IBM and Seiko in that it possesses not only relevant technological expertise but also detailed knowledge of the electronic assembly submarket. It too is not involved in licensing the technology of other firms.

A distinguishing feature of the collaborations of this group is that they include some equity joint ventures. Examples include GMF and Cybotech, both of which are international joint ventures. The link between ASEA and ESAB and also Hobart and Yaskawa through Torsteknik is similar in nature to the GMF and Cybotech joint ventures, although neither is a traditional joint venture in that both ESAB and Torsteknik existed prior to their involvement in robotics. In the GMF and Cybotech joint ventures, both partners make substantial contributions while also lacking important expertise provided by the other partner. In the GMF joint venture, GM had user knowledge, sensor knowledge, and had developed a painting system but

Table 7-8. Principal Collaborations of User Firms.

Firm	Partner(s)	Nature of Collaboration	Motives
GMF	GM and Fanuc	Joint venture	Exploit marketing and technological expertise of partners
"	Melton Machine and Control, Lincoln Electric, Niko GmbH, Oshap, Tecnomatix, Rishworth and Mehaffey, EPP, Elof, Hansson	Marketing licenses	Expand distribution
"	United Technologies	GMF acquired a marketing license	Exploit distribution network
"	Niko GmbH	GMF acquired a marketing license and supplied components	Exploit distribution network and expand technological capacity for Niko's robot
"	Robcam	GMF acquired a marketing license	Exploit distribution network
"	Applied Robotics	Marketing license	Exploit distribution network
"	Eaton-Kenway	GMF secured a technology license to E-K's AGV technology and exclusive rights to market it to the auto industry and nonexclusive rights to other industries	Exploit distribution network and expand technological capacity
"	IRI	Contract for technology/manufacturing license	Expand technological capacity
Graco Robotics	Graco and Edon Finishing Systems	Joint venture	Exploit marketing and technological expertise of partners
"	Ole Molaug Engineering	Technology license	Expand technological capacity and exploit distribution network
IBM	VAR's	Marketing licenses	Expand distribution
"	Sankyo Seiki	Contract for supply, marketing license	Exploit technological expertise

Table 7–8. continued

Firm	Partner(s)	Nature of Collaboration	Motives
Cybotech	Ransburg and Renault	Joint venture	Exploit marketing and technological expertise of partners
"	Tokico	Marketing license	Exploit distribution network
"	Purdue	Joint technology development	Expand technological capacity
Seiko	Diverse distributors	Marketing licenses	Expand distribution network
ESAB	ASEA	Acquisition of controlling interest	Expand distribution of ASEA
"	ASEA	Joint technological development	Expand technological capacity of both partners
Hobart	Yaskawa	Marketing license	Exploit distribution network
"	Yaskawa	Joint ownership of Torstetnik	Exploit distribution network and expand technological capacity
Advanced	Metallurgical Industries	Marketing license	Expand distribution network
"	Nachi-Fujikoshi	Marketing license	Exploit distribution network
"	GM and other partners	Joint technological development	Expand technological expertise
"	Ohio State	Joint technological development	Expand technological expertise
"	Odelft	Joint technological development	Expand technological expertise
"	Caterpillar	Equity financing/ license on Caterpillar data	Sale of expertise and expand technological capacity
Nordson	Basfer	Marketing license	Exploit distribution network
"	Yaskawa	Marketing license	Exploit distribution network
Admiral	Yaskawa	Marketing license	Exploit distribution network

lacked a general technological capacity to design and produce robots. Fanuc had technological and production knowledge in robots and a history of success in its own markets but lacked extensive market knowledge and was not particularly strong in sensing and software. No other potential partner had nearly as good a fit for GM (Conigliaro and Chien, 1983, pp. 50–53). Since it was not feasible for either partner to have acquired the other, the result was a joint venture between the two firms. In the Cybotech joint venture, Renault had user and technological knowledge but lacked knowledge of the U.S. market and a U.S. production base. Ransburg possessed those skills and had some expertise relevant to robotic arc welding and painting. While it might have been possible, although difficult, for Renault to have acquired Ransburg, in the process Renault would have acquired a company mainly involved in markets unfamiliar to Renault. The more attractive alternative was to form a joint venture organized solely around robotics.

These two joint ventures can be compared to ESAB and Torsteknik. Both ESAB and Torsteknik are small companies specializing in robotics related activities (i.e., arc welding). Consequently, the easiest way for ASEA and Hobart and Yaskawa to develop ongoing relationships with their partners was via acquisition. In contrast, in the case of GMF and Cybotech none of the partners was small nor highly specialized to robotics related activities. Consequently, a joint venture was the most economical way to forge an ongoing relationship.

Note that in this group of collaborations there was only one limited equity investment (Advanced-Caterpillar), and even that collaboration possessed other features (the supply of valuable information to Advanced by Caterpillar). Unlike the electronic controls or software specialists, the application specialists were not generally producing frontier technological developments. In addition, the application specialists were typically well established firms with a greater internal supply of capital than the electronic controls/software specialists. Consequently they had less need for limited equity and/or R&D investments and were less attractive targets for limited equity and/or R&D investments than the electronic controls or software specialists.

Collaborations of the Factory-of-the-Future Firms

The collaborations engaged in by the factory-of-the-future firms and their motives are summarized in Table 7–9. Almost all of the agree-

Table 7-9. Principal Robotics Collaborations of the Factory-of-the-Future Companies.

Firm	Partner	Nature of Collaboration	Motives
GE	DEA	Manufacturing license	Expand product line
"	Hitachi	Manufacturing license	Expand product line
"	Volkswagenwerks	Manufacturing license	Expand product line
"	Mitsubishi Electric	Marketing license	Expand product line
"	Nachi-Fujikoshi	Marketing license	Expand product line
"	RPI	Robotics Research Center	Expand technological capacity
"	Graco/LTI	Consortium to recommend each other's products	Expand distribution
GCA	PaR Systems	Acquisition	Expand product line
"	Dainichi Kiko	Marketing and joint technological development	Expand product line
Westinghouse	Mitsubishi Electric	Marketing license/ joint technological development	Expand product line
"	Mitsubishi Heavy Industries	Joint technological development	Expand product line
"	Komatsu	Marketing license	Expand product line
"	Olivetti	Manufacturing license	Expand product line
"	CMU	Robotics Research Center	Expand technological capacity
"	Unimation	Acquisition	Expand product line
"	Adept	Limited equity investment	Monitor technological developments to expand technological capacity
Bendix	Yaskawa	Marketing license	Expand product line
"	Comau	Limited equity investment/marketing license	Expand product line

ments involve the acquisition of technology. Each of the factory-of-the-future firms has licensed the technology of firms in other countries. All the firms made acquisitions or limited equity investments in robotics-related firms. GE purchased Calma, a major U.S. producer of interactive graphics equipment, and purchased a minority interest in Perceptron of the United States, a leading vision firm. GCA purchased Par Systems, a U.S. producer of remotely controlled manipulators, Westinghouse purchased Unimation, maintained a minority interest in Adept, and purchased a minority interest in Perceptics, a manufacturer of image processing equipment. Bendix purchased a minority interest in Comau, a subsidiary of Fiat of Italy, and set up a separate company in which it owns 90 percent, Bendix-Comau Systems, to market and test automation equipment. In addition to these collaborations, both GE and Westinghouse sponsor major university robotics laboratories that work on their problems.

The motives for these collaborations are very similar to the motives of the firms making limited equity and/or R&D investments in the electronic controls and/or software specialists: to remain abreast of technological developments in robotics. None of the factory-of-the-future firms have engaged in any robotics equity joint ventures. This reflects the fact that they have little valuable technology or specialized user experience to share.

Review of Robotics Collaborations

U.S. firms are engaged in collaborations to acquire technology, sell technology, and exploit market knowledge. Many of these collaborations are international. The principal types of collaborations include

- OEM and/or marketing agreements and consortiums in which firms recommend each other's products
- Manufacturing licenses
- Technology licenses
- Contracts for specific items
- Joint technology development on specific items
- Broad R&D funding ventures
- Limited equity investments
- Equity joint ventures
- Acquisitions of controlling interest

Different types of firms tend to engage in different types of collaborations. Joint ventures tend to occur among partners that, at least initially, are of comparable size and make contributions to the venture of comparable value. They typically involve partners that are involved in many other activities not directly related to the joint venture. GMF and Cybotech are both examples of this type of joint venture. Other examples are the joint ventures involving American Cimflex and Visual Machines and Machine Intelligence Corporation and Yaskawa. When the potential partners are of different size and the smaller one is highly specialized, the collaboration typically takes the form of an acquisition. The Westinghouse acquisition of Unimation and ASEA's acquisition of a controlling interest in ESAB are examples of this.

When partners wish to collaborate only on specific, well-defined projects the collaboration may take the form of a product purchase, technology production contract, or a specific joint development contract. Examples of the former type of collaboration are American Cimflex and GM's purchases of IRI vision hardware and Cincinnati Milacron's purchase of Control Automation's vision system. Examples of technology production contracts are IBM's purchase of robots from Sankyo Seiki, Cincinnati Milacron's purchase of robots from Dainichi-Kiko, and Prab's acquisition of software technology from Matra Datavision. Examples of joint technology development projects include GMF's agreement with Meta Machines concerning the Meta Torch and Intelledex's project with Applied Materials to develop clean room robots.

In other instances one firm may want to monitor developments in an area characterized by rapid technological change, such as vision. Then a limited equity investment may be employed. Examples include Ford and BMW's investments in American Cimflex and Westinghouse's investment in Adept. An alternative way to achieve a similar result is through broad R&D funding, which often accompanies limited equity investments. Examples include GM's funding of Automatix's R&D and BMW's funding of American Cimflex's R&D.

Finally, when collaborators are unequal in size and/or expertise and one desires technology already produced by the other, a marketing, manufacturing, or technology license is often used. The robotics industry is characterized by many examples of this type of arrangement, especially between firms in different countries. A major motivation for these agreements rather than direct export or foreign investment is the difficulty of enforcing patent rights internationally[4] and also the difficulty of gaining knowledge about the domestic user market.

The range of robotics collaborations involving U.S. firms indicates that collaborations tend to occur at nearly every stage of the development, production, and marketing of robots and related devices.

This is partly a reflection of the fact that robotics technology is still evolving at a rapid pace and market shares are still in flux. Moreover, unlike other industries, the nature of robotics technology to date has not had an important effect on the form of collaborative efforts.

Note the absence of government policies having any direct effect on the type of collaborations pursued in robotics. Unlike other industries, robotics has not yet been influenced by government procurement policies, nor has it been the subject of international trade negotiations. Thus offsets and orderly marketing arrangements are nonexistent in robotics and consequently have not shaped the nature of international collaborations. In addition, the large number of robotics producers and the rapid rates at which market shares have been changing in recent years means that antitrust concerns are not prominent in robotics. Consequently, international agreements are not at all the result of restrictions on domestic collaborations. Rather, they reflect the very different types of expertise possessed by firms in different countries.

Evaluation of International Equity Collaborations

In this section each of the international robotics equity collaborations detailed in the prior section is reviewed. The success of the venture, how it is managed, and the nature of any transfer of technology is explored.

GMF.   Begun in 1983 as a 50-50 joint venture of GM and Fanuc of Japan, GMF was initially capitalized at $10 million and headquartered in the United States, near GM. Most of its management, as well as many of its employees, are from GM. It derives its robot production principally from Fanuc in Japan, which is the source of most of its robots.

Until GM's recent cutback on automation expenditures, GMF appeared to be a big success. To understand the basis for its success, it is necessary to consider the backgrounds and contributions of its partners. Fanuc is the world's leading producer of computer numerical controls. It is also a leading international producer of motors and a leading Japanese robot producer. Prior to the formation of GMF, its robot line was fairly narrow. It concentrated initially on robots to service machine tools. Beginning prior to GMF but accelerating after GMF was formed, Fanuc expanded its robot line to include process and assembly robots. GMF has exclusive rights to Fanuc's robots in the United States and nonexclusive rights in Europe. Fanuc now produces all of GMF's robots except for its painting robot and is basically GMF's robot producer.

GM is the leading U.S. user of robots. It uses robots for a wide range of tasks, including spot and arc welding, machine loading and unloading, materials handling, spray painting, and assembly. It had acquired vast internal experience in using robots prior to the formation of GMF. This experience has been transferred to GMF through its applications engineers, many of whom were hired by GMF. They work in a special unit that houses experts in various robot applications. GMF is given very high evaluations by users for its applications services (*Robotics Today*, 1986).

Prior to the formation of GMF, GM had also been involved in the development of robots. A high-level GM employee served as an industrial advisor on one of the early robotics projects sponsored by the National Science Foundation. This led to the issuance of the specifications for the PUMA robot ultimately developed by Unimation (Ayres, Lynn, and Miller, 1983). GM also developed the painting robot that GMF markets. GMF planned to produce the robot in a state-of-the-art plant making wide use of flexible manufacturing systems (*Industrial Robot*, 1986b). However, due to the recent cutback in GM's automation expenditures, plans for the plant have been shelved (*Business Week*, 1986).

GM also was involved in a considerable amount of research on robotics. It had long been doing research in robotics software and had developed one of the early robotic vision systems. Many of its research personnel are employed by GMF, including Lothar Rossol, who heads research at GMF and is acknowledged to be one of the leading robotics researchers in the world. Fanuc had also been conducting an extensive amount of research in robotics prior to the formation of GMF. Working together at GMF's headquarters in the United States, the two companies have developed a number of new products, sometimes alone and sometimes in collaboration with other firms. GMF developed its own programming language that can be used to tie together vision, off-line programming, and robots. It developed a sophisticated vision system using IRI hardware and its own software and algorithms. It developed a software simulation system with Intergraph that provides tools to define and manage a project, compose a complete work cell, and simulate the performance of robotic systems. It is working with Meta Machines to integrate the Meta Torch into its robots, eliminating duplicate hardware and providing greater application flexibility and simplified programming. Finally, it licensed the Heron CAD/CAM software of Robcad of Israel and Applied Robotics line of robot hand exchange systems and end effectors, thereby increasing its systems capability.

In many respects, though, GMF is greater than the sum of its parts. To understand this, consider some of the accomplishments GM and Fanuc have been able to achieve working together. The S-3 series of welding robots produced by Fanuc is the result of a GMF perceived need based on user interactions. It took only four months for Fanuc to design a full-scale version of these robots, which is a remarkably short turnaround time (*Industrial Robot*, 1983c). GMF perceived a need for a gantry robot. Initially it licensed a Niko GmbH of West Germany gantry robot from United Technologies, which possessed the marketing rights to the robot in the United States. Later it negotiated directly with Niko and arranged to have Fanuc provide controls, drives, and motors for the robot and for the robot to be programmed with GMF's programming language (*Robot News International*, 1986b). In a similar deal negotiated with Eaton-Kenway of the United States, GMF secured the right to Eaton Kenway's AGV technology. It plans to use it to manufacture AGV's in Japan through Fanuc. It also hired fifty Eaton-Kenway engineers to continue R&D on AGV's in the United States (*Robot News International*, 1986a).

The success of GMF can be gauged from its sales and employment statistics. In 1983 its sales were $22.3 million, which constituted 10 percent of the sales of all U.S. based firms. In 1984 its sales skyrocketed to $102.8 million, giving it 25 percent of the market, and further increased to $180 million and 31 percent of the market in 1985 (Table 7-2). Its employment at its U.S. headquarters has also increased dramatically, rising from just a small work force to 600 at the end of 1985, although the work force was recently cut back from 700 to 500 after GM reduced its automation expenditures (*Business Week*, 1986). Although a sizable portion of its sales are to GM, GMF also sells to outsiders. Estimates of the fraction of sales accounted for by GM vary greatly. One source estimates that in 1984 between 25 and 30 percent of GMF's sales were to nonauto companies (*Industrial Robot*, 1985a), with 20 percent to nonauto companies in 1985 (*Industrial Robot*, 1986a). These figures would make GMF the leader among U.S. based firms in sales to nonauto producers.[5] Over half of GMF's value added has been estimated to be attributable to its U.S. operations (*Industrial Robot*, 1984).

GMF's activities also span a broad range of products and regions. It produces a wide range of robots, accounting for 60 percent of the sales of finishing and coating robots, 8.4 percent of the sales of small parts material handling and assembly robots, and 6 percent of the sales of arc welding robots among U.S. based firms in 1985 (Conigliaro and Chien, 1985). GMF also has a major presence in Europe and throughout the world. It opened a European center in West Germany to serve as warehouse, workshop, laboratory and engineering school for its customers' employees and it has numerous distributors located around the world.

The amount of technology transferred to GM as a result of its collaboration with Fanuc seems modest. Fanuc continues to design and produce all but GMF's painting robots. In the United States GMF concentrates on the development of software and software related products such as vision. These were areas of specialty of GM prior to the formation of GMF, although they have certainly been developed further by GMF. Thus, while GMF appears to exploit synnergistically the skills of its partners, the collaboration does not appear to have led to a substantial expansion in GM's robotics capabilities. Moreover, Fanuc recently decided to engage in a joint venture with General Electric to develop control systems for automated production lines, which infringes directly on the expertise GM brings to GMF. If the joint venture with GE reflects Fanuc's dissatisfaction with the performance of GMF, as has been suggested (*Business Week*, 1986), it raises an ominous sign concerning GMF's future, especially in light of the substantial cutback in automation expenditures recently made by GM.

Cybotech. Cybotech began in 1980 as a joint venture between Ransburg of the United States and Renault of France, with Ransburg owning 51 percent of the company and Renault 49 percent. Its expertise in large part was derived from Renault. Its robots are generally based upon Renault designs. It builds on Ransburg expertise only to a limited extent. Cybotech developed a robotic arc welding system, which is an area in which Ransburg has some experience. However, Ransburg's main market is electrostatic painting, and Cybotech has made virtually no inroads on its own into the market for finishing and coating robots. Its main representation in this market is through a painting robot it licenses from Tokico of Japan, an affiliate of Ransburg.

The early major market for Cybotech's robots was the AMC-Renault joint venture. Subsequently it expanded its market considerably, especially to aerospace companies who use its robots primarily for drilling, spraying primer, and transporting parts. It has developed considerable expertise in systems engineering, with two-thirds of its sales in 1985 estimated to be from systems development (*Robot News International*, 1985d). It is now doing considerable research on off-line programming of its robots, an area in which Renault has been active. In 1985 it received funding from the state of

Indiana to pursue research on off-line programming of robots jointly with Purdue University (*Robotics World*, 1985). Ransburg had previously supported robotics research at Purdue.

Ransburg and Renault executives have met twice a year to share information on new projects and developments (*Robot News International*, 1982), with the venture regularly reviewed by Renault's chairman (Conigliaro and Chien, 1983). Sometimes Renault employees have provided help to Cybotech, and in other instances it has been Cybotech providing the assistance to Renault. Historically each company has had the right to license the other's technology (*Robot News International*, 1982). Over time, Renault's financial involvement in the company has declined. It has been estimated that Ransburg has put in $20 million into Cybotech since its formation (*Robot News International*, 1985d). Currently Ransburg owns 90 percent of Cybotech's stock, with Renault's 10 percent holding primarily to monitor technology developments at Cybotech (*American Metal Market*, 1985).

Cybotech has developed a fairly entrenched position in the robotics industry. In 1983 its sales were only $2.3 million whereas by 1985 its sales had risen to $12.3 million, accounting for 2.2 percent of the sales of U.S. based firms. Arc welding robotic systems currently account for almost half of its sales, and in 1985 it ranked sixth among U.S. based arc welding robotics firms with 10 percent of the market (Conigliaro and Chien, 1985). It manufactures in the United States and recently moved to a new, larger facility. The company has consistently lost money, as have most of the robotics firms, but it was predicted that it would be in the black by mid-1986 (Conigliaro and Chien, 1985), although recently it appears that Renault has begun competing with Cybotech for sales to AMC (*Industrial Robot*, 1985b).

Overall, Cybotech appears to have benefited greatly from Renault's technology. It appears to have used it to launch a now virtually independent entity with its own distinct expertise and markets.

ESAB.   As noted earlier, ESAB is not a traditional U.S. equity joint venture. Although it has a unit in Colorado that has been an important source of technology, it is based in Sweden. Moreover, the company was not originally formed as a joint venture. What qualifies it as a joint venture is that ASEA owns a controlling interest in the company, which it has used to forge close cooperation between it and ESAB, including ESAB's U.S. subsidiary.

ESAB derives all of its robots from ASEA. It has also developed a number of its own products to supplement ASEA's robots, sometimes with ASEA's cooperation. It developed a positioner that orients pieces to be welded. The positioner is coordinated with the robot through the robot controller. It adds considerable flexibility to the robotic welding system. ESAB also developed other products that expand the reach of ASEA's robots, and it developed a seam finding unit in conjunction with ASEA and its own welding seam tracking systems. Recently ESAB's U.S. subsidiary designed an easy-to-use robotic arc welding system that is basically a robot. It was the result of a two-year, multimillion dollar R&D project. Currently the system is being manufactured in the United States and exported around the world. In the future it may be produced outside the United States (*Robot News International*, 1985b).

ESAB has been very successful in the arc welding submarket. Among U.S. based vendors it ranked first in the sales of arc welding robots in 1985 with $8 million, which amounts to 13.3 percent of the market (Conigliaro and Chien, 1985). This is impressive in light of the fact that it sells only to nonauto users, with ASEA servicing the welding needs of the auto industry. Sales of its new robotic arc welding system are projected to quite high. It continues actively to perform R&D and to collaborate with ASEA.

Torsteknik. As noted earlier Torsteknik is a Swedish arc welding specialist. It is 55 percent owned by Hobart of the United States and 45 percent owned by Yaskawa of Japan. It is another unconventional U.S. equity joint venture in that the company was not originally a joint venture nor did it originally involve U.S. participation.

Torsteknik's initial entry into the robotics industry was in 1978 when it signed to handle Yaskawa's robots in Scandinavia. Subsequently, Torsteknik secured the U.K. rights to distribute Yaskawa's robots through Yaskawa. In Japan Yaskawa makes use of Torsteknik's expertise in welding and it also uses Hobart's technology. In the United States Hobart uses Yaskawa's robots and is backed up by the fixtures of Torsteknik. In Scandinavia Torsteknik is the principal agent for Yaskawa's and Hobart's technologies. There appears to be little direct technology transfer or cooperative R&D among the three companies (*Industrial Robot*, 1983b).

Torsteknik has developed a fairly sizable presence in robotics in recent years. In 1985 it sold over 120 arc welding robots in Scandinavia (*Industrial Robot*, 1985d).

Machine Intelligence Corporation—Yaskawa. Machine Intelligence Corporation and Yaskawa set up two companies, one in the United States and the other in Japan, to market jointly developed products.

They developed one product jointly soon after their agreement. It consists of a Yaskawa robot with a vision system and an orienting table. It was used to detect defects on pressed plates and to separate defective from good plates (*Industrial Robot*, 1983a). In 1985 the two companies introduced a system for robotic assembly of high-precision electronic components such as thin-film transistors and magnetic heads. It consists of a Yaskawa robot, a conveyor, three vision sensing units, and a controller. The vision system is specially designed to produce very precise images. Sales of the system are just beginning in Japan, where there is a sizable market for the assembly and testing of thin magnetic heads for floppy and hard disc magnetic storage equipment (*Robot News International*, 1985a).

Visual Machines.   Visual Machines is a vision company based at the University of Manchester which was started by American Cimflex, Rediffusion Simulation, and the University of Manchester. It was set up to develop new image processing technology based on work conducted at the University of Manchester in England over the past ten years. It has developed a system that can be used alone or to control robots and MC machine tools. American's role in the company appears to be limited to providing primarily expertise gained from the design, manufacture, and development of computer controlled robot systems. In contrast, American appears to have incorporated Visual Machine's technology directly into its own vision efforts. Visual's system became part of American's product offerings when it developed its vision subsidiary in 1984 using BMW funding. Recently Visual Machines has been infused with new capital from British venture capitalists, causing American's holdings in the company to fall to 15 percent. At the time of the refinancing the company had sold twenty vision systems, twelve in the United States, primarily through American (*Robot News International*, 1985c).

Rediffusion Simulation.   American Cimflex acquired 42 percent of Rediffusion, a U.K. company, when it was reorganized in 1985. Rediffusion is a licensee of the Merlin robot of American Cimflex, which it manufactures and incorporates into systems sold in Europe. When the company was reorganized, American also took a license on Rediffusion process management hardware and software (*Robot News International*, 1985e). There is a potential for future technology transfer from Rediffusion to American and American to Rediffusion. It is too early to tell the extent to which such transfers will occur.

BMW-American Cimflex. As noted earlier, BMW invested $5.6 million of R&D and equity capital in American Cimflex in 1984, giving it a seat on American's board. The money was used to launch a subsidiary specializing in vision products for the automobile and electronics markets. Its first products were a system for inspecting complex assemblies and a vision tracking system for seam location. BMW stations a representative at the U.S. subsidiary to consult on vision projects. The principal transfer of technology in this agreement is from American to BMW, as the main purpose of the agreement is to allow BMW to keep abreast of machine vision developments. However, BMW does provide information, through its U.S. representative, about actual factory problems.

THE FUTURE

Current and Future State of
International Joint Ventures

Currently there are few major U.S. firms producing a sizable number of robot arms of their own design. Those U.S. robot arm producers who entered the industry early, such as Unimation, Cincinnati Milacron, and Prab, are not prospering. They are being displaced by GMF, which gets its robots principally from Fanuc, and other foreign firms with a U.S. base such as ASEA, Kuka, ESAB, and Seiko. The U.S. firms that are prospering are principally those specializing in electronic controls and software for CIM. Most of these firms secure their arms from foreign producers. Some of these firms have been the object of international collaborations, such as Machine Intelligence Corporation and Object Recognition Systems, while others have been subject to limited equity investments, such as Automatix and American Cimflex.

There have been two types of equity joint ventures involving U.S. firms: (1) those involving specialized robot users and robot producers, and (2) those involving electronic controls/software firms and either robot producers or vision users. The first type of joint venture, between users and producers, is likely to occur less often in the future. With the slowdown in entry by U.S. producers, it is unlikely that many new firms with specialized user knowledge will enter the industry. Moreover, users typically become a less important source of information about buyer preferences and the technological means to satisfy them as new technologies develop (Abernathy, 1978). Consequently, there are likely to be less users in the future who possess sufficiently valuable information to motivate a full-fledged equity joint venture involving a leading robot producer.

The second type of joint venture is more difficult to forecast. It would seem likely that the number of limited equity investment joint ventures will decline in the future. The principal motive for these collaborations is to allow the investor to keep abreast of technological developments in the investee's field. However, most new products experience a slowdown in technological change, especially more dramatic technological changes, as they mature. Typically dominant designs eventually emerge for the new product and market shares of producers stabilize (Abernathy, 1978). In such an environment it becomes easier to keep abreast of technological developments and limited equity investments are likely to become less valuable.

The incidence of collaborations between electronic controls/software companies and robot producers is more difficult to forecast. Based on the typical development of new industries, recent trends causing the robotics industry to disintegrate vertically may well continue in the future. If it becomes possible for users to combine economically different components of robotic systems—arms, vision systems, end effectors, controllers, software interfaces, and so forth—on a modular basis, then such collaborations will probably decline. Alternatively, if modular combinations involve costly duplication of hardware and software and limit user flexibility, then there may be an increasing number of collaborations between component specialists and robot producers. Whether they would take the form of equity joint ventures, such as the MIC-Yaskawa venture, or more limited agreements, such as the GMF-Meta Machines collaboration, is more difficult to predict. Most likely both types of collaborations would occur. Furthermore, since the United States has many specialized component producers but not many robot arm producers, many of these collaborations involving U.S. firms are likely to be international.

One other important but difficult to predict factor is the role that national governments will play in the future in their domestic robotics industries. If they become more involved, as already seems to be taking place in countries like France, Sweden, and Great Britain, international collaborations may increase. Already some non-U.S. firms have responded to French and British initiatives to collaborate with domestic robotics firms.[6] If this trend continues it is likely to contribute to an increasing number of international joint ventures, some of which undoubtedly will involve U.S. firms.

Welfare Effects of U.S. Robotics
International Joint Ventures

There are two dimensions of international joint ventures that have welfare implications for the United States. First, they allow U.S. firms to exploit their expertise in electronic controls/software and knowledge of the user market. Second, they discourage U.S. producers from developing a capability to design and produce robot arms, allowing producers from other countries, principally Japan, to dominate the international market for robot arms. Clearly, the former effect is an unequivocal benefit. It has resulted in powerful synergistic combinations like GMF and the development of leading specialized producers like Automatix. The latter effect is clearly detrimental although it does not occur in all joint ventures—for example, the Cybotech joint venture enabled Ransburg to become a robot arm producer. However, by and large, international robotics joint ventures, as well as licensing and other types of international collaborations, have not resulted in many U.S. firms developing a capability to design and produce robot arms.

While it is clearly not desirable to discourage the development of U.S. robot arm production, it is not clear how U.S. interests could have been better served by restrictions on international collaborations. If such collaborations had been restricted, it is not clear that U.S. producers with specialized knowledge could ever have exploited their expertise. While foreign firms might have been at a disadvantage in those specialized areas, their advantage in robot arm technology might have been sufficiently great to have enabled them to dominate the U.S. market. Alternatively, suppose that specialized U.S. producers would have been able to have survived. Then firms like Unimation and Cincinnati Milacron most likely would have had greater U.S. sales. Would this have been beneficial? Currently, these firms are losing out to foreign firms or U.S. firms who secure their robot arms from foreign firms. Would U.S. robot buyers have benefited by having less access to the best robots available? Clearly no. It might be possible to justify such effects if the robotics industry were an infant industry. However, the U.S. robotics industry developed before any other country's robotics industry. Perhaps it did not develop as fast as the robotics industries of some other countries because the government did not become as involved as in other countries. If so, the solution, if one is desired, is for the U.S. government to support robotics producers, not to restrict the agreements in which they can engage.

The backdrop of this debate is that robots and CIM are critical to the future competitiveness of U.S. industry. Even if restrictions on international collaborations would have benefited U.S. robotics producers, it might have greatly damaged nonrobotic U.S. firms who depend now or will depend in the future on robots and CIM. Moreover, the trend in CIM is that the robot arm itself is becoming a less significant part of robotic installations, with electronic controls and software becoming more important. International collaborations of all kinds have enabled U.S. firms to develop a leading position in many of the control and software areas that seem slated for the greatest future growth. In the end, even though international joint ventures in robotics may have had undesirable consequences, it is not clear that any other policies could have mitigated these consequences without causing more serious problems than they were intended to cure.

NOTES

1. See Abernathy (1978, Ch. 4) for a discussion of the development of new industries.
2. One example of this is the widespread diffusion of MAP, a protocol for coordinating CIM products that was introduced by GM.
3. Many reasons have been advanced for the faster growth of the robotics industry in Japan than the United States, including government aid, fear of labor shortages, and Japanese expertise in production engineering. See Lynn (1983).
4. See the assessment of Joseph Engleberger quoted in the *American Machinist*, April 1982, p. 63.
5. However, it was recently estimated that in 1986 over 85 percent of GMF's sales were accounted for by GM (*Business Week*, 1986).
6. For example, Danichi Kiko of Japan has teamed up with Jaguar Cars and British-owned Danichi Sykes Robotics to develop new automated production systems for Jaguar automotive facilities with funding anticipated from the British government. See Office of Technology Assessment (1984, p. 359). See also U.S. International Trade Commission, "Competitive Position of U.S. Producers of Robotics in Domestic and World Markets," USITC Publication 1475, 1983, pp. 31–32, for efforts by the French government to encourage collaborations between foreign robotics firms and French producers.

REFERENCES

Abernathy, William J. 1978. *The Productivity Dilemma*. Baltimore: The Johns Hopkins University Press.

American Metal Market. 1985. "Cybotech Moves Manufacturing Operations." September 9, p. 9.

Ayres, Robert U., Leonard Lynn, and Steve Miller. 1982. "Technology Transfer in Robotics between the U.S. and Japan." In *Technological Exchange: The U.S.-Japanese Experience*, Cecil H. Uyehara, ed. (Washington, D.C.: University Press of America), pp. 89–90.

Baranson, Jack. 1983. *Robots in Manufacturing.* Mt. Airy: Lomond Publications.

Business Week. 1986. "GM Throws a Monkey Wrench into the Robot Market." August 25, p. 36.

Conigliaro, Laura, and Christine Chien. 1983. Prudential-Bache Securities. *CIM Newsletter.* August 2, pp. 50–53.

_____. 1985. Prudential-Bache Securities. *CIM Newsletter.* June 24.

Industrial Robot. 1983a. "Emphasis on Cheaper Robots." March, p. 48.

_____. 1983b. "Looking for a Big Place in UK Arc Welding." December.

_____. 1983c. "Towards the Intelligent American Robot." December, p. 288.

_____. 1984. "Exploding the Myths That Surround GMF." September, p. 171.

_____. 1985a. "GMF Robotics Outlines Its Plans for '85." March, p. 4.

_____. 1985b. "Lasers Lead Technology Advance at Essen." December, pp. 260–1.

_____. 1986a. "U.S. Robots Growth Slows." March, p. 6.

_____. 1986b. "Investing in Tomorrow's Technology." March, pp. 46–49.

Lynn, Leonard. 1983. "Japanese Robotics: Challenge and Limited Exemplar." *Annals of the American Academy of Political and Social Sciences* (November).

Office of Technology Assessment. 1984. *Computerized Manufacturing Automation.* Washington, D.C.: U.S. Government Printing Office.

Reich, Robert B., and Eric D. Mankin. 1986. "Joint Ventures with Japan Give Away Our Future." *Harvard Business Review*, March-April, pp. 78–86.

Robot News International. 1982. "Why Cybotech Finds the Going Tough." May, p. 5.

_____. 1985a. "Robots for Semiconductor Production." February, p. 8.

_____. 1985b. "Easy-to-use Robot Welder from ESAB." March, p. 10.

_____. 1985c. "£1,000,000 Investment in UK Vision Firms." December, p. 1.

_____. 1985d. "Ransburg Still Pins Its Faith on Robotics." December, p. 2.

_____. 1985e. "Rediffusion Robots Gets a Facelift from American Robots." December, p. 4.

_____. 1986a. "GMF Chooses Eaton as AGVS Partner." May, pp. 1–2.

_____. 1986b. "Some of the Glitter Goes Out of Robots 10." May, p. 4.

Robotics Today. 1983. "Westinghouse Advances the Art of Assembly." February, pp. 33–36.

_____, 1986. "Survey Rates Robot Vendors." February, p. 45.

Robotics World. 1985. "Cybotech Develops Software." July, p. 16.

Tech Tran Corporation. 1982. *Industrial Robots.* Napierville, Ill.

U.S. International Trade Commission. 1983. "Competitive Position of U.S. Producers of Robotics in Domestic and World Markets." USITC Publication 1475, p. 16.

8 MULTINATIONAL JOINT VENTURES IN THE STEEL INDUSTRY

Leonard H. Lynn

Steel has traditionally been less international than most of the other U.S. industries examined in this book. In the years after World War II, U.S. producers scarcely had the capacity to satisfy their home market. And, having been plagued by grossly excessive capacity during the 1930s, they were unwilling to make the huge long-term investments that would have been necessary to produce steel for potentially unstable foreign markets (Hogan, 1971). While the major U.S. steelmakers did invest in overseas sources of raw materials, they saw little reason to commit capital to foreign production. Nor did these U.S. firms have control over strategic production technologies that might have offered them niches in such countries as Japan.[1] All in all, the U.S. market was large and stable and the major steel producers had developed a comfortable modus vivendi under the leadership of U.S. Steel (Borrus, 1983).

This indifference toward foreign steel producers disappeared by degrees as the competitiveness of U.S. firms became problematic in the U.S. market. Beginning in the late 1970s the major U.S. steelmakers began to turn to their foreign competitors for assistance. The assistance they required in the case of the integrated steel producers was comprehensive, encompassing massive needs for infusions of new technology, better management, and more capital. Often this included a desire on the U.S. side to maximize the foreign equity holding (indeed, to sell out altogether if a willing customer could be found). By the mid-1980s most major integrated U.S. steel producers were involved in some sort of joint venture arrangement with foreign steel producers. Some entailed foreign purchases of equity in the integrated firms themselves. Others were start-up joint ventures for the production of steel sheet or other products. The U.S. partner typically contributed a site (often an abandoned plant) and the foreign partner contributed capital and technology.

Foreign producers had earlier entered the minimill segment of the U.S. steel industry. This segment grew in importance in the 1960s as small steel-producing firms were organized using new technologies to occupy various geographic or product niches in the U.S. market. Minimills seemed to offer attractive opportunities for foreign firms (particularly European and Canadian) to enter the U.S. industry, frequently through direct ownership, but occasionally through joint ventures. In some instances foreign owners sought comparative advantage through the use of new technology. International alliances have also been formed by firms in the specialty steel and steel distribution segments of the U.S. steel industry. Foreigners have offered capital in these segments, but even more so have offered new technology.

Since the circumstances in the integrated, minimill, specialty, and distribution sectors of the industry each have their own special features, it is best to discuss each separately.

INTEGRATED STEELMAKERS

Business has not only been poor for the integrated U.S. steelmakers in recent years, it has been disastrous. They have made little profit, and indeed in many years have suffered huge losses. Major firms have disappeared and some analysts expect no more than two or three to survive until the end of the century. The firms have little capital to develop or introduce new technology, and many find the potential return on investment in almost any other business activity so exceeds that in steelmaking that the only reasonable business strategy is one of diversification.

Table 8-1 tracks the fate of the dozen leading steelmakers of 1976 over the subsequent eight years. It should be noted that the steel industry had been characterized by very high stability for a generation or more before 1976. The big eight steel firms of 1976, U.S. Steel, Bethlehem, National, Republic, Inland, Armco, J&L, and Youngstown, were (in slightly different order) the big eight steel firms of 1950. Nor had there been any drastic changes in this list of firms since the Depression years. Even the group of smaller integrated firms had been fairly stable for a long period of time. Wheeling-Pittsburgh was formed by a merger of the firms that had ranked

Table 8-1.   Ten Largest U.S. Steel Producers, 1976 and 1984.

Raw Steel Production (1,000 net tons)			
1976		1984	
U.S. Steel	28,278	U.S. Steel	15,100
Bethlehem	18,900	Bethlehem	12,166
National[a]	10,770	LTV[g]	9,971
Republic[b]	9,621	Inland	6,479
Inland	7,947	Armco	5,911
Armco	7,611	National	4,812
J&L/LTV[c]	6,979	Weirton[h]	2,795
Lykes-Youngstown[d]	5,054	Nucor[i]	1,725
Wheeling-Pittsburgh[e]	3,948	Florida[i]	1,010
Kaiser[f]	2,561	Chaparral[i]	981
McLough Steel	2,007	CF&I	770
CF&I	1,507	Northwestern	744

a. National spun off its Weirton Division. Half of its steel interests were purchased by NKK of Japan.
b. Absorbed by LTV.
c. Absorbed Lykes-Youngstown and Republic.
d. Absorbed by LTV.
e. In bankruptcy proceedings in 1985.
f. Liquidated.
g. Product of merger of J&L, Youngstown and Republic.
h. Spun off by National.
i. Minimill. Not listed in 1976.
Sources: *Iron Age.* 1985. "Steel Industry Financial Analysis," May 3. U.S. Fair Trade Commission. 1977. *Staff Report on the United States Steel Industry and Its International Rivals.* Washington, D.C.: U.S. Government Printing Office.

ninth and thirteenth in the industry in 1950. CF&I was tenth in the industry in 1950, and twelfth in 1976. Kaiser was a little behind CF&I in production in 1950, somewhat ahead of it in 1976. Only McLouth had grown substantially to enter the list of top integrated firms.

Given this history of stability, the eight years after 1976 are extraordinary. The leading steelmaker, U.S. Steel, produced only a little more than half as much steel in 1984 as in 1976. The Corporation dropped its plans to build a new integrated steel works in the late 1970s and in 1982 spent $6 billion to buy Marathon Oil. In 1986 it absorbed another oil company, Texas Oil and Gas, for $3 billion. Meanwhile the Corporation abandoned some 15 percent of its steelmaking capacity. The result has been that U.S. Steel reduced its dependence on steel from 70 percent of sales in 1979 to 30 percent in 1985. In 1986 U.S. Steel changed its name to USX.

The second largest integrated steelmaker, Bethlehem, reduced its steel production from 18,900,000 tons in 1976 to 12,166,000 tons in 1984. Bethlehem did not follow other major steel firms in a strategy of diversification, resulting according to some analysts, in the company's major losses in recent years. In 1982 Bethlehem lost nearly $1.5 billion. Things improved in 1983 and 1984, but the company was still losing money. Some analysts are concerned about the company's long-term viability.

The third largest integrated steelmaker in 1976, National Steel, pursued a strategy of diversification with extraordinary singlemindedness. The company changed its name from National Steel to National Intergroup in 1983, spun off one of its major works in an employee buyout plan, and sold a 50 percent interest in the remainder of its steel operations to Nippon Kokan. National reportedly would now like to sell the other half of its steel operations.

The fourth largest producer in 1976, Republic Steel, disappeared in a merger in 1984. The fifth largest, Inland, reported losses of some $182 million in 1982, its first full year of losses in a half century. The sixth largest, Armco, lost $135.6 million in 1984. The seventh largest, J&L, absorbed the steelmakers that had ranked third and eighth in 1976. The new firm produced only slightly more steel in 1984 than the largest of its three components had eight years earlier. Worse, this company suffered heavy losses in the early 1980s, and filed for bankruptcy protection in 1986.

If the "big eight" integrated steelmakers did badly, the smaller integrated firms did even worse. Wheeling-Pittsburgh filed for Chapter 11 bankruptcy protection in 1985. Kaiser completely closed down its iron and steelmaking operations in 1983. McLouth Steel filed for Chapter 11 bankruptcy in 1981 and was on the verge of being liquidated before being put back into operation in late 1982 by the owners of a steel distribution company. CF&I permanently closed its blast furnaces, basic oxygen furnaces and several of its rolling mills in 1984, ceasing operations as an integrated steelmaker (Hogan, 1984; McManus, 1982).

As Table 8-2 shows, in 1982 and 1983 *all* the major integrated firms suffered heavy losses. U.S. steel returned to profitability in 1984, but only because of profits from its nonsteelmaking operations such as Marathon Oil.

Even when times were better, the major U.S. steelmakers did not invest heavily in the development of new technology. In their authoritative study of the U.S. steel industry, Barnett and Schorsch (1983) point to this as an element in the poor corporate strategy they see as having contributed to the precipitate decline of the U.S. industry.

Table 8-2. Return on Stockholder's Equity for Integrated Steelmakers, 1979-1984.

	1979	1980	1981	1982	1983	1984
U.S. Steel	-6.0	9.5	17.2	-5.6	-20.7	8.3
Bethlehem	11.7	4.7	8.0	-53.2	-14.1	-12.4
LTV	24.7	20.2	38.9	-12.9	-16.0	-30.2
Republic	8.6	3.4	12.6	-14.4	—	—
Inland	10.3	2.3	4.4	—	—	—
Armco	12.9	13.6	13.7	-15.5	-41.1	-25.8
National	8.9	5.8	5.8	—	-19.4	3.1
Weirton	—	—	—	—	—	—
Wheeling-Pittsburgh	12.3	3.5	12.6	-14.4	—	—
Kaiser	9.3	27.6	-166.8	—	—	—
CF&I	7.3	9.1	17.9	—	-85.7	-34.4
McLouth	5.6	[bankruptcy proceedings]				

Source: *Iron Age.* Various years. "Financial Analysis of the Steel Industry." Firms were no longer listed after they ceased integrated operations or were absorbed by another firm.

Data reported by the Office of Technology Assessment show that U.S. ferrous industry spending on R&D was a comparatively low 0.7 percent of sales in 1963. Interestingly, Japanese steel industry spending on R&D was also about 0.7 percent of sales in 1963. By 1978, however, U.S. spending had declined to 0.5 percent while Japanese spending had increased to 1.08 percent of sales (Barnett and Schorsch, 1983; Office of Technology Assessment, 1980; Japan Science and Technology Agency, various years). Not only did the integrated U.S. steelmakers invest little in research, but the investment they did make was concentrated in product development, rather than in production technology. As a result, it later seemed reasonable that intensive involvement by foreign firms in the management of the U.S. firms could produce major gains in productivity.

In short the major U.S. steelmakers found themselves in a situation where they desperately needed both new cost-cutting technologies and infusions of capital to implement the new technologies. Given their low level of investment in technology and low (or negative) profitability, it is not surprising that U.S. steelmakers could find neither the technology nor the capital they needed in the United States. They found both in Japan.

In 1981 *American Metal Market* reported that most major American firms had entered into programs to receive technical assistance from Japanese steelmakers. U.S. Steel had an agreement for "comprehensive cooperation" with Nippon Steel and one for help with its cold strip mill and continuous casting facilities with Sumitomo; Bethlehem had gone to Kawasaki for help in improving yields, to Nippon Kokan for continuous annealing technology and to Nippon Steel for coke oven technology; Republic had an agreement with Kawasaki; Armco had a comprehensive cooperation agreement with Nippon Steel and asked Nippon Steel to do a "plant diagnosis" of Armco's Houston mill; Inland used Nippon Kokan as a consultant in planning a new blast furnace; J&L was getting help from Sumitomo on continuous casting and seamless pipe; Kaiser and Ford both went to Nippon Kokan for help in modernizing their steel works (later Nippon Kokan considered buying the steelmaking operations of both of these firms (Murakami, 1981).

Descriptions in the press are suggestive of the sorts of aid the American firms were receiving from the Japanese. Some were more in the nature of management than technology. *Forbes* magazine, for example, quoted an Armco executive as saying:

> We found Nippon Steel could run one of its blast furnaces for 900 shifts before they had to reline the furnace. We were struggling to get 600. As it turned out they weren't using better bricks, they just had better workmanship and were running their furnaces better. Even walking through our plant they can see things like inventories, production controls, even changes in scheduling which could make a difference (Wiegner, 1980).

A Japanese newspaper article on the technical assistance Sumitomo gave to U.S. Steel said that both the Sumitomo and U.S. Steel engineers were surprised at the gap in the use of technology between the two firms. The article noted numerous failings in the management of technology by the Americans, especially with regard to scheduled maintenance programs, energy conservation, and quality control (*Asahi Shimbun*, 1980).

Much of the technology the American steelmakers required from the Japanese, then, required the transfer of "tacit knowledge"— which is substantially unpatentable and which includes a substantial component of difficult to codify experience. The transfer of tacit knowledge requires a very high level of trust and good faith since providers of the knowledge can easily hold back some of the knowledge promised and buyers can easily claim results were unsatisfactory and withhold payment. If the supplier is to receive payment through the profits of the joint venture, he is well motivated to perform efficiently (Hennart, 1986). And, indeed, several of these technical agreements did evolve into agreements for equity participation by the Japanese.

Equity participation might have been rational for both sides given that both sides were determined to effect technology transfer, but why should the Japanese have been interested in investing in U.S. steel firms when American sources of capital found them so unattractive? In most cases there has been a complex intertwining of reasons. Perhaps the best way to understand this is by looking at some of the major investments of the Japanese in integrated U.S. steel firms.

NIPPON KOKAN AND NATIONAL STEEL

The largest Japanese involvement in a U.S. integrated steelmaking operation was consumated on August 31, 1984 when Nippon Kokan (NKK) paid National Intergroup $292 million to purchase 50 percent of National's steel group. NKK had been interested in investing in a U.S. steelmaker for several years. While providing technical assistance to Kaiser Steel in the late 1970s NKK had engaged in preliminary discussions regarding capital participation in Kaiser. These arrangements fell through, however, and NKK was then approached by Ford. Here again the initial exploratory dealing was in the form of a technology exchange. In January 1981 a five-member team from NKK inspected Ford's Rouge Works to see what technical contributions NKK could make to the modernization of the plant's high-tensile steel operations. At the end of the year NKK began providing technical assistance to Rouge.

Ford hoped to sell its steel works outright to NKK, then discussed the possibility of a joint venture. Aside from providing assurance that NKK would not be closed out of the U.S. market, purchase of an interest in the Rouge Plant could have allowed NKK a share in the supply of steel to Honda and Nissan as well as to a Ford-Toyota joint venture that was then being discussed (this joint venture also later fell through). Both Honda and Nissan are NKK customers in Japan. Aside from this, Rouge had two electric furnaces that were only six years old and a modern hot strip mill. NKK reportedly had some $500 million to invest in the plant, $200 million to buy a share in it and the rest to make it a "technological showpiece." Negotiations finally broke down because NKK was concerned about labor costs at Ford (*Japan Insight*, 1981; *Business Week*, 1982; Thompson, 1984).

The next candidate for NKK's equity participation in a U.S. steel-maker was National Steel. Because of the low return on investment in steel, the top management of National had been shifting investments out of the steel industry for several years. In 1980, when Howard Love became chief executive officer, 85 percent of National's sales were accounted for by steel. That year National purchased First Nationwide Financial Corporation, which in turn expanded by acquiring savings and loan firms in various parts of the United States. These efforts at diversification were sharply increased after a consulting report commissioned by the company projected zero growth for the U.S. steel industry (National had been expecting 5–7 percent annual growth). In 1984 National spun off one of its two integrated steel works to employees and initiated talks with NKK. These negotiations were suspended when National accepted an offer by U.S. Steel to buy National's steelmaking operations, but resumed after that deal was called off in the face of antitrust concerns expressed by the Justice Department (Magnet, 1985).

NKK felt it could upgrade the technology at National to make a profit on its investment, while also ensuring its access to the U.S. market. The two firms had been associated in research projects for some fifteen years. National was one of the stronger American integrated steelmakers. Between 1980 and 1984 it had cut its production capacity in half while cutting its steelmaking work force from 27,000 to 11,000. Its mills included two of the six lowest cost mills in the United States. But NKK saw substantial room for further improvements in National's steelmaking operations. National's yield of finished steel from raw steel was 75 percent compared to 90 percent for NKK. NKK reportedly believed that over time it could improve National's yields by 4 percent a year. An NKK executive vice president noted that if the percentage of National's steel produced by continuous casting were raised from its 1984 level of about 70 percent to NKK's level of 90 percent, National's operating costs could be cut by about $44 million (*Economist*, 1984b). There was also some concern with the quality of National's products. This too was an area where NKK felt it could make major contributions (Symonds, 1985a; *Business Week*, 1984a).

NKK was also interested in the U.S. market for steel sheet for the automotive market. National had planned to build an electrolytic galvanizing line at its Great Lakes Works near Detroit. Plans had included the use of technology developed by another foreign company. These plans were changed to make use of NKK technology (*NKK News*, 1984).

The balance of NKK's marketing and technological interest was reflected in the three people it sent to be in the top management of National Steel. The senior of the three, Haruki Kamiya, was an NKK executive vice president with a background in sales. One of the other two, Yukio Tani, was the NKK director with major responsibilities

for technology. Tani was closely involved in the planning of the joint
venture as leader of NKK's National Steel Project Technology Team.
The other senior executive sent to National, an NKK director named
Sosuke Doi, had a background in international trade.[2]

Although only a short time has passed since NKK purchased its
share in National Steel, it has already been quite active in trying to
upgrade National's technology, sometimes acquiring a market for its
own technologies in the process. A plan was announced to invest
nearly $1 billion by 1989. In December 1985 National commissioned
a new 400,000 ton per year electrogalvanizing line. NKK received
the order for the design and engineering of the line including manufacture and procurement of the main galvanizing section. This was
the first large-scale technical assistance provided to National after the
joint venture agreement was initiated. The new line was the first of
its type in the United States, indeed it represented the first export
order NKK received for the technology (a second was received from
the Spanish national steel corporation shortly thereafter). Total investment for the facility came to $120 million. Marubeni, a Japanese
trading company, helped arrange financing (*NKK News*, 1986). NKK
also received an order from National for the construction of a 250
ton ladle furnace and supporting facilities for National's Granite City
Works, and then another contract to supply a molten steel surface
level control system for continuous casting molds at Granite City
(*NKK News*, 1985b).

Much of the technological upgrading of National Steel has taken
place with little or no new investment. In an effort to promote this
the joint venture formed a new technical coordinating and planning
department. The new department is staffed by both National and
NKK people and is intended to introduce NKK process and production technology at National. A June 1985 report claimed that NKK
experts had helped identify more than 300 areas where costs could
be cut. NKK found, for example, that National used twice as much
fuel as NKK to power reheating furnaces and suggested ways to cut
the difference.

Less information is available about NKK's successes on the marketing side, but a recent report indicates that NKK had begun to sell
surface treated steel sheets to Japanese auto makers operating in the
United States by acting in cooperation with National (*Japan Economic Journal*, 1986).

Meanwhile National Intergroup has made other moves to further
reduce its dependence on steel. In October 1984 it attempted to
merge with Bergen Brunswig Corporation, a drug distributor. If the

merger had succeeded, the National Intergroup would have been dependent on steel for only one-fourth of its revenues (*Business Week*, 1984b). More recently there have been reports that National Intergroup would like to sell its remaining share of National Steel to NKK or to others.

KAWASAKI AND CALIFORNIA STEEL

California Steel Industries represents a complex multinational arrangement. It is half owned by a British born investor, one-quarter owned by the American subsidiary of a Brazilian firm, and one quarter owned by Kawasaki Steel. Kawasaki and the Brazilian firm also jointly own a Brazilian steel plant with Italy's top steel producer. This "Brazilian" firm supplies steel slabs for finishing by California Steel.

Ironically, this multinationalism is centered in the plant of a firm that once strongly opposed imports, Kaiser Steel. After failing to attract investment from NKK and other sources, Kaiser Steel closed its integrated facility in Fontana, California, in 1984. In May 1984 a group of investors seeking to revive some of Kaiser's facilities approached Kawasaki. The group reportedly hoped to get capital, new plate-making technology and (possibly) help in becoming a supplier for the new joint venture in California between General Motors and Toyota. Kawasaki, which had previously spent more than a year studying the possibility of acquiring the Kaiser works, joined the group which purchased Kaiser's facilities for $100 million. At the end of 1984 parts of the Kaiser plant were put back into operation as California Steel Industries, Inc. Kawasaki provided technical support for revamping the plant's finishing mills and sent an executive to be in charge of technology and production.

California Steel imports steel slabs from Brazil and finishes them into hot-rolled, cold-rolled and galvanized sheets and plates. The company's initial production is scheduled to be 700,000 tons per year of such products as hot-rolled and cold-rolled sheets and galvanized sheets. It was expected to buy some 800,000 tons of slab in its first year of operation, most of it from Companhia Siderurgica de Tubarao (CST) of Brazil. CST is itself a joint venture that was formed in 1984 with 51 percent ownership by the Brazilian government, with the rest split between a Japanese consortium headed by Kawasaki and an Italian group led by Finsider. CST went on stream in 1983 with a capacity of 3 million tons of slab per year (*Newsletter from Kawasaki Steel Corporation*, 1985).

NISSHIN AND WHEELING-PITTSBURGH STEEL

One of the more troubled of the integrated U.S. steelmakers, Wheeling-Pittsburgh, reportedly spent five years approaching all of the major Japanese steelmakers in search of financial and technological assistance. In 1982 Kobe Steel and Wheeling-Pittsburgh discussed an arrangement whereby Kobe would invest in Wheeling-Pittsburgh and the two firms would jointly produce seamless pipe. The deal collapsed when the market for tubular goods failed.

Finally, in early 1984 an agreement with Nisshin Steel was announced. Under the agreement Nisshin, Japan's sixth largest steel producer and a member of the Nippon Steel group, was to pay $17.5 million for 10 percent of Wheeling-Pittsburgh, and the two companies were to build a $40 million steel coating line at one of Wheeling-Pittsburgh's plants. The chairman of Nisshin Steel also joined the board of directors of Wheeling-Pittsburgh. The revamped plant was to be run by a joint venture, Wheeling-Nisshin Coaters, and is to turn out galvanized sheet for the auto and appliance industries. Nisshin and Wheeling-Pittsburgh would each supply half of the sheet to be coated. The agreement was complicated by Wheeling-Pittsburgh filing for bankruptcy protection in 1985, but this did not stop plans to construct the new plant (*Japan Economic Journal*, February 8, 1986).

Nisshin's main incentive for participating in this venture was to gain better access to the U.S. market, most notably to General Motors, a major buyer of products from Wheeling-Pittsburth (*Economist*, 1984a). Quotas were doubtless a factor here as well, since some 17 percent of Nisshin's sales were to the United States. Wheeling-Pittsburgh in addition to getting capital and technology, would strengthen an area of weakness, its lack of modern flat-rolled finishing facilities.

OTHER INTERNATIONAL JOINT VENTURES
WITH INTEGRATED STEELMAKERS

Other joint ventures have been set up more recently between integrated U.S. and Japanese steelmakers. In early 1985 LTV and Sumitomo Metals formed a 60–40 joint venture called L-S Electro-Galvanizing Company. The joint venture will have a new $125 million electrogalvanizing line on the site of a former Republic mill in Cleveland, Ohio. The new company will receive financial help from Mitsui and will use Sumitomo-developed technology. It will be jointly managed. This seems to be yet another instance of an American firm getting capital and technical assistance from a Japanese firm to serve a new and growing need in the U.S. market (*Iron Age*, 1985b).

U.S. Steel sought to establish joint ventures with several foreign companies. Many of U.S. Steel's blast furnaces and steelmaking furnaces are obsolete and would be extremely expensive to replace or update. A solution would be to import steel slabs from foreign producers for rolling at U.S. Steel plants. Discussions were held with British Steel under which U.S. Steel would have purchased slabs from British Steel to roll at its Fairless Works. The blast furnaces and open hearths at Fairless would have been shut down and British Steel would have become part owner of the works. This plan fell through in late 1983 after generating considerable controversy. An agreement was concluded in 1985 with Pohang Iron and Steel Company (Posco) of South Korea under which U.S. Steel and Posco are to be 50–50 partners in a joint venture firm. The new firm is to acquire U.S. Steel's Pittsburg, California plant and invest approximately $300 million in a four-year project to renovate it. Posco agreed to pay $90 million for its share of the works. The Pittsburg works had been supplied with steel for rolling from the World War II vintage open hearths at U.S. Steel's Geneva (Utah) Works. Rather than undertaking the expensive (and perhaps futile) effort of updating the Geneva works, U.S. Steel can use low-cost coils from Posco's new steel production facilities. The works will import 1 million tons of coil per year from Posco for processing into sheet and tin. Aside from bringing in capital for the modernization of the Pittsburg works, the agreement also will allow U.S. Steel to shut down parts of the Geneva works and reduce its sheet production costs on the West Coast by about $40 per ton.

Posco, like the Japanese firms, has been concerned about the threat to its U.S. sales posed by protectionism and has seen investment in the United States as a counter to this threat. Posco also has a new integrated greenfield steel mill coming on stream in the late 1980s. It will need to find markets for the products of the new mill. Earlier, it had established a coal mining subsidiary in the United States and explored the possibility of taking over the old Gadsden works of Republic Steel. In 1984 Posco bought a 45 percent interest in Feralloy Corporations coil process operations in Pittsburg, California. Posco, in return, would receive a stable market for its coil.

INTEGRATED STEELMAKING JOINT
VENTURES: SOME OBSERVATIONS

While there is considerable diversity among integrated steelmaking joint ventures, it is possible to posit, tentatively, several observations. Most of the U.S. firms involved appear to have been seeking two related goals: the reduction (or elimination) of their dependence on steelmaking and the lowest possible cost maintenance of the viability of their remaining steelmaking operations. For National Intergroup, the NKK joint venture represented a substantial withdrawal from the steel industry and increased the possibility of a total withdrawal at some future point. If the efforts to upgrade the National plants do not succeed, National Intergroups will lose far less than if it had not taken a partner. If the efforts do succeed, largely through the introduction of new technology by Nippon Kokan, National's investment will be greatly increased in value. By seeking sources of slab from British Steel and finally arranging a joint venture with Pohang, U.S. Steel sought to be able to close down obsolete blast furnaces and open hearths without losing the use of its more efficient rolling facilities and its access to markets. LTV and Wheeling-Pittsburgh were able to remain suppliers for the increasingly demanding U.S. automobile industry by forming joint ventures for which the Japanese supplied most of the technology and investment, with the U.S. partners offering semiabandoned plant sites and access to markets.

The Japanese had various reasons for investing in joint ventures in the United States. First, Japanese steelmakers were interested in supplying the automakers and other Japanese manufacturing firms that have been establishing operations in the United States. Joint ventures provided a means of doing this with less risk of having these markets suddenly cut off due to protectionism. Such firms as Honda, Nissan, Toyota, Mazda, Isuzu, and Suzuki had or were establishing operations in the United States that could provide a good base of customers. As of March 1984 some forty Japanese auto parts suppliers had also set up marketing or manufacturing operations in the United States and more were on the way (Furukawa, 1984b).

More generally, the Japanese were concerned about the loss of the American market due to protectionism. In the 1960s and 1970s the Japanese could partially moderate pressures for protectionism by slowing their U.S.-bound exports. As more and more countries became steel exporters, the Japanese found themselves unable to exert this sort of control. Given the near collapse of the integrated U.S. steelmakers in the early 1980s it seemed clear that barriers to foreign steel would be erected. Indeed, in late 1984 a "quota" system was imposed that would restrict the sale of Japanese steel in the United States. According to one report, investment in the integrated U.S. firms was favored as a matter of policy by MITI to help ease trade frictions. MITI was said to welcome the agreement between NKK and National, for example, and to have promised it support, possibly in the form of easier availability of low-interest government loans (Furakawa, 1984).

In at least one case, Kawasaki's investment in California Steel, the acquisition of a stake in an American steelmaker fit a broader strategy of a multinational rationalization of production.

The Japanese saw genuine opportunities to make profits through U.S. steel firms by upgrading their technology and management. At the same time there may have been a shortage of more attractive routes to diversify that would have made use of the employees of Japanese steel firms—no small consideration when permanent employment is customary. The Japanese steelmakers have generally sought to find a way out of their dilemma of slow growth by reducing employment through attrition and through increased exports of technology and engineering services. The number of researchers in the Japanese steel industry has continued to grow, doubling since the mid-1960s

Some Japanese firms were attracted by the new market for electrogalvanized steel sheet for automobile bodies in the United States as automakers sought to offer new quality assurance programs to customers. In December 1983 General Motors asked producers of galvanized sheet to give a presentation on their capacity to supply GM with galvanized sheet that would meet requirements for the 1987 model year. GM and other automakers wanted to be able to offer extensive guarantees against corrosion. To do this they wanted to use a coated sheet that is paintable, weldable, and formable. The conventional hot-dipped galvanizing process most commonly used in the United States is less likely to meet these needs than electrolytic galvanizing. American suppliers soon began announcing plans for new electrolytic galvanizing facilities. Some American firms found it useful to get the technology and some of the capital for the new facilities via joint ventures with Japanese firms (Fierman, 1985; McManus, 1984).

Finally, the Japanese saw opportunities to enhance their own technological capabilities through these investments, both through justifying increased investment in research and through the ability to acquire American technologies.

Given this willingness of Japanese and other foreign interests to contribute capital and technology to joint ventures in the United States, why did they seek U.S. partners rather than buying out or establishing wholly owned subsidiaries? A major consideration seems to have been the desire to minimize the risk in their U.S. investments. A U.S. partner could help solve problems with respect to labor, for example. In cases such as NKK's participation in the management of National Steel, the joint ventures did not involve the creation of a new plant with a new work force, but rather the management of an existing unionized work force. It is clear that NKK was greatly concerned about this problem in its earlier negotiations with Kaiser and Ford. A U.S. partner could also help reduce uncertainty with regard to markets. National Steel, Kaiser, U.S. Steel, LTV all are well set up to sell the products of the new joint ventures. One might wonder about the prospects for joint ventures in which the major offering of the U.S. partner is the reduction of uncertainty about U.S. labor and markets. In these cases the joint venture may well be no more than a transitional form of organization with a foreign takeover occurring later. Finally, given the low (or nonexistent) profitability of integrated U.S. steel firms, it may be that foreign investors wanted to minimize the amount of their investment to the smallest amount that would ensure access to the U.S. market. It might be sensible for a foreign firm to put money into a low-return U.S. investment to help protect markets, but it would not make sense to put any more money into such an investment than was necessary.

In some instances the foreign interest in the U.S. industry was part of an international restructuring of the steel industry. One aspect of this has been a "disintegration" of the steelmaking process. International comparative advantage may differ from one part of the steel production process and another. Countries, such as Brazil that have traditionally exported ironmaking raw materials may integrate forward to the production of iron and then steel slabs. This can result in a substantial savings in shipping costs (since slabs weigh far less than the coal and iron required to produce them). Conversely, U.S. steelmakers may have lost comparative advantage for the production of slabs because of higher labor costs but retain it for the production of coated sheets and other products because of their presence in the world's largest market. Foreign steelmakers in countries that are now building major new steel industries, such as Korea, may also find it useful to have U.S. joint venture firms take their semifinished products until they complete their own finishing mills.

The upshot is that firms in Korea and Brazil find it useful to have partners in the United States that can make use of their slab and ensure a stable market. The U.S. partners have or can build at relatively low cost finishing facilities and provide an outlet for final products. They can also avoid the need to build or refurbish blast furnaces and steelmaking equipment. Thus the California Steel and U.S. Steel-Pohang ventures. The Japanese firms can go a little further along the production path, providing sheet for electrogalvanizing lines in the United States. Thus the LTV-C. Itoh and Nisshin-Wheeling-Pittsburgh joint ventures.

In all of these cases, the foreign partners, are well motivated to upgrade the technological level of the joint ventures they are participating in. It should be stressed, however, that while the Japanese may introduce new technology and management practices to joint ventures that will increase the efficiency of American steel producers, there is little cause for optimism that this will lead to a reestablishment of these firms as major international competitors. Even the Japanese integrated steelmakers are finding themselves under pressure from foreign producers with lower wage costs. Like their American counterparts they are attempting to reduce their dependency on steel, though unlike the Americans they are moving rather slowly and they are moving into related fields to which they can bring some relevant experience. In June 1984 Nippon Steel, Japan's (and the world's) largest producer, amended its articles of incorporation to include as the company's lines of business not just steelmaking but "the production and sale of nonferroalloys, fine ceramics, chemicals and plant engineering." In July 1984 Nippon Steel established new departments of New Materials Development, Titanium Development, and a Bureau of Oil Drilling Machinery. Nippon Steel's goal appeared to be to have its nonsteel activities account for some 30 percent of total sales by the year 2000 (Yonekura, 1984). Nippon Kokan, Japan's second largest steelmaker, established a "New Materials Division" in January 1985 and announced a goal of having the new division account for 25 percent of sales by the year 200 (*NKK News*, 1985a). Kawasaki Steel, Japan's third largest producer, initiated a five-year plan in April 1986 that is designed to raise the contribution of its nonsteel revenues from the present 18 percent to 40 percent by the year 2000 (*Newsletter from Kawasaki Steel Corporation*, 1986).

MINIMILLS

There have long been smaller nonintegrated steelmakers in the United States. These firms typically used open hearths and other technologies similar to those used by the larger firms, but often with even less efficiency. In the 1950s and 1960s a new type of smaller steelmaker began to appear. These "minimills" were smaller than the integrated steelmakers, to be sure, but they also differed from them in other important respects. They used modern electric furnaces to melt scrap and typically were very quick to introduce new technologies such as continuous casting. They were generally located in regional markets and thus could save on shipping costs in reaching their customers. They concentrated on relatively simple products such as wire rod or concrete reinforcing bar.

Some of these firms were extremely efficient and highly profitable. It has been claimed that one of them, Nucor, in good times and bad has always been the most profitable producer of carbon steel in the world (McManus, 1985). Over the five-year period 1978-1983 Nucor realized a return on equity of 18.8 percent, nearly double that of the most profitable integrated firm (*Iron Age*, 1984). Not all minimills were successful, of course, and some failed. Nonetheless, the minimill segment of the steel industry was consistently far more profitable than the integrated producers in the 1970s. From 1977 to 1981 the minimills had a return on equity of 17 percent, while that of the integrated steelmakers was only 5.6 percent (Barnett and Schorsch, 1983, p. 97).

Some minimills have grown to the point that "mini" is no longer an accurate description of them. As Table 8-3 shows, four of these firms can now produce 1 million or more tons of steel per year. Nucor, North Star, and Florida now rank among the ten largest producers of steel in the United States. They have also expanded their geographic scope and some claim to be national rather than regional suppliers. Nucor and North Star each have plants in four states. Minimills produce steel in twenty-seven states. There is even a small plant in Hawaii. As they become national marketers the minimills increasingly encroach on the traditional domain of the major integrated firms. Recently, they have begun to pose still another threat to the integrated producers by expanding the range of products they offer (McManus, 1980).

At the beginning of 1984 there were approximately 50 minimills in the United States supplying approximately 15-18 percent of the U.S. market for steel. One expert predicts that the share of the minimills will rise to 20-24 percent by 1990 and reach a peak of around 34 percent by the middle of the 1999s (Miller, 1984). Given the profitability and prospects of the U.S. minimills it is perhaps not surprising that they have attracted substantial foreign interest.

Table 8-3. U.S. Mini-midi Mills Ranked by Capacity.

Firm	Plant Locations	Total Capacity (Tons per Year)
1. Nucor Corporation	S.C., Neb., Tex., Utah	2,000,000
2. North Star Steel	Minn., Iowa, Mich., Tex.	1,610,000
3. Florida Steel	Fla., N.C., Tenn.	1,440,000
4. Chaparral Steel	Tex.	1,000,000
5. Atlantic Steel	Ga.	750,000
6. Georgetown Steel	S.C.	700,000
7. Raritan River Steel	N.J.	650,000
8. Bayou Steel Corporation	La.	650,000
9. Newport Steel Corporation	Ky.	510,000
10. Roanoke Electric	Va.	500,000
11. Sheffield Steel	Okla.	400,000
12. Structural Metals	Tex.	360,000
13. Ohio River Steel	Ky.	350,000
14. Roblin Industries	N.Y.	290,000
15. Steel of West Virginia	W.Va.	250,000
16. Auburn Steel	N.Y.	240,000
17. Cascade Steel Rolling Mills	Ore.	240,000
18. Kentucky Electric	Ky.	240,000
19. New Jersey Steel	N.J.	240,000
20. Birmingham Bolt	Ala.	225,000
21. Razorback Steel	Ark.	220,000
22. Northwest Steel	Wash.	200,000
23. Border Steel Mills	Tex.	180,000
24. Mississippi Steel	Miss.	180,000
25. Knoxville Iron	Tenn.	180,000
26. Tamco	Calif.	175,000
27. Judson Steel	Calif.	160,000
28. BW Steel	Pa.	150,000
29. Marathon Steel	Ariz.	150,000
30. Soule Steel	Calif.	100,000
31. Intercoastal Steel	Va.	100,000
32. Ameri-Steel	Pa.	100,000
33. Marathon Le Tourneau	Tex.	75,000
34. Hawaiian West	Haw.	60,000
35. Texas Steel	Tex.	24,000
36. Oklahoma Steel	Okla.	18,000
Total Capacity		14,717,000

Source: Compiled from information in Association of Iron and Steel Engineers. 1984. *Directory of Iron and Steel Plants: 1984.* Pittsburgh: AISE.

FOREIGN INVOLVEMENT IN U.S. MINIMILLS

An examination of the thirty-six minimills and midimills listed in Table 8-3 shows the importance of foreign involvement in this sector of the U.S. steel industry. The Korf group of West Germany designed, built and operated the largest plant of North Star Steel (second largest producer on the list) and the plant of Georgetown Steel (sixth on the list) before going bankrupt in 1983. Co-Steel International of Canada established Chapparal Steel (fourth on the list) and Raritan River (seventh on the list). Another Canadian company, Ivaco, purchased Atlantic Steel Company (fifth on the list) in 1979. Austria's Voest-Alpine built Bayou Steel (eighth on the list) in 1981. German, Saudi, and Brazilian financing and technology were involved in the building of Ohio River (thirteenth on the list). Kyoei Steel of Japan built and operates Auburn Steel (sixteenth). A Swiss firm has controlled New Jersey Steel (nineteenth). A British firm has owned Knoxville Iron Company (twenty-fifth). Two Japanese firms own half of Tamco (twenty-sixth). Ameri-Steel (thirty-second) is a division of Ulme International.

The most conspicuous foreign actor in this sector of the U.S. steel industry has been Willy Korf, a flamboyant German entrepreneur. Korf's Georgetown, South Carolina minimill was the first foreign-owned steel company in the United States. Korf later built minimills in Texas and Connecticut. Korf began his activities in the United States through various dealings with Midland-Ross Corporation of Ohio. In 1967 he purchased rights to Midland-Ross's Midrex iron ore direct reduction process.[3] A year later Korf established Georgetown Steel Corporation in South Carolina. Midland-Ross purchased 49 percent of the new minimill and established a subsidiary that used the Midrex process to produce iron for Georgetown. Midland-Ross also bought 50 percent of a Korf minimill in West Germany. Midland-Ross hoped through these holdings to obtain knowledge about the processing of metallized pellets into steel. In 1971, however, Midland-Ross reduced its ownership of Georgetown Steel to less than 10 percent and sold all of its share of the German plant to Korf. When the price increases for natural gas in 1973–1974 made the Midrex Process unattractive for use in the United States, Midland-Ross sold the technology to Korf for a reported $25 million. Korf established a new firm, Midrex Corporation, to handle the process and quickly turned to selling the technology outside the United States.[4]

In 1975 Korf, short of money, secretly sold 30 percent of his German and American holding companies to the Kuwaiti government.[5]

In 1976 Korf opened his second minimill in the United States, the Georgetown-Texas Steel Corporation. By 1980 his two plants had a capacity of nearly 1.5 million tons of steel per year. In 1982, however, some of the Korf companies suffered heavy losses, and in early 1983 Korf's German holding company was declared bankrupt. Various Korf holdings were sold off in Europe. The semigovernmental Austrian Steelmaker Voest-Alpine, which had owned 49 percent of Korf Engineering, increased its holdings to 66 percent and took control of the former Korf engineering arm. The Georgetown-Texas Steel Corporation was merged into North Star Steel. Midrex was sold to Kobe Steel of Japan. Korf Industries (USA) was reorganized in 1983 with the Kuwaiti's increasing their ownership from 30 percent to 51 percent.[6]

In 1984 Korf was rebuilding his empire, using strategies based on technology as he had before. This time, instead of the Midrex process, he was promoting the KR process. The KR process also directly reduces iron ore into iron suitable for use in electric furnaces but is better suited for use in the United States because it uses coal rather than natural gas as a fuel. Korf also established Connecticut Steel, a new minimill that is to be a showplace of technologies Korf is trying to sell.

Korf has not been the only foreign steelmaker to attempt to use new technologies in seeking a niche in the minimill segment of the U.S. steel industry. In 1981 the Austrian steelmaker, Voest-Alpine, spent $300 million to establish Bayou Steel in Louisiana. Unfortunately, the mill brought 650,000 tons of annual capacity on stream just as demand began contracting. Bayou reportedly lost about $153 million before Voest-Alpine gave up and sold it to an American firm at the end of 1985. In establishing two of the largest American minimill firms, Chaparral Steel and Raritan River, Co-Steel of Canada sought to introduce new technology that would minimize production costs. In the case of Chaparral, Co-Steel was approached by a U.S. firm to be a joint venture partner. Co-Steel designed and built the mill using technology it had developed at its Canadian plant. Chaparral came on stream in 1975. By the mid-1980s Chaparral had a capacity of 1 million tons and was marketing its steel in virtually every part of the United States. Co-Steel built a wholly owned minimill, Raritan River, in New Jersey in 1980. This mill, with some 650,000 tons per year capacity is also one of the largest nonintegrated facilities in the United States. Co-Steel's rapid expansion, however, ended with serious financial difficulties in late 1985, and the company sold its interest in Chaparral.

There have also been instances where foreign firms have upgraded the technology of existing minimills in the United States. Tamco Steel was formed in California in 1974 as a joint venture of Ameron (50 percent), Tokyo Steel (25 percent), and Mitsui (25 percent). The initial plan was to have Tamco process billets produced in Japan. After a period of technical problems Tamco absorbed part of the steel and wire division of Ameron and Japanese operating executives from Tokyo Steel and Mitsui were put into Tamco's management. New Jersey Steel was taken over in 1977 by the Italian subsidiary of Von Roll, a Swiss firm. Its facilities were substantially modified using the technology of an Italian engineering firm.

Other movements of foreign capital into the American minimill segment, of course, have been simple investments, with few direct technological implications. A few have been part of the growing international integration of the steel industry. Tuscaloosa Steel in Alabama, for example, was recently formed with participation by British Steel. British Steel may provide slabs for the new firm.

OBSERVATIONS ON MINIMILLS

Foreign interests have frequently sought to enter this profitable sector of the U.S. steel industry. Most have done this via direct investment, sometimes bringing new technology with them as a basis for comparative advantage. While in some cases American capital has been involved, there have not been many instances comparable to those where integrated American steelmakers were sought as partners because of their expertise in the management of a U.S. work force or access to markets. Korf did establish a tie with Midland-Ross to obtain technology, but this lasted only a few years.

It may be that foreign interests have not seen a need to have U.S. partners in operating minimills in the United States because it is easier to manage labor at a minimill than at an integrated steel plant. The size of the work force is much smaller. Some minimills have managed to keep out the United Steel Workers union. A more important reason is that foreign-owned minimills have moved into small market niches, often encouraged by chambers of commerce and local industry, and thus have had less obvious need for help with marketing. Nonetheless few of the foreign-run minimills in the United States have been successful over the longer term and many have ended up in the hands of U.S. interests.

Given the prominence of Japanese joint ventures in the integrated sector of the U.S. steel industry, it might be wondered why there has been so little Japanese involvement in the minimill sector. One reason for this is simply that minimills have not been strong in Japan. Prices of scrap and electricity are high in Japan, and there is a technologically efficient integrated sector. With only a few exceptions (Tokyo Steel for one) there have not been strong nonintegrated steelmakers that could come to the United States. Many of the nonintegrated Japanese steelmakers are weak affiliates of integrated firms.

SPECIALTY STEELS

The prospects for technology transfer both to and from the United States have been important in motivating joint ventures in the specialty steel sector. One such joint venture was discussed by Copperweld and Japan's Daido Steel in 1985. Daido was reportedly interested because two of its customers for hot-rolled bars in Japan, Nissan and Honda, have moved into the United States. Steel import quotas have limited Daido's ability to supply the U.S. plants of these firms. Copperweld cannot supply these customers without help because its quality standards are not high enough.[7]

A transfer of technology to the United States was also involved in a recent small joint venture between Ellwood City Forge (ECF) of the United States and Uddeholm Tooling AB of Sweden. ECF's main contribution to the joint venture, aside from providing 80 percent of its capital, is a commitment to use most of the mills output. The Swedish firm's major contribution is to be its technical know-how in the production of specialty grades of steel. This will allow ECF to expand beyond its previous market of standard carbon and low-alloy grades of steel. The major benefit to Uddeholm is that it can reduce its lead time and freight costs in reaching the rich U.S. market for alloy tool steel (*Iron and Steel Engineering*, 1985).

In both the Copperweld and Ellwood City cases, firms in the United States were interested in joint ventures because they provided opportunities for the acquisition of technology. One joint venture in the specialty steel industry was halted because it appeared to offer opportunities for the transfer of U.S. technology to a foreign firm. In 1983 Nippon Steel sought to follow its diversification strategy by purchasing Special Metals Corporation, a subsidiary of Allegheny Corporation. Special Metals produces superalloy metals that are used in military jet engines. It also uses advanced melting technologies and additionally engages in some research for the U.S. Department of Defense. The result was that "objections by the Defense Department, unforeseen by both negotiating parties, make it impractical to proceed with the sale of Nippon" (Prizinsky, 1983).

Another foreign investment in a U.S. specialty steel maker had less involvement of technology transfer. In 1976 the French specialty steelmaker Creusot-Loire (C-L), bought a share of Phoenix Steel and later that year took control of Phoenix's management. C-L invested heavily in upgrading the Phoenix plants, but in the early 1980s both Phoenix and C-L suffered losses. C-L was forced to liquidate as the French government withdrew from the steel industry and Phoenix filed for bankruptcy protection in 1983 (Johnson, 1985).

These four cases, then, represent a range of examples. In two of them U.S. firms are motivated by the prospect of receiving technology that will allow them to expand their business, while their foreign partners are concerned about expanding their markets in the face of protectionism or (in the Ellwood City case) constraints on growth. The foreigners offer technology, the Americans offer markets. Nippon Steel apparently was interested in Special Metals as part of its strategy (shared with most of the other major Japanese steelmakers) of becoming a producer of an ever wider range of new high-technology materials. The technology would have gone from the U.S. Phoenix upgraded some of its facilities as a result of the C-L investment, but the motivation on the U.S. side was simply to get the capital needed to improve its facilities and the motivation on the foreign side seems to have had little to do with opportunities to be gained through the introduction of technology.

STEEL SERVICE CENTERS

A growing share of carbon steel in the United States is handled by service centers. These are firms that purchase steel from mills, selling it to final users. Most also process the steel for their customers. A service center may, for example, have extensive equipment for the bending, cutting, sawing, slotting, punching, deburring, leveling, and surface preparation of steel. In 1985 an estimated 12 percent of the service centers in the United States had some foreign ownership, by 1990 the percentage could be 20 percent (*Iron Age*, 1985a).

European interests have long been involved in this segment of the U.S. steel industry. Uddeholm Corporation, for example, started centers to market Swedish tool steels back in 1927. Krupp and Klockner of West Germany have also had steel service centers in the United States. It is the Japanese, however, who have been most active in acquiring total or partial ownership of steel service centers in the United States. In some instances the Japanese actors have been steelmakers or trading subsidiaries of steel firms, but more often it has been the major trading companies. As Table 8-4 shows, approxi-

Table 8-4.   Japanese Investments in U.S. Steel Industry.

Year	Japanese Partner(s)	U.S. Partner(s)	Firm and Activity
1961	Sumikin Bussan [Sumitomo Metals]		Sumikin Bussan, U.S. steel, coal trade
1964	Marubeni (36.3%)	Phil Steinberg (63.7%)	Crest Steel, service center
1965	Kawasaki Trading		Kawasho International, trade, especially steel
	Hitachi Metals		Hitachi Metals International, sale of products
1966	Sumitomo Metals (50%) Sumitomo Trading (50%)		Quality Metals
	Shinsho Shoji		Shinsho American, trade
1968	Sumitomo Trading (80%)	A. Geldner (20%)	Western Tube and Conduit, pipe manufacture
1970	Koyo Trading		Metals Exports, steel importer
1971	Mitsubishi (82%)	W. Rawn (18%)	RJM steel sales
1972	Kanematsu Gosho		Southern metal Service steel fabrication center
	Nippon Steel		Nippon Steel USA info coll.
1973	Shibamoto Industries		Shibamoto America trade in steel
1974	Mitsui		Sea-Port Steel, import of steel
	Tomen (80%)	D. Hall (20%)	Diamond Perforated Metal, fabrication/sale flat steel
	Nissho-Iwai (35%) Nippon Koshuha Steel (35%)	K. Ritter (18%)	Alloy Tool Steel, fabrication/sale alloy tools
	Tokyo Steel (25%) Mitsui (25%)	Ameron (50%)	Tamco minimill

Table 8–4. continued

Year	Japanese Partner(s)	U.S. Partner(s)	Firm and Activity
	Nippon Steel (5%) Mitsui (45%)	Amax (50%)	Alumax, aluminum products
	Tokyo Steel		Tokyo Steel (USA), market studies, investments
1975	Sumitomo Trading (80%) Kyoei Steel (20%)		Auburn Steel, minimill
1976	Toshin Steel (20%) Asahi Bussan (20%)	AVA (60%)	AVA Toshin Service and Supply, sale of electric furnace parts
1977	C. Itoh		S&W Import, sale of pipe and pallet nails
	Nittetsu Shoji		Nittetsu Shoji America trade in steel, etc.
1978	Tomen		First Metals import of steel products
	Sumitomo Corporation (55%)	Harry Ong (45%)	Industrial Metals, sale of stainless, etc.
	Maruichi Kokan (38%) Maruichi Kohan (8%) Nissho Iwai (30%) Mitsubishi (15%) Sumitomo Bank (4%) Tokai Bank (3%) Tokyo Bank (2%)		Maruichi American, sale of welded pipe
	Japan Steel Works		Japan Steel Works America, import JSW products
	Kawasho		Hayward Steel and Sheet, service center
1979	Daiwa Kokan Kogyo		Century Tube, produc- tion of pipe
	Shinko Wire (95%) Mitsui (5%)		Shinko Wire America, production of PC wire
1980	Marubeni		Archer Pipe and Tube, sale of steel pipe

(Table 8-4. continued overleaf)

Table 8–4. continued

Year	Japanese Partner(s)	U.S. Partner(s)	Firm and Activity
	O&K (95%) Shinko Trading (5%)		O&K Steel, drawn wire
	Mitsui	Reliance Steel and Aluminum [took over in 1982]	Reliance Steel, service center
	Tokyo Steel (60%) C. Itoh (40%)		TCI Trading, sale of wire rope
1981	Daiwa Kokan Kogyo		American Daiwa Steel, production of pipe
	Sumitomo (51%)	C. Rossi et al. (49%)	Distributor Metals, sale of stainless
	Tokyo Steel (55%) Nippon Steel (5%) Mitsubishi (20%) C. Itoh (20%)		ATR Wire and Cable, sale of steel cord for tires
	Kawasaki Steel		Kawasaki Steel Amer- ica, information, trade facilities
	Kobe Steel		Kobe Steel America, market research
1982	Sumitomo Trading		Summit Stainless, processing and sale of stainless steel
	C. Itoh (81%)	Lafayette Metals (19%)	Lafayette Metal Service, sale of fabricated steel
	Daiwa Kokan		American Daiwa Steel, pipe and tube imports
1983	C. Itoh		C. Itoh Pipe and Tube, sale of pipe and tube
	Kobe Steel		Midrex, development and sale of Midrex Process
	Marubeni		Texma Investment, oil country tubular goods
	Sumitomo Metals (49%) Sumitomo Corporation (49%) Sumitomo Bank (2%)		Tube Turns, production, sale of steel

Table 8–4. continued

Year	Japanese Partner(s)	U.S. Partner(s)	Firm and Activity
	Mitsui		Mitsui Tubular Products, sale of oil well pipe, tube
	Daido Steel (60%) Daido Industries (40%)		Daido Steel (America), import of industrial equipment
1984	Nissho Iwai		N-I Tubulars, sale of steel pipe
	Nissho Iwai (85%)		Nisco Steel Services, steel service center
	Kawasaki Steel (25%)	M. Wilkinson (50%)	California Steel Industries, production of steel
	Nippon Kokan (50%)	National (50%)	National Steel
	Nippon Kokan		NKK Project Management, plant related
	Nisshin	Wheeling-Pittsburgh	Wheeling-Pittsburgh
1985	Mitsubishi		Coilplus, fabrication and sale of steel
	Marubeni		Bleim Steel, steel service center
	C. Itoh	Armco	steel service center
	Nissho Iwai		Berwick Steel, steel service center
	Nisshin		Thinsheet Metals, produce alloys
	Kawasho		Alerco Manufacturing service center
Unknown date of entry			
	Mitsubishi		Acvem Corporation, dealer in steel products
	Nippon Kokan (40%)	Martin-Marietta (60%)	Martin-Marietta Aluminum, production of titanium alloy

Sources: *Shukan Toyo Keizai.* 1985. *Kaigai shinshutsu kigyo soran.* Reports in *American Metal Market.*

mately twenty-five U.S. steel service centers have been fully or partially owned by Japanese firms.

In 1985 all the big eight Japanese general trading firms, Mitsui, Mitsubishi, Sumitomo, Marubeni, C. Itoh, Kanematsu Gosho, Nisho-Iwai, and Tomen, had wholly owned subsidiaries among the U.S. steel service centers. Marubeni purchased a little more than one-third interest in Crest Steel Corporation in 1964. Within a decade Marubeni had been joined by Sumitomo, Mitsubishi, Kanematsu Gosho, Mitsui, Tomen, and Nissho-Iwai. C. Itoh followed in 1977. In 1984 and 1985 alone, at least a half dozen new entries were made into this sector by Japanese general trading firms.

The movements of the major Japanese trading companies have been motivated in part by fears of protectionism and in part by an effort to serve Japanese manufacturing operations in the United States. When the trigger price mechanism was implemented in the late 1970s it was alleged that foreign controlled service centers could nominally sell steel at the trigger price, but in effect be selling at a discount by offering customers extra processing and other services at no cost. Some spokesmen of U.S. steel service firms charged that this was the major reason foreign firms were buying major stakes in existing firms. Whatever the truth of this allegation, several Japanese firms did acquire a full or partial interest in U.S. steel service centers in 1978-1982.

In late 1984 the U.S. introduced a "voluntary" trade quota system whereby foreign suppliers of steel would each be restricted to a certain percentage of the U.S. market. The Japanese, for example, were to supply no more than 5.8 percent of the U.S. market—in effect, not merely curtailing future expansion, but cutting back sales below past levels (Lynn and McKeown, 1988). One response to this decrease in volume by the Japanese trading firms was to seek to increase the value added through their services to each ton of steel. A way to do this is by increasing their investment in steel service centers, preferably by developing centers able to offer a broader range of services. In some cases that has meant the introduction of technology from Japan.

One, perhaps unanticipated, consequence of the steel quotas, has been that the major trading firms have sought more ties with U.S. domestic producers of steel. These firms have built up an investment in the United States with experts on the steel industry and markets for steel and with the reduction of Japanese supplies of steel have sought domestic replacements.

C. Itoh took the most direct approach in this regard. In 1985 it formed a joint venture with Armco Steel to operate a series of steel service centers. The joint venture, at least initially, would concentrate on the sale of Armco steel products, though the possibility of later selling Japanese steel has been left open. Armco is to be responsible for marketing, C. Itoh for the management of the plants (Furukawa and Collier, 1985). In other "post quota" instances, Japanese trading companies have established or bought out U.S. steel service centers with the announced intention of handling domestic steel. Such was the case, for example, with Mitsubishi's establishment of Coilplus, a coil processing plant in Alabama in 1985.

It will be interesting to see if the Japanese trading firms maintain their relationship with domestic steel producers if trade barriers are lowered. It may be that the increased strength in the service centers will allow an even greater infusion of imports than occurred before.

Another reason for the recent movement of Japanese trading firms into U.S. steel service centers is to provide a basis for serving some of their traditional clients with new U.S. manufacturing plants. Marubeni, for example, acquired Blein Steel Company in Toledo, Ohio, in 1985 to improve its ability to serve the Honda and Nissan plants in the United States. A year earlier, Nissho-Iwai, another major general trading firm, established a service center, at the urging of Sanyo's operations in Arkansas. This service center, Nisco, also supplies Sharp and Nissan in Tennessee. One advantage the Japanese owners of service centers may enjoy with respect to Japanese customers is their familiarity with the somewhat distinctive Japanese "just-in-time" inventory control systems, such as Toyota's *kanban* system, in which suppliers make frequent small deliveries to minimize the customer's need to maintain inventories of raw materials. This apparently has been a factor in Nisco, a subsidiary of Nissho-Iwai formed in 1984, getting business from other Japanese firms (Teplitz, 1984; Collier, 1985). It is possible that in this regard there may be some transfer of a managerial technology to U.S. firms.

As can be seen from Table 8-4 most of the major Japanese steel firms also have a direct or indirect interest in American steel service centers. Sometimes this is via subsidiary trading firms such as Nittetsu Bussan (Nippon Steel), Sumikin Bussan (Sumitomo Metals), or Kawasho (Kawasaki Steel). Sometimes the steelmakers jointly own American affiliates with related Japanese partners. This has not been common, however. In a few cases two or more Japanese firms (including a trading firm) jointly own a steel distribution company. Three firms in the Sumitomo group, Sumitomo Metals, Sumitomo Corporation, and Sumitomo Bank, for example, jointly hold Tube Turns.

These joint ventures and wholly owned foreign subsidiaries have sometimes brought in new technologies. Nissho-Iwai and Mitsubishi announced plans to bring in high-speed slitters built by Watanabe

Iron Works in Japan to their new Nisco and Coilplus subsidiaries. Both are also planning to bring technicians from Japanese steel supply firms to improve operations at Nisco and Coilplus. Nissho-Iwai announced its intention to invest in new equipment at Berwick, a service center it acquired in 1985. Marubeni announced similar plans for its recently acquired Blein Steel Company (Furukawa, 1984a). Finally, as noted, it is possible that new managerial practices will be brought in by the Japanese. (Interestingly, it is C. Itoh, not Armco, that will manage the service center set up by the two firms.) The introduction of new managerial practices might be especially significant with regard to inventory control systems. On the other hand, the deep intrusion into the American steel marketing system by foreign steelmakers and firms closely connected with them may reduce yet another competitive advantage the domestic industry has had, putting yet more pressure on U.S. producers.

IMPLICATIONS FOR POLICY

U.S. trade and other policies have clearly played roles in the increasing number of international joint ventures in the United States steel industry. Trade barriers and the threat that they might be extended were major reasons in the decisions of foreign firms to establish production capabilities in the United States in the integrated and mini-mill segments of the industry. Restrictions in the volume of Japanese steel imports also led the trading companies both to participate in joint ventures in the distribution of steel and to establish subsidiaries. On the other hand, the voluntary restraint agreements and other mechanisms used to "protect" the U.S. industry have been used as justification by the Justice Department for discouraging a restructuring of the U.S. industry through mergers. One consequence of this was that U.S. antitrust policy has been criticized for forcing U.S. firms to seek foreign rather than domestic merger partners. National Steel, for example, turned to Nippon Kokan after being prevented from becoming part of an enlarged U.S. Steel.[8]

Should policymakers be faulted for this outcome? Has the result been a net loss of high-skill jobs as research and other functions are transferred offshore? Or has the result been a revitalization of the steel industry saving jobs and industrial capacity for the United States? While the evidence presented in this chapter does not allow a comprehensive answer to these questions it is suggestive.

First, it might be noted that U.S. firms have been withdrawing from the steel industry. When they have had capital, they have most often used it to pursue policies of diversification. A common sense of the situation seems to be that expressed by *Business Week* in mid-1986: "For weaker [steel] companies, the only course may be to allow their businesses to liquidate gradually. For stronger companies it may be to diversify out of steel" (p. 90). Thus government policies designed to allow U.S. steelmakers increases in profits with the idea that these profits would be used to increase efficiency have not had that outcome (see Borrus (1983), for example). On the other hand, while foreign capital and technology may not have allowed a resurgence of the U.S. steel industry, they may well have slowed down the process of decline. One report suggests that NKK has been able to obtain "a large portion" of the $1.2 billion National Steel needs to modernize at favorable rates from Japanese sources (Glasgall, 1986). It is difficult to imagine where National could have raised money on this scale in the United States.

There is reason to believe that Japanese firms are improving the technological level of the U.S. steel industry, particularly in the integrated steel, specialty steel, and steel distribution sectors. In the minimill segment much of the technology used has come from European and Canadian sources. Some of this too, is a result of protectionist moves. Japanese trading companies shifted their expertise from importing Japanese steel, to gaining control of parts of the U.S. distribution system and upgrading it to serve both Japanese and American firms in the United States. It may be that higher level functions supporting the operations of joint ventures in the United States are being transferred offshore, but it is not clear that these functions would have remained in the United States even without foreign ownership. USX has remained American owned, but has substantially cut its research staff and budgets.

While it is difficult to tell what would have happened if U.S. Steel had taken over National Steel, the major instance of restructuring by U.S. steelmakers, the absorption of Youngstown Sheet and Tube and Republic Steel by LTV did not produce much of a turn around. Indeed, in 1986 LTV filed for bankruptcy court protection.[9] Further, since U.S. Steel has not recently been noted for either investing heavily in its steel plant and equipment or in research, it is not clear that it would have been able (or willing) to provide either more capital or more technology to allow improvements in the efficiency of National Steel than NKK.[10]

NOTES

1. The Japanese and others did import considerable steel production technology from the United States, but most of this technology was developed

by manufacturers of steel plant equipment, not by steelmakers. A list of Japanese technology imports between 1950 and 1957 includes twenty-six imports from the United States. Only five were from steelmakers. See Nippon Tekko Renmi, 1959, pp. 828–831. The U.S. firms were strong in the development of new product technologies, but these technologies could typically be transferred under arm's length arrangements such as licensing.

2. NKK also sent several other executives to Pittsburgh, and received visits from National engineering teams.

3. The Midrex Process uses natural gas to produce iron that can be refined in electric furnaces—providing a substitute for scrap in minimills. It has been used in many countries but has been particularly attractive in areas where natural gas is cheap and steel scrap in short supply, most notably in the Middle East.

4. Material on the earlier history of Korf in the United States is drawn from *Steel* (1968); Neal (1969); Ball (1982), and news articles in *American Metal Market*.

5. This deal did not become publicly known until 1978. See *Economist* (1978).

6. Based on news articles in *American Metal Market*.

7. According to one Copperweld executive Copperweld is more interested in the access an agreement would give them to Daido technology than in the additional volume they would get.

8. Arrangements for a buy out of National Steel by U.S. Steel were terminated because of the Justice Department's opposition on antitrust grounds.

9. Of course, there might have been an even greater loss of employment and productive capacity if these mergers had not taken place. The point is simply that the restructuring was at best a holding action.

10. In recent years U.S. Steel typically has ranked at or near the bottom in percentage of sales invested in research in the American steel industry.

REFERENCES

Arenson, Karen W. 1984. "U.S. Steel and National Drop Plan to Merge Steel Divisions." *New York Times*, March 10, pps. 1, 37.

Asahi Shimbun (evening). 1980. "Tekko nippon koko ni ari." December 9.

Ball, Robert. 1982. "A German Maverick Pioneers in Steel." *Fortune*, October 4, pp. 131–134.

Barnett, Donald F., and Louis Schorsch. 1983. *Steel: Upheaval in a Basic Industry*. Cambridge, Mass.: Ballinger.

Borrus, Michael. 1983. "The Politics of Competitive Erosion in the U.S. Steel Industry." In John Zysman and Laura Tyson, eds., *American Industry in International Competition*. Ithaca: Cornell University Press, pp. 60–105.

Business Week. 1982. "Why NKK Wants a Losing U.S. Steel Mill." December 27, p. 40.

_____ . 1984a. "Steel Forges a Japanese Connection." May 7, p. 30.

_____. 1984b. "National Tries to Move Even Further Away from Steel." October 22, p. 40.

_____. 1986. "Steelmakers Are Running Out of Options." June 23, 1986.

Collier, Andrew. 1985. "Japan Entry Takes Three Forms with Big Expansion Plans." *American Metal Market*, May 13, p. 14.

Economist. 1978. "Quiet Kuwaitis", November 25, p. 89.

_____. 1984a. "Wheeling-dealing." 291, February 11, pp. 62–64.

_____. 1984b. "Japanese Steel Follows the Carmakers to America." 291, April 28, p. 73.

Fierman, Jaclyn. 1985. "Sleeker Skins for Finicky Car Buyers." *Fortune*, January 7, p. 78.

Furukawa, Tsukasa. 1984a. "Japan's Challenge." *American Metal Market*, May 14, p. 14a.

_____. 1984b. "Japan Secures U.S. Beachhead." *American Metal Market*, August 29.

_____, and Andrew Collier. 1985. "Joint Armco, Itoh Venture Plans Series of Steel Process Centers." *American Metal Market*, June 14.

Hennart, Jean-Francois. 1986. "A Transaction Cost Theory of Equity Joint Ventures." Unpublished paper presented at the Academy of Management, August.

Hogan, William T. 1971. *Economic History of the Iron and Steel Industry in the United States*. Lexington, Mass.: Lexington Books.

Glasgall, William. 1986. "Japanese Capital Finds a Home in Middle America." *Business Week*, July 14, p. 52.

Iron and Steel Engineer. 1985. "Mini-mill Joint Venture to Feature Latest Technology." April, p. 63.

Iron Age. 1984. "Iron Age Financial Scoreboard." p. 31. September 3.

_____. 1985a. "Service Centers Face Growth the Hard Way." May 3, pp. 41–56.

_____. 1985b. "Steel Summary: Steelmakers Pursue Joint Ventures to Avoid Overexpansion." 228 (August 16): 16.

Japan Insight. 1981. "Ford Seeks Japanese Technical Assistance on Steel." January 23, p. 3.

Japan Science and Technology Agency. *Indicators of Science and Technology*. Tokyo: Science and Technology. Various Years.

Johnson, Mary C. 1985. "How Two White Knights Plan to Rescue Phoenix." *Iron Age*, May 17, pp. 30–31.

Kidd, J. D. 1985. "Posco, U.S. Steel Form Firm to Buy Pittsburg, Calif. Mill." *American Metal Market*, December 17, p. 1.

LaRue, Gloria T. 1985. "Copperweld Must Meet Quality Standards to Be Daido Partners." *American Metal Market*, October 8, p. 2. Copperweld, incidentally has been controlled by French interests since 1975.

Lynn, Leonard H., and Timothy J. McKeown. 1988. *Organizing Business: Trade Associations in Japan and America*. Washington, D.C.: University Press of America and American Enterprise Institute.

Magnet, Myron. 1985. "How Top Managers Make a Company's Toughest Decision." *Fortune*, March 18, pp. 52–57.

McManus, George. 1980. "Mini-mills Begin to Make Noises in a Big Way." *Iron Age*, May 5, pp. MP5–MP15.

_____. 1982. "State-of-the-Art R&D Couldn't Help McLouth." *Iron Age*, January 4, pp. 19-21.

_____. 1984. "Detroit Forces the Issue in Galvanizing." *Iron Age*, March 19, pp. 57-59.

_____. 1985. "Minimill Report: The Honeymoon Is Over." *Iron Age*, March 1, pp. 26-37.

Murakami, Mutsuko. 1981. "Closing the Circle." *American Metal Market/Metalworking News*, Annual Steelmaking Today Supplement.

Neal, H. R. 1969. "Americans, German Marry for Technology." *Iron Age*, January 30, p. 49.

Newsletter from Kawasaki Steel Corporation. 1985. "Overseas Operations Entering a New Phase." March–April.

Nippon Tekko Renmei. 1959. *Sengo Tekkoshi*, Tokyo: Nippon Tekko Renmei.

NKK News. 1984. "NKK to Acquire 50% Interest of National Steel Corporation." Remarks by James E. Haas, president of National Intergroup, at NII/Kokan Press Conference, August 22, Pittsburgh.

_____. 1985a. "New Materials Division to Form Fourth Corporate Pillar." February–March.

_____. 1985b. "NKK to Supply Ladle Furnace to National Steel." May.

_____. 1986. "New Electrogalvanizing Line Commissioned at National Steel." February–March, p. 2.

Office of Technology Assessment. 1980. *Technology and Steel Industry Competitiveness.* Washington, D.C.: U.S. Government Printing Office.

Prizinsky, David. 1983. "Allegheny Unit Sale to Nippon Steel Off." *American Metal Market*, July 4, p. 1.

Yonekura, Seiichiro. 1984. "The Winter Age of the Japanese Steel Industry." Harvard Business School Case 0-685-050, p. 5.

Steel. 1968. "German Steelmaker in U.S. to Buck Rebar, Wire Imports." December 9, pp. 60-61.

Symonds, William. 1985a. "National Steel's New Game Plan Is Made in Japan." *Business Week*, June 3, p. 78.

_____. 1985b. "To Beat the Foreign Competition, U.S. Steel Joins It." *Business Week*, December 30, p. 55.

Teplitz, Ben. 1984. "Trade Firm's US Entry May Widen." *American Metal Market*, May 14, p. 14a.

Thompson, Donald B. 1984. "Can a Cause of a Problem Solve It?" *Industry Week*, May 14.

Wiegner, Kathleen. 1980. "Steel Turnabout." *Forbes*, November 10.

9 MULTINATIONAL JOINT VENTURES IN MOTOR VEHICLES

James P. Womack

A striking feature of the motor vehicle industry today is its size, organizational complexity, and degree of internationalization. In 1985 production of cars and trucks in the world's market economies totaled 41.2 million units. These vehicles were assembled from an average of about 15,000 parts in a complex process undertaken by about thirty final assemblers worldwide, each aided by several thousand suppliers of components, materials, and tools. After assembly, 42 percent of these vehicles—17.3 million units—were shipped across national boundaries for sale (Motor Vehicle Manufacturers Association, 1987).

An equally striking feature of this industry during its first century of development has been the periodic emergence of new producing regions with powerful competitive advantages based on new systems of production organization and new product strategies. The emergence of new producers in new regions has repeatedly threatened established producers, creating both the need and the opportunity for the multinational joint ventures to be examined in this chapter. The emergence of Japan as the current claimant to competitive dominance has caused a powerful wave of joint venture formation in the 1980s that promises to change the structure of the entire world industry in the years immediately ahead.

This chapter is based largely on twenty-five interviews with executives of auto assembly and component firms, government officials, bankers, and financial analysts from the United States, Japan, and Korea. For obvious reasons most respondents requested to remain anonymous.

This chapter examines this process of industry evolution and analyzes the types of joint ventures currently forming. It also inquires about the consequences of the current surge in joint venture formation for the future of the American motor vehicle industry and concludes with some observations about public policies toward these ventures.

A CENTURY OF TRANSFORMATIONS[1]

The European Low-Volume Specialists

The motor vehicle industry as a practical, commercial activity dates to the mid-1880s in Germany and France. During its first two decades, competition between the many small companies assembling vehicles focused on rapid improvements in product performance. Typically the vehicle designer and final assembler had a highly skilled work force, depended on independent machine shops and foundaries to supply most of the vehicle's components and was willing to alter the product extensively to customer order. Not surprisingly product costs were high, buyers were well-to-do, and number of units produced was small. Nevertheless, as late as 1906 the small French and German producers accounted for 59 percent of world motor vehicle production (totaling 82,000 units) (Motor Vehicle Manufacturers Association, 1987, p. 10). They exported a considerable fraction of their output to the United States and were acknowledged as the industry's technology leaders.

The American Mass Producers

This situation changed dramatically after 1908 when Henry Ford introduced the Model T, the first motor vehicle consciously designed for mass manufacturing through careful attention to simplifying the fabrication of each part. In 1913 Ford introduced a second major innovation: continuous flow assembly in combination with thoroughgoing Taylorist work organization. This approach brought the many parts together in a remarkably efficient manner.[2] In 1920–1921 Alfred Sloan at General Motors devised the divisional corporate structure and product strategy to guide and coordinate the giant enterprises that Ford's manufacturing techniques seemingly made inevitable.[3]

In combination, these American contributions to industrial organization transformed the fundamental character of the industry and gave overwhelming competitive advantage to American companies.

By the late 1920s they were producing more than 85 percent of the world's motor vehicles and accounted for more than 70 percent of world exports of motor vehicles (Motor Vehicle Manufacturers Association, 1987, pp. 10, 32).

The key elements of this Ford/Sloan transformation were in striking contrast to the small-scale, craft-oriented structure of the European industry:

- High scale, particularly in major mechanical components produced with single-purpose machines

- Specialization of work tasks at every level from the shop floor to the design, engineering, and financial staffs

- Concentration of the industry at the assembler level into the familiar "Big Three"

- Vertical integration of final assembly and components manufacturing with the objective of coordinating an extremely complex process with multiyear lead times and enormous capital investments.

Given the new logic of the motor industry after 1908, the Big Three found little use for joint ventures or other forms of collaboration. They had ample production volume to achieve full economies of scale without needing to collaborate with domestic rivals and would have been barred from cooperation on antitrust grounds in any case. In situations where foreign investment proved economic or necessary (to lower shipping costs or hurdle trade barriers) they generally spurned local partners for fear of losing control. GM was the most adamant, taking the position that it would have no involvement in any project where it did not have 100 percent equity and management control.[4]

The European High-Volume Specialists

While Sloan always talked of a "product for every purse and purpose," the Ford/Sloan system in practice narrowed the range of product offerings to a "standard size" car and light truck able to share under-the-skin mechanical components, particularly engines and transmissions, where cost savings from scale economies were greatest. Visible differentiation was energetically pursued but through the introduction of differing trim levels and "hang on" options rather than alternatives to the standard-size vehicle.

This approach, long thought to be simple common sense in a high-scale industry, provided the competitive opening for European producers in the period after World War II. Because of differing road conditions, tax policies, and income distribution patterns in the various European countries, no standardization on a single type of vehicle had occurred during the prewar period. The isolation of national markets by trade barriers meant that no economies of scale were available either and the industry had languished despite the efforts of many assemblers to copy the organizational advances of Ford and Sloan. The postwar integration of the European market provided the necessary scale while historical circumstance provided an extraordinary range of producers and models.

The European producers used this range of products to attack the Americans, beginning with third-country export markets where small European cars routed large American cars during the 1950s. The American share of world motor vehicle exports fell from 55 percent in 1947 to 10 percent in 1959 as American exports declined by 50 percent. (The Japanese were not yet a factor, garnering only 0.7 percent of world exports in the latter year, according to the Motor Vehicle Manufacturers Association (1986, p. 32).) The Europeans next turned to the United States, making their initial attack with small cars during the 1958 recession. This was repulsed by U.S. produced compact cars and Japanese imports, but the Europeans were able to shift to luxury and sporty models and captured practically the entire world luxury-car market by the late 1970s.[5]

The basic features of "European approach" to motor vehicle manufacture, in comparison with Ford/Sloan practice, might be summarized as follows:

- Intermediate scale, balancing economies of scale against the need for truly differentiated products with different physical attributes and images. The Europeans discovered that selling prices can fall faster than production costs if production is pushed to a level where a product is perceived as a "commodity."

- Intermediate levels of concentration at the assembler level, which consists in the 1980s of a six high-volume producers (including GM and Ford) and another half-dozen luxury- and performance-car producers.

- Lower levels of vertical integration, coupled with a technologically sophisticated components industry.

The postwar European industry, it should be clear, could not ignore the need for minimum scale, particularly in complex mechanical components. However, licenses, long-term purchase arrangements, and joint ventures between companies who were otherwise competitors were found to be a workable alternative to American-style mergers and increasing concentration.

An example is the three-way venture between Volvo, Renault, and Peugeot to produce a V-6 engine needed for each producer's luxury car. Sales volumes were modest in this segment in the 1960s, making a solo project impractical given significant scale economies in engine production up to about 500,000 units per year. Yet a direct purchase from another producer carried cost and dependency penalties. The solution was a three-way joint venture (the Société Franco-Suéddise de Moteure-PRV, or FSM) at Douvrin in France, initiated in 1974.

More recent examples include the joint venture between PSA of France and Iveco (Fiat) in Italy to produce a light van (commencing in 1979), the collaboration between Saab, Alfa Romeo, and Fiat/Lancia to design an executive car (produced in a different version by each company beginning in 1985), and the collaboration between Volkswagen and Renault on a four-speed, electronically controlled automatic transmission (set for introduction in 1987).

The Flexible Japanese Mass Producers

While the European producers succeeded in truly differentiating their products, they did not achieve any advance on the Sloan/Ford model in terms of manufacturing efficiency and production system flexibility. Their shop-floor organizational techniques and product development processes, although varying by country within Europe, were remarkably similar to Detroit's. This sharply limited the European producers' ability to compete directly against Detroit when both regions offered comparable products. It also made it difficult for them to transfer production to North America when currency shifts in the 1970s eliminated their postwar cost advantage. (Witness the disastrous performance of Volkswagen's and Renault's U.S. assembly operations.) The failure of both American and European producers to move beyond the Sloan/Ford system eventually provided the opening for Japanese exporters to attack both regions in the 1970s.

From the beginning of the postwar period the leaders of the Japanese motor industry believed that they would not be able to compete with Detroit on the basis of scale. This was because the protected Japanese domestic market demanded a wide range of products and was crowded with a number of producers, each backed by a massive industrial group (converted from the prewar *zaibatsu* to the postwar *keiretsu*). Waiting for a few producers with very high scale to emerge from an attrition or consolidation process might take decades and might not happen at all.[6] Thus to compete successfully in export markets a new strategy was needed.

After a decade of experimentation this emerged as a new approach to the organization of the production system, pioneered in particular by Taiichi Ono at Toyota. The key feature of the Toyota production system, which now commends itself as a new organizational paradigm for complex manufacturing, was low-cost flexibility. (For a concise statement of the Japanese approach to low-cost specialization, see Friedman (1983).)

Toyota set out to build a manufacturing system that could produce a wide range of models at moderate volumes, like the European producers, but without a cost penalty. One element was flexible, multiskilled work teams on the shop floor using flexible machines that could process a number of different parts. (Monden (1983) provides the definitive description of the Toyota system on the shop floor.) A second element was flexible, multiskilled suppliers able to take on much of the design and engineering work done in the United States and Europe by the final assembler. A third element was a team approach to market analysis, product design, and manufacturing engineering that united the efforts of the suppliers and the assembler to permit the rapid development of new products (Cusumano, 1985, Ch. 6).

In combination, these Japanese inventions produced a domestic industry with the following features:

- Intermediate production scale, but without a cost penalty
- Intermediate levels of concentration at the assembler level, with seven independent producers and several additional affiliated producers
- A components supply system that is neither hierarchical in the vertically integrated GM sense nor "arms-length" and market-based in the fashion of the independent American and European components firms. Instead assemblers entered into long-term alliances with suppliers rather like the collaborations and joint ventures that are the focus of this volume.

As the Japanese system began to emerge it became apparent, perhaps to the surprise of its inventors, that the amount of human effort, tooling, and in-process inventory needed to design and manufacture a car or truck was considerably lower in a Toyota-type system operating at intermediate scale than it was in a GM-style system operating at very high scale. Product development time was compressed as well and the accuracy of the manufacturing process was greatly improved. By the late 1970s this translated into a vast competitive imbalance between the Japanese producers perfecting this system and their Western rivals, an imbalance painfully exposed by the second energy shock.

Because of the inherent flexibility of Japanese production systems and the rivalry between the industrial groups, joint ventures among Japanese firms were very rare. However, transnational arrangements did find a use because of the technical weakness of Japanese components producers and the market protection practices of the Japanese government. The consequence was a number of joint ventures in the 1960s designed to transfer essential technology to a Japanese firm in return for access to the Japanese market for a Western partner.

An example is the automatic transmission venture in Japan between Borg Warner (U.S.) and Aisin Seiki, a member of the Toyota group. No Japanese producer in the 1960s possessed the technology to make an automatic transmission, a device essential for success in the U.S. market. However, the automatic transmission and its production process are so complicated that licensing would have been very cumbersome. Direct purchases from foreign producers or foreign investment in Japan, either alone or with a domestic partner, were more practical. However, at that time the Japanese government blocked majority foreign investments in the auto sector and placed very high tariffs on imported components. A transnational joint venture in Japan was therefore the one approach acceptable to MITI that met the needs of the commercial partners.

Although a number of these ventures were formed, generally involving Western components firms with the weakest market positions, their importance declined sharply over time as Japanese technology caught up with the West.

THE CURRENT ROLE OF JOINT VENTURES IN THE MOTOR INDUSTRY

Since the full emergence of the Japanese industry in the late 1970s the rate of joint venture formation in the motor sector has accelerated dramatically. More than 100 transnational joint ventures have been initiated worldwide since 1980, the majority since 1984.[7] (These are listed in Appendix 9A.) Equally striking, the American Big Three and the largest American parts makers are among the most energetic venturers. Why is this happening?

Some ventures are still motivated by the classic objective of increasing scale and these now extend beyond Europe to include the Japanese. For example, Fuji Heavy Industries and Isuzu Motors have formed a venture to jointly operate an assembly plant in the United States producing products for both companies. Since neither company has the distribution network to absorb the output of a full-scale assembly plant, this makes eminent sense. However, joint ventures to gain scale account for only a small fraction of the ventures now forming.

Another fraction of the new wave of ventures is motivated by three special circumstances in the world industry not necessarily assignable to the emergence of Japan—the growth of niche markets, overcapacity, and the need to incorporate new technologies.

Serving Special Niches

It is now widely agreed that the motor vehicle market is "fragmenting," especially in North America. The number of distinctive body styles and product configurations is growing rapidly while the sales volume in traditional segments is falling. Whether this is due more to the flexibility of the Japanese producers or to the normal tendency for product offerings to proliferate in mature markets is open to debate, but the need for the American Big Three to respond is not. Thus collaborations are now forming for the objective of *reducing* scale and gaining a distinctive product image, without an excessive cost penalty.

Two recent examples are the collaborations between Chrysler and Maserati (Italy) and between Cadillac (GM) and Pininfarina (Italy). In both cases the American company wanted a low-volume, luxury sports car with a distinctive image. They desired a car with a Chrysler or Cadillac badge that could compete with the luxury imports from Europe. Selecting Italian companies with a history of distinctive products to design and build these cars made obvious sense for Detroit while the small Italian partners needed the investment funds and distribution network the Americans can provide. In addition, it appears that low-volume products can be developed cheaper and faster outside the engineering and product design bureaucracies of the American companies while the use of existing mechanical components from Detroit's high-volume products can keep manufacturing costs down.

Market Exit

As the markets of North America, Europe, and Japan have become increasingly integrated over the last decade, the number of competitors in each market segment has grown greatly. In addition, deregulation of the trucking industry in the United States has changed the mix of commercial vehicles demanded, deemphasizing the largest trucks. In consequence a number of manufacturers, particularly of heavy commercial vehicles, are concluding that there is no long-term prospect for profitability.

Exit from a single segment of the truck or car market is not a straightforward matter, however. Each producer's distribution network needs a full range of products to be competitive so that dropping heavy trucks, for example, could threaten the rest of a producer's range. One solution is to take a minority stake in a joint venture with a competitor to assure supply of products for a particular segment. This approach may be able to provide a better guarantee of an appropriate product at a reasonable price than would a purchase agreement with the same competitor, which might be cancelled at any time.

General Motors has recently taken this approach with Volvo. A joint venture, with Volvo in the majority, will absorb all of GM's manufacturing in heavy trucks in North America and is a clear case of exit for GM from a manufacturing presence in this segment. However, GM hopes that its 35 percent equity stake in this venture will guarantee a supply of GM-badged products of suitable specification for its distribution network.

Ford has recently agreed to a similar venture in Europe with Iveco (Fiat). Ford could see no end in sight to its losses in heavy trucks but wished to stay in the light truck business. Iveco's sole business is trucks, but the company needs to increase its capacity utilization and volume to be profitable. The solution is a joint venture with majority control by Iveco that absorbs Ford's heavy truck manufacturing while guaranteeing a supply of Ford-badged products to Ford's distribution system.

Given excess capacity in many segments of the world motor industry it is likely that more of these "exit ventures" will form in the period immediately ahead. Indeed, the joint venture formed early in 1987 from Ford and Volkswagen operations in Brazil and Argentina (to be called Autolatina) seems to have a similar objective.

Marriage of Technologies

The motor industry now stands at the juncture of the mechanical and the electronic ages and perhaps at a transition between ferrous and nonferrous structural materials as well. Practically every system in the motor vehicle formerly managed mechanically or electromechanically is likely to be converted to electronic control in the years immediately ahead—electronic antiskid brakes, electronic steering, electronic transmission controls, fully automatic climate controls, and so on. Similarly many vehicle components formerly made of iron or steel are likely to be made of aluminum, reinforced plastics, or ceramics—aluminum fenders, composite floor pans, plastic gas tanks, ceramic pistons, and other parts.

This presents a special problem for components suppliers because those firms traditionally supplying the industry with ferrous, mechanical components do not understand the new technologies. At the same time, firms in other sectors advancing these technologies have no experience in production at the volumes the motor industry requires. Additionally, many of the new vehicle components require the marriage of several new technologies, typically a new type of material with electronic controls.

Active suspension provides an interesting example. This new technology may replace mechanical springs and shock absorbers with a hydraulic system controlled by a microcomputer. The advantages are manifold: a dramatic reduction in total part counts, substantial weight savings, and a capacity to instantly tune the vehicle to any desired driving style, road conditions, and passenger or cargo load. However, the supplier of these systems must be master both of electronics and hydraulics and have the capacity to engineer and produce complete systems at high volumes.

Joint ventures appear to be a promising means to do this. Lotus, a British subsidiary of GM, and Moog, an American supplier of precision hydraulic components for the auto and aircraft industries, have recently agreed to collaborate in supplying active suspension systems to final assemblers. Lotus is the world leader in development of the electronic controls in active suspension systems but has no particular expertise in hydraulics or high-volume manufacturing. Moog is a specialist in manufacturing precision hydraulics at substantial volumes. Jointly they can marry the necessary technologies and manufacturing expertise. Each firm apparently feels that more is to be gained from collaboration in this new activity, whose future dimensions are unclear, than from licensing or contract engineering its expertise to the other. A number of ventures of this type are now forming and it seems likely that this will be a very active area of joint venture formation in the period immediately ahead.

THE CRITICAL FUNCTION OF TRANSNATIONAL VENTURES

If scale, carving a niche, exit, and technology absorption were the only motivations for multinational joint ventures, interest in this phenomenon would probably be modest. The ventures cited, while numerous, are small-scale and in many cases could as easily be intra- as international. What has caught the attention of industry executives, government policymakers, and the general public is the smaller number of very large-scale ventures involving some of the largest enterprises in the world economy—GM and Toyota, Ford and Mazda, Chrysler and Mitsubishi, BL and Honda. These joint ventures in the areas of product design and manufacture are in direct response to the emergence of Japanese competitive advantage in motor vehicles.

For a brief period after 1979, this advantage could be expressed through rapid growth in exports and market shares in the United States and Western Europe. However, as domestic producers began to falter, governments in practically every automobile-producing country instituted some type of trade restraint. In addition, even the most optimistic Japanese auto executives recognized that the sheer magnitude of the world motor vehicle market created problems for ever growing Japanese exports. For example, American consumption of cars, trucks and replacement parts, at wholesale, was about $240 billion in 1986. Capturing this entire market through finished unit exports seemed impractical, even if the Japanese share increased only gradually. The American motor vehicle trade deficit (which grew to $55.5 billion by 1986; see Table 9-1) was severely straining

Table 9-1. Net U.S. Trade Balance, Motor Vehicles and Parts, 1973-1986 ($ Billions).

	Parts	Cars, Trucks, and Parts
1973	− .3	− 4.8
1974	.4	− 4.3
1975	1.6	− 1.7
1976	.1	− 5.0
1977	− .5	− 7.3
1978	− 1.5	−11.5
1979	− 1.3	−10.5
1980	− .6	−12.5
1981	2.8	−12.1
1982	1.5	−17.8
1983	− 1.6	−24.2
1984	− 3.1	−32.8
1985	− 6.2	−42.7
1986	−10.2	−55.5

Source: 1973-1984: U.S. International Trade Commission. 1985. "The U.S. Automotive Industry: U.S. Factory Sales, Retail Sales, Imports, Exports, Apparent Consumption, Suggested Retail Prices, and Trade Balances with Selected Countries for Motor Vehicles, 1964-1984," (Mimeo). Washington, D.C.: I.T.C., pp. 92, 98. 1985 and 1986: Calculated by the USITC.

the trading system and it seemed certain that a radical realignment of currencies, comprehensive trade protection, or both, would eventually halt export growth.[8]

Reluctantly, but long before the dramatic strengthening of the yen in 1986–1987, Japanese producers began to think about offshore production. This in turn suggested three new roles for joint ventures.

The two logical alternatives facing the Japanese assemblers were to invest directly in North American and European production facilities or to develop production platforms for export from developing countries not covered by American and European quotas on Japanese products. In both cases multinational joint ventures offered means of overcoming key problems. In North America and Europe they minimized risk and investment outlays as Japanese producers experimented with adapting their techniques to a radically different environment. In developing countries, such as Korea, Taiwan, and Malaysia, a joint venture was often the price of access. Governments in practically every country with the necessary infrastructure had carefully studied the Japanese development model and were demanding local equity participation rather than 100 percent direct investment.

For beleaguered American and European assemblers and components suppliers the transnational joint venture had something to offer as well. The two short-term means out of their competitive dilemma were revitalization of domestic production operations or a rapid move to low-wage production locations in developing countries.[9] Joint ventures were useful and perhaps essential in either strategy: In the United States and Europe, they encouraged the Japanese to conduct what amounted to clinics in organizational best practice for the benefit of their Western venture partners. In developing countries they were essential for gaining access from governments demanding the same investment terms from the Americans and Europeans as from the Japanese.

Thus, a great boom in joint ventures commenced. These may be divided broadly between those designed to transfer Japanese manufacturing practices to the United States or Europe and ventures in a few developing countries—notably Korea, Taiwan, and Mexico—designed to produce low-cost products for export to the United States to compete with Japanese products.

Transnational Ventures in the United States and Europe

As of early 1987 the vogue in joint venturing had yielded Japanese-American and Japanese-European linkages among final assembler firms as shown in Table 9-2. Final assembly accounts for only about 20 percent of the manufacturing activity in the motor vehicle sector and there is now a second wave of joint venturing in progress involving components makers, including the components divisions of some of the major assemblers.

The urgency in this second wave of ventures is due in part to the remarkable success of the initial Japanese-owned or managed auto assembly plants in the United States (Honda at Marysville, Ohio, 1982; Nissan at Smyrna, Tennessee, 1983; and NUMMI at Fremont, California, 1984). Production cost at these plants is dramatically lower and the quality is dramatically higher than in the existing American-managed assembly plants. Although additional imports of finished units are indefinitely blocked by trade barriers (and perhaps by the strengthening yen as well),[10] there is no clear limit to how much of the market the Japanese producers can capture from their American assembly plants. Four additional Japanese-managed plants are under construction in the United States, three more are under construction in Canada, and Ford and Nissan are negotiating on yet another joint venture plant. Thus, Japanese-managed North American assembly capacity seems certain to total more than 2.0 million units by 1989.[11] This could give the Japanese an additional 15-20 percent of the car market beyond the 22 percent they hold in 1986, with no change in the "voluntary" import quota on finished units.

This prospect does pose a long-term trade problem for the Japanese, however. As their U.S. assembly plants started to consume large amounts of imported parts after 1982 and the American assemblers, partly in response, began to substitute offshore for domestic parts, the motor vehicle trade balance started to move negative even more rapidly than it had before imposition of trade restraints in 1981.

Given the implausibility of an ever growing deficit in the motor vehicle account (which leads to new trade barriers, a stronger yen or both), the Japanese realize they must now produce a much larger fraction of the vehicle in the United States. The American assemblers face this challenge as well since additional U.S. trade barriers or a precipitate drop in the dollar may close off their access to cheap foreign parts.

The question for the Japanese assemblers, therefore, is whether they can develop an efficient components supply system in North America to manufacture a large fraction of the motor vehicle near the point of final assembly. The U.S. manufacturers are addressing the same issue from the opposite direction, asking how they can rehabilitate their existing North American component manufacturing base so that it can compete with Japanese components suppliers now investing in the United States and Canada. The recent surge in U.S.-

Table 9-2. Ventures between Japanese and Western Motor Vehicle Assemblers.[a]

Joint Ventures

Name of Venture	Partners	Date Initiated	Location	Activity
Alfa Romeo Nissan Automobiles (ARNA)	Nissan/Alfa Romeo	1980	Naples, Italy	Assembly of cars and light trucks, some joint design of the body
New United Motor Manufacturing (NUMMI)	General Motors/Toyota	1984	Fremont, Calif.	Assembly of a preexisting Toyota design
Diamond-Star Motors	Chrysler/Mitsubishi Motors	1985	Bloomington, Ill.	Assembly of a small car, some joint design of the body
	General Motors/Suzuki	1986	Ingersoll, Ont.	Assembly of preexisting Suzuki design

Collaborations[b]

Partners	Activity	Date Initiated
Honda/BL	Joint design and shared production of XX and YY models	1978
Daimler-Benz/Mitsubishi Motors	Joint design and production of a light commercial vehicle in Spain	1984
Ford/Mazda	Production in a Mexican Ford facility of a Mazda-designed product using Mazda's process technology and process engineering/management assistance. A very large fraction of the output of this plant will be exported to the United States. (Ford has also agreed to buy half the output of Mazda's new assembly plant at Flat Rock, Mich. However, no design collaboration is involved in this project nor is Ford involved in managing the plant. Thus it is less a collaboration than the other examples cited.)	1984

a. This listing does not include several license arrangements between Japanese and Western companies. Nissan is currently building Volkswagen Santanas in Japan under license and practically all of Isuzu's passenger car range is based on General Motors designs from the United States or Europe on license. These are instances of Japanese firms filling out their product lines by buying designs, rather than true collaborations of the sort under study here.

b. "Collaboration" as used here means the joint design or manufacture of products without the creation of a shared-equity, legal entity. For example, Honda and BL have jointly designed a large car (sold in the United States as the Acura Legend and the Rover Sterling). In addition to the design collaboration, BL will produce Honda badged cars in the United Kingdom for sale in Europe while Honda produces Rover-badged cars in Japan for sale in Japan and Australia. The degree of cooperation involved goes beyond that in the typical joint venture yet no merger or long-term amalgamation of the two companies is planned. Throughout this chapter the term *joint venture* applies to such collaborations as well as to more traditional, "legal" joint ventures.

Japanese joint ventures in components indicates a widely shared perception that such linkages may be an important means to this end. This is particularly so because of the unique nature of the Japanese components supply system.

THE STRUCTURE OF JAPANESE COMPONENT SUPPLY SYSTEMS

As is widely known by now, the Japanese motor vehicle producers, led by Toyota, pioneered a remarkable system of "group" organization in the period after World War II.[12] As Toyota and the other companies began to grow, they spun off most of their components supply operations and even a considerable fraction of their assembly operations into legally separate companies. In addition, through loans of personnel and equipment and sharing of design and engineering functions, strong links were formed with many independent suppliers in which the assembler held only a tiny equity share.[13] By the early 1980s Toyota was about 20 percent vertically integrated using standard Western measures (based on majority equity) but in fact about 70 percent vertically integrated in group terms. Most important parts in the vehicle were produced by organizations to which Toyota had close and lasting ties through equity cross holdings, personnel interchanges, loans of equipment and investment funds, and informal but very real commitments to a shared destiny.[14]

There are also a number of major suppliers in Japan who sell in large volumes to two or more assemblers and who are not part of any assembler's group. In these cases as well, the relation between the supplier and the assembler seems to be much closer to Japanese group practice than to historic American practice. A simple contrast between typical Japanese and American supplier-assembler relations brings several differences into focus. Historically, American assemblers have prepared the specifications and drawings for most of the component parts in a new vehicle and put these out to bid. This is at a point perhaps a year before the beginning of production after all major design decisions have been made. Both to sustain price competition and to protect against supply interruptions, orders usually have been placed with a number of vendors and for short periods.

The Japanese by contrast have generally involved their suppliers from the beginning of the design process and have expected these suppliers to design, engineer, and test components, as well as produce them. In addition, almost the entire burden of inventory management and quality control has been placed on the supplier. A supplier is typically assigned a component for the life of the model and is expected to continually reduce the cost of the component during that period, allowing only for increases in materials costs. There is still competition, to be sure, and in fact it can be much fiercer than in the United States because a common Japanese practice is to source a component with two companies, both highly dependent on the one assembler for a large fraction of their business. By continually shifting orders to the higher quality and lower cost supplier, the assembler can alter the profitability of the two businesses dramatically. Not surprisingly, the suppliers are very attentive to the desires of the assembler.

This system seems to provide the advantages of traditional vertical integration as pioneered by General Motors in the period after World War I with the advantages of truly independent cost and profit centers found in arms-length component purchasing arrangements in the West. That is, it contains elements of both hierarchies and markets, to use the traditional Western dichotomy, but seems to work better than either alone.

For present purposes another aspect of the Japanese group system is equally important. It presents formidable barriers to outside firms wishing to do business with a Japanese assembler. The experience of an American components supplier seeking to sell to Nissan after it announced an assembly plant in the United Kingdom is illustrative:

> I went to Japan, visited Nissan headquarters and asked to see their parts specification so I could prepare a bid. Their response was straightforward but hardly what I had expected: "We don't have a specification. In fact, we know very little about that part. What we do have is two suppliers in Nissan 'group' who have met all our needs for that type of component for many years. If you want to sell to Nissan you will have to make some sort of arrangement with those suppliers."[15]

Rather than an evasion, the American discovered that this was the simple truth. Direct sales into the Nissan system would be very difficult without first reaching an accommodation with Nissan's long-term group suppliers in whom the assembler had great trust (not to mention equity cross links, loaned personnel, and shared equipment). After much negotiation it turned out that a workable means of doing business was a joint venture between the American firm and one of the Japanese suppliers. The former provided the capital investment for a new plant next to the Nissan assembly plant now under construction at Washington in the United Kingdom, as well as vital knowledge of British business practices which the Nissan supplier felt it lacked.[16] The Nissan group member in turn contributed the product technology, process machinery, and the essential ability to work smoothly with the assembler.

Oddly, vertical integration in the American production chains, although significantly reduced from the level of a decade ago, presents a similar commercial challenge for the Japanese.[17] Doubtless many a Japanese components supplier has asked, "How do we sell to General Motors? We know we can provide lower costs and higher quality, even from an American manufacturing location, compared with the existing in-house GM parts supplier (for example, Delco Moraine, Harrison, Inland, Saginaw, AC, Fisher Guide). However, there is tremendous corporate resistance to abandoning the very large investments in in-house parts."

An additional, although unspoken, problem for the Japanese is the need to introduce competitive manufacturing systems in the United States and Europe without posing too much of a threat to the existing suppliers. The arrival of the Japanese assemblers has been accepted, indeed encouraged, by the Americans and the British (although even this is too much for most of continental Europe) but the process of shouldering out thousands of small, often family-owned suppliers may create new and more difficult tensions.[18] The joint venture, at least in the short run, may be a way to avoid this problem since it leaves a role for the existing U.S. suppliers.

Given the joint venture's ability to deal with a number of problems at the supplier level it is not surprising that many are now in formation. GM has recently signed a joint venture with Akebono Brake Industry to construct a U.S. plant in an arrangement that may prove prototypical. Akebono is an "independent" supplier in Japan, delivering brake components to all of the major assemblers while maintaining a close working relationship with each. Thus it can provide the vital "introduction" and guarantee of quality that GM's Delco Moraine Division needs to sell brake components to the new Japanese assembly plants under construction in the United States. Similarly, Delco Moraine can provide Akebono entree to General Motors, access that Moraine would otherwise oppose since it would come at the Division's direct expense. (Moraine now supplies practically all brake components to GM's assembly divisions.)[19]

Beyond this first venture GM is known to be considering ventures with Japanese suppliers having strong "group" relations with Japanese assemblers. A range of ventures with Hitachi (a close ally of Nissan) in vehicle electronics and with members of Toyota group are possibilities. Toyota, for its part, has made it widely known that only the three largest of its group members—Nippondenso, Aisin Seiki, and Toyoda Gosei—will invest in the United States through wholly owned ventures. The other group members, about 200 companies in all, will be encouraged to form joint ventures with American suppliers or to provide licenses and liaison assistance (*Japan Economic Journal*, 1985).

For Chrysler and Ford, with less vertical integration, the need for components joint ventures in the United States is less pressing. However, the American-based independent components companies supplying Ford and Chrysler face the immediate challenge of rapidly improving quality while lowering costs. Otherwise they face elimination either by Japanese competitors investing in the United States or by imported parts. Not surprisingly, a host of joint ventures involving American and Japanese components companies are now being announced. (See Appendix 9A.) While it is too early to tell how large this phenomenon will become, it has the potential to radically alter the supply system in North America. Indeed, the logic of the situation, as shown by the GM-Akebono arrangement, is that the same joint ventures may serve two purposes at once, feeding both Japanese and American assembly plants in the United States.

Finally, it is important to note that American-Japanese and European-Japanese joint ventures motivated by a similar logic are being formed for components production in Japan as well. There is no longer a problem with direct investment barriers, as was the case with the Aisin-Warner joint venture cited at the beginning of this chapter. Wholly owned direct investment is now possible and a few Western companies are pursuing this approach. However, the problem remains of selling to Japanese assemblers who demand tight coordination with suppliers and high standards of quality. To achieve this, foreign companies need an introduction to Japanese assemblers and this is where the joint venture comes into play.

One example is GM's recently announced venture with Nihon Radiator, a key member of Nissan group. The venture will manufacture a new type of energy-efficient air conditioner compressor using a variable-capacity feature developed by GM's Harrison Radiator Division (*Metal Working News*, 1986). GM could have gone solo on Japanese production of this item since it has a technological lead, but the company concluded that an alliance with Nihon would assure sales to Nissan and probably to some of the smaller assemblers as well. In the absence of such an arrangement GM might still have garnered some initial orders at Nihon's expense, but Nihon would have worked very hard to duplicate GM's technology and regain its traditional role as Nissan group's air conditioning specialist. A joint venture, even given the well-known tendency for these to dissolve if the partner's interests diverge, seemed the most promising means for

GM to sell to Nissan over the long term, particularly if Harrison keeps advancing its technology so that it continues to be an attractive partner for Nihon.

TRANSNATIONAL JOINT VENTURES IN THE DEVELOPING COUNTRIES

If moving production from Japan to the United States is one solution to the current competitive imbalance in the motor vehicle sector, a logical alternative is to move production from Japan and the United States to developing countries with low wage rates. A number of such efforts have been announced recently in Korea, Taiwan, Mexico, and Brazil. In each case the logic leading to joint ventures rather than other arrangements seems to be the same.

Specifically, governments in these countries are determined to keep their motor industry in domestic hands to the greatest extent possible. While assembler operations in the past were sometimes permitted as wholly owned foreign activities (in Mexico and Brazil) or at least with controlling foreign equity (Taiwan), all four countries discourage majority foreign ownership in the components sector. Therefore, companies wishing to produce parts there find that a local partner either essential or highly advantageous.[20]

The multinationals, when forced to choose, find some sort of long-term venture with a local partner more attractive than arms-length purchases from locally owned parts makers or assemblers in which they have no continuing interest. This is consistent with the new logic of assembler-supplier relations, based on Japanese practice, which the multinational producers are trying to introduce wherever they operate. In addition, the American multinationals seem to have abandoned their historic reservations about 50-50 ventures or even minority equity stakes provided a sound basis for an enduring relationship can be established with the foreign partner.[21]

The third party involved in these negotiations—local companies in developing countries—lack the technology and management to produce motor vehicles and components at large scale for export markets in the developed countries. They need a transnational partner as well.

As was the case in Japan in the 1960s, the joint venture is the one technique that meets the minimum needs of developing country governments, domestic companies, and the multinationals. In consequence, there has been a rapid proliferation of joint ventures in developing countries and a large fraction of the export oriented expansion in motor vehicle and component production now underway in these countries is in the form of joint ventures.

THE CONSEQUENCES OF JOINT VENTURES FOR TECHNOLOGY TRANSFER AND AMERICAN COMPETITIVENESS

Given their number and continuing growth it is important to ask what these ventures mean for technology transfer and the competitiveness of American manufacturing. Because Japanese-American ventures in the United States and ventures by American companies in the developing countries have different objectives, they may have different consequences and need to be examined separately.

Japanese-American Joint Ventures in the United States

Practically all of these ventures, at both the final assembly and component supply levels, involve the same activities. A core of Japanese managers from the Japanese partner are brought to the United States by the joint venture to direct the operation. This consists of assembling a vehicle or fabricating a component that has been designed in Japan, although generally with some input on styling from the American partner.

The first question to ask, therefore, is whether these ventures can succeed in their own terms. Can they recreate Japanese manufacturing superiority in North America? Because the "technology" to be teansferred in these ventures consists entirely of new organizational techniques, ventures that fail to produce superior products at lower cost through transplant of these methods can hardly be expected to transfer the relevant technology or to alter the competitive position of their American partners.

The NUMMI Case[22]

At the assembly plant level in North America there is only one case far enough along to evaluate: the NUMMI venture linking GM and Toyota.[23] However, the results to date are so remarkably positive that one can no longer argue that such ventures cannot succeed.

NUMMI uses a California facility operated by General Motors from its completion in 1963 until 1982, when it was closed due to lack of West Coast demand for General Motors products. When the plant was taken over by the joint venture in 1984 only minor modifi-

Table 9-3. Labor Productivity: NUMMI, Toyota-Japan, and GM-United States (Hours per Car).[a]

	GM Low-Tech Plant 1986	GM High-Tech Plant 1987	NUMMI 1986	Toyota Takaoka 1986
Hours per car	33.4	27.0	19.0	15.7
Percentage Difference from NUMMI	+76	+42	—	-17

a. To obtain these productivity estimates it has been necessary to standardize among the four plants for the number of manufacturing steps being performed, the size and complexity of the product, and the number of hours actually worked in relation to hours paid. Therefore, only welding, painting, final assembly, check out, and rectification operations are included in these figures. (Some auto assembly plants also perform stamping, produce plastic moldings, build seats, etc.). The Toyota Corolla is used as the standard product. Only hours worked are included. (If hours paid were used instead, the U.S. plants would be less efficient compared with Toyota because of larger amounts of paid but nonproductive relief time.) John Krafcik and James P. Womack. "Comparative Manufacturing Practice: Imbalances and Implications," Appendix A, provides full details of these adjustments. (This document is available from the International Motor Vehicle Program, Massachusetts Institute of Technology.)

cations were made to the buildings. The United Auto Workers union organized the plant and over 80 percent of the work force on the plant floor was taken from the union rolls of former employees when it was under GM management.[24] A stamping operation (in a new building) was added to the activities performed and new process machinery was installed throughout. However, this equipment was quite conventional by international standards and the level of automation in the refurbished plant is below that of the most recently retooled General Motors plants (labeled "High-Tech" in the Table 9-3).

The improvement in efficiency, nevertheless, has been remarkable. Table 9-3 provides a comparison of NUMMI's performance with that of its sister Toyota plant in Japan (producing an identical product) and with typical "low-tech" and "high-tech" General Motors plants today.

Equally important, the quality level of the vehicles produced at NUMMI is a great improvement over GM plants. In the summer of 1986 Chevrolet quality inspectors were frequently awarding perfect marks to the NUMMI cars on GM's corporate quality audit. This is unprecedented in the General Motors manufacturing system.[25] While comprehensive comparisons with Toyota Corollas emerging from the Takaoka plant are not available, a leading American consumer magazine tested both a Corolla and a Nova and was unable to find any differences in "fit and finish" or the number of delivered defects. (The one significant defect found, a clutch that "shuddered" on engagement, occurred in both the Corolla and the Nova, indicating a design rather than a manufacturing problem.) (*Consumer Reports*, February 1986, pp. 119–126, and September 1985, pp. 542–549.)

The reasons for success at NUMMI are hardly secrets. The senior managers with operational responsibilities are entirely from Toyota and every effort has been made to implement the Toyota production system (Monden, 1983). The key elements in this system are those listed at the outset of this chapter in characterizing the Japanese contribution to manufacturing practice: multiskilled workers in teams on the shop floor, a new approach to supplier relations, relentless efforts to eliminate inventories, and a philosophy of continuous improvement.

Work teams of five to seven members are trained to handle a range of duties on the shop floor including decisions about how to accomplish the assembly tasks, assembly itself, and quality inspection. Each worker gains a multitude of skills in this system and can fill in for any other team member. Equally important, the team leader, who is also a union member, has no fixed operational duties but instead fills in for absentee workers. This creates strong peer pressure against unscheduled absenteeism and accounts in considerable degree for NUMMI's 2–3 percent unscheduled absentee rate compared with double digit absenteeism at the old Fremont facility.

Suppliers at NUMMI are also treated as part of a team. NUMMI engineers routinely visit supplier plants to suggest ways to improve operations and the burden of inspections and quality is placed on suppliers through a system that documents every defective part found and requires that suppliers explain how the problem has been rectified.

Finally, NUMMI strives to standardize operations and rigorously document work tasks so that deviations from best practice can be detected by the work teams and continuous, incremental improvements can be achieved. No level of performance short of perfection is acceptable.

The United Auto Workers have fully cooperated with efforts to permit flexible use of workers and the level of grievances has been remarkably low by American standards. As a result of teamwork, cooperation, and high standards, inventories are much lower than in the former plant (about two days compared with two months) and vast numbers of relief workers, quality checkers, shop stewards, rework specialists, and machine repair specialists are missing. With each worker acting as a quality inspector, quality is much higher as well and the amount of scrap is greatly reduced.

Indeed, if the entire American motor vehicle manufacturing system were as efficient and high quality as NUMMI, a large part of the import threat would be over. Compared with older "low-tech" GM plants, NUMMI has eliminated more than 40 percent of the labor hours involved with the manufacturing steps it performs (33.4 hours versus 19). Perhaps more surprising, NUMMI uses 30 percent less labor and vastly cheaper process machinery than GM's latest and most automated manufacturing plants. If similar productivity improvements could be achieved in components fabrication as well, the total amount of human effort needed to produce a car in the United States would fall very nearly to the Japanese average (remembering that Toyota is the most efficient of the Japanese producers) at a time when Japanese wages are nearly equal to American wages.

But what difference can NUMMI make beyond this one plant? First, note that none of the "technology" available for transfer through this joint venture is technology in the hardware sense. Rather it is a set of techniques for harmonizing the efforts of workers and very conventional machines. Thus transfer depends critically on the ability of General Motors to instill these techniques in its own personnel so that they may be diffused to the company's other assembly and component manufacturing facilities.

LEARNING FROM NUMMI

General Motors is using three techniques to learn from NUMMI. First, fifteen managers are loaned to NUMMI to work under more senior Japanese managers for a period of three years. Second, GM has established a liaison office near NUMMI which systematically documents NUMMI's techniques and makes this knowledge available to all interested personnel in General Motors. This is done by producing videotapes and written documentation on NUMMI production methods and by developing a NUMMI database accessible by computer at all GM assembly plants. In addition, the liaison office has arranged brief tours of NUMMI for more than 2,000 GM manufacturing managers and officials of UAW locals. Third, GM has established a program for management trainees attending graduate management and engineering schools at GM expense who undertake research projects during summer internships at NUMMI. These students will assume manufacturing positions in GM when they complete their degrees.

The first rotations back from NUMMI have already occurred. For example, NUMMI's first head of purchasing was given a similar position at GM's new Saturn subsidiary. Another manager has been sent to Europe to implement NUMMI-style changes there. Four other managers have been given the task of "NUMMIzing" GM's Van Nuys, California assembly plant, which has recently negotiated a NUMMI-style, flexible labor contract with the UAW.

The experience of these managers has been highly positive but GM faces a major problem in the simple fact that NUMMI's ability to produce "NUMMized" managers is minuscule in comparison with the current needs of GM. Because rotation of GM employees through NUMMI must stop in 1992 (under the terms of settlement of Chrysler's civil antitrust suit attempting to block the venture), only 45–50 GM managers will obtain direct NUMMI experience under the three-year rotation system. This is only about 1.5 NUMMI experienced managers per North American assembly plant.

General Motors strategists are convinced that a critical mass of NUMMIzed managers must be placed in older plants to turn them around and the company is currently negotiating with the joint venture on shortening each manager's stay at NUMMI and increasing the number of managers involved. Even so, only a trickle of managers can be produced by a single joint venture. To go much faster or involve many more managers will either give the managers an incomplete education or degrade the performance of NUMMI itself or both.

Unfortunately, plant tours, video tapes, and manuals seem to be a poor substitute for hands-on experience. Recent interviews by the author with several manufacturing managers in the GM system who have been exposed to NUMMI instructional materials and taken on NUMMI tours reveal a very partial understanding of NUMMI's procedures, and in many cases a defensive conviction that NUMMI techniques can never work in their plant. In the words of one manager, "all that NUMMI talk is pretty unpopular around here."

Toyota by contrast has a much easier task in learning from NUMMI. Its managers are fully trained in the Toyota production system. What they need is experience in teaching it to Americans, and NUMMI is able to provide this on a scale proportional to Toyota's future needs.

Toyota sent 30–35 senior managers to NUMMI at the start of the venture on three to five year rotation. Thus far only one of these managers, a personnel specialist, has been transferred to Toyota's new American manufacturing staff and it appears that most of the others will return to Japan. While these managers are available for reassignment to North America at some future point it appears that the main conduit for transferring experience gained at NUMMI to

Toyota's new plants in Kentucky and Ontario lies with personnel at the shop floor level.

NUMMI has been continuously staffed with 30-60 lower level managers and production engineers on loan from Toyota for 3-6 month periods. In the early days, these Toyota employees trained the work team leaders and production engineers hired by NUMMI as well as the GM managers on loan. More recently these workers have been compiling detailed quality charts and learning curves for various NUMMI operations, information that will be of great use in starting up new North American plants.

More than 300 of these "trainers" have now received a minimum of three months experience at NUMMI and hundreds more will cycle through NUMMI before the Kentucky and Ontario facilities open. Many of these Toyota employees have already received their orders to move to North America with their families for multiyear tours at the new plants and it seems very likely that Toyota will open those plants with a highly experienced training staff on hand.

Thus one may well ask whether General Motors or Toyota will learn more of practical value from NUMMI, and the same may be asked of the Chrysler-Mitsubishi venture. This, it should be clear, is not for lack of systematic efforts to learn by GM and Chrysler but rather because the lessons Toyota and Mitsubishi need to learn are easier and they need only produce enough "Americanized" managers to run one or two new plants at a time while GM and Chrysler need immediately to retrain managers throughout vast production systems.

MULTINATIONAL VENTURES IN THE DEVELOPING COUNTRIES

The example just discussed is a case of technology transfer from Japan to the United States, the key question being who in the United States—the American firm or the Japanese—will make the best use of the opportunity. An equally important issue is the likely consequence of the many joint ventures under development by American firms in a select group of developing countries now poised to make a substantial push into the world motor vehicle industry. In particular, what are the technology transfer implications of these ventures and what will they mean for American competitiveness?

A Korean venture involving General Motors is perhaps the most interesting example. GM has recently entered into an arrangement with the Daewoo Corporation to produce a small car in Korea. Most of the output is earmarked for export to the United States where it will be sold through GM's Pontiac Division as an entry level car to replace the American-made T1000 model. An unusual feature of this enterprise is its scope. Through a series of separate joint ventures between Daewoo's group companies and the different assembly and components divisions of GM, General Motors is undertaking to transfer designs and process technology to build practically the entire car—bodies, engines, transmissions, electrical systems, brakes, steering, and ancillary parts—at world-scale production volumes. In a very real sense, GM is teaching the personnel of the joint venture everything it knows about auto manufacturing.

The joint ventures do not involve the transfer of design or engineering knowhow. The product in question is sold in Europe as the Opel Kadett and was designed and engineered several years ago by GM's Opel subsidiary in Germany. However, the obvious question is what would happen if Daewoo could master design and engineering skills as well. It might then be able to develop its own products for sale in the United States and elsewhere without the hindrance of GM licensing restrictions. What further use would it have for GM? What reason is there to think it would not began direct exports to North America, in competition rather than in collaboration with its erstwhile mentor?

Interviews with managers on both sides of these joint ventures and at General Motors in the United States reveal a consensus agreement that there is none. GM managers acknowledge that Daewoo may try to "eat our lunch" but argue that it will take Daewoo decades to master the necessary engineering, design, and marketing skills to break away. In the meantime, assuming the venture succeeds, it will supply GM with profitable low-cost products with which to compete with the Japanese in Asia and the United States.

Even assuming that Daewoo quickly finds an alternative source of engineering and design skills, and develops its own marketing channels—the approach successfully employed by its Korean rival, Hyundai—the GM view is that a host of American and European rivals would have quickly provided Daewoo with the same manufacturing know-how.[26] Thus GM also views the Daewoo venture as a maneuver to block immediate North American competition from Daewoo in collaboration with some competing Western producer.

There are also some less flattering reasons to question whether this venture and others undertaken recently by the Big Three in developing countries (see Appendix 9A), will create a long-term threat to American based manufacturing. What is notably missing in the Daewoo venture is a transfer of state-of-the-art production management. Indeed, the present venture entails a 50-50 split in equity but with practically all operating managers provided by the Daewoo parent. This arrangement is the result of a crisis in 1981 when it became apparent that a former joint venture, with the same equity split but run by GM expatriate managers, had been a failure. It had not been able to compete with Hyundai in Korea, much less to export. This failure traces to the simple fact that the key "technology" in today's auto industry—Toyota-style production organization—is not in GM's possession to transfer. This creates a very real question, incidentally, of whether the American-Korean joint ventures can actually produce a product of sufficient quality and cost low enough to be competitive either with Japanese exports to the United States or with vehicles produced in the United States by Japanese companies.

On the other side of the ledger, the Japanese producers definitely feel a risk in transferring their production organization know-how to venture partners in Korea or elsewhere in the developing world. Their domestic market is, after all, the only developed-country market not experiencing significant foreign penetration to date and a combination of low wages and Japanese-style production management in the possession of an independent, developing-country producer could be a very powerful threat both in the Japanese home market and elsewhere in the world. To delay this possibility as long as possible, the Japanese producers have tried to enter into very narrow agreements for licensing of designs and the sale of process machinery to developing-country auto firms. In particular, they have sought to avoid joint ventures on the U.S. model of Toyota and Mitsubishi where Japanese managers are in actual control of the operation and necessarily teaching their methods to Koreans, Taiwanese, Mexicans, or Brazilians. For a country in Japan's position this makes eminent sense.

PUBLIC POLICY TOWARD JOINT VENTURES IN THE MOTOR VEHICLE SECTOR

We must conclude this chapter by asking what public policy stance toward joint ventures is appropriate, both for ventures between Japanese and American firms in the United States and for those involving American firms in "new entrant" countries. Do these ventures create a stronger American motor vehicle industry? Is this issue even important? Do they create the risk of reconstructing a tight oligopoly in this industry, now at a world rather than a national scale?

Several points of clarification are essential at the outset. First, almost all of the ventures currently in operation or under consideration involve only joint manufacturing activities although a few involve joint design activities as well. Very few involve basic research, applied research, or the introduction of fundamentally new types of products with new technologies. Thus they are at the manufacturing end of the research-development-manufacturing continuum and rarely involve the transfer of "technology" in the sense of hard engineering or scientific knowledge. Rather they involve the transfer of management methods from one location to another.

Second, the magnitude of motor vehicle consumption in the United States, about $240 billion per year for cars, trucks, and replacement parts, suggests that there will always be a motor vehicle industry of substantial size in the United States. If trade protection doesn't guarantee this, a weak dollar will. The question, therefore, is what activities this industry will undertake and how efficiently.

Third, competition in the American motor vehicle market, even with trade restraints on the Japanese, is greater than at anytime since the 1920s. Twenty-three independent companies are offering volume cars in the American market and this number could easily grow to twenty-five or more companies by the early 1990s.[27] In addition, the importers are steadily expanding the range of products offered as the Japanese move up into larger cars and the Europeans move into midsize and sporty cars. This means that the former oligopoly of the Big Three will be very difficult to reconstruct, particularly through the mechanism of joint ventures.

This is doubly true because of the Japanese conglomerate group structure noted earlier. These vast industrial alliances offer a number of advantages over the more fragmented American model of industrial organization, but in particular they offer remarkable cyclical endurance and comeback potential for the weaker players in a maturing industry. Instead of two or three strong participants, the Japanese auto industry, which is now fully mature domestically, has seven significant players—Toyota, Nissan, Honda, Mazda, Mitsubishi, Suzuki, and Isuzu. The last four by all logic of American competition should have been out of the game by now but instead they have been kept in, even in cases of catastrophic miscalculation (notably at Mazda in 1974; see, for example, Rohlen and Pascale (1983). The reason is almost too simple: enormous financial resources available from other conglomerate group members and an ability to draw on the managerial and technical resources of the group to revitalize a company during a crisis.

The point is that these same enterprises now promise to become leading players in American-based manufacturing. Even if one can imagine some sustainable method of collusion between GM and Toyota or Chrysler and Mitsubishi, one must make the additional leap to mergers or noncompetitive understandings between Toyota, Nissan, Honda, Mazda, Mitsubishi, Suzuki, Isuzu, and Suburu. More likely than too little competition in the years to the end of this century is so much competition between American and Japanese firms that it produces a political reaction. This may manifest itself shortly in an overcapacity crisis in North American as the Japanese direct investments and joint ventures come on line.

With these points in mind, what policy prescriptions seem appropriate with regard to Japanese-American joint ventures in the United States? Remarkably, government should worry not that there are too many but that there are too few. The American owned motor vehicle industry at the assembly plant level consists of fifty-one facilities. None of these facilities is at present competitive with NUMMI on cost and quality. Yet we have seen the limited capacity of a single joint venture to produce managers with state-of-the-art techniques and attitudes to turn around these existing plants. General Motors, at least, is gaining a second source of management reeducation from its Suzuki venture in Ontario. Unfortunately, the rest of the decisions have been made on the first wave of Japanese plants in the United States. These, with the exception of Chrysler-Mitsubishi, are 100 percent direct investments by Japanese firms reluctant to joint venture with the Big Three.[28] When they come on stream in the late 1980s they will create an overcapacity and policy crisis that might have been avoided if most had instead been undertaken as joint ventures with GM, Ford, and Chrysler.

That opportunity is past, but many immediate opportunities are available at the components supply level. Government policies must not discourage potential cross-national ventures.[29] If a joint venture proposes to bring existing component factories up to world class standards, a case might even be made for tax incentives and other inducements. Otherwise, the capacity crisis now approaching in assembly will likely be replicated in components. The danger is that the situation will get out of hand politically and that very rigid trade management measures or even investment controls will be instituted in an attempt to embalm the status quo. This will produce the worst possible outcome: a large but inefficient and low-quality American motor vehicle manufacturing system.

Finally, what government attitude is appropriate toward the joint ventures of American producers in Korea, Taiwan, and other newly industrializing countries? The fundamental reality here is that venture partners in those countries have a range of alternatives to American companies. If Daewoo had not formed a venture with General Motors it almost surely would have done so with a Japanese or European firm. In addition, these ventures are not transferring engineering and scientific know-how but rather organizational techniques, an area of expertise where American firms lag far behind the

Japanese. Thus these ventures are not likely to create independent rivals to American firms. Even if they did, the realities of the trading situation are such that these new entrants' market access is likely to be quite limited by trade barriers[30] or continuing declines in the value of the dollar. A more appropriate question, but one better answered by company managers than governments, is whether joint ventures in less developed countries are a misguided diversion of corporate energy from the pressing need to reform the American production base.

APPENDIX 9A: A LISTING OF MULTICOMPANY COLLABORATIONS IN THE MOTOR VEHICLE INDUSTRY, JUNE 1987

The following is a list of 127 collaborations in the automobile and commercial vehicle industry worldwide. Note, however, the following definitions and caveats.

A *collaboration* is a cooperative effort between two independent production organizations, often rivals in other areas, to design and manufacture a component or finished vehicle. This definition does not include ventures common in developing countries where the local partner is a silent equity holder involved in the project to meet government requirements for local equity participation but making no contribution of management or other expertise. Nor does the term *collaboration* as used here include licensing agreements, direct purchase arrangements, marketing tie-ups, or ventures involving long-term research where no commercial product is expected to result.

The *motor vehicle industry* includes the design and manufacture of cars, trucks, buses, and their component parts. It does not include the design and manufacture of process machinery, off-road vehicles, military equipment, or motorcycles.

The listing is based on a review of the English language trade press (*Wards Automotive Reports, Automotive News, American Metal Markets, The Wall Street Journal, The Financial Times, The Japan Economic Journal*, and others) since 1981. In addition, a few listings are from company annual reports and from Dodwell's *The Structure of the Japanese Auto Parts Industry*, 1983 Edition. From this it will be apparent that coverage of collaborations entered into prior to 1980 is incomplete.

The listing of the collaborations is by country of production. In a number of cases, such as the BL-Honda collaboration on the Legend/Sterling, activities occur in two or more countries. Collaborations of this sort are listed at the end under "multicountry."

Collaborations, By Country of Operation By Date of Commencement (127)

Partners	Venture Name	Date Est.	Products
Australia (1)			
Nihon Radiator (Japan) [Nissan] 51%/ Kanematsu-Gosho (Japan) 9%/ Air International (Australia) 40%	Nichira International	1984	Assembly of air conditioners
Brazil (4)			
GM, Saginaw (U.S.) 35%/ DHB Industries (Brazil) 65%		1984	Steering gears
Rockwell International (U.S.) 49%/ Randon SA (Brazil) 51%	Freios Master Equipamentos Automotivos	1986	Truck brakes
Yuasa Battery Co. (Japan) 50%/ Lucas Industries (U.K.) 50%	Lucas-Yuasa de Brasil	1986	Auto batteries
ZF (FRG) 48%/ Mangels SA (Brazil) and ZF do Brasil 52%		1986	Truck transmissions
Canada (6)			
Magna International (Canada)/ Niles Buhin (Japan) [Nissan]		1984	Electronics
Woodbridge Group (Canada)/ Inoue MTP (Japan)		1985	Auto seat cushions
Waterville Cellular Products (Canada)/ Inoue MTP (Japan)	Waterville-Inoue	1985	Instrument panels, trim
General Motors (U.S.)/ Suzuki (Japan)		1986	Mfg. of small cars and trucks
Rockwell International (U.S.) 60%/ Mitsubishi Steel (Japan) 30%/ Mitsubishi Corp. 10%	Rockwell International Suspension Systems	1986	Coil springs, stabilizer bars, torsion bars for cars and trucks
VDO AG (FRG)/ Yazaki Corp. (Japan)	VDO-Yazaki	1987	Auto instruments
China (3)			
AMC (France) 31.4%/ Beujing Automotive Works 68.6%	Beijing Jeep	1983	Assembly of jeeps
Volkswagen (Germany) 50%/ Shanghai Tractor and Auto Co. 25%/	Shanghai-Volks.	1984	Assembly of cars

Appendix 9A. continued

Partners	Venture Name	Date Est.	Products
China (3) (*cont.*)			
Bank of China 15%/ China National Auto Industry Corp. 10%			
PSA (France) 22%/ Guangzhou Auto (China) 46%/ Banque National de Paris 4%/ China International Trust and Investment (China) 28%	Guangzhou-Peugeot	1985	Assembly of trucks
Egypt (1)			
GM (U.S.) 30%/ El Nasr Auto (Egypt) 30%/ Misr Iran Development Bank (Egypt)/ Export Development Bank (Egypt)	General Misr	1986	Manufacture of cars
France (3)			
Volvo (Sweden) 33%/ Renault (France) 33%/ PSA (France) 33%	FSM	1971	Engines
Clarion (Japan) [Nissan] 51%/ Jean Besis Group (France) 49%	Clarion France	1982	Stereos
Stanley Electric (Japan) [Honda] 31%/ Renault (France) 45%/ 5 French and 1 Italian minority shares	IDESS	1984	Liquid crystal displays
India (6)			
Maruti Udyog (India) 74%/ Suzuki (Japan)		1982	Auto manufacture
Hindustan Motors (India)/ Isuzu (Japan)		1984	Auto assembly
Toyota (Japan)/ DCM (India)	DCM Toyota	1985	Truck manufacture
Nippondenso (Japan) [Toyota]/ Shri Ram Fibers	SRF Nippondenso	1985	Electrical equipment
Asahi Glass (Japan)/ Maruti Udyog (India)	Asahi India Safety Glass	1985	Auto glass

(*Appendix 9A. continued overleaf*)

Appendix 9A. continued

Partners	Venture Name	Date Est.	Products
India (6) (*cont.*)			
Champion Spark Plug Co. (U.S.) 40%/ Modine Industries (India) 60%/ Indian public 20%		1986	Spark plugs
Italy (4)			
PSA (France) 50%/ Fiat (Italy) 50%	Sevel	1978	Commercial vans
Alfa Romeo (Italy) 50%/ Nissan (Japan) 50%	ARNA	1980 1986	Auto assembly Utility vehicle assembly
Rockwell (U.S.)/ Iveco (Italy) [Fiat]	Rockwell CVC	1981	Truck axles
Eaton (U.S.) 50%/ SKF (Sweden) 50%			Valve lifters
Japan (19)			
Borg Warner (U.S.)/ Aisin Seiki (Japan) [Toyota]/ Toyota (Japan)	Aisin-Warner		Automatic transmissions
Torrington (U.S.)/ Nippon Seiko (Japan)	NSK-Torrington		Needle bearings
Nissan (Japan) 65%/ Mazda (Japan) 35%	Jatco		Automativ transmissions
Uniroyal (U.S.)/ Nitta Bearing (Japan)	Unitta		Timing belts
Borg Warner (U.S.)/ Tsubakimoto Chain (Japan)	Tsubakimoto-Morse		Gears, clutches
Borg Warner (U.S.)/ Nippon Seiko (Japan)	NSK-Warner		Clutches, seat belts, etc.
Tokyo Buhin (Japan)/ Rockwell International (U.S.)		1983	Truck brakes
Mazda (Japan) 34%/ Hiroshima Press (Japan) [Masda] 51%/ Nihon Radiator (Japan) [Nissan] 15%		1985	Exhausts
Kawasaki Heavy (Japan) 50%/ Isuzu (Japan) 50%		1985	Bus manufacture
Goodyear (U.S.)/ Toyo Tire and Rubber (Japan)	Toyo Giant Tire	1985	Tire manufacture

Appendix 9A. continued

Partners	Venture Name	Date Est.	Products
Japan (19) *(cont.)*			
GKN Sankey (U.K.) 60%/ Mitsubishi Steel (Japan) 40%	Translite	1985	FRP springs
GM, Harrison (U.S.) 49%/ Nihon Radiator (Japan) [Nissan] 51%	Galsonic Harrison	1986	Air conditioning compressors
GM, Inland (U.S.) 45%/ NHK Spring (Japan) 55%	NHK Inland	1986	FRP springs
Mitsubishi Electric (Japan)/ Mikuni (Japan)/ Robert Bosch (FRG)	Nippon Injector	1986	Electronic fuel injection
SKF (Sweden)/ Koyo Seiko [Toyota] Japan		1986	Clutch bearings
NHK Spring (Japan) < 50%/ Suzuki (Japan) > 50%		1986	Seat manufacture
Walbro Corp. (U.S.)/ Mitsuba Electric Manufacturing (Japan)	Mitsuba-Walbro Inc.	1987	Electric fuel pumps
Electrolux Autoliv (Sweden)/ Fuji Kiko (Japan)	Fuji-Autoliv KK	1987	Seat belts
Volvo (Sweden)/ Mitsui Corp. (Japan)/ Fuji Heavy Industries (Japan)		1987	Bus manufacture
Korea (13)			
GM (U.S.) 50%/ Daewoo Corporation (Korea) 50%	Daewoo Motor	1984	Auto manufacture
GM, Delco Remy (U.S.)/ Daewoo Precision Industries (Korea) [Daewoo]	Daewoo Automotive	1984	Electronics components
GM, Fisher Guide (U.S.)/ Kosco (Korea) [Daewoo]	Koram Plastic	1985	Plastic bumpers
GM, Delco Moraine, Harrison, and Saginaw (U.S.)/ Daewoo Precision Industries (Korea) [Daewoo]	DHMS Industries	1985	Steering, brakes, radiators, axles, air conditioners, etc.
Chrysler (U.S.) 50%/ Samsung (Korea) 50%		1985	Auto parts

(Appendix 9A. continued overleaf)

Appendix 9A. continued

Partners	Venture Name	Date Est.	Products
Korea (13) (*cont.*)			
Ford (U.S.) 50%/ Mando Machinery (Korea) 50%		1985	Radiators
LOF (U.S.) 30%/ Nippon Sheet Glass (Japan) 30% Hankuk Glass (Korea) 40%	Hankuk Safety Glass	1985	Auto glass
TRW (U.S.)/ Kia (Korea)		1985	Steering gears
Degussa (FRG)/ Oriental Chemical (Korea)	Ordeg	1985	Catalysts
AE Group (U.K.) 50%/ Yoosung Enterprise 50%	Dongsuh Industries	1985	Pistons
Nifco (Japan) 57%/ Mitsubishi (Japan) 3%/ Yun Higiun (Korea) [Sangyong]	Korean Industrial Fastener	1985	Fasteners
Samsung Radiator (Korea) 34%/ Blackstone Corp. (U.S.) 33%/ Nihon Radiator (Japan) 33%		1986	Aluminum radiators, condensors, evaporators
Dong Hwan Ind. (Korea) 55%/ Nihon Radiator (Japan) 45%		1986	Air conditioners, heaters
Malayasia (1)			
Heavy Industry Corporation (Mal.) 70%/ Mitsubishi Motors (Japan) 15%/ Mitsubishi Corporation (Japan) 15%	Proton	1983	Auto manufacture
Mexico (7)			
GM, Delco Prod. (U.S.) 40%/ Mexican interests 60%	Aralmex		Suspension components
GM, DDA (U.S.) 40%/ DINA (Mexico) 60%	Moto Diesel Mexicana		Engines and pistons
Nippon Sheet Glass (Japan) 50%/ LOF (U.S.) 50%	L-N Safety Class		Windshields
GM, Saginaw (U.S.) 40% TBO (Mexico) 60%	Compania Nacional de Direcciones Automotrices		Steering gears

Appendix 9A. continued

Partners	Venture Name	Date Est.	Products
Mexico (7) *(cont.)*			
GM, Packard Electric (U.S.) 40%/ Mexican interests 60%	Promotera de Partes Electricas Automotrices		Wiring harnesses
Ishino Gasket (Japan)/ Dana Corp. (U.S.)		1985	
NHK Spring (Japan)/ Rassini Rhem (Mexico ?)		1985	Springs
Netherlands (1)			
Fiat (Italy) 24%/ Volvo (Sweden) 29.5%/ Dutch government 36.5%	Van Doorne Transmission		CVT belts
Spain (2)			
Kayaba Industry (Japan) 49%/ TI Silencers (U.K.) 51%	TI Suspension	1983	Shock absorbers
Stanadyne (U.S.)/ Fraymon (France) [Valeo]		1985	Valve lifters
Taiwan (5)			
Hino (Japan) [Toyota] 42% Mitsui (Japan) 3%/ Ho-Tai Motors (Taiwan) 55%	Kuozui Motors	1984	Manufacture of trucks and buses
PSA (France)/ Yeu Tyan Machinery (Taiwan)		1985	Engines and parts
Nissan (Japan) 25%/ Yue Loong Motors (Taiwan)		1985	Auto assembly
Fuji Heavy Industries (Japan) 35%/ Taiwan Vespa (Taiwan) 65%	(Pending govt. approval)	1986	Manufacture of light trucks and cars
Yue Loong Motors, China Motor Corporation (Taiwan) 75%/ Mitsubishi Motors (Japan) 25%	(Pending govt. approval)	1986	Assembly of light trucks and vans
Thailand (2)			
Toyota Motor Corporation (Japan) 40%/ Siam Cement Corporation (Thailand) 60%		1987	Engine manufacture
Nissan Motor Corporation and Nissan Diesel (Japan) 30%/ Siam Motor Corporation (Thailand) 70%		1987	Engine manufacture

(Appendix 9A. continued overleaf)

Appendix 9A. continued

Partners	Venture Name	Date Est.	Products
United Kingdom (5)			
Austin Rover (U.K.)/ Perkins (U.K.)		1982?	High-speed direct-injection diesel
Nihon Radiator (Japan) [Nissan]/ TI Silencer (U.K.)	TI-Nihon	1982	Mufflers, exhausts
Hoover Universal (U.S.)/ Ikeda Bussan (Japan) [Nissan]		1985	Seating
Cosworth (U.K.)/ Comalco (Australia)		1986	Aluminum engine blocks and heads
General Motors, Bedford (U.S.) 60%/ Isuzu (Japan) 40%		1987	Van manufacture
United States (24)			
Tokyo Rope (Japan)/ Mitsubishi (Japan)/ C. Itoh (Japan)	ATR Wire and Cable	1981	Electrical equipment
Nifco (Japan)/ Nitto Seiko (Japan)/ Illinois Tool Works (U.S.)	Nippon Metal	1983	Metal fasteners
Hella North America (FRD) 51%/ Koito (Japan) [Toyota] 39%/ Ichikoh (Japan) [Nissan] 10%	North American Lighting	1984	Halogen lighting
Wynn's International (U.S.) 50%/ Diesel Kiki (Japan) 50%	Wynn-Kiki	1984	Air conditioners
IHI (Japan)/ Borg Warner (U.S.)	Warner-Ishi	1984	Turbochargers
Chrysler (U.S.) 50%/ Mitsubishi Motors (Japan) 50%	Diamond-Star	1985	Auto assembly
Sheller-Globe (U.S.) 45%/ Ryobi (Japan) 55%	Sheller-Ryobi	1985	Die castings
General Motors (U.S.) 50%/ Toyota (Japan) 50%	NUMMI	1985	Auto assembly
GM, Delco Moraine (U.S.) 50%/ Akebone (Japan) 50%		1985	Brakes
Federal-Mogul (U.S.)/ NTN Toyo Bearing (Japan)	NTN-Bower [?]	1985	Bearings

Appendix 9A. continued

Partners	Venture Name	Date Est.	Products
United States (24) (*cont.*)			
Daikyo (Japan) [Mazda] / Magna International (Canada)		1986	Plastic parts
Volvo (Sweden) 65%/ GM, GMC (U.S.) 35%	Volvo GM Heavy Truck Corporation	1986	Heavy trucks
Isuzu (Japan) 50%/ Fuji Heavy Industries (Japan)		1986	Light truck assembly
Sanoh Industrial (Japan) 50%/ ITT Higbie Manufacturing (U.S.) 50%	Hisan Corporation	1986	Automotive steel tube components
Moriroku Corporation [Honda] (Japan)/ Capitol Plastics (U.S.)	Greenville Technology Corporation (proposed)	1986	Plastic components
B. F. Goodrich (U.S.) 50%/ Uniroyal (U.S.) 50%	Uniroyal Goodrich Tire	1986	Automobile tires
GM, DDA (U.S.) 50%/ Deere and Company (U.S.) 50%		1986	Truck diesel engines
Inoue MTP (Japan) 49%/ Woodbridge Group (Canada) 51%		1986	Dashboards
Yuasa Battery (Japan)/ General Battery (U.S.)		1986	Automobile batteries
Wickes Manufacturing (U.S.)/ Cycles Peugeot (France)		1986	Automotive seating
NHK Spring (Japan) 55%/ Barnes Group (U.S.) 45%	NHK-Associated Spring Suspension Components	1986	Auto springs
Douglas and Lomason (U.S.)/ Namba Press Works (Japan)	Bloomington Seating	1987	Auto seats
VDO AG (FRG)/ Yasaki Corporation (Japan)	VDO-Yazaki Corporation	1987	Auto instruments
Clevite Industries (U.S.)/ Bridgestone Corporation (Japan)	Clevite-Bridge-stone	1987	Suspension and steering components

(Appendix 9A. continued overleaf)

Appendix 9A. continued

Partners	Venture Name	Date Est.	Products
Federal Republic of Germany (3)			
GHH, MAN Commercial Vehicles (FRG)/ VW (FRG)		1979	Manufacture of medium trucks
Engelhard (U.S.)/ Kali-Chemie (FRG)		1984	Catalytic converters
United Technologies (U.S.) 75% Grundig (FRG) 25%	United Technologies Grundig	1984	Wiring harnesses
Yugoslavia (1)			
GM (U.S.) 49%/ Yugoslavian interests 51%	IDA		Foundry, component machining
Multicountry Collaborations (16)			
Honda (Japan)/ BL (U.K.)		1980	Joint design/ production of XX and YY cars
Fiat (Italy)/ PSA (France)		1980	Joint design of auto engine
Saab (Sweden)/ Alfa (Italy)/ Fiat-Lancia (Italy)		1980	Joint design of an executive car
Renault (France)/ VW (FRG)		1983	Joint design/ production of automatic transmissions
GM, Cadillac (U.S.)/ Pininfarina (Italy)		1984	Joint design/production of a luxury car
Chrysler (U.S.)/ De Tomaso Industries (Italy)		1984	Joint design/production of luxury cars
Renault (France)/ Matra (France)		1984	Joint design/ production of a passenger van
Eaton (U.S.)/ Clark (U.S.)		1985	Truck transmission manufacture
Daimler-Benz (FRG)/ Mitsubishi Motors (Japan)		1985	Joint design/ production of a commercial van
Mitsubishi Motors (Japan)/ Hyundai Motors (Korea)		1985	Joint production of an executive car and a midsize car
MAN (FRG)/ Eaton (U.S.)		1985	Joint design/production of truck axles

Appendix 9A. continued

Partners	Venture Name	Date Est.	Products
Multicountry Collaborations (16) (*cont.*)			
Ford (U.S.)/ Chausson (France)		1986	Joint design/production of sport car
Moog Inc. (U.S.) 60%/ GM, Lotus (U.S.) 40%	Moog Lotus Systems	1986	Active suspension systems
Matra (France) 35%/ Fiat (Italy) 65%		1986	Carburetors and dashboard instruments
Ford (U.S.) 48%/ Fiat, Iveco (Italy) 48%/ Credit Suisse First Boston 4%	Iveco Ford Trucks	1986	Manufacture of medium and heavy trucks
Volkswagen AG (FRG) 41%/ Ford Motor Company (U.S.) 49%	Autolatina	1986	Manufacture of autos in Brazil and Argentina
Terminated Collaborations			
France			
Allied, Bendix (U.S.) 49%/ Renault (France) Bought out by Allied	Renix	1978– 1985	Electronics
Lucas (U.K.)/ Valeo (France) Bought out by Valeo	Ducellier		Electronics
United States			
Hoover Ball Bearing (U.S.)/ Nippon Seiko (Japan) Bought out by Nippon Seiko	Hoover-NSK	1973– 1975	Bearings

NOTES

1. Much of the material in this section is adapted from Chapter 2 of Altshuler et al. (1984).
2. For a brief summary of Ford's contributions see Abernathy (1978), ch. 2.
3. Chandler (1962, ch. 3) provides the classic account of Sloan's accomplishments.

4. This was not only GM's stated policy; it was also its practice. When the Indian government in 1951 demanded that GM's Indian operations be reorganized as a joint venture with 50 percent Indian equity, the company refused and withdrew from India. The agreement to take a minority share in Isuzu in 1971 was GM's first acknowledgment that even the world's largest company would have to bend to the demands of foreign governments blocking 100 percent equity direct investments.

5. In model year 1985, practically all cars sold in the United States for more than $20,000 were European. The European imports in that year averaged twice the customs value of Japanese imports, $12,472 per unit versus $6,346. (Calculated from U.S. International Trade Commission, 1986.)

6. The Ministry of International Trade and Industry, which fully embraced the Sloan/Ford model of high-scale manufacturing, did its best to create an industry in Detroit's image through a succession of proposals for industry consolidation. At the assembler level it proposed that two or three companies be formed with production divided between them on the basis of product size. At the component level MITI floated a number of plans to merge all suppliers of a given component, such as alternators or springs, into a single firm to supply the whole industry. Because this approach did not mesh with the desire of each industrial group to play an independent role in the motor vehicle sector, it was never implemented. See Duncan (1973).

7. These numbers are necessarily approximate. Most ventures are reported in the trade press, but the use of the term "joint venture" is exasperatingly imprecise. Many reported joint ventures turn out upon investigation to be little more than licensing agreements with a bit of production engineering thrown in. Appendix 9A is an earnest effort to construct an accurate list but should be treated with caution.

8. Data on the size of the motor vehicle market are calculated from U.S. Department of Commerce, *Survey of Current Business.* Trade data for this sector are summarized in the U.S. International Trade Commission. "The U.S. Automobile Industry: Monthly Report on Selected Economic Indicators." The expression "consumption . . . at wholesale" is significant because this represents the value of motor vehicle products coming out of U.S. factories plus the net trade balance at the border. This, rather than the commonly cited retail sales figure (including distribution costs and dealer profits), is the portion of the motor vehicle market which is up for grabs in international trade.

9. There is a longer term means as well based on truly epochal innovations in production process technology that slash labor content, boost quality, and increase flexibility. GM in particular has made much of this approach, but the first factory complex based on these principles (Saturn) is still three years away. Even if successful, the extension of these techniques and technologies through the entire American industry would require a decade or more. Thus this approach will not be considered further here. The chapter on robotics, however, is centrally concerned with the role of joint ventures in the advance of American process technology.

10. "Voluntary restraints" on Japanese finished units were introduced in 1981. Since that time the level of permissible imports has been as follows:

1981	1,762,500
1982	1,762,500
1983	1,762,500
1984	1,940,850
1985	2,412,950
1986	2,412,950
1987	2,412,950

The expectation in the industry is that the current level will continue indefinitely. This is partly because the largest Japanese producers—Toyota, Honda, and Nissan—find the present quotas a convenient way to thwart the North American advance of their smaller Japanese rivals. (The quotas for individual producers are determined by MITI on the basis of historical performance in the U.S. market, favoring the companies entering the United States early.) More important, the ever growing deficit in automotive trade between the United States and Japan points in the direction of more rather than less trade protection or of additional strengthening of the yen. In addition, the Japanese will soon have about 1.7 million units of assembly capacity in the United States, reducing any incentive to push for relaxation of the current restraints.

11. Japanese managed auto assembly operations in the United States by 1989 will be as follows:

Company	Product	Location	Capacity	Start Date
Honda	Accord, Civic	Marysville, Ohio	360,000	1982
Nissan	Sentra/pickup	Smyrna, Tenn.	240,000	1983
NUMMI	Nova/Corolla FX16	Fremond, Calif.	250,000	1984
Mazda	MX-6/Probe	Flat Rock, Mich.	300,000	1987
Diamond-Star	Mirage/Colt	Bloomington, Ill.	240,000	1988
Toyota	Camry	Georgetown, Ky.	200,000	1988
Suburu/Isuzu	Small car/ small truck	United States (?)	120,000	1989
			1,710,000	

In addition, Honda has just opened a plant in Canada and Toyota and Suzuki plants are under construction:

Company	Product	Location	Capacity	Start Date
Honda	Accord	Alliston, Ont.	80,000–150,000	1987
Toyota	Corolla	Cambridge, Ont.	50,000–100,000	1988
Suzuki-GM	Sprint/Samari	Ingersoll, Ont.	200,000	1989

This could yield 450,000 units of capacity in a country with only a 1.1 million unit car market. Thus it is very likely that most of the cars assembled in these plants will be destined for the United States as well. Even if the Japanese firms producing in Canada do not qualify for free entry to the U.S. market under the terms of the 1965 U.S.-Canada Auto Pact, they will face no quotas and only a 2.6 percent tariff.

12. The best treatment of the Toyota and Nissan production groups is Cusumano (1985, esp. pp. 241–261).

13. The typical pattern of equity holding within these groups is for each member to hold a small fraction of the equity of many other members. In consequence, the companies in a group will often collectively hold the majority of the groups' equity even though no firm has a large or controlling stake in any other firm.

14. The details on the structure of the Japanese automotive production groups, including a list of the members of each group as well as independent companies, can be found in Dodwell (1983).

15. Interview with Eugene Goodson, Group Vice President, Hoover Universal, Ann Arbor, Michigan, January 1986.

16. The firm in question, although American owned, had been the largest supplier of the component in question in the United Kingdom, from its UK plants, for fifty years.

17. At present GM is about 70 percent vertically integrated, Ford about 45 percent, and Chrysler about 25 percent. Although Chrysler has lower volume in most product lines, its lead in outsourcing to suppliers with lower labor costs, both in the United States and abroad, is now giving the company a $600 per car production cost advantage over GM. That company's one-time competitive advantage in the form of the industry's highest level of vertical integration has now become one of its greatest weaknesses.

18. This is a topic of great concern among Japanese assemblers who cite recent remarks by U.S. Trade Representative Clayton Yuetter (1986) as an indication that the terms of the trade debate may be changing. Yuetter, in a recent speech at the University of Michigan offered a warning: "We welcome the large investments made in the U.S. by Japanese automobile manufacturers during the past few years, but we are concerned with trends that suggest that these firms do not allow competition from American suppliers for key parts contracts. In many cases, the contracts to bring Japanese suppliers into the U.S. are signed in Japan before production ever starts in the U.S. . . . We will expect free market forces and open competition to prevail among Japanese companies assembling cars in the United States. That is the way we do business."

Marcy Kaptur and Sander Levin, two midwestern Democratic Congressmen, have recently made this argument even more strongly (*New York Times*, 1986).

19. Akebono's President Nobomoto made direct reference to this advantage of joint ventures when the project was announced: "A joint venture in the U.S. is preferable to a wholly-owned subsidiary. Both companies will learn from each other and dual ownership expands the potential base of business beyond that available to either company individually." (*Financial Times*, August 7, 1985, p. 4.)

20. Unlike many import-substituting joint ventures in developing countries in the 1950s and 1960s, these ventures export most of their output directly or sell it to assemblers who export the finished units. Thus negotiation on the degree of foreign ownership often focuses on the fraction of the ven-

ture's output to be exported. For example, Toyota withdrew from a proposed joint venture in Taiwan in 1985 because it demanded majority equity control, but the government was unwilling to allow this unless the venture guaranteed meeting very ambitious export targets.

21. As a veteran of GM's international operations remarked in an interview: "We used to think equity was the key to a relationship and we demanded all or nothing. Gradually it has become clear that our technology, management skills, and marketing channels are the key elements we bring to developing country operations. The local partner can supply all of the equity yet be effectively tied to us for the long-term. By the same token, we've had operations where we had all of the equity but no influence due to local government interference in day to day operations. Thus we are now much more flexible in our thinking about the key elements in a venture with local partners."

22. The basic data about NUMMMI are from John Krafcik, "Learning from NUMMI," (September 1986), a working paper prepared with the aid of the author for MIT's International Motor Vehicle Program. Krafcik was a quality control engineer at NUMMI during its first two years of operation.

23. The Chrysler-Mitsubishi joint venture under construction in Illinois will not produce its first vehicle until 1988.

24. However, it should be noted that NUMMI needed only 2,060 hourly workers compared with 6,200 on the Fremont payroll at its output peak in 1978. Any company able to pick the 25-30 percent of its work force with the best work records for reassignment to a new plant would presumably be able to improve quality and productivity in the new plant.

25. This information was provided by General Motors and independently confirmed by the author.

26. They point specifically to an offer by PSA in France to provide Daewoo with assistance in manufacture of the Peugeot 205 for export.

27. Independent producers selling in the United States in volume (more than 10,000 per year) as of 1987:

United States	General Motors, Ford, Chrysler
Japan	Toyota, Nissan, Suburu, Honda, Mazda, Mitsubishi, Isuzu, and Suzuki
United Kingdom	Jaguar, Rover
France	PSA, Renault
Sweden	Saab, Volvo
Korea	Hyundai
Yugoslavia	Zastava (Yugo)
West Germany	Daimler-Benz, BMW, Volkswagen/Audi, Porsche

Independent new entrants by 1990 are likely to include the following:

Italy	Alfa Romeo (presently selling in the United States but at very low volume)
Korea	Kia (in collaboration with Mazda and Ford)
Malayasia	Proton

In addition, Daihatsu (a member of Toyota group), Seat (the Spanish sub-sidiary of Volkswagen), Citroen (a member of PSA group), Autolatina (the joint venture of Ford and Volkswagen in Brazil and Argentina), Daewoo (the GM-Daewoo Group joint venture in Korea), Ford of Mexico, and Ford, Nissan, and Mitsubishi joint ventures in Taiwan are very likely to begin exports to the United States.

28. With the exception of further ventures between GM and Toyota, there is no evidence that American antitrust policy discouraged joint venturing. Rather, the more adventuresome Japanese producers (which turned out to include everyone but Toyota and Mitsubishi, two of the most conservative companies in Japan) judged they could do better on their own than with an American partner who "knew the territory."

29. The public policy case for joint ventures between American assemblers or between the largest American parts makers is much more problematic. The argument is sometimes still heard in Detroit that American antitrust policy in the past discouraged joint ventures between American assemblers and between American parts makers which would have made the current American-Japanese ventures unnecessary. However, this line of reasoning is difficult to accept. What American motor vehicle firms have critically lacked has been state-of-the-art production organization, not scale or any other factor a joint venture might provide. Thus ventures between American firms would have been collaborations of the weak, probably destined for the same fate as the defensive mergers of a previous era.

30. Indeed, the Japanese may do their best to shut it. Yet another of the ironies of this age of internationalization is that the Japanese producers, to the extent their U.S. based operations begin to feel the pressure of imports from less developed countries, may become the most energetic protectionists in the United States. They are already pushing hard to limit Korean access in Canada.

REFERENCES

Abernathy, William J. 1978. *Production Dilemma.* Baltimore: Johns Hopkins University Press.

Altshuler, Alan, Martin Anderson, Daniel Jones, Daniel Roos, and James Womack. 1984. *Future of the Automobile.* Cambridge, Mass.: MIT Press.

Chandler, Alfred D., Jr. 1962. *Strategy and Structure.* Cambridge, Mass.: MIT Press.

Cusumano, Michael. 1985. *The Japanese Automobile Industry: Technology and Management at Toyota and Nissan.* Cambridge, Mass.: Harvard University Press.

Dodwell Consultants. 1983. *The Structure of the Japanese AutoParts Industry.* Hong Kong: Dodwell.

Duncan, William Chandler. 1973. *U.S.-Japan Automobile Diplomacy: A Study in Economic Confrontation.* Cambridge, Mass.: Ballinger.

Friedman, David. 1983. "Beyond the Age of Ford: The Strategic Basis of the Japanese Success in Automobiles." In John Zysman and Laura Tyson, eds., *American Industry in International Competition*. Ithaca, N.Y.: Cornell University Press.

Japan Economic Journal. 1985. "Three Toyota Motor Affiliates to Make Parts in U.S." December 28.

Metal Working News. 1986. "GM, Nihon Radiator in Compressor Venture." March 24.

Monden, Yasuhiro. 1983. *The Toyota Production System*. Atlanta: Institute of Industrial Engineers.

Motor Vehicle Manufacturers Association. 1987. *World Motor Vehicle Data*. Washington, D.C.: MVMA.

New York Times. 1986. "Crucial Negotiations on Trade with Japan." October 17, p. A23.

Rohlen, Thomas, and Anthony Pascale. 1983. "The Mazda Turnaround." *Journal of Japanese Studies*, 9, no. 2 (Summer): 219-264.

U.S. International Trade Commission. 1986. "The U.S. Automobile Industry: Monthly Report on Selected Economic Indicators." (Mineo). Washington, D.C.: USITC.

Yuetter, Clayton. 1986. "Remarks of Ambassador Clayton Yuetter." University of Michigan U.S.-Japan Automotive Industry Conference, Ann Arbor, April 1, pp. 6-7.

10 CONCLUSIONS AND POLICY IMPLICATIONS

David C. Mowery

The analyses of collaborative ventures between U.S. and foreign firms in previous chapters show that the importance, structure, and locus of collaboration vary greatly among these manufacturing industries, as do the amount and direction of technology transfer. As a result, the competitive consequences of international collaboration will differ considerably among these industries. Among other things, this heterogeneity suggests that any public policy that attempts to regulate international collaboration in these and other industries is inadvisable and infeasible.

This chapter's evaluation of international collaborative ventures is based on the premise that such collaborations are a modest tributary in a quickening flow of international technology transfer. International technology transfer operates through a wide variety of channels, of which international collaboration is only one. Neither this larger and more rapid international flow of technology nor the greater economic and technological sophistication of other industrial nations that drive them is undesirable. They are one result of a period of economic development and political stability since 1945 that has been a key objective of U.S. foreign policy. U.S. managers and public policymakers must develop creative and effective responses to this new environment, rather than try to turn back the clock.

COLLABORATIVE VENTURES
IN EIGHT INDUSTRIES

Telecommunications Equipment

International collaboration between U.S. and Japanese firms and between U.S. and European firms has grown rapidly within this industry during the past decade. Collaborative ventures appear to be more significant than alternative channels for the exploitation of technological and other forms of firm-specific capabilities. The focus of international collaboration is product development, manufacture, and marketing. The dominant motive for collaboration is market access, which includes both access by foreign firms to the large U.S. market and access by U.S. firms to foreign markets.

Market access is an important motive for collaboration in this industry for two reasons. The restructuring of the U.S. telecommunications industry in 1984 opened up the large U.S. market to foreign suppliers, who had to develop marketing networks rapidly to compete with the substantial AT&T enterprise that remained. This settlement also freed AT&T to compete in new domestic markets (primarily computer hardware) and new foreign equipment and (potentially) service markets. AT&T has utilized collaborative ventures with foreign firms to expand its domestic product line and to gain access to foreign markets.

The importance of the market access motive, especially in European markets, reflects the prominent role of government entities (mainly postal and telephone ministries) as purchasers in this industry. Access to these markets for U.S. firms in many cases requires the participation of a local firm. Other motives for collaboration include risk-sharing, as the costs of new product development continue to grow, a lack of international standards, which creates a need for exchanges of sensitive data between supplier and purchaser firms, and the growing interdependence of computer and telecommunications equipment technologies, which means that firms in the computer industry have a strong incentive to develop technological expertise in telecommunications through collaboration with telecommunications firms, and vice versa.

The competitive consequences of collaboration are difficult to evaluate. Rather than supporting a one-way flow of advanced technologies from U.S. to foreign firms, most international collaborative ventures in this industry include significant foreign contributions of technology. AT&T, one of the U.S. firms that has been most active in establishing international collaborative ventures, would face greater obstacles in overseas markets if it did not pursue such collaboration. AT&T historically has not pursued these markets, and there exist significant impediments to access to many of them. Moreover, the level of technological capabilities within a number of foreign telecommunications equipment suppliers is already sufficiently high, and the amount of technology transfer within collaborations between U.S. and foreign telecommunications equipment firms sufficiently low, that international collaborative ventures are unlikely in and of themselves to significantly increase near-term competitive pressures on established U.S. firms.

Commercial Aircraft

Joint ventures between U.S. and foreign firms and among foreign firms (such as Airbus Industrie) are of great importance within this industry. Virtually all of the major commercial transports and engines developed by U.S. firms since the early 1970s have enlisted significant foreign involvement. Other channels for technology transfer, such as licensing and direct foreign investment, are less important in the development and production of commercial aircraft and engines for the global market.

The focus of international collaboration within this industry is product development and manufacture. This reflects the fact that the critical competitive assets are those of design and production management, and is due as well to the need for marketing and product support to be controlled by the organization in charge of design and production. The primary motives for collaboration are market access, risk-sharing, and access to low-cost capital for U.S. firms. Market access is a particularly important incentive for collaboration because foreign markets for commercial aircraft, like those for telecommunications equipment, are characterized by substantial government involvement. Foreign governments also have become increasingly interested in collaboration with U.S. firms, either to sustain an established aircraft production and design capability or to develop such a capability through technology transfer within collaborative ventures.

In most cases joint venture agreements between U.S. and foreign firms have involved outflows of technology from U.S. to foreign firms. Technology transfer between U.S. and foreign firms, however, is not a one-way flow. Although Boeing and General Electric clearly have transferred technology to foreign firms through their joint ventures, the "balance of trade" in technology transfer within the now defunct joint venture between Saab-Scania Aircraft and Fairchild, or the International Aero Engines consortium, appears to be more even.

International collaboration has not yet produced serious competitive threats to major U.S. aircraft and engine firms. Technology transfer within these collaborations is insufficient to enable foreign participants to mount a credible entry into the world commercial aircraft industry as a "prime contractor" in the near future. Indeed, inasmuch as the rise of Airbus Industrie (a development that owes little to U.S.-European collaboration in commercial aircraft) has motivated a portion of the collaboration between U.S. and foreign firms in this industry, such collaboration is a result, rather than a cause, of intensified international competition.

International collaborative ventures have increased foreign competitive pressures, however, on the U.S. firms engaged in components and parts production for commercial airframes and engines. International collaboration within this industry is one aspect of a larger trend toward worldwide sourcing of parts and components by both U.S. and foreign prime contractors. This development is benefiting U.S. supplier firms, who have expanded their exports during the 1980s. Nonetheless, continued high levels of international collaboration will in the long run require these firms to improve their technological and competitive performance and may lead to increased international collaboration within this segment of the industry.

Integrated Circuits

The pattern of international collaboration in the microelectronic integrated circuit industry is complex. In some cases, as in biotechnology, foreign firms have provided risk capital to start-up firms in order to gain access to advanced technology. Collaborative ventures between U.S. and foreign firms, however, historically have not been widespread within this industry, particularly by comparison with licensing.

Before 1980 collaborative ventures within this industry were motivated by market access considerations. The importance of these motives reflected the desire of foreign firms to penetrate the U.S. market, as well as the desire of U.S. firms to penetrate markets in both Japan and Europe. Since 1980, improved Japanese technological capabilities also have led to a limited number of collaborations between U.S. and Japanese producers of microprocessors and memory components that focus on joint development of new processes and products. Continued U.S.-Japanese trade frictions and negotiations over access to the Japanese and U.S. markets are likely to result in additional collaboration between U.S. and Japanese firms in the future.

The flow of technology transfer through international collaborative ventures in this industry does not consist exclusively of an outflow of U.S. technological capabilities, and some recent collaborative ventures establish the potential for a considerable transfer of Japanese integrated circuit technology to U.S. firms. The consequences of international collaboration for the future competitiveness of the U.S. integrated circuit industry appear to be modest—the industry's current competitive challenges reflect more fundamental problems of capital formation and, possibly, industry structure. International collaborative ventures provide one solution to both of these problems and therefore have the potential to strengthen segments of the U.S. industry.

Pharmaceuticals

Collaborative ventures are of relatively minor importance in this industry (outside of ventures involving small biotechnology firms, discussed in Chapter 6), particularly by comparison with the licensing of pharmaceutical products. The modest role of collaborative ventures reflects the strength of patent protection and the relative ease with which pharmaceuticals product technology can be transferred via contract.

Some collaboration between U.S. and foreign firms has developed, however, in the marketing within the United States of pharmaceuticals developed by foreign firms. These marketing-centered collaborative ventures are the result of the increasing costs of pharmaceuticals innovation, which has reduced the ability of some U.S. firms to develop new products, and the desire of foreign pharmaceuticals producers for access to U.S. markets. The high costs of testing and marketing new drugs within the United States mean that marketing collaborations with established U.S. firms are attractive to many prospective foreign entrants. Recent collaborative ventures between Japanese and U.S. firms may nevertheless be a transitional, rather than a permanent, business strategy. Over time, as these foreign producers develop a wider range of pharmaceutical products, establish relationships with members of the U.S. medical profession who are able and willing to administer clinical trials of new drugs, or develop a wholly owned domestic marketing and distribution network, the incentives for such international collaboration could dwindle.

The limited technology transfer that occurs within these ventures consists of inflows of new products from foreign sources that allow U.S. firms to utilize their expertise in drug testing and marketing. The competitive status of U.S. firms within this industry thus is not likely to be affected by international collaboration. As in several of the other U.S. industries discussed in these studies, international collaboration between U.S. and foreign pharmaceuticals firms is a result of changes in the competitive status of U.S. firms within the global industry, rather than a cause of these changes.

Biotechnology

Collaborative ventures appear to be significant mechanisms for the exploitation of technological capabilities in this industry, especially collaborations between new firms (the developers of biotechnology products and processes) and established firms from the pharmaceuticals and other industries (the distributors, users, and marketers of processes and products embodying these new technologies). The motives for and types of collaboration are similar for both domestic and international collaborations, reflecting the fact that gaining access to the U.S. market by a new U.S. firm, especially one producing pharmaceuticals for human use, is often nearly as difficult as gaining access to a foreign market for this firm. Another important motive for collaboration is the need of newly established firms in this industry for capital.

The focus of most collaborative ventures is research and marketing, which provides access by established firms to biotechnologies developed by the new firms and a marketing and distribution network for the products of the small biotechnology firms. There appears to be little or no biotechnology research or marketing collaboration among established firms, nor is there extensive collaboration among the new biotechnology firms.

International collaborative ventures in which U.S. biotechnology firms are involved support an outflow of technological assets and capabilities developed by these firms to foreign, established firms. Although the long-term consequences of this outflow for the competitiveness of U.S. biotechnology firms may be detrimental, these impacts must be balanced against the consequences for young U.S. biotechnology firms of the insufficient capital or access to foreign markets that might occur in the absence of collaboration. The evidence cited in Chapter 6 suggests that biotechnology firms are gradually integrating forward into production and marketing as they mature, which means that domestic collaborative ventures in this industry may decline in importance. International collaboration in marketing, however, may remain an important means of supporting access by U.S. biotechnology firms to foreign markets, reflecting the regulatory barriers to access to these markets.

Robotics Equipment

Several joint ventures between automobile firms and robotics producers have been formed during the past decade, but such collaboration is not widespread within the industry. The collaborative ventures between General Motors of the United States and Fanuc of Japan and between Renault of France and Ransburg of the United States relied at their inception on the exchange of sensitive information about auto manufacturing processes and robotics design between the partners. As the market for robotics machinery has broadened beyond automobile producers, however, the incentives for these development-centered collaborative agreements between suppliers and major users have weakened.

Other joint ventures in this industry recently have sprung up between supplier firms. These ventures, which also focus on product development and manufacture, may become more common if robotics technologies evolve to require greater investments in the integration of systems produced by different firms, as in the integration of microprocessor-based controllers or vision systems with robot hardware. Licensing and technology exchange agreements are more important than joint ventures in other segments of the robotics industry. The international "balance of trade" in robotics technology transfers through these licensing and technology exchange arrangements appears to consist largely of inflows, as U.S. firms gain access to foreign expertise in the production of hardware through such arrangements. The lack of success of U.S. firms in producing robotics hardware does not appear to be a direct result of international collaborative ventures. Instead, collaboration is one result of the lack of competitiveness of U.S. firms in hardware production and allows them to participate in the global industry without having to develop such expertise.

The outlook for collaborative ventures in robotics, as opposed to technology exchange and licensing agreements, is mixed. Since governments do not play a major role in most markets for robotics equipment, market access is a less salient motive for international collaboration. The incentives for user-supplier joint ventures also have diminished. Robotics technologies in which technical interfaces are becoming more complex, however, as in vision systems, may be an area of expanding international collaboration among suppliers in the future. The competitive impacts of these and other international collaborative ventures on the U.S. robotics industry are likely to be modest. Licensing, joint ventures, and technology exchange agreements allow U.S. firms to gain access to the technological assets of foreign producers. These activities have supported the entry and participation of U.S. firms as suppliers of applications software, advanced controllers, and integrated factory automation systems and therefore, if anything, have strengthened their competitiveness.

Steel

International collaborative ventures in this industry are motivated largely by the need for foreign producers of basic steel (primarily Japanese firms) to obtain access to the U.S. market, which is protected by agreements among the European Community, Japan, and the United States. Established U.S. producers of basic steel also need advanced process and managerial technologies in steelmaking, even as they reduce their financial commitment to the domestic U.S. steel market. Collaboration is centered on joint production, employing foreign production and management technologies in U.S. plants. Other collaborative ventures in the basic steel industry (for example, that between Pohang Iron and Steel of South Korea and U.S. Steel) are based on long-term commitments to share the output of a specialized production facility, exploiting scale economies.

Licensing and technical assistance agreements between Japanese and U.S. firms preceded many of these collaborative agreements, but could not provide the technological and management assets or capital needed by U.S. firms. Direct foreign investment in the United States by Japanese firms, an alternative method of gaining access to the U.S. market, is risky and unattractive in a global industry characterized by excess capacity.[1] In other segments of this industry (specialty steel and minimills), direct foreign investment in the United States has been significant.

Technology transfer within these international collaborative ventures consists primarily of inflows of advanced production and management technologies from foreign sources. Collaboration appears to offer one path to the partial rejuvenation of the U.S. basic steel industry. Although the capital and technology inflows within these ventures are unlikely by themselves to restore the basic steel industry to its former levels of employment and sales, its prospects would be even bleaker in the absence of these collaborative ventures.

Automobiles

The motives for collaborative ventures in this industry and the form taken by these ventures closely resemble those in the steel industry. Collaborative ventures in the automobile industry involve the import by U.S. firms of advanced technologies of production management and are centered on joint production of automobiles and, increasingly, automotive parts and components. Japanese auto producers seek access to the U.S. market through collaborative production agreements, while U.S. parts suppliers collaborate with Japanese firms to supply Japanese auto producers in the United States and Japan. U.S. automobile and auto parts producers also want access to the managerial technologies and production methods employed by Japanese automobile firms and can gain such access most effectively through collaboration, rather than licensing. As in steel, domestic collaboration among U.S. firms does not provide access to these technological and management capabilities.

Collaborative ventures within this industry support a substantial flow of technology from foreign to U.S. firms. These collaborative ventures thus carry with them the potential to improve the competitiveness of U.S. firms. The long-term outlook for international collaboration among the auto producers is uncertain—Japanese auto firms appear increasingly to be entering the U.S. market via direct investment, having in some cases employed collaborative ventures to gain experience in dealing with the U.S. work force. Within the automotive parts industry, however, collaboration is likely to remain significant because of the smaller size of the U.S. firms and their desire to improve sales to Japanese auto producers in both the United States and Japan.

A PRELIMINARY EVALUATION

Although the full implications of international collaboration for U.S. managers and policymakers will not be apparent for some time, this cross-industry comparison does not support the critical view of international joint ventures presented in such works as Reich and Mankin (1986), for several reasons. Technology transfer within these ventures is more modest in scope and less uniformly "outward bound" from the United States than some assessments assume. Just as U.S. industries vary in their current account balances on goods trade, the net inflows or outflows of technology through international collaborations vary across industries. Requiring balance in technology transfer on an industry-by-industry basis makes no more sense than does a requirement for such balance in goods trade. Moreover, in a number of industries, international collaboration has the potential to improve the international competitiveness of the U.S. participants.

Reich and Mankin's critical assessment of joint ventures also appears to assume that certain assets or capabilities, such as research, product development, and design, are more significant than others for the establishment or maintenance of industrial competitiveness. These industry studies, however, support the work of Teece (1986) and others in demonstrating the importance of a wide range of capabilities for the realization of commercial profit from innovation. The relative importance of research, production, or marketing capabilities, as well as the strength of the complementarities among them, vary across industries. Indeed, these variations explain many of the differences among industries in the structure and locus of collaboration among firms.

The structure of collaboration in the eight industries discussed in this collection appears to be determined largely by the motives of the U.S. and foreign participants. In a majority of cases the motive for collaboration is access to markets, whether in the United States or foreign nations. The asset provided in exchange for market access is technology. The form in which the technology is provided, which is determined by both the motives of the participants in the collaborative venture and the characteristics of the technology, also plays a central role in structuring the collaboration. Thus, where the technology is provided in essentially "embodied" form (that is, in a finished product), collaboration focuses largely on marketing, as in the pharmaceuticals industry, or may be of minor importance altogether.

If the technical interfaces among the components that must be combined to produce a final product are stable or standardized, supply or licensed production agreements can substitute for collaborations, as in the collaborations between U.S. applications engineering firms and foreign producers of robotics hardware or the technology exchange agreements of the integrated circuit industry. Further development of technical standards in robotics, telecommunications equipment, and integrated circuits thus could reduce reliance on collaborative ventures that are based on technology exchange.

In cases in which the incentives of the participants require greater access to the technological assets, or in which the nature of the technology prevents embodied transfer, as in the steel, automobile, telecommunications equipment, biotechnology, and commercial aircraft industries, collaboration tends to focus on activities upstream from marketing, including product development and manufacture. In commercial aircraft, telecommunications equipment, and segments of the integrated circuit industry, the desire of U.S. firms for access to foreign capital or technology provides an additional impetus to collaboration in research and product development.

International collaborative ventures also are closely linked to structural change. Increased technological pluralism within the world economy is a central cause of increased international collaboration among firms. In addition, most of the industries considered in this collection have experienced significant structural change as a result of developments in both technology and policy. Greater reliance on collaborative ventures is one response to such change.

The global telecommunications equipment industry, for example, is being restructured as a result of U.S. regulatory and judicial decisions, technological change, and increased pressure on a number of foreign nations to open their domestic markets to imports. The U.S. integrated circuit industry is being challenged by both foreign competition and the development of new technological capabilities, which have increased its demands for capital and have altered its structure. The U.S. pharmaceuticals industry has undergone a "shakeout" in its middle ranks as a result of the increased costs of new product development. The U.S. automobile, commercial aircraft, and steel industries also have experienced dramatic structural change in recent years. In most of these industries, international collaboration will accelerate structural change but is not directly responsible for such change.

Will international collaboration be a permanent characteristic of global competition in all of these industries? The long-term outlook differs across industries. Industries in which international collaboration in product development is motivated by a desire to reduce risk, gain access to technology, or deal with the effects of a major governmental presence as a purchaser or as an arbitrator of international trade disputes will continue to rely on international collaboration. These industries include telecommunications equipment, commercial aircraft, and (potentially) integrated circuits. Technological evolution in both integrated circuits and some segments of the robotics industry may provide additional motives for international collaboration.

International collaboration in the U.S. steel industry is likely to continue because of the reluctance of Japanese firms to assume ownership of additional production capacity in an industry plagued by domestic and international excess capacity and the likelihood that foreign access to the U.S. market will remain restricted. International collaborative ventures also will remain significant in the U.S. auto parts industry because of the substantial obstacles faced by U.S. firms in gaining access to Japanese management and production systems and Japanese markets.

In other industries, however, international collaboration may be a more transitory phenomenon. Japanese collaboration with the major U.S. automobile firms may have peaked, as Japanese firms now are investing in wholly owned U.S. production capacity. International collaboration that is motivated by market access concerns in industries in which governments do not play a major role as purchasers also may decline in importance in the long term. These industries include biotechnology and segments of the robotics industry, where the maturation of the industry is likely to reduce incentives for collaboration, and pharmaceuticals, where marketing collaborations will decline somewhat in importance if foreign entrants expand their product lines and presence in the United States.

The fact that technology transfer is at the center of many joint ventures renders very important the management by partner firms of both technological development and the processes of technology transfer. Managers must recognize the potential clash in incentives between technological leaders, reluctant to allow the transfer of key technological capabilities, and technological followers, whose participation may hinge on the amount of technology transfer within joint ventures. The success of a project may be undercut by the attempts of partners, motivated by their desire to maximize technology transfer and learning, to participate in all aspects of the project. Nevertheless, the importance of technology transfer as a source of cohesion within ventures between a dominant and subordinate firm means that these ventures may be more durable and successful than those among technological equals (Killing, 1983).

The structure of international collaborative ventures, especially those that focus on joint research and product development, raises additional challenges: How are decisions among equals to be made? How is feedback from prospective purchasers to be integrated into the design process? How are product support responsibilities to be handled, and how is this source of operating experience to be incorporated into design modifications? Under some circumstances, an autonomous management structure, charged with responsibility and the power for a wide range of design, marketing, production, and product support issues, may be preferable. While attractive under specific circumstances, however, such a structure is also costly. There is no single optimal management structure for a collaborative venture—the appropriate design will depend, among other things, on the character and magnitude of the contributions and capabilities of the participants.

POLICY IMPLICATIONS

The complexity of international collaborative ventures, the fact that the pattern and impact of these ventures vary considerably across industries, and the historical evidence that restrictions on technology transfer are either ineffective or perverse in their impacts (Harris, 1986; Committee on Science, Engineering, and Public Policy Panel on the Impact of National Security Controls on International Technology Transfer, 1987) all argue against the development of policies to restrict international collaborative ventures involving U.S. firms. Such controls currently are imposed on collaborative ventures in technologies with potential military applications in the commercial aircraft and other industries. Nevertheless, the incentives for U.S. firms to enter international collaborative ventures and the payoffs from these ventures for U.S. firms and the U.S. economy are heavily influenced by U.S. trade and research policies.

The industry studies in this volume provide little evidence to support the argument that U.S. antitrust policy is a central factor in the decisions of American firms to collaborate with foreign enterprises. In most instances, international collaborative ventures are not partial substitutes (or inferior ones, from the viewpoint of public policy) for the collaboration among U.S. firms that might develop in the absence of antitrust restrictions. The primary motive for many collaborative ventures, access to foreign markets, is not affected by the structure or enforcement of restrictions on collaboration between U.S. firms. In other cases, such as the collaborative ventures in the automobile and steel industries, U.S. firms collaborate with foreign firms in order to gain access to technological and other assets that are not available from other U.S. firms. Antitrust policy also is largely irrelevant to precommercial research collaboration among U.S. firms in the wake of the National Cooperative Research Act of 1984, and antitrust rarely applies to "vertical" collaborations, such as risk-sharing subcontracting relationships.

Antitrust policy has played an indirect role, however, in motivating or structuring international collaborative ventures in several industries. The 1982 Modified Final Judgment in the case of *United States v. AT&T* opened the domestic U.S. market to foreign telecommunications equipment suppliers and unleashed AT&T to compete in markets outside of telecommunications and in foreign markets for telecommunications equipment. The limited duration (eight years) of the NUMMI joint venture between General Motors and Toyota is a direct result of the settlement reached in the antitrust suit against NUMMI filed by the Chrysler Corporation. There is some evidence in the commercial aircraft engine industry that the U.S. Department of Justice has allowed international collaboration between competing firms of a sort that would not have been allowed between the major U.S. firms, based on an inappropriate distinction between the domestic and international markets for these products. The evidence is not conclusive in this case, however, and the example appears to be an isolated one.

Restrictions on imports in other industries have provided a basis in antitrust policy for distinguishing between domestic and international collaborations involving U.S. firms. The conjunction of antitrust and trade restrictions influenced the joint venture between National Steel and Nippon Kokan Steel, one of the most significant collaborative ventures in the industry. This venture was established in the wake of the Justice Department's opposition to the sale of a number of National Steel properties to the U.S. Steel Corporation, based on the Department's judgment that the domestic U.S. market was protected from imports. Paradoxically, restrictions on imports in this industry led to collaboration between U.S. and foreign firms that was prohibited among U.S. firms.[2] The consequences of this collaboration, however, do not appear to be harmful to the long-term competitiveness of the U.S. firms involved, as was noted above. Moreover, the tendency of trade restrictions to create such incentives for international collaboration is another reason to avoid such policies, rather than an argument for the relaxation of antitrust restrictions in protected industries.

Although trade policy has played a very significant role in the development of international collaborative ventures, these ventures appear to raise relatively few novel issues for trade policy. They arise in part from restrictions on market access and government involvement in procurement decisions, both of which have received increased U.S. government attention in recent years. Other policy implications of these collaborative ventures reflect their role in supporting technology transfer; although important, however, international collaboration is but one of a number of channels of technology transfer.

Foreign governments increasingly employ nontariff trade barriers in a strategic fashion so as to improve access to the technological assets of U.S. and other foreign firms. Limitations on the access by U.S. firms to foreign markets through restrictions on exports or direct investment, government involvement in procurement transactions, and the provision of risk capital to local firms that are either partners of or competitors with U.S. firms all are examples of such policies. Although most analyses of strategic trade policy have focused on the ability of governments to affect the entry and output decisions of foreign and domestic firms (see Brander and Spencer, 1985, Brander, 1986; and Krugman, 1986), these policies are intended to affect the technology transfer decisions of foreign firms. These policies have influenced collaboration between U.S. and foreign firms, but there are few if any examples of substantial transfer within such collaborations of the technological assets that will rapidly increase foreign competitive threats to the U.S. firms involved. In many cases, collaborative ventures between U.S. and foreign firms followed, rather than led, the development of significant foreign competition.

The trade-restricting actions of foreign governments also are matched by recent actions of the U.S. government in a number of industries. Restrictions on imports of selected goods, restrictions on the pricing of these imports, restrictions on foreign investment, and intervention in government procurement decisions all have provided strong incentives for foreign firms in the steel, auto, and microelectronics industries seeking access to the U.S. market to form collaborative ventures with U.S. firms. The Fujitsu-Fairchild case is one example of the use by the federal government of moral suasion to restrict the investment decisions of a foreign firm; in the wake of that episode, Fujitsu and other foreign electronics firms may resort to collaborative ventures to establish a production presence in the U.S. market. Extensive use of "Buy America" restrictions in U.S. military and a wide range of nonmilitary procurements also restrict foreign access to this market and establish an incentive for collaboration.

Research and product development subsidies are another potential inducement to international collaboration and have been cited as a contributor to the tilt of the international trade "playing field" away from U.S. advantage. With the exception of spectacular cases of subsidized product development in the commercial aircraft industry (Airbus Industrie, which by some estimates benefited from public subsidies totaling $2.5 billion during 1968-1982; see Krugman, 1984), however, most recent programs of public support for Japanese and European technology development programs are both relatively modest in scale (absolutely and by comparison with U.S. programs) and focus on precommercial research, rather than the development of specific products. Indeed, some observers have argued that Japanese programs of public support for precommercial cooperative research are an effort to offset the results of limited labor mobility and venture capital supplies in the Japanese economy (Saxonhouse, 1986). European programs of precommercial cooperative research, including the European Strategic Program in Information Technology (ESPRIT) and the European Research Coordinating Agency (Eureka), also are intended in part to overcome the fragmentation of the European market for high-technology products by encouraging collaboration among heretofore rivalrous "national champions." Where the results of these publicly supported research programs are published in the open scientific literature, such programs can in fact benefit nonparticipant U.S. firms, who may gain access to the results of the basic research without having to bear all of the costs.

Two of the three major areas of policy that affect collaboration, government subsidies and procurement, are now covered by multilateral treaties ("codes of conduct") under the General Agreement on Tariffs and Trade that were negotiated during the Tokyo Round of trade talks. In addition, the commercial aircraft industry is covered by an Agreement on Trade in Civil Aircraft that specifies rules of acceptable conduct. To the extent that international collaboration poses a serious long-term threat to U.S. international competitiveness and is motivated by trade-distorting practices in these areas, additional strengthening of the codes, as well as the Agreement on Trade in Civil Aircraft, is necessary.

The "Uruguay Round" of trade talks began in 1986 and will consider the treatment of foreign investment, including the "right of establishment" by firms of production and other operations in foreign markets. Negotiation of multilateral rules for the treatment of foreign investment would have a considerable impact on the last group of government trade policies, restrictions on foreign investment, that affect international collaboration. These negotiations also may produce a multilateral agreement on international trade in telecommunications services and equipment, codifying the rules of acceptable behavior and (potentially) controlling abuses in an industry in which international collaboration has been considerable. Government involvement (as owners or buyers) in high-technology industries other than commercial aircraft and telecommunications equipment, however, is limited in most industrial nations. This fact may restrict the possibilities for other sectoral agreements that could control the trade-distorting policies that lead to international collaboration in some industries.

As Chapter 6 noted, the development and enforcement of stronger forms of intellectual property protection, another subject of the current multilateral negotiations, also might facilitate the licensing of process and product technologies to foreign firms and reduce one incentive for collaborative ventures in such industries as biotechnology. Stronger intellectual property protection probably will have little impact, however, on international collaboration in most of the industries examined here.

The increased salience of bilateral negotiations in U.S. trade policy, especially negotiations affecting access to foreign (frequently Japanese) markets, also may lead to additional collaborative ventures between U.S. and foreign firms. These talks often take as a measure of success the achievement by U.S. firms of some target market share in a foreign market (see Bhagwati, 1987; World Bank, 1987). Achievement of this outcome in many markets, especially the domestic Japanese market, will require either direct foreign investment by U.S. firms or the formation of long-term collaborations between U.S. and foreign firms. Bilateral talks between the U.S. and Japanese governments over automobile components and semiconductors are likely to be followed by negotiations covering other industries. If these talks and the associated government monitoring of trade outcomes expand, so too will international collaborative ventures.

The implications of international collaboration, as with other forms of technology transfer, for science and technology policy seem clear. In a world in which scientific and technological knowledge crosses national boundaries more rapidly than ever before, public policy should focus on supporting the rapid adoption of new technologies by domestic firms, rather than focusing solely on the generation of new scientific and technical knowledge. In the case of the United States, as the recent report of the Committee on Science, Engineering, and Public Policy's Panel on Technology and Employment (1987) pointed out, such a reorientation of science and technology policies may require, among other things, greater funding for civilian "gray area" research, involving cooperative work by industry and government in demonstration and applications of generic technologies.

International collaborative ventures in many cases convey substantial benefits to U.S. firms and the U.S. economy, and more often than not are the result, rather than the cause, of intensified international competition. The development of policies to exploit the global environment of technological parity between the United States and other industrial nations in a growing range of industries will be far more beneficial than efforts to transform this environment or to resist trends toward growing interfirm collaboration in some industries. The recent wave of such ventures may have crested in some industries, even as it continues to build in others. Nevertheless, international collaborative ventures now are firmly established in a wide range of industries and cover a broader set of activities than in the past. Experimentation and growth in collaboration between U.S. and foreign firms in an expanding set of industries are likely to continue.

NOTES

1. This motive for international collaboration in the steel industry bears a strong resemblance to the situation in the integrated circuit industry, where

international collaborative ventures are being employed to rationalize production capacity in some product lines.

2. Hufbauer and Rosen (1986, p. 62) have noted this tendency, arguing that "a pattern has arisen in which transnational associations raise fewer antitrust concerns than combinations involving two domestic producers. . . . The numerous equity purchases plus one joint venture in the auto industry, as well as several joint ventures in steel, exemplify this phenomenon. While this is the logical consequence of import restraints, it was probably an unintended effect."

REFERENCES

Bhagwati, J. 1987. "Trade in Services and the Multilateral Trade Negotiations." *The World Bank Economic Review*, 1: 549–569.

Brander, J. A. 1986. "Rationales for Strategic Trade and Industrial Policy." In P. Krugman, ed., *Strategic Trade Policy and the New International Economics*. Cambridge, Mass.: MIT Press.

_____, and B. J. Spencer. 1985. "Export Subsidies and International Market Share Rivalry." *Journal of International Economics*, 18: 83–100.

Committee on Science, Engineering, and Public Policy (COSEPUP), Panel on the Impact of National Security Controls on International Technology Transfer. 1987. *Balancing the National Interest: U.S. National Security Export Controls and Global Economic Competition*. Washington, D.C.: National Academy Press.

Committee on Science, Engineering, and Public Policy (COSEPUP), Panel on Technology and Employment. 1987. *Technology and Employment: Innovation and Growth in the U.S. Economy*, edited by R.M. Cyert and D.C. Mowery. Washington, D.C.: National Academy Press.

Harris, J. 1986. "Spies Who Sparked the Industrial Revolution." *New Scientist*, May 22, pp. 42–47.

Hufbauer, G. C., and H. F. Rosen. 1986. *Trade Policy for Troubled Industries*. Washington, D.C.: Institute for International Economics.

Killing, J. P. 1983. *Strategies for Joint Venture Success*. New York: Praeger.

Krugman, P. 1984. "The U.S. Response to Foreign Industrial Targeting." *Brookings Papers on Economic Activity*: 74–121.

_____. 1986. "Industrial Organization and International Trade." National Bureau of Economic Research Working Paper No. 1957.

Saxonhouse, G. R. 1986. "Why Japan Is Winning." *Issues in Science and Technology*, 4: 72–80.

Teece, D. J. 1986. "Profiting from Technological Innovation: Implications for Integration, Collaboration, Licensing, and Public Policy." *Research Policy*, 15: 285–305.

World Bank. 1987. *World Development Report: 1987*. New York: Oxford University Press.

INDEX

Labor costs, 273, 287
Lancia, 305
Large-scale integrated (LSI) circuit, 114
Lata Switching Generic Equipment, 44
"Latch up," 141 n. 9
Lathiere, Bernard, 107 n. 35
Learning economies, 26, 27, 75, 86
Legend/Sterling, 331
Levin, Sander, 344 n. 18
Libya, 104
Licensing, 4-8; and automobile industry, 304-305, 327; and biotechnology, 8, 43, 189-190, 197; and commercial aircraft industry, 79, 351; and integrated circuits, 112, 118, 119-120, 122, 123, 141 n. 10; and pharmaceuticals industry, 8, 43, 153; and protectionism, 6, 18; and robotics industry, 8, 223, 232-233, 238-240, 246-247, 252, 253, 263, 355-356; and steel industry, 356; and technology transfer, 9-10, 18 ns. 8 and 9; and telecommunications industry, 43, 54
Local area networks (LANs), 37, 45, 48
Lockheed, 73, 92
Lotus, 310
Love, Howard, 273-274
L-S Electro-Galvanizing Co., 277-278
LSI Logic, 130, 131-132, 134, 135
LTV, 277-278, 279, 281

McAuto, 241
McDonnell Douglas, 71, 72, 82-86, 90, 106 n. 106; and Fokker, 71, 72, 106 n. 24; and robotics, 241
Machine Intelligence Corporation (MIC), 230, 243, 246, 253, 259-260, 262
Machine Vision International, 231
McLouth, 269, 270
Malaysia, 312, 345 n. 27
Management of collaborative ventures, 10-11, 16-17, 107 n. 34, 360; and automobile industry, 327-328, 330, 357
Management-information systems, 225
MAP protocol, 264 n. 2

Marathon Oil, 269, 270
Market access, 10, 14-15, 358, 360, 361, 362, 364-365; and automobile industry, 312; and biotechnology, 214, 354, 360; and commercial aircraft, 90, 101, 103, 105; and steel industry, 277, 356, 359; and telecommunications, 38, 39, 350-351
Market homogeneity, 13-14
Marketing, 5, 11, 19 n. 11; and automobiles, 306; and biotechnology, 12, 189, 198, 210-211, 212, 354; and commercial aircraft, 19 n. 10, 78-79, 90, 91, 93, 97, 100, 106 n. 28, 107 ns. 31 and 35, 351; costs, 8, 24; and pharmaceuticals, 12, 154-155, 166-168, 174-175, 360; and robotics, 223, 226-235, 243; and telecommunications, 39-49, 56, 63-65
Marshallian conception of firms, 158, 163, 172
Martin, 73
Marubeni, 275, 294, 295, 296
Marysville, Ohio, 313
Maserati, 308
Mask makers, 120
Matra, 125-126, 241, 242, 253
Maturity of industry, 11
Mazda, 279, 311, 329
MCI, 35, 55
MD-11 aircraft, 73, 106 n. 23
MD-80 aircraft, 73, 75, 90, 106 n. 23
MD-89 aircraft, 93
MDF100 aircraft, 71, 82-86, 99, 100, 105 n. 21
Mead, Carver, 136
Medi-Physics, 210
Merck, 147, 160, 163, 173; and biotechnology, 190, 193
Mercure 100, 105 n. 19
Mercure 200, 22, 82-86, 99, 100, 105 n. 20, 106 n. 24
Mergers, 10, 23, 149, 216-217
Merlin robot, 260
Meta Machines, 247, 253, 255, 262
Meta Torch, 247, 253, 255
Metro aircraft, 91
Mexico, 328
Microelectronics and Computer Technology Corporation, 3, 111, 140

ABOUT THE EDITOR

David C. Mowery is associate professor of economics and social sciences in the Social and Decision Sciences Department of Carnegie-Mellon University. During 1988, Dr. Mowery is working in the Office of the U.S. Trade Representative as a Council on Foreign Relations International Affairs Fellow. He has published a number of papers on the economics and management of technological change, has served as a consultant to several corporations and government agencies, and has testified before Congress on science and industrial policy issues. He was a member of the National Academy of Engineering's Panel on the Competitive Status of the U.S. Civil Aviation Manufacturing Industry, which issued its report in 1985, and served as study director for the Panel on Technology and Employment of the National Academy of Sciences, National Academy of Engineering, and Institute of Medicine. Dr. Mowery received his Ph.D. in economics from Stanford University.

ABOUT THE CONTRIBUTORS

Steven Klepper is professor of economics and social sciences in the Social and Decision Sciences Department of Carnegie-Mellon University. He received his Ph.D. in economics from Cornell University and has published a number of papers in applied and theoretical econometrics, industrial economics, criminal justice, and the economics of technological change.

Leonard H. Lynn is associate professor of management policy at Case Western Reserve University in Cleveland. He is the author of *How Japan Innovates: A Comparison with the U.S. in the Case of Oxygen Steelmaking* (the Japanese edition of which was recently published), coauthor of *Organizing Business: Trade Associations in Japan and America*, and author of numerous articles and book chapters on technology policy and the management of technology in Japan. He is currently working on two major comparative studies: one on the management of engineers, the other on the impact of new communications technology on the organization of businesses in the United States and Japan.

Gary P. Pisano is a doctoral candidate in the School of Business Administration at the University of California, Berkeley. His research interests include industrial organization, the economics of technical change, and the management of technology. He is currently completing his dissertation on the sources and organization of innovation in biotechnology.

385

Michael V. Russo is a doctoral candidate in the Business and Public Policy program in the School of Business Administration at the University of California, Berkeley. His research interests include strategic management of regulated firms, business-government relations, organizational economics, and technology policy. He is currently completing his dissertation, a longitudinal study of diversification in the electric utility industry.

Weijian Shan is an assistant professor at the Wharton School of Business, University of Pennsylvania. He completed his Ph.D. in business administration at the University of California, Berkeley. His dissertation examined collaborative arrangements in the biotechnology industry. His research interests include international business, industrial organization, and innovation.

W. Edward Steinmueller is deputy director of the Center for Economic Policy Research at Stanford University. His research interests include the economics of the international semiconductor industry; the growth of new, high-technology industries; and the economics of the newspaper industry. He received his Ph.D. in economics from Stanford University.

David J. Teece is professor of business administration and director of the Center for Research in Management at the University of California, Berkeley. His current research interests include industrial organization, the economics of technical change and innovation, international business, energy, and public policy. He holds a Ph.D. in economics from the University of Pennsylvania.

Lacy Glenn Thomas is professor of business at the Columbia University Graduate School of Business. He received his Ph.D. in economics from Duke University and has been a member of the faculty of the University of Illinois and a research fellow at the Brookings Institution. His research has focused on the economics of strategic planning and innovation in the pharmaceuticals industry.

James P. Womack is research director of the International Motor Vehicle Program at the Massachusetts Institute of Technology. He was previously a research associate with the Future of the Automobile Program at M.I.T. and a coauthor of *The Future of the Automobile*. He received his Ph.D. in political science from M.I.T.